Intranet
PUBLISHING

Intranet PUBLISHING

Paul Bodensiek

with

Gordon Benett

Jane "JC" Calabria

Rick Darnell

Paula Jacobs

Guy "Rob" Robinson Kirkland

Diane Koers

Michael Marchuk

Tony Wasson

Intranet Publishing

Copyright© 1996 by Que® Corporation.

Library of Congress Catalog No.: 96-68579

ISBN: 0-7897-0803-5

98 97 96   6 5 4 3 2 1

Interpretation of the printing code: the rightmost double-digit number is the year of the book's printing; the rightmost single-digit number, the number of the book's printing. For example, a printing code of 96-1 shows that the first printing of the book occurred in 1996.

Screen reproductions in this book were created using Collage Plus from Inner Media, Inc., Hollis, NH.

Credits

President
Roland Elgey

Vice President and Publisher
Marie Butler-Knight

Publishing Director
David W. Solomon

Title Manager
Kathie-Jo Arnoff

Editorial Services Director
Elizabeth Keaffaber

Managing Editor
Michael Cunningham

Director of Marketing
Lynn E. Zingraf

Production Editor
Julie A. McNamee

Editor
Sarah Rudy

Stategic Marketing Manager
Barry Pruett

Assistant Product Marketing Manager
Christy M. Miller

Technical Editor
Bill Vernon

Technical Specialist
Nadeem Muhammed

Acquisitions Coordinator
Carmen Krikorian

Software Relations Coordinator
Patty Brooks

Editorial Assistant
Carmen Krikorian

Book Designers
Barbara Kordesh
Kim Scott

Cover Designer
Jay Corpus

Production Team
Steve Adams
DiMonique Ford
Trey Frank
Jason Hand
Damon Jordan
Clint Lahnen
Bob LaRoche
Ryan Oldfather
Casey Price
Julie Quinn
Laura Robbins
Bobbi Satterfield
Kelly Warner
Paul Wilson
Donna Wright
Jody York

Indexer
Cheryl Dietsch

Cover photograph by Jean Miele.

Composed in *Officina Sans* and *Century Light* by Que Corporation.

Acknowledgments

A book arrives on the shelves of your local newsstand out of the blue, with no indication of the work involved in writing it or the vast number of people who were instrumental in taking the raw text and making it into a finished work.

First and foremost, I have to thank my wife, Mary, who put up with my almost total absence for the months that this book took to create. You inspired me and kept me going when I thought I couldn't keep up the breakneck pace any longer. This book is dedicated to you.

Thank you to Kathie-Jo Arnoff of Macmillan, who first approached me with the idea of *Intranet Publishing* and who has been invaluable in keeping me in line with our concept of the book and on time with what originally looked to be impossible deadlines.

A very large portion of this book would not have been possible without the help of eight talented writers: Gordon Benett, Jane Calabria, Rick Darnell, Paula Jacobs, Guy Robinson Kirkland, Diane Koers, Michael Marchuk, and Tony Wasson. Thank you all for applying your particular talents under fierce deadlines.

A big thank you to all of ParaGrafix's customers who have been patient with me as their projects were placed on hold. I'm back!

Last but not least, thank you to the staff of Macmillan Computer Publishing who made our manuscripts look great.

About the Authors

Paul Bodensiek is a mechanical engineer specializing in innovative heating element design and technical writing. He also runs ParaGrafix, an advertising and desktop publishing company. In his spare time, he writes short fiction, sails tall ships, and is working toward his private pilot's license. Mr. Bodensiek is blessed to share his life with wife, Mary, and daughter, Melissa.

Gordon Benett is president of Techne Group, a systems consultancy founded in 1995 to create efficiencies through technology integration. Mr. Benett builds on 15 years of industry experience, during which he architected systems for computer start-ups, General Electric Company, and a Fortune 500 utility. He built his first Web site in 1994 and hasn't looked back. When not in cyberspace, Mr. Benett enjoys life in Waltham, MA with his wife, Susan, four year-old daughter, and infant son.

Jane "JC" Calabria and **Guy "Rob" Robinson Kirkland** live together, work together, and network the computers at home together, where Jane swears she's going to install a 1-900 phone number for their friends who call with their computer problems. She is a trainer, consultant, and writer for Rockey & Associates, Malvern, PA. He is an independent trainer, consultant, and writer. Jane teaches classes in desktop applications, groupware, and the Windows operating system. Rob teaches Novell Netware, Lotus Notes, Windows NT, communications software, numerous application programs, and hardware management. As consultants, she develops PC support models for organizations and provides software solutions, and he sets up networks, designs applications, and subdues unruly hardware or software. As writers, they develop training manuals and are involved with several projects at Que. She is a Certified Lotus Professional (CLP) and a Certified Lotus Notes Instructor (CLI) as well as a Microsoft Certified Professional (MCP). He is a Certified Novell Engineer (CNE), a Microsoft Certified Product Specialist (MCPS) for Windows NT, and a Certified Lotus Notes Instructor (CLI). In his spare time, Rob picked up a law degree. In her spare time, Jane is a correspondent for Philadelphia's KYW News Radio 1060 AM where she broadcasts weekly as "JC on PCs" with her computer news and tips. They can be reached on CompuServe at **74750,3360**, or on the Internet at **Jane_Calabria.Rockey_&_Associates@Notes.Compuserve.Com.**

Rick Darnell is a midwest native currently living with his wife and two daughters in Missoula, MT. He began his career in print at a small weekly newspaper after graduating from Kansas State University with a degree in broadcasting. While spending time as a freelance journalist and writer, Rick has seen the full gamut of personal computers since starting out with a Radio Shack Model I in the late 1970s. When not in front of his computer, he serves as a volunteer firefighter and member of a regional hazardous materials response team.

Paula Jacobs is a Boston-based journalist and consultant who specializes in cyberspace and management strategy issues. She has written on the Internet and related topics for leading magazines and trade journals. Her e-mail address is **pjacobs@world.std.com**.

Diane Koers owns and operates All Business Service, a software training and consulting company formed in 1988 that services the central Indiana area. Her area of expertise has long been in the word processing, spreadsheet, and graphics area of computing as well as providing training and support for several popular accounting packages. Diane's authoring experience includes developing and writing software training manuals for her clients' use.

Michael Marchuk has been involved with the computing industry for over 17 years. Michael currently manages the development research department for a mid-sized software development firm while consulting for small businesses and writing leading-edge books for Que. Along with his bachelor's degree in Finance from the University of Illinois, he has received certification as a Netware CNE and a Compaq Advanced Systems Engineer.

Tony Wasson is a freelance writer and consultant. He owns and edits *Desert Computing Magazine* of Yuma, Arizona. You may reach him at **wasson@primenet.com**.

We'd Like to Hear from You!

As part of our continuing effort to produce books of the highest possible quality, Que would like to hear your comments. To stay competitive, we *really* want you, as a computer book reader and user, to let us know what you like or dislike most about this book or other Que products.

You can mail comments, ideas, or suggestions for improving future editions to the address below, or send us a fax at (317) 581-4663. For the online inclined, Macmillan Computer Publishing has a forum on CompuServe (type **GO QUEBOOKS** at any prompt) through which our staff and authors are available for questions and comments. The address of our Internet site is **http://www.mcp.com** (World Wide Web).

In addition to exploring our forum, please feel free to contact me personally to discuss your opinions of this book. I'm **72410,2077** on CompuServe, and **karnoff@que.mcp.com** on the Internet.

Thanks in advance—your comments will help us to continue publishing the best books available on computer topics in today's market.

Kathie-Jo Arnoff
Title Manager
Que Corporation
201 W. 103rd Street
Indianapolis, Indiana 46290
USA

Contents at a Glance

Table of Contents

25 Microsoft FrontPage

Introduction

The Internet, and its graphical offshoot, the World Wide Web, have been garnering vast amounts of attention in the popular press over the last couple of years. Touted as the Information Superhighway by pundits and politicians, this worldwide computer network is supposed to bring vast amounts of data to everyone's desktops. With an estimated 30 million users (and thousands more joining every day), the Internet is the world's largest computer network.

Almost unmentioned in all of this hoopla is an even faster growing series of computer networks: *intranets*. Another "child" of the Internet, intranets use the same technology as the World Wide Web (server programs, routers, and browsers) to help everyone in a company communicate quickly and efficiently. Netscape, perhaps the most successful company marketing World Wide Web software, estimates that over 80 percent of its sales are not for the Web at all, but for corporate intranets.

Good communications is the most important tool a company can possess. It drives every aspect of operations from Research and Development to Human Resources, and improved communications can help make any business run more smoothly. Companies throughout the world have found that for a relatively modest investment, they can create a "homegrown" workgroup network that rivals the power of such giants as Lotus Notes. When used in combination with these more traditional workgroup solutions, an intranet provides a way to bring individual workers closer together and have them functioning at peak efficiency.

Who Is This Book Written for?

This book has been designed as both a reference and a guide to help anyone create and maintain his or her own portion of the corporate intranet. From basic HyperText Markup Language (HTML) used to create intranet pages to advanced features such as online forms and databases, we have assembled a complete text on what building intranet content entails. Any member of a company can use *Intranet Publishing* as a personal tutor.

Though written specifically for users running Microsoft Windows 95 and Windows NT, the vast majority of this book is applicable to any kind of computer system. One of the greatest advantages of an intranet is that it is designed to be *platform independent*. This means that no matter what kind or mix of computers your company uses, every user on every type of machine can communicate back and forth without worrying about file formats and data structures. When documents are created for the intranet, they are created for all the computers that the network contains.

 When we called this book *Intranet Publishing*, we meant it. The CD-ROM that we have included is chock-full of hundreds of browsers, utilities, graphics and even full intranet-server programs for your publishing needs. You'll see a CD icon, as shown here, next to parts of the book that discuss things included on the disc. Between the software on the CD and the instructions in the following pages, everything you need to get your intranet up and running is included.

How This Book Is Organized

We have organized *Intranet Publishing* in a logical fashion so that it progresses from the most basic principles of creating individual intranet pages to the more advanced subjects of security and site management. You can work at your own pace, moving from one chapter to the next, or use the book as a reference during your creative process.

Intranet Publishing is divided into three main sections to help you begin creating intranet content right away. The remaining two sections and three appendixes help give you ideas for making your intranet work more effectively, how to use your intranet and where to get more information. Following is the breakdown of the *Intranet Publishing*'s sections.

Part I, "Getting Started," gives the beginning reader a broad overview of how an intranet works and how the HTML language lets you create documents to be viewed by other people in your organization.

Part II, "Creating Intranet Content," leads you through all of the different ways to create content for distribution over the intranet.

Part III, "Managing Content," covers how to actually make your content available to other users. You learn tips and techniques for creating multiple-page intranet sites, how to place your content on the intranet server, and how to protect your site from accidents and tampering.

Part IV, "Putting Intranets to Work," provides an overview of how other companies are putting their intranets to work. We have included pictures of their actual computer screens to help you use their techniques to improve your own sites.

Part V, "Exploring Publishing Tools," explores the high end of intranet publishing tools. This sampling of programs will help advanced readers choose a system to create complex intranet sites incorporating all manner of data from other applications.

Part VI, "Appendixes," supplies additional information to help you make the most of your intranet, from creation to actual use. Following is a summary of each appendix:

> Appendix A, "What's on the CD," provides a complete listing of all the programs, utilities, and documents that we have included on the CD-ROM. This software can be invaluable in helping you create your intranet sites.

> Appendix B, "Using an Intranet," gives you an introduction to using a browser program to navigate and interact with your company's intranet.

> Appendix C, "For Further Reading," has a list of books and World Wide Web sites that give further information on intranets, the programs used to create them, and other topics of related interest.

Conventions Used in This Book

The ways to use specific commands in programs is almost as varied as the number of programs you can use to create intranet content. Using the Windows 95 or NT interface, you can choose options from pull-down menus, select specific commands from toolbars, use combinations of keys pressed at the same time, or pull up context-sensitive menus using the right mouse button. Some tasks are easier using one method, some using another, and some just depend on your own preference.

We have included methods for using all of these ways of issuing commands for the programs that are used in this book. When the keys are used for menu commands, we show the key letter underscored, while the rest of word is "normal" (for example, "choose <u>F</u>ile, <u>S</u>ave" means that the F in File and the S in Save are the key letters in these menu commands). We have also included the function key equivalents for menu and dialog box commands, where appropriate. These are indicated by the names of two or more keyboard keys combined by a + sign (for example, Ctrl+B means that you should press the Ctrl key and the B key at the same time).

Most mice have at least two buttons. Throughout the book, we generally assume that the primary mouse button is on the left and the secondary button is on the right. You may have changed these buttons around using the Windows control panel, so take note of what the command is telling you to do. Most active commands use the primary mouse button (highlighting, choosing options from menus) while the secondary mouse button brings up context-sensitive menus or provides other program-specific commands.

We have used several typefaces to set specific text apart. Text that you should type is printed in **bold** or in `computer type` if it is a long passage. Terms that you may not be familiar with are set in *italics*. HTML code is always presented in capital letters (<A HREF>).

▶ **See** "What Is An Intranet?," **p. 10**

We have included cross-references pointing to pages with other sections that have related information throughout the book. You'll usually find these at the end of sections within a chapter.

Additional information is included in Tips, Cautions, and Notes. Tips, Notes, and Cautions are boxed, as shown here.

TIP

Tips provide short techniques to help you avoid problems or improve productivity.

NOTE

Notes contain lengthier information that expands on topics covered in the text. They may also be used as an aside.

CAUTION

Cautions warn you of actions that may cause unexpected events, such as loss of data.

From Here...

It's appropriate to end this introduction, as we will end every main chapter in this book, with the From Here... section. Once you've completed a chapter and are wondering what's next, the From Here... section helps you plan your learning process. Usually there are at least three chapters included that directly, or indirectly, build on what you've just learned.

On behalf of all the talented writers and the also talented staff at Macmillan Computer Publishing, I'd like to take this opportunity to thank you for purchasing *Intranet Publishing*. We trust it will be an invaluable aid in creating an intranet system that you and your company find useful and can be proud of.

Paul Bodensiek
Barrington, Rhode Island

P.S. From Here...

- Chapter 1, "Understanding Your Intranet Site," provides a quick introduction for those who have never written HTML code before, or want a quick refresher of its power.

- Chapter 4, "Creating Content with Your Desktop Applications," is the first of six chapters that lead you through creating all manner of content for your intranet.

- Appendix B, "Using an Intranet," helps you get the most of your intranet by introducing two of the most popular browsers.

- Acknowledgments.   Please take a moment to read the acknowledgments at the beginning of this book. Without the people listed, and many more who weren't, this book would never have come to pass.

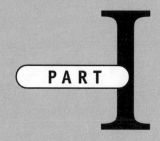

Getting Started

1

Understanding Your Intranet Site

By Paul Bodensiek

Intranets are powerful tools for enhancing all manner of communications over your company's existing computer network using the graphical interface that has made the World Wide Web so popular. There are no more network drives to search, no more subdirectories to sift through. By simply pointing and clicking, almost all the information on the network is available to authorized users. Setting up an intranet and making information, or content, available is relatively easy.

This chapter first gives an introduction to the power and depth of an intranet. The chapter then shows you examples of some of the dynamic ways your company can use an intranet.

In later chapters, you learn how to use HTML to create your own intranet pages, forms, and comment systems.

In this chapter, you learn about

- The definition of an intranet
- The major components of an intranet
- How an intranet compares to the Internet and the World Wide Web
- Some of the ways your company can use an intranet

What Is an Intranet?

In its simplest form, an intranet is just your company's existing network with some software that lets it route HTML (HyperText Markup Language) documents. Using the same graphic based software developed to run the World Wide Web, an intranet allows for easy access to all manner of information located on any computer connected to your network.

Intranet versus World Wide Web

The Internet (Net) is a world-wide network of computers originally began as an experiment by the United States Department of Defense in the 1970s. This network was to be so stable that even if some of the computers were destroyed, the flow of important information would be uninterrupted. The experiment was so successful that the military, defense contractors, and research institutions all got "online" to make exchanging data easier. As the Internet grew, finding information became increasingly difficult for users.

The World Wide Web (WWW or Web), now the single biggest and fastest growing component of the Internet, began as a set of specifications written by Tim Berners-Lee of the European Laboratory for Particle Physics (CERN) in 1989. He proposed a series of protocols, or *tags*, that would allow one document (also called a *page*) to link to another and make navigating the huge Internet easier for researchers. These links are called *hypertext links* and are familiar to anyone who has used the help system in Windows. Collected together, the protocols form what is known as the HyperText Markup Language (HTML). The graphical nature of the World Wide Web also drew "civilians" to the new network in droves and it is where almost all commerce over the Internet takes place.

In addition to links, HTML tags define how a page looks on your screen and even what and where graphics should be displayed along with the text. Web pages are incredibly easy to use. Just point to a link, click your mouse button, and you are instantly in contact with a computer across town or across the world. You don't need to know anything about where the other computer is, or even what type it is. The World Wide Web protocols ensure that everything works smoothly.

The first *browsers*, programs that use these protocols, were introduced in 1993. In just over two years, the Web has become the most popular computer network in the world. With more than 35 million users worldwide, and thousands more joining every day, the Web shows no sign of slowing down its growth.

It was only a matter of time before someone figured out that a company's computer network could be set up with a program that allows it to function as a miniature Internet and transmit Web documents to everyone in the organization. Dubbed an *intranet*, this new form of corporate networking is growing at an astonishing rate. Netscape estimates that between 70,000 and 140,000 companies have intranets and that number is expected to rise rapidly over the coming years.

▶ **See** "What Is HTML?," **p. 22**

How an Intranet Works

A central computer, typically your company's network server, handles all the data traffic associated with sending and receiving files. These files may be HTML code to be displayed by a browser program, data files used by another program, or any combination of the two. A program called the *web server* tells the central computer how to deal with requests and transmissions so that any computer can communicate on an intranet regardless of what kind it is or what operating system it is using.

When you start your browser program, it sends a request to the web server. This request asks the server to send a file to the browser, which displays the file for you. Typically the first page displayed is a department or corporate *home page* that contains basic information and links to other files and pages on the intranet (see fig. 1.1).

Fig. 1.1
The first page you typically see when starting your browser is your company's home page.

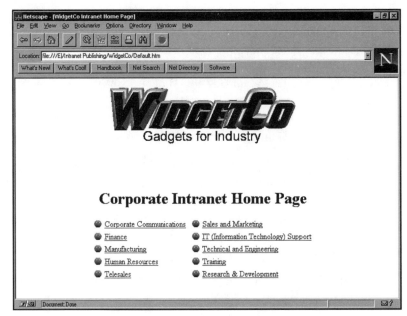

Clicking a link to, say, the Human Resources department sends a new request to the server which then transmits the Human Resource department's home page to your browser.

The HTML and other files that the server sends to your browser all have to originate from the server's hard drive. There are advantages and disadvantages to having files centrally located like this.

If you could write a page and keep it on your desktop computer, it would be much easier for you to make changes to it, but it would increase the network traffic on your machine. Since the files are all on one computer (or more if your company has more than one server) there is always a specific place for browsers to look for information, making it much easier to link pages together.

Once your intranet is up and running, it is completely seamless. You don't ever have to think about what the network is doing, just point and click.

▶ **See** "Aspects of Security," **p. 237**

▶ **See** "Updating Files Locally," **p. 256**

What Is an Intranet Page?

An *intranet page* is a single HTML document. A collection of related intranet pages is called a *site*. Unlike a piece of paper, an intranet page can be as long or as short as needed. Even if the document is longer than one screen (that is, you have to use the scroll bars to see everything) it is still considered one page (see fig. 1.2).

Fig. 1.2
No matter how long an intranet document is, it is still considered one page.

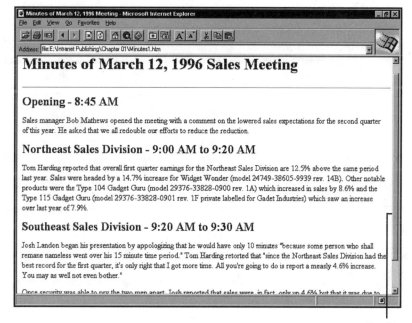

Scroll bar

Intranet content can be created by almost any program you currently use: word processors, spreadsheets, databases, even the paint program that comes bundled with Windows 95. Because an HTML document is an unformatted text file (usually you see text files with names like BOB-MEMO.TXT) any program that can save or print to a text file can create the basis for HTML content. Although the paint program can't create text files, it can make the graphics that have helped make the Web and intranets so popular.

Using HTML-specific editing programs has advantages and disadvantages: while HTML editors generally make inserting HTML tags easier, you are already familiar with the workings of your other desktop applications and this can make production faster. As you work through Part II: "Creating Intranet Content," you'll get some guidance as to when a particular technique is applicable. Part V: "Exploring Publishing Tools," introduces some high-end publishing tools that help automate many facets of intranet content production.

One of the major debates raging over HTML is who has control over how a page is displayed—the person who created it or the person viewing it. Historically, the display has been controlled by the person viewing it. He or she set options in the browser program to instruct it what color to make the page and text and how big it should display on the screen.

This was fine when the only information being displayed on the Web was straight text, such as shown in figure 1.3. The simple tags for this example are shown in figure 1.4. With the explosion of advertising over the Web, designers want their *vision* of the page to be displayed on every computer screen. New tags are being developed to give the designer, also known as a *content provider*, more control.

This does not mean that you have to exercise this control. A simple page can contain only the basic tags necessary to let it be displayed, while a more elaborate page can have a certain style. See figures 1.5 and 1.6 for an example of how the same information shown in the preceding figures can be formatted differently. If you just want to make information available to others in your company, you might want to leave out the fancy formatting.

Fig. 1.3
A basic page created to display information quickly.

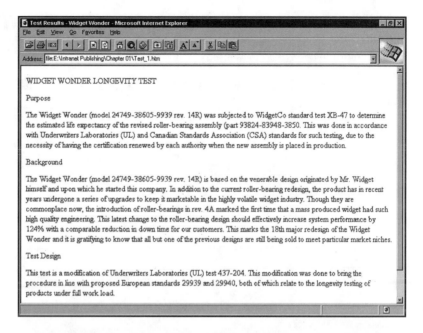

Fig. 1.4
The HTML code that displays the page shown in figure 1.3.

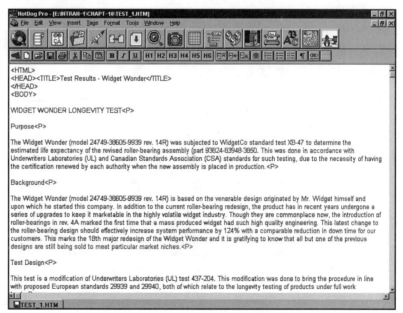

Fig. 1.5
The same information shown in fig. 1.3, but formatted to give it more style.

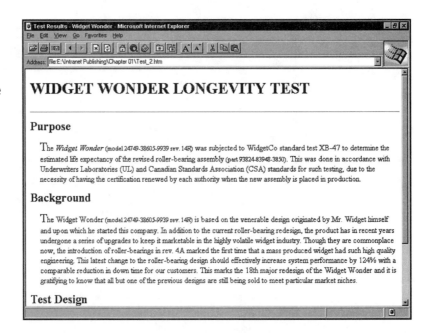

Fig. 1.6
The code used to produce the page shown in fig. 1.5.

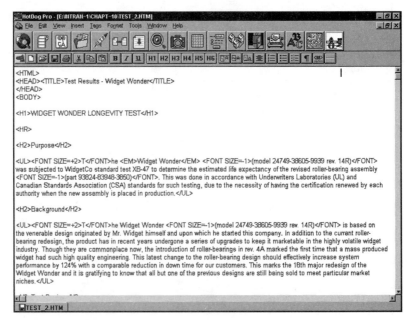

▶ **See** "Working with Text Files," **p. 84**

How Can You Use Your Intranet?

Your use of an intranet is limited only by your imagination. Part IV, "Putting Intranets To Work," provides real world examples of how companies are using intranets to make their businesses run more smoothly. The following examples are intended to get you thinking of new applications and ways an intranet can help you.

Newsletter

Does your office or department put out a newsletter for its members? How much time do you spend printing, photocopying, and distributing it?

If you publish your newsletter as an intranet page or pages, as shown in figure 1.7, as soon as you have finished writing, it can be available for everyone to read. See Chapter 14, "Corporate Communications," for examples. You can even set up a link that allows readers to respond via e-mail to any issues raised. All they have to do is click a highlighted e-mail symbol and their browser opens an e-mail window and automatically inserts your address.

Fig. 1.7
A departmental newsletter can be available as soon as it has been written.

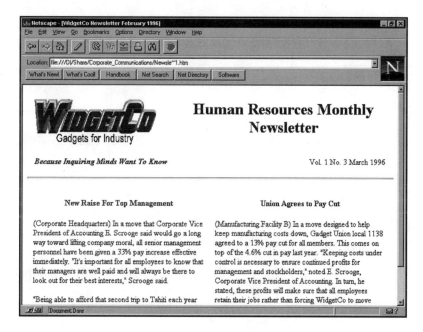

Product Database

A product database used by the sales department can be created using HTML pages. This greatly simplifies both creating and updating. By using links to engineering drawings, marketing information, and financial calculations, each product's information is always up-to-date.

For example, if engineering changes the design of a part, this change is automatically shown in the page's figure. No alteration needs to be made to the HTML code, and the change is transparent to the sales force (see fig. 1.8).

Fig. 1.8
A product sales page seamlessly pulls together information from many different departments.

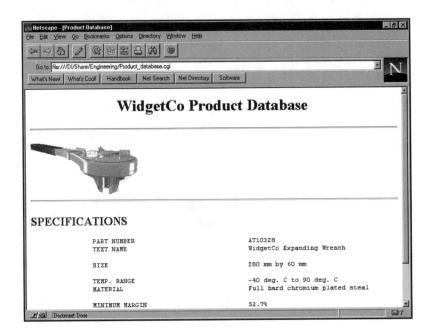

▶ See "Linking Documents," **p. 113**
▶ See "Content Implementation," **p. 278**

Employee Handbook

As company policies change, keeping an employee handbook up-to-date and distributed can become a difficult and costly operation. If the handbook is published as an intranet site, as shown in figure 1.9, however, every change can be fully documented and available to any employee at any time. Links can be included for health benefits, pension plans, even access to employee records (providing that the appropriate security safeguards are in place).

Fig. 1.9
Employee hand-books are con-stantly being changed. By publishing it as an intranet site, everyone has instant access to the latest infor-mation.

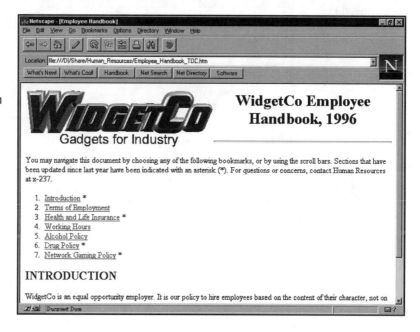

▶ **See** "Sample Uses in Human Resources," **p. 289**

▶ **See** "Aspects of Security," **p. 237**

Manufacturing

Making sure that assemblers have the latest work instructions and drawings is always a problem. As orders arrive on the shop floor, a quick look at a product's HTML page can confirm drawing and work instruction dates (see fig. 1.10). If the assembler does not have the latest information, a quick click on a link pulls up the appropriate drawing or word processing document and allows it to be printed out immediately. If computers are available at the as-sembly station, the documents can be simply left on the computer screen, saving time and large amounts of paper. See Chapter 20, "Manufacturing," for examples of ways your manufacturing department can use an intranet.

Fig. 1.10
All information about a product, from material lists to engineering drawings, is instantly accessible.

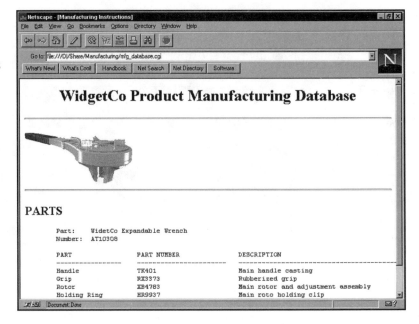

This page can access the same information used by a sales database, eliminating duplicated paperwork.

From Here...

Intranets are becoming a powerful tool in all manner of communications, from corporate information to sales and marketing data. This chapter provided a brief introduction to intranets, the HTML language that lets them work, and some of the ways your company can put them to use.

The following chapters provide specific information about the topics discussed and help you begin your own intranet publishing:

- 🌑 Chapter 2, "HTML Primer: Planning a Document," teaches you how to set up and publish your page.

- 🌑 Chapter 3, "Formatting Documents," builds on the knowledge learned in Chapter 2. This chapter teaches you how to format your document using more advanced HTML tags and link the document to others.

- 🌑 Part IV, "Putting Intranets To Work," gives you real life examples of intranets. Each example provides screen shots and HTML code to help you think of ways to use your intranet and implement your ideas.

2

HTML Primer: Planning a Document

By Paul Bodensiek

The one thing that most dictates how you construct your intranet documents and how they look is *HTML*, the *HyperText Markup Language*. Designed to make World Wide Web and intranet publishing relatively easy, HTML's main drawback is its limited page layout capabilities. Without a lot of work, your pages will not be as intricate as those you design with a page layout program (such as QuarkXPress) or even your word processor.

On the other hand, HTML is extremely powerful for linking all types of document files together. From other HTML pages to text files, and from graphics to spreadsheets, HTML helps you weave your computer network together to make all types of communication faster and more efficient.

This chapter teaches you the basic structure of an intranet document and walks you through the building stage of your first intranet page. By the end of the chapter, you'll have all the skills necessary to create simple intranet pages. In future chapters, you learn how to format your documents for maximum readability and ease-of-use, use advanced graphics features, and add strength to your documents by incorporating tables, databases, and messaging.

In this chapter, you learn

- What HTML is
- The parts of an intranet page

● How to name intranet pages
● How to enter and format text

What Is HTML?

HyperText Markup Language (HTML) is the collection of instructions, or *tags*, that tell the browser program how to display a document. Most people who create HTML documents for a living will tell you that the language is *so* complicated that you are much better off paying them to produce your Web documents rather than learning to make your own. Nothing can be further from the truth.

If you can write a letter using a word processor, you already have most of the skills necessary to make your own HTML documents. In fact every time you reference a previous letter, memo, or report, you are making a link to that document (see fig. 2.1). The only difference between your letter and an HTML document is that a person reading the letter has to physically look through a file cabinet to find the referenced document, while a browser automatically loads any referenced document you choose.

Fig. 2.1
An average business letter contains many references that perform the same function as an HTML hyperlink.

Reference—

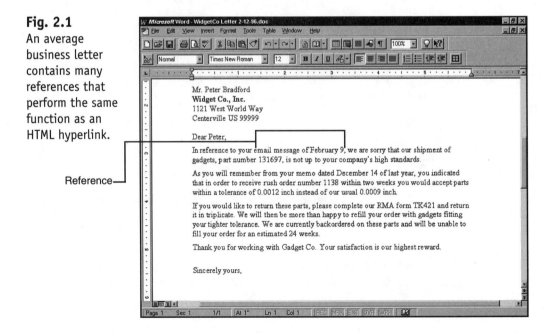

Your word processor saves you from having to enter special codes for print-ing bold or italic text: All you do is highlight a word and click the appropriate button. The word shows up bold or italic on your screen, and you think noth-ing more about it. The file containing your letter, however, has tags at the beginning and end of the word that tell the printer to start and end "bolding" (see fig. 2.2).

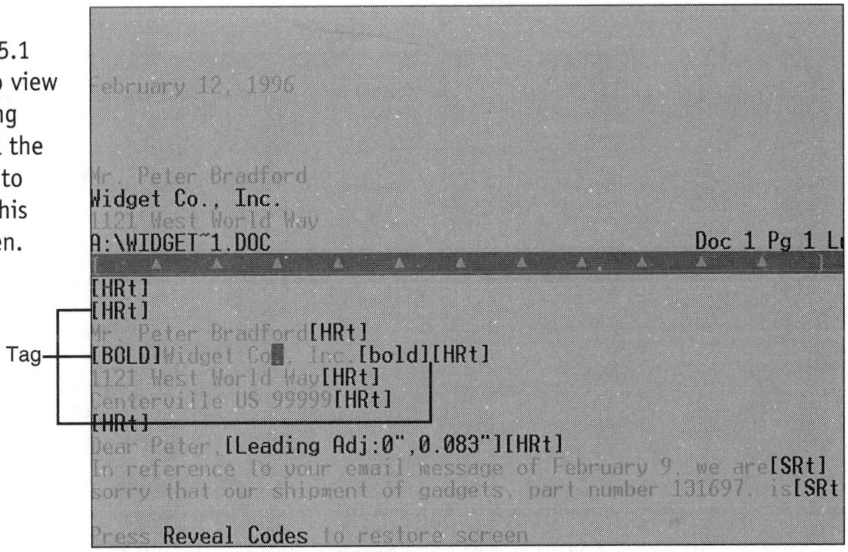

Fig. 2.2
WordPerfect 5.1 allows you to view the formatting tags that tell the printer what to do. Usually this view is hidden.

HTML is no different than the preceding example, and it's not difficult to learn. Most HTML tags require a beginning and ending entry. Luckily they are not difficult to distinguish; the ending tag just adds a slash (/) to the be-ginning tag. For example, a bold word would be surrounded by the tags <B> and </B>. In the previous sentence, the word *and* would show up bold on a browser screen. The beginning and ending tags taken together are called a *container*.

If you remember the "old days" of word processors, being shielded from for-matting tags was not possible. I cut my teeth writing research papers on my college's mainframe computer. Being able to update text on-screen before printing it out was worth the trouble of typing in bizarre commands to indent paragraphs or change a type style. I can't remember a single one of those commands now, but being able to use them then relegated my typewriter to mothballs.

Typically you write HTML documents in one of two ways: you use a basic text editor, like Notepad, and type out your text and every HTML tag by hand or you use an HTML editor that automatically inserts tags around a highlighted word or phrase. Either way, the document you're editing displays your HTML tags, and you have to load the file into a browser to see what it looks like (see figs. 2.3 and 2.4).

▶ **See** "HTML Editing Programs," **p. 101**

Fig. 2.3
An HTML document can look confusing while it's being edited.

Tag ——

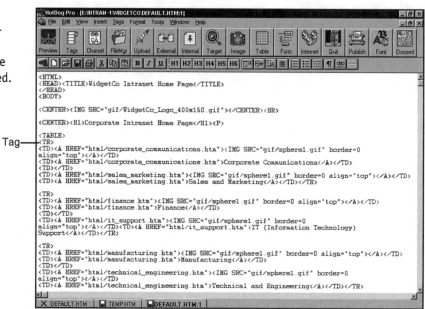

Now what-you-see-is-what-you-get (WYSIWYG) HTML editors are becoming available. Microsoft started with its Microsoft Word Internet Assistant. It was very basic and left out many of the more advanced HTML formatting options, but for making simple documents, it was a godsend. It has since been updated to include some of the higher-end commands, and now other editors are also available like Netscape Navigator 2 Gold and Microsoft FrontPage. These new tools are cutting down the learning curve and removing many of the arguments that professional Web designers have used to sell you their services.

Either way, using a text-based or WYSIWYG editor, HTML editing is not difficult.

Fig. 2.4
The code shown
in figure 2.3
produces the
WidgetCo home
page.

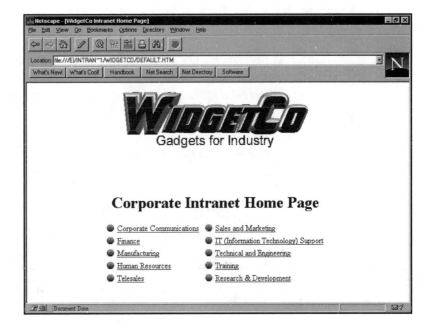

HTML Strengths

HTML's greatest strength is listed right in its name: *HyperText*.

▶ **See** "Linking Documents," **p. 113**

In addition to links from one page to another, hypertext allows you to link
your document to a file not even viewable by a browser. For example, an
engineering department might be looking for comments on its new widget.
The department produces a page that has text describing the widget and
includes a link to its computer-aided design (CAD) drawing file. Anyone who
wanted to look at the drawing could click the drawing's link and either have
the file downloaded to his or her computer, or the appropriate program
would start and automatically load the file so that it could be studied.

A great deal of creativity can be expressed in the layout of a page. The use of
graphics (logos, icons, and buttons) can help you make a page that is both
useful and interesting to look at. Studies have shown that documents using
color and graphics are more easily read and have a higher retention level
than those that are in black and white and don't use any graphics. See figure
2.5 for an intranet page with graphic embellishments.

NOTE

You don't have to be a great artist to include color graphics in your intranet pages. The CD-ROM included with this book contains a collection of graphic accents, icons, and buttons to help you put together interesting pages with a minimum of effort. See Appendix A, "What's on the CD," for a list of included graphics.

Your company may also have its logo available in a file that can be used in your page.

Fig. 2.5
The use of graphics and some creative layout can make your intranet pages more interesting to read.

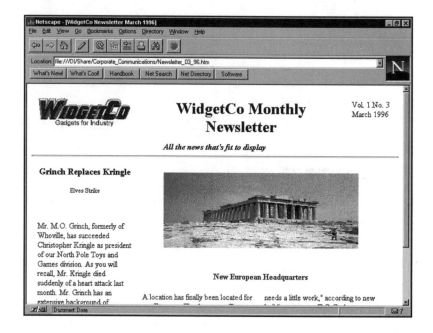

As with any type of layout, remember not to go overboard. Too many graphics and colors can make a page totally unreadable. Be subtle and keep your readers in mind when laying out your intranet pages.

HTML Limitations

Looking at an HTML page might give you the impression that the programs used to produce it are as robust and flexible as a desktop publishing program (see fig. 2.6). They are not. Even the new breed of WYSIWYG HTML editors are nowhere near as powerful as the page layout programs of 10 years ago.

There is a lot of catching up to be done and many opportunities for companies that can make page layout for HTML easier.

Fig. 2.6
Although some Web pages look complex, their underlying structure is still quite simple.

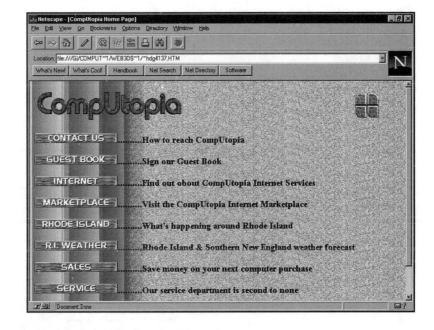

In general your pages are limited to displaying text in one of two faces: proportional or fixed width. A proportional typeface is one in which each letter uses only as much space as it needs, like **Times Roman**. In a fixed width typeface, like `Courier`, each letter uses exactly as much space as every other.

For example, most of the text in this book is printed in a proportional typeface so the space used by a "W" is much wider than that used by an "I." In a fixed width typeface, a "W" and an "I" each take up the same space on a line (see fig. 2.7).

You may have used a word processor or desktop publishing program to set up two or more columns of text in your company newsletter. While it's possible to do this in an HTML document, it's not straightforward and you can forget having the text wrap around an irregularly shaped graphic (see fig. 2.8).

Fig. 2.7
In a proportional typeface each letter space is in proportion to the width of the letter, while in a fixed width typeface all spaces are the same.

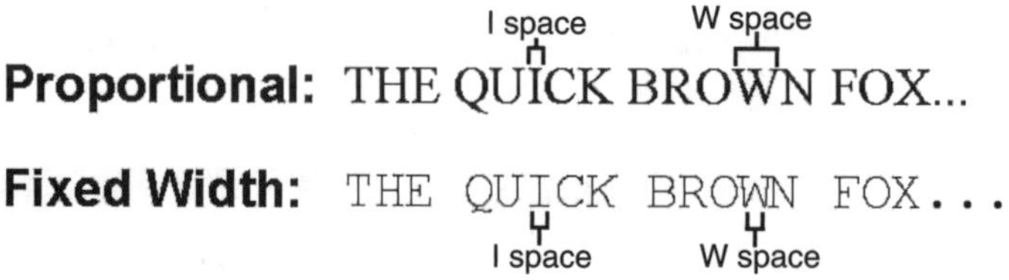

I space   W space

Proportional: THE QUICK BROWN FOX...

Fixed Width: THE QUICK BROWN FOX...

I space   W space

Fig. 2.8
Desktop publishing programs allow you to wrap text around the outline of an irregularly shaped graphic.

▶ **See** "Before You Start Writing," **p. 211**

Updating documents can also be difficult if proper care is not taken. One important fact to keep in mind is that a document is defined not only by its name, but also its location. If an intranet page file is moved from one subdirectory or computer to another, all links to that page will be lost.

In addition, unlike most word processing files, graphics do not become part of the HTML files. This means that the relative location of the HTML page and any graphic elements it references must also remain constant.

Parts of a Page

A page must contain a head section and a body section. Within each of these portions is the information that you want displayed on the client's screen. Almost everything added to a page is part of these two sections. Figure 2.9 shows the relationship between the head and body. Additionally, a signature section tells the person viewing the page who created it (see fig. 2.10).

Fig. 2.9
A bare intranet page shows the relationship between the head and body sections.

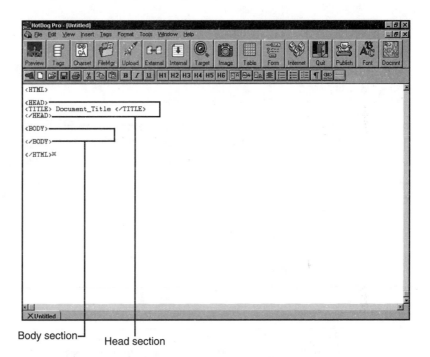

Body section ⌐   Head section

A page always starts with the tag <HTML> and ends with </HTML>. This alerts your browser program that the following text file should be interpreted as HTML code so that it will display it properly.

NOTE

The <HTML>...</HTML> container is not strictly necessary. Most browsers will interpret an HTML page properly without it, but sometimes your documents may be read by a browser that does need it. To be on the safe side, always include this tag in your code.

The Head Section

Located between the <HEAD> and </HEAD> tags, the head section is like the header in a word processing document. You use it to provide information about the document, such as its title and a base location for any further documents that it may reference. The title is generally displayed in the title bar of the browser program, while other tags in the head are usually not displayed.

▶ **See** "Reuse, Reuse, Reuse," **p. 219**

▶ **See** "Linking Documents," **p. 113**

The Body Section

The body section contains everything that you want shown in your document. For example, if you have written a list of possible health care providers serviced by an insurance agency, it would be placed in the body section.

The Signature

The signature section is a courtesy to your readers. It's not strictly necessary, but is generally provided to let people know who created the page and how to contact that person.

The signature is defined by the <ADDRESS>...</ADDRESS> container. It can contain any other HTML formatting like a reference to your e-mail address or your home page's URL (Uniform Resource Locator). Figure 2.10 shows the HTML code of an example signature section.

Fig. 2.10
The signature
section of a page
gives the reader
information about
how to get in
contact with you.

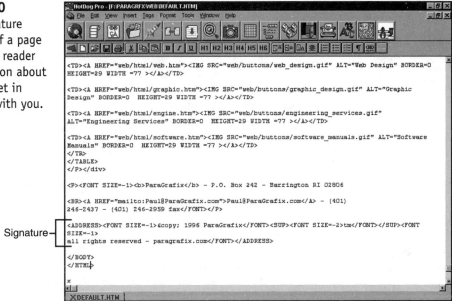

```
HotDog Pro - [F:\PARAGRFX\WEB\DEFAULT.HTM]
File  Edit  View  Insert  Tags  Format  Tools  Window  Help

<TD><A HREF="web/html/web.htm"><IMG SRC="web/buttons/web_design.gif" ALT="Web Design" BORDER=0
HEIGHT=29 WIDTH =77 ></A></TD>

<TD><A HREF="web/html/graphic.htm"><IMG SRC="web/buttons/graphic_design.gif" ALT="Graphic
Design" BORDER=0  HEIGHT=29 WIDTH =77 ></A></TD>

<TD><A HREF="web/html/engine.htm"><IMG SRC="web/buttons/engineering_services.gif"
ALT="Engineering Services" BORDER=0  HEIGHT=29 WIDTH =77 ></A></TD>

<TD><A HREF="web/html/software.htm"><IMG SRC="web/buttons/software_manuals.gif" ALT="Software
Manuals" BORDER=0  HEIGHT=29 WIDTH =77 ></A></TD>
</TR>
</TABLE>
</P></div>

<P><FONT SIZE=-1><b>ParaGrafix</b> - P.O. Box 242 - Barrington RI 02806

<BR><A HREF="mailto:Paul@ParaGrafix.com">Paul@ParaGrafix.com</A> - (401)
246-2437 - (401) 246-2959 fax</FONT></P>

<ADDRESS><FONT SIZE=-1>&copy; 1996 ParaGrafix</FONT><SUP><FONT SIZE=-2>tm</FONT></SUP><FONT
SIZE=-1>
all rights reserved - paragrafix.com</FONT></ADDRESS>

</BODY>
</HTML>
```
Signature

DEFAULT.HTM

Basic Body Tags

The body of your document is composed of text and graphics formatted to convey the information you want to appear. Using the body tags listed below, you can start writing simple HTML documents right away.

Paragraph Tags

Paragraph tags tell the browser how to format paragraphs. In HTML, new lines of code are used to make editing and updating code easier. This is part of HTML's background as a pseudo-programming language. Software writers often use indents and carriage returns to organize their code into logical sections. This legacy is carried on by HTML and can be extremely handy, if a bit confusing at first.

One of the hardest parts of HTML to get used to is that you don't automatically create a new paragraph when you hit the Enter key. To make sure there are breaks in paragraphs where you want them, you have to use the Paragraph or Line Break tags.

NOTE

Note that WYSIWYG editors automatically add the appropriate line break tags for you.

The line break tag, <BR>, places a single return at the end of a paragraph. It's useful when you want to keep the spacing between parts of a page small. If you have long paragraphs of text, a single <BR> tag may leave your page difficult to read.

The paragraph tag, <P>, adds an extra return between paragraphs. This is extremely useful when you have long passages of text.

TIP

The paragraph tag <P> can also be used as a container. See "Using the Paragraph Tag as a Container" in Chapter 3 for advanced uses of this tag.

Figures 2.11 and 2.12 show an example of text formatted with and without line break tags.

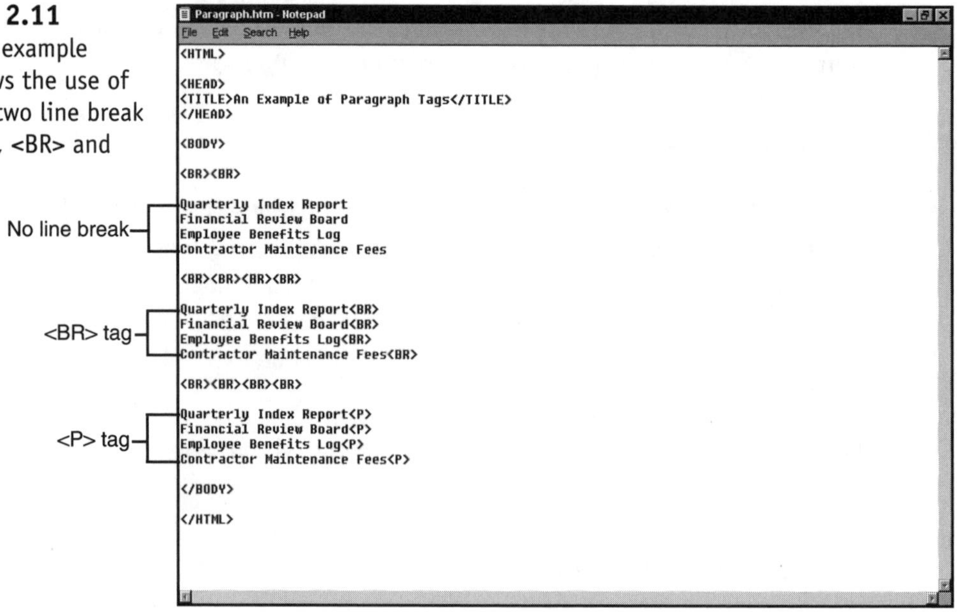

Fig. 2.11
This example shows the use of the two line break tags, <BR> and <P>.

```
Paragraph.htm - Notepad
File  Edit  Search  Help
<HTML>

<HEAD>
<TITLE>An Example of Paragraph Tags</TITLE>
</HEAD>

<BODY>

<BR><BR>

Quarterly Index Report
Financial Review Board
Employee Benefits Log
Contractor Maintenance Fees

<BR><BR><BR><BR>

Quarterly Index Report<BR>
Financial Review Board<BR>
Employee Benefits Log<BR>
Contractor Maintenance Fees<BR>

<BR><BR><BR><BR>

Quarterly Index Report<P>
Financial Review Board<P>
Employee Benefits Log<P>
Contractor Maintenance Fees<P>

</BODY>

</HTML>
```

No line break—

 tag—

<P> tag—

Fig. 2.12
The results of using the line break tags shown in figure 2.11.

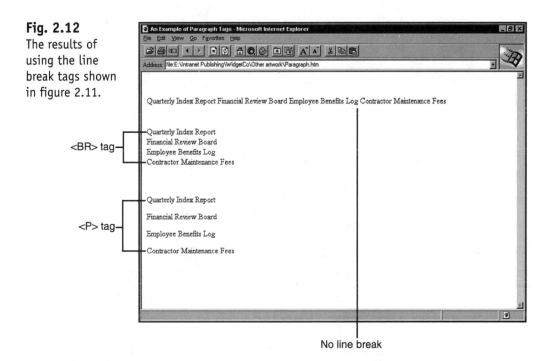

 tag

<P> tag

No line break

Character Tags

As noted earlier in this chapter, individual words or letters can be modified by adding formatting tags before and after them. You can make words bold, italic, or both, and even change their color.

Bold and Italic

The easiest two tags to use are the bold and italic containers. Each of these is a simple one-letter tag surrounded by angle brackets. Table 2.1 shows the use and structure of these two tags.

TABLE 2.1   The Bold and Italic Tags

Name	Tags	Description
Bold	<B>…</B>	Causes the text in the container to be bold. Example: this is <B>Bold</B> Result: this is **Bold**

continues

TABLE 2.1   Continued

Name	Tags	Description
Italic	<I>...</I>	Makes the text in the container italic. Example: this is <I>Italic</I> Result: this is *Italic*

Size and Color

The font tag is a bit more complicated. With it you can set the size and color of individual words or letters.

Unlike word processing documents in which you can use an almost unlimited number of type sizes, you are limited to seven letter sizes in an HTML document. While this may seem like a small number, you'll rarely want or need to deal with more than this. See figure 2.13 for an example of the seven letter sizes allowed in an HTML document. Figure 2.14 shows the HTML code used to produce these different sizes.

Fig. 2.13
Although an HTML document is limited to seven letter sizes, this covers quite a range.

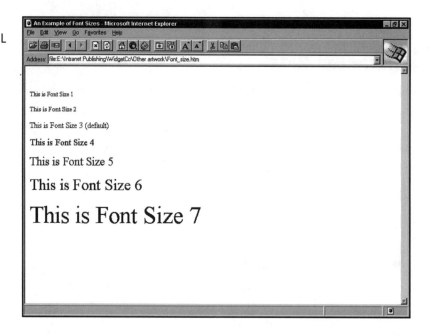

By default, all text displayed in an intranet document is size 3. To set the size of letters or words, you use the <FONT SIZE="#">...</FONT> container (see fig. 2.14). For example, to make a particular word size 6, type in the following tag:

```
<FONT SIZE="6"> this is size 6 </FONT>
```

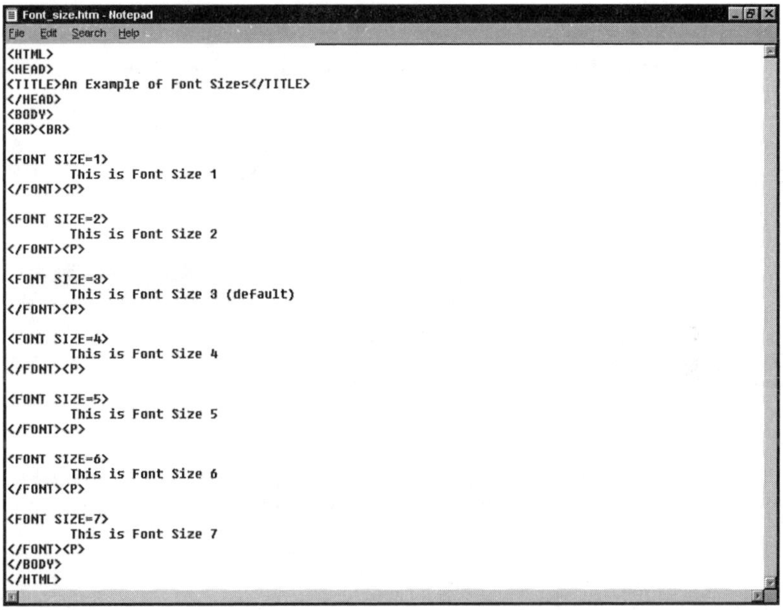

Fig. 2.14
To set the absolute size of words or letters, use the <FONT SIZE=#>...</FONT> container.

```
Font_size.htm - Notepad
File  Edit  Search  Help
<HTML>
<HEAD>
<TITLE>An Example of Font Sizes</TITLE>
</HEAD>
<BODY>
<BR><BR>

<FONT SIZE=1>
        This is Font Size 1
</FONT><P>

<FONT SIZE=2>
        This is Font Size 2
</FONT><P>

<FONT SIZE=3>
        This is Font Size 3 (default)
</FONT><P>

<FONT SIZE=4>
        This is Font Size 4
</FONT><P>

<FONT SIZE=5>
        This is Font Size 5
</FONT><P>

<FONT SIZE=6>
        This is Font Size 6
</FONT><P>

<FONT SIZE=7>
        This is Font Size 7
</FONT><P>
</BODY>
</HTML>
```

TIP

The quotation marks in the font tag are not strictly necessary. Use them to make your code easier to read.

A major strength in HTML's control of letter size is the ability to set relative sizing. If you want to emphasize certain text by making it larger or smaller than the surrounding text, simply use a + or - sign before the number you enter in the font tag. The number is the amount larger or smaller than the surrounding text you want.

TIP

Relative font size is especially useful when you don't know what default font size a person accessing your screen has set for his or her browser.

For example, if you want to make some text two sizes bigger than the surrounding text, type in the following tag (replacing the text within the container with whatever you want)

```
<FONT SIZE="+2">this is 2 sizes larger</FONT>
```

To make text two sizes smaller than the surrounding text, type in the following tag (replacing the text within the container with whatever you want)

```
<FONT SIZE="-2">this is 2 sizes smaller</FONT>
```

Figures 2.15 and 2.16 give an example of different text sizes. All were based on the default text size of 3.

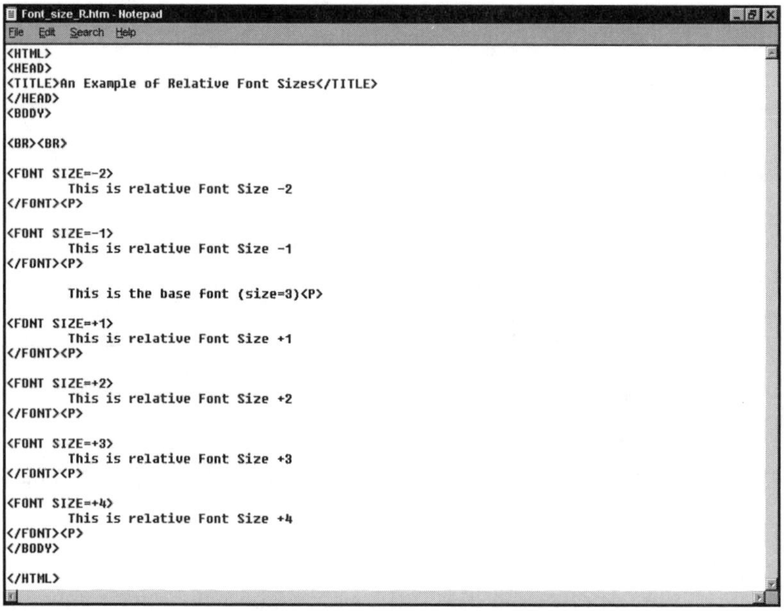

Fig. 2.15
To set text to relative sizes, use plus (+) or minus (-) signs before numbers in the <FONT SIZE=#> tag.

```
<HTML>
<HEAD>
<TITLE>An Example of Relative Font Sizes</TITLE>
</HEAD>
<BODY>

<BR><BR>

<FONT SIZE=-2>
        This is relative Font Size -2
</FONT><P>

<FONT SIZE=-1>
        This is relative Font Size -1
</FONT><P>

        This is the base Font (size=3)<P>

<FONT SIZE=+1>
        This is relative Font Size +1
</FONT><P>

<FONT SIZE=+2>
        This is relative Font Size +2
</FONT><P>

<FONT SIZE=+3>
        This is relative Font Size +3
</FONT><P>

<FONT SIZE=+4>
        This is relative Font Size +4
</FONT><P>
</BODY>

</HTML>
```

NOTE

Not all browsers display text formatted in different colors. If you are going to use colored text, make sure its meaning is not lost if all the text in your document is the same color.

Changing a word's color works exactly the same way as changing its size, with the exception that the colors you pick are specified as 6-digit numbers in hexadecimal (hex) format. The first two digits control the amount of red in the color, the second two the amount of green, and the third two blue.

Fig. 2.16
The result of setting type size relative to the base size.

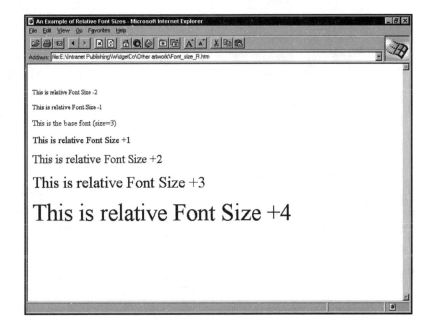

N O T E

Without getting into too much detail about hexadecimal numbers, each digit (single number) ranges from 0 to 15, unlike how we normally count whereby each digit ranges from 0 to 9. Since we only have 10 individual numbers, 10 through 15 are represented by the letters A through F.

The number 16 is represented in hex as 10. Numbers above 16 are built up just as you do with regular numbers by adding on to the base. So 17 is represented as 11, 18 as 12, 31 as 1F and 32 as 20.

A two-digit hex number can range from 0 (represented as 00) to 255 (represented as FF).

TIP

The CD-ROM contains a really useful utility, The Color Machine, that generates hex numbers for any color. You don't have to guess at the hex number, just create the color on screen using three sliders (one each for red, green, and blue) and the hex numbers are automatically displayed. You can even copy the numbers to the clipboard to paste them into your file.

To make text a particular color, type the following tag (replacing "text" with the text you want colored).

```
<FONT COLOR="######">text</FONT>
```

The number 000000 represents the color black, while FFFFFF represents white. Table 2.2 gives a list of different colors and their hexadecimal numbers.

TABLE 2.2 Common Colors and Their Hexadecimal Numbers

Color	Hexadecimal	Decimal (base 10)
Black	000000	0-0-0
White	FFFFFF	255-255-255
Light Gray	C8C8C8	200-200-200
Medium Gray	7F7F7F	127-127-127
Dark Gray	373737	55-55-55
Red	FF0000	255-0-0
Green	00FF00	0-255-0
Blue	0000FF	0-0-255

Font size and color tags can be combined together for interesting effects. For example, to set the phrase "buy this book" in size 3, red letters, type in the following tags

```
<FONT SIZE="3" COLOR="FF0000">buy this book</FONT>
```

N O T E

Netscape Navigator 2.0 also accepts written words for colors. Acceptable colors are red, green, blue, cyan, magenta, yellow, black, white, turquoise, and pink. For example, you can write the previous line as

```
<FONT SIZE=3 COLOR="RED">buy this book</FONT>
```

Make sure that you include both quotation marks or you could experience some very weird results.

Create Your First Intranet Page with HTML

Now it's time to put all the tags you've learned in this chapter together to produce your first intranet page.

▶ **See** "HTML Editing Programs," **p. 101**

For this first example, you will be writing your code in Notepad and entering all the HTML tags by hand. As you become more proficient in writing intranet pages, you'll find editors specifically tailored to adding HTML tags invaluable. Part V, "Exploring Publishing Tools," introduces some high-end publishers that could be useful if you are creating a lot of intranet content.

Write the Basic Page Text

To begin the example, type in the HTML tags for the head, body, and address, and then enter the text for the page. To do this:

1. Start Notepad by opening the Start menu, selecting Programs, Accessories, Notepad.

2. Turn on word wrap by opening the Edit menu and selecting Word Wrap.

3. Type in the text exactly as shown below. It should look like figure 2.17.

```
<HTML>

<HEAD>

<TITLE>
```

```
     Intranet Publishing Kit Example Document
</TITLE>

</HEAD>

<BODY>

WidgetCo
Corporate Intranet Home Page

Departments

Corporate Communications
Sales and Marketing
Human Resources
Education and Training
Legal and Finance
Manufacturing
Documentation
Research and Development
Customer Service and IT Support

</BODY>

<ADDRESS>
     BodensiekP
</ADDRESS>

</HTML>
```

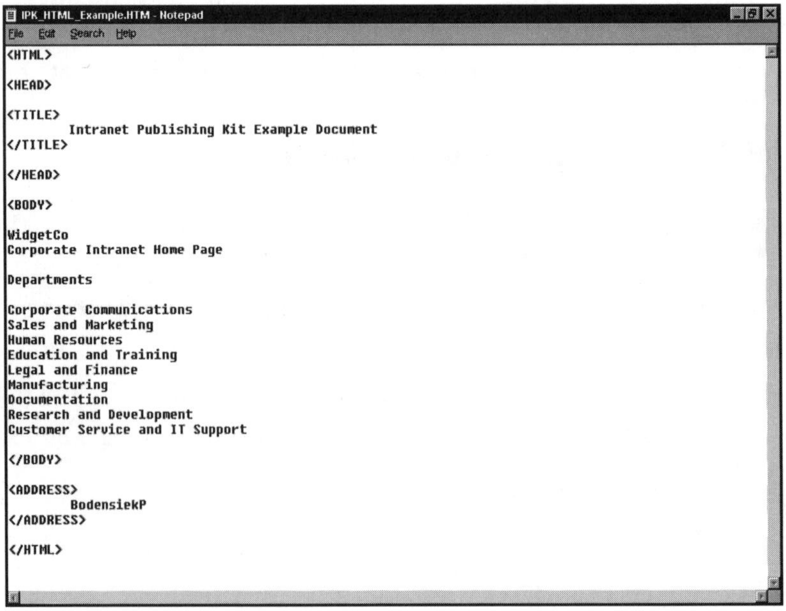


```
<HTML>

<HEAD>

<TITLE>
     Intranet Publishing Kit Example Document
</TITLE>

</HEAD>

<BODY>

WidgetCo
Corporate Intranet Home Page

Departments

Corporate Communications
Sales and Marketing
Human Resources
Education and Training
Legal and Finance
Manufacturing
Documentation
Research and Development
Customer Service and IT Support

</BODY>

<ADDRESS>
     BodensiekP
</ADDRESS>

</HTML>
```

Fig. 2.17
The text used for the Chapter 2 HTML example.

4. Choose File, Save.

5. Create a new folder on your hard drive by choosing the Create New Folder button. Name the new folder **HTML_Example**.

6. Double-click the New Folder icon you have created to open the folder.

7. Enter **IPK_HTML_Example.HTM** in the File Name text box and choose the Save button.

TIP

Don't use spaces in your file and folder names when saving HTML documents since some browsers may not recognize your folder or file later if you don't. A good way to avoid spaces in long file names is to use an underscore (_) between words.

8. Leave Notepad running since we'll be coming back to this example later.

View Your HTML Document

Now that you have saved your HTML code, view it using MS Internet Explorer. If you have not installed Internet Explorer, we have included the latest version on the CD along with a number of other browsers. Although the following instructions are based on Internet Explorer, the steps will be similar if you use another program.

To view your HTML file:

1. Start Microsoft Internet Explorer by doubling-clicking its desktop icon or selecting it from the Start menu.

    You may have to minimize Notepad first by choosing the minimize button at the upper right-hand corner of the screen.

2. Immediately press the Esc key or choose View, Stop.

3. Open your new HTML file. Choose File, Open then click the Open File button and navigate your hard drive to find the file you just saved. Choose the Open button.

N O T E

If you are using a different browser program, you may have to type the following in the address text box

file:///C|/HTML_Example/IPK_HTML_Example.HTM

where C is the letter of your hard drive. The | symbol after the C is typically made by pressing Shift+\, though your keyboard may be different. If your file is in another folder, you may have to alter the path.

Your very first intranet page is displayed on your screen (see fig. 2.18). But, we forgot to tell the browser to put breaks between our lines of text.

Fig. 2.18
Your very first intranet page is displayed without any line breaks.

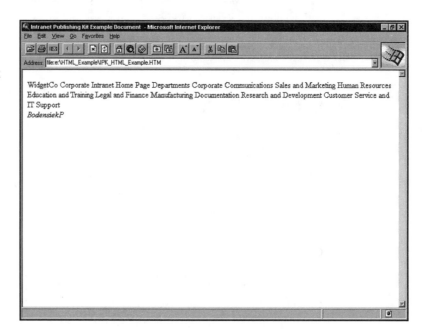

Add Line Breaks

Everywhere we want to have a line break needs to have a tag telling the browser to start a new line. To do this:

  1. Open Notepad by selecting it from the taskbar or by pressing Alt+Tab until your Notepad document is highlighted.

2. Add **
** and **<P>** tags at the end of each line as shown in figure 2.19. The <BR> tags will make the list of departments fit neatly together, while the <P> tags give some spacing between the different portions of your page.

Fig. 2.19
Update your HTML code to include breaks between lines to make your text readable.

3. Save your file by choosing File, Save.

4. View your changes by switching back to Internet Explorer. Either select Internet Explorer from the taskbar or press Alt+Tab until Internet Explorer is highlighted. Your page should look like figure 2.20. Note that you may have to choose View, Refresh to make Internet Explorer reload the file with your changes.

Do not exit Notepad as we will be coming back to it later.

Add Some Character Formatting

Well, your new intranet page is readable, but it does leave a little something to be desired from a style point of view. To add character formatting to your page, follow these steps:

1. Return to your HTML code in Notepad.

2. To make the name of the company large, place the cursor at the beginning of the word *WidgetCo* and type **<FONT SIZE="6">**. At the end of *WidgetCo* (before the <BR> tag) add the tag **</FONT>** so that only WidgetCo is large.

3. To make *WidgetCo* bold, add the **<B>** and **</B>** tags at the beginning and end of the word.

Fig. 2.20
With the addition of line breaks, your intranet page is now much more readable.

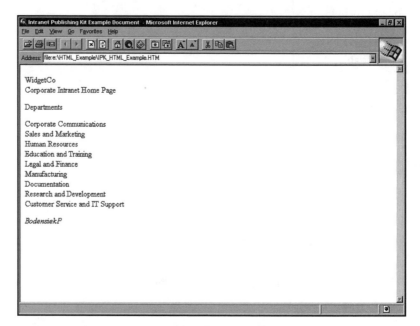

NOTE

Make sure you "nest" your tags when writing code by having your end tags in the opposite order of your start tags. For example, after steps 1 and 2, the WidgetCo line should read:

```
<FONT SIZE="6"><B>WidgetCo</B></FONT><BR>
```

Some older browsers won't understand tags if they are not nested properly. It's also a good HTML habit to write your code this way since it makes changes easier.

4. To add some style to the Corporate Intranet Home Page text, add the italic tags, **<I>** and **</I>** at the beginning and end of its line. Also,

increase the size of the text to 5 by adding the tags **<FONT SIZE= "5">** and **</FONT>** at the beginning and end of "Corporate Intranet Home Page."

Note that you should place the </I> and </FONT> tags before the line break tag, <P>.

5. As an added enhancement to the "Corporate Intranet Home Page" text, make it red by adding the color tag to the font tag. Simply type **COLOR="FF0000"** after SIZE="5" in the font tag.

Your file should now look like figure 2.21.

Nested font tags

Fig. 2.21
Your intranet home page HTML file after adding tags to give the first two visible lines some style.

Nested bold tags —

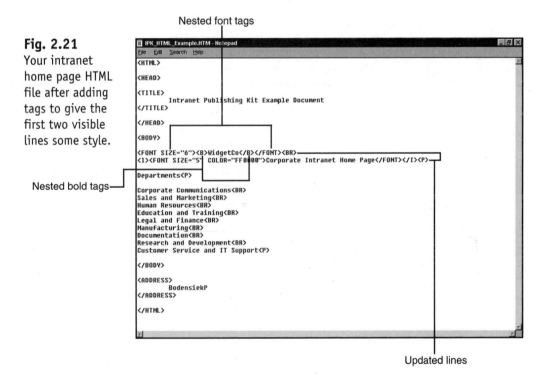

Updated lines

6. Save the page and switch to Internet Explorer to view your work. Your file should look like figure 2.22.

Make the Code Easier To Read

Even with very few formatting tags included in your HTML code, your new page is getting kind of difficult to understand. By adding tabs and space between lines of code, you can keep your code neat and easy to deal with during any future changes you might make.

Fig. 2.22
The result of adding character formatting tags to the first two visible lines of text.

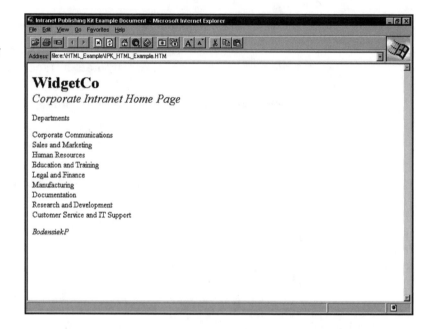

Figure 2.23 shows the same text we've been dealing with throughout this example. The only change since figure 2.21 is moving the character and paragraph formatting tags to different lines from the text they modify. Note that all the tags and lines of text are in the same relative positions, though.

Putting the formatting on separate lines is not always desirable. For example, breaking a line of text to display a bold tag, as in figure 2.24, is more confusing than leaving the line intact.

Fig. 2.23
A browser displays
this neat text file
in exactly the
same way it does
the relatively
messy code of
fig. 2.21.

```
IPK_HTML_Example.HTM - Notepad
File   Edit   Search   Help
<HTML>

<HEAD>

<TITLE>
          Intranet Publishing Kit Example Document
</TITLE>

</HEAD>

<BODY>

          <FONT SIZE="6"><B>
WidgetCo
          </B></FONT><BR>
          <I><FONT SIZE="5" COLOR="FF0000">
Corporate Intranet Home Page
          </FONT></I><P>

Departments<P>

Corporate Communications<BR>
Sales and Marketing<BR>
Human Resources<BR>
Education and Training<BR>
Legal and Finance<BR>
Manufacturing<BR>
Documentation<BR>
Research and Development<BR>
Customer Service and IT Support<P>

</BODY>

<ADDRESS>
          BodensiekP
</ADDRESS>
```

Fig. 2.24
Keeping all the
text with a line
or paragraph
together is
generally prefer-
able to breaking
up the text to
accentuate the
formatting tags.

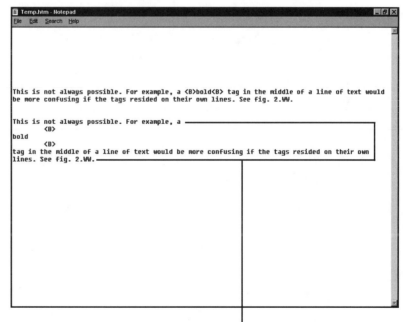

This formatting is confusing.

From Here...

In this chapter, you've learned the basics of writing HTML code and even wrote a simple intranet page. In the coming chapters, you'll learn more about HTML code and how to use it to link all your applications and data files together.

- ● Chapter 3, "Formatting Documents," builds on the knowledge you gained in this chapter and teaches you how to format your document using more advanced HTML tags and create simple links to the other documents.

- ● Chapter 4, "Creating Content with Your Desktop Applications," teaches you to use almost any application currently on your computer to create intranet content.

- ● Chapter 5, "Integrating Content from All Your Desktop Applications," shows you how to combine content from any application into your intranet site using hypertext links and OLE. Learn how to reference files using UNIX file conventions.

Formatting Documents

By Paul Bodensiek

In Chapter 2, "HTML Primer: Planning a Document," you learned the basic HTML tags to make text bold or italic and how to add breaks between lines of text. You also created your first intranet page using Notepad and viewed it in Microsoft Internet Explorer.

In this chapter, we expand on your ability to lay out intranet pages so that they convey the information you want with the least amount of effort.

At the end of the chapter is a handy HTML reference that lists all the tags you have learned so far.

In this chapter, you learn how to

- Add headings
- Center text
- Add horizontal lines
- Set the default font
- Create lists and multiple columns of text
- Add preformatted text and long quotations
- Add a dictionary-style definition
- Add a graphic

More Paragraph Tags

In addition to introducing line feeds, paragraphs can be formatted in a number of other ways. You can format entire paragraphs in larger text, center them across the width of the page, and use a number of other options detailed in the following sections. These additional formatting tags can help you make your intranet pages pleasing to the eye, and easier to read and understand.

Adding Headings

In Chapter 1, "Understanding Your Intranet Site," you created the headings for your first intranet page by making the text very large and bold. HTML provides an easier way to get the same effect using the <H#> tag. This tag provides six levels of headings you can use to organize your pages. Each heading style corresponds to a number between one and six. One is the highest heading level and six is the lowest.

To add a heading, simply insert **<H#>** before the heading text and **</H>** after, where the pound sign (#) is the number of the heading style you want.

One nice feature of the heading tag is that it automatically adds a line feed after the heading line so that you don't need to include the <P> or <BR> tag. Headings are like a combination of a paragraph and a character tag because they modify the character settings and also add the line feed.

See figures 3.1 and 3.2 for examples of the six heading styles.

TIP

This book is printed using three different heading levels. Your readers may find it confusing to use many more levels than that in your intranet pages.

Fig. 3.1
The six headings
provided by HTML
help you organize
your HTML page.

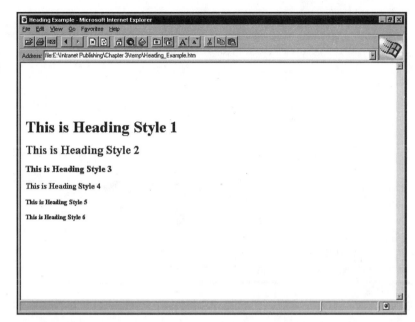

Fig. 3.2
HTML headings
are added using
the <H#>...</H>
container.

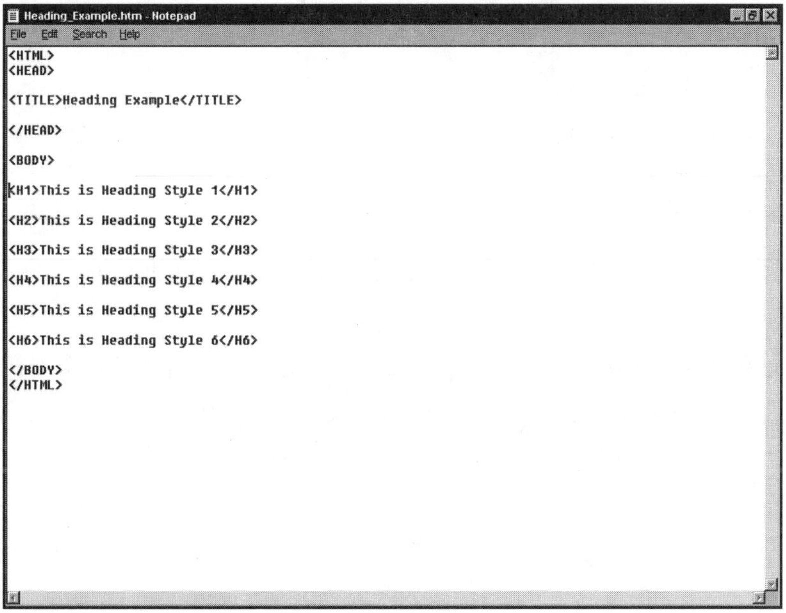

▶ **See** "Character Tags," **p. 33**

Centering Text

Often you want to center text, headings, or graphics. Use the <CEN-TER>...</CENTER> container. One nice thing about centered text is that it doesn't matter what size window the viewing browser is using. In other words, if a user changes the size of the browser window, the centered text automatically moves to maintain its centering.

See figures 3.3 and 3.4 for examples of centered headings and text.

Fig. 3.3
Centered text remains centered no matter what size the viewing window is set to.

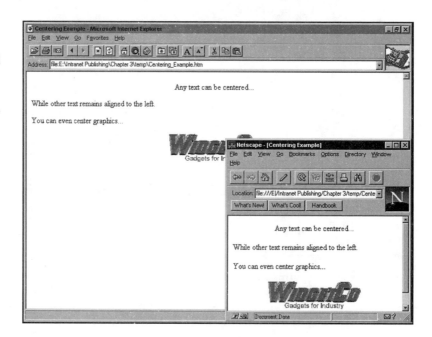

Using the Paragraph Tag as a Container

In Chapter 2, you used the <P> tag to add a line break between two paragraphs. This tag may also be used as a container that allows you to align particular paragraphs to the left, right, or center.

Fig. 3.4
To center a
portion of your
document, simply
add the <CENTER>
container around
your text or
graphic.

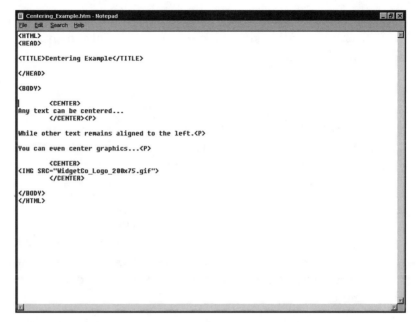

```
Centering_Example.htm - Notepad
File  Edit  Search  Help
<HTML>
<HEAD>

<TITLE>Centering Example</TITLE>

</HEAD>

<BODY>

        <CENTER>
Any text can be centered...
        </CENTER><P>

While other text remains aligned to the left.<P>

You can even center graphics...<P>

        <CENTER>
<IMG SRC="WidgetCo_Logo_200x75.gif">
        </CENTER>

</BODY>
</HTML>
```

There are two main advantages to the <P> container. First, it is the only tag
that allows you to align text to the right; and second, you can interrupt a
centered section of text for a left or right aligned paragraph without making
any changes to the surrounding code.

To use the <P> container, enter **<P ALIGN="*a*">** at the beginning of the
paragraph and close the container with **</P>** at the end of the paragraph.
Replace *a* with either **LEFT**, **RIGHT**, or **CENTER**.

▶ **See** "Paragraph Tags," **p. 31**

Adding Horizontal Rules

Another way to separate sections of a page without using headings is to add a
horizontal rule (line). By default, a horizontal rule extends from one side of
the screen to the other, with a dark top and light bottom to give it an engraved look. The <HR> tag includes a number of enhancements that make it

particularly useful as a graphical tag in your pages. The <HR> tag gives you control over the line's thickness, width, and alignment. You can also remove the embossed look to make a solid line.

TIP

Although the <HR> tag adds a full paragraph break both before and after the line, place a carriage return after the paragraph before the line using the <BR> tag. If you ever remove the line, this will keep the text before and after the line from running together.

The horizontal rule tag has four modifiers (SIZE, WIDTH, ALIGN, and NOSHADE) that may be used in any combination. See table 3.1 for a description of these modifiers. Figures 3.5 and 3.6 show examples of using the <HR> tag modifiers. Figure 3.7 gives an example of the <HR> tag used in an intranet page.

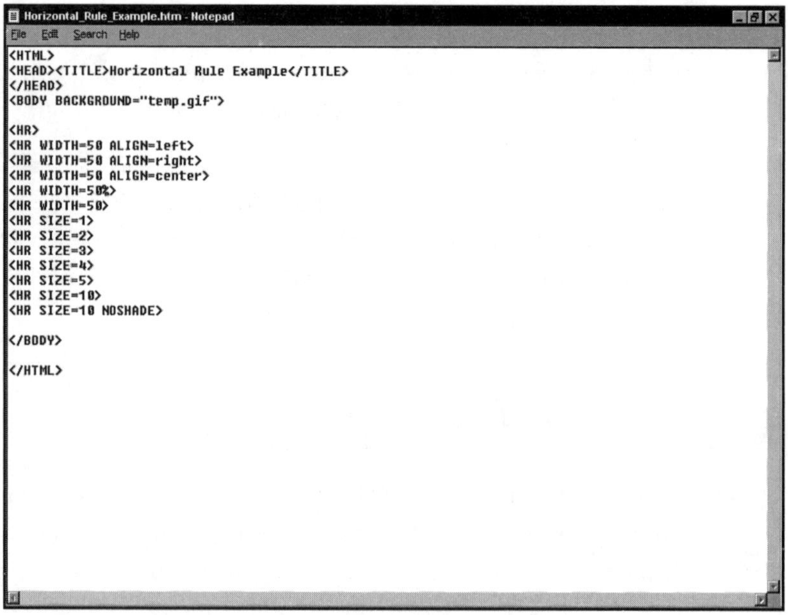

Fig. 3.5
The horizontal rule modifier may be used in any combination for a variety of effects.

```
Horizontal_Rule_Example.htm - Notepad
File  Edit  Search  Help
<HTML>
<HEAD><TITLE>Horizontal Rule Example</TITLE>
</HEAD>
<BODY BACKGROUND="temp.gif">

<HR>
<HR WIDTH=50 ALIGN=left>
<HR WIDTH=50 ALIGN=right>
<HR WIDTH=50 ALIGN=center>
<HR WIDTH=50%>
<HR WIDTH=50>
<HR SIZE=1>
<HR SIZE=2>
<HR SIZE=3>
<HR SIZE=4>
<HR SIZE=5>
<HR SIZE=10>
<HR SIZE=10 NOSHADE>

</BODY>

</HTML>
```

Fig. 3.6
Depending on the background color, the engraved look of horizontal rules may not be visible.

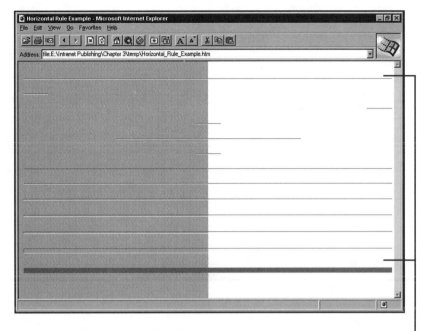

Embossing not visible

Fig. 3.7
Horizontal rules can be used to create a dramatic effect.

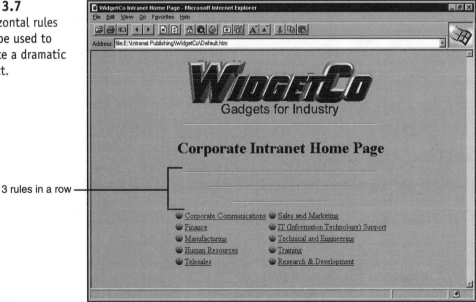

3 rules in a row

TABLE 3.1   Horizontal Rule Modifiers

Modifier	Description
SIZE	Sets the thickness of the horizontal rule in pixels. Example: <HR SIZE="5">
WIDTH	Sets the width of the horizontal rule. Example: <HR WIDTH="10"> (width is 10 pixels) Example: <HR WIDTH="10%"> (width is 10 percent of viewing window's width)
ALIGN	Determines whether the horizontal rule is aligned left, right, or center. Unless the width is less than the viewing window's width, this modifier has no effect. The default alignment is center. Example: <HR ALIGN="right">
NOSHADE	Turns off the embossed look of the horizontal rule. Example:<HR NOSHADE>

More Character Tags

You have a great amount of control over how your audience views text in your intranet pages. In addition to bold and italic text as outlined in Chapter 2, you can also tell your viewers' browsers to override their default settings and use many other controls that you might see in a standard word processing program.

▶ **See** "Character Tags," **p. 33**

Setting the Base Font

Browser programs generally have a series of default settings that display text in a certain way. If you don't place any specific commands in your HTML code, all text will be displayed in these defaults. Suppose, however, that you want the majority of text in your page displayed in blue at size 5 with some text displayed in green, size 3. You could either incorporate an endless series of font size and font color tags or you could impose your own default font characteristics and only add tags for the rare differences. Working this way can save a lot of time and make updating much easier.

N O T E

The two tags outlined in this section do not work with some viewers. They work just fine with Netscape viewers, but the basefont tag is ignored by Microsoft Internet Explorer. Test browsers used throughout your company to make sure these tags work before basing your content on them.

Because these tags will be ignored by programs that don't support them, you may find that your pages are not displayed as you would like them. You might want to avoid these tags if you know that a significant portion of your audience uses viewers that do not support these tags.

Font Size

In Chapter 2, you learned how to make text in any of seven different sizes using the <FONT SIZE="#"> container. You can set the default, or *base*, font size using a similar tag—the <BASEFONT SIZE="#"> tag. Sizes specified using basefont may be any of the seven sizes previously described. Place the <BASEFONT SIZE="#"> on its own line directly after the <BODY> tag to ensure that all text in your page will be displayed correctly (see fig. 3.8). There is no closing tag for the <BASEFONT SIZE="#"> tag.

Fig. 3.8
Place the <BASEFONT SIZE="#"> tag on the first line after the <BODY> tag.

The <BASEFONT SIZE="#"> tag

```
Default.htm - Notepad
File  Edit  Search  Help
<HTML>
<HEAD><TITLE>WidgetCo Intranet Home Page</TITLE>
</HEAD>
<BODY>

<BASEFONT SIZE=7>

<CENTER><IMG SRC="gif/WidgetCo_Logo_400x150.gif"></CENTER>
<HR WIDTH=400>

<CENTER><H1>Corporate Intranet Home Page</H1>
<HR WIDTH=400>
<HR WIDTH=300>
<HR WIDTH=200>

<TABLE>
<TR>
<TD><A HREF="html/corporate_communications.htm"><IMG SRC="gif/sphere1.gif" border=0 align="top"></
<TD><A HREF="html/corporate_communications.htm">Corporate Communications</A></TD>
<TD></TD>
<TD><A HREF="html/sales_marketing.htm"><IMG SRC="gif/sphere1.gif" border=0 align="top"></A></TD>
<TD><A HREF="html/sales_marketing.htm">Sales and Marketing</A></TD></TR>

<TR>
<TD><A HREF="html/finance.htm"><IMG SRC="gif/sphere1.gif" border=0 align="top"></A></TD>
<TD><A HREF="html/finance.htm">Finance</A></TD>
<TD></TD>
<TD><A HREF="html/it_support.htm"><IMG SRC="gif/sphere1.gif" border=0 align="top"></A></TD><TD><A

<TR>
<TD><A HREF="html/manufacturing.htm"><IMG SRC="gif/sphere1.gif" border=0 align="top"></A></TD>
<TD><A HREF="html/manufacturing.htm">Manufacturing</A></TD>
<TD></TD>
<TD><A HREF="html/technical_engineering.htm"><IMG SRC="gif/sphere1.gif" border=0 align="top"></A><
<TD><A HREF="html/technical_engineering.htm">Technical and Engineering</A></TD></TR>
```

Since this tag sets the default font size for your page, you may not use relative font sizes in the tag itself. However, you may still use relative font sizing for any particular section of text in your page. For example, if you have set the base font size to 5, you may then use the <FONT SIZE="-2">...</FONT> container to make some text smaller (in this case the resulting text will be size 3).

Font Color

Setting the default font color for a document is slightly different than setting its size. Default font color is a modification of the body tag.

As with the <FONT COLOR="#"> tag, colors are set by a six-digit hexadecimal number. Each two-digit group sets the amount of red, green, and blue respectively from 000000 (black) to FFFFFF (white). The color blue is represented by 0000FF. See "Size and Color" in Chapter 2 for a table that contains a list of common colors and their hexadecimal numbers.

To set the default font color, add **TEXT="#"** to the standard body statement of your HTML page. For example, to set all text in a page to blue, your body statement would read

```
<BODY TEXT="0000FF">
```

Striking Out Text

Struck out text is an effective way to show where changes have been made in an intranet document (see fig. 3.9). To strike out text, place the <S>...</S> container around the desired text:

```
<S>Struck Out Text</S>
```

Fig. 3.9
In addition to
bold and italic, an
intranet page may
incorporate many
other type styles.

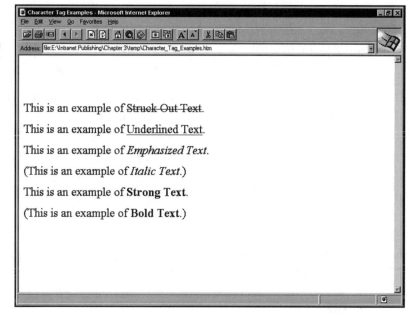

Underlined Text

Underlining is set using the <U> tag:

```
<U>Underlined Text</U>
```

Underlined text in an HTML document may sometimes be mistaken for a link
to another document. If you are going to use underlined text, make sure that
you format the text in a color which is easily recognizable as different from
links.

▶ **See** "Linking Documents," **p. 113**

Logical Text Tags

Logical text tags are a little different from the styles we have been discussing
until now. In all the previous text tags, you have been specifying exactly what
you wanted done to the font: it was either made bold, italic, underlined, or
any combination.

Logical text tags, on the other hand, leave the exact change to the text totally up to the browser application. Headlines are a logical tag because your page just tells the browser, "make this text a headline type 1," and the browser decides how big the text should be and whether it should be bold.

From the author-centric point of view, logical text tags provide almost no control over how the page will be viewed, while from the viewer-centric point-of-view, all text with a certain logical style looks identical. The main advantage for the author, though, is that you can apply what would normally take a couple of tags with a single tag (for example, <H1>...</H1> instead of <B><FONT SIZE="7">...</B></FONT>). At some time in the future, someone (probably at Netscape) will come up with new tags to make formatting text easier and more exact. Until then, we have logical styles.

Figure 3.9 (shown earlier) contains examples of the two following logical text styles.

Emphasizing Text

In general, emphasized text is displayed by viewers as italicized, so the emphasized tag is effectively the same as the italic tag (<I>). To make text emphasized, use the <EM>...</EM> container

```
<EM>Emphasized Text</EM>
```

Making Text "Strong"

Strong text is generally displayed as bold, so there is no difference between using the strong or the bold tag (<B>). To make text strong, use the <STRONG>...</STRONG> container:

```
<STRONG>Strong Text</STRONG>
```

Advanced Paragraph Tags

The following four types of paragraph tags provide some special purpose formatting that can be very useful when setting up the longer documents that a corporate intranet site may incorporate.

Lists

Lists are specifically set up to aid in organizing large, well, lists of information that have a logical hierarchy, such as departments and personnel or the chapters of a book. Both ordered and unordered lists provide automatic indentation for the various levels of information.

> **N O T E**
>
> Note that this indentation has nothing to do with how you write your code. Although figure 3.11, later in this chapter, shows the text indented, this is simply to make the code easier to read while editing. It's the list codes themselves that create the indentation when the intranet page is displayed on a browser.

Ordered Lists

An ordered list appears like a standard outline with numbered or letter headed rows. Ordered lists are a different type of tag from what has been discussed thus far in that you may nest ordered lists within other ordered lists to add a further indentation level (see fig. 3.10).

Fig. 3.10
An ordered list allows you to set up an outline that incorporates many levels of information.

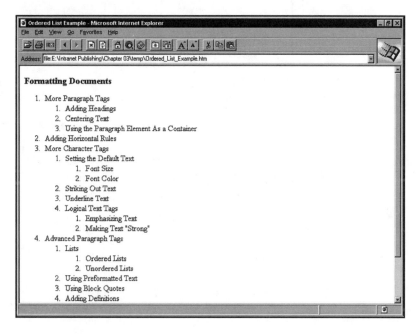

TIP

You can make ordered lists more readable by having each sublevel of the list have a different prefix style, such as A. B. C., or i. ii. iii. and so on.

An ordered list also incorporates more than one type of tag. There is the tag used to start the list <OL> and the tag to start each new line in the list <LI> (see fig. 3.11). While you must close a list using </OL>, you do not need to close a list item. Also, you do not need to include line breaks in a list; the <LI> tag automatically inserts them for you.

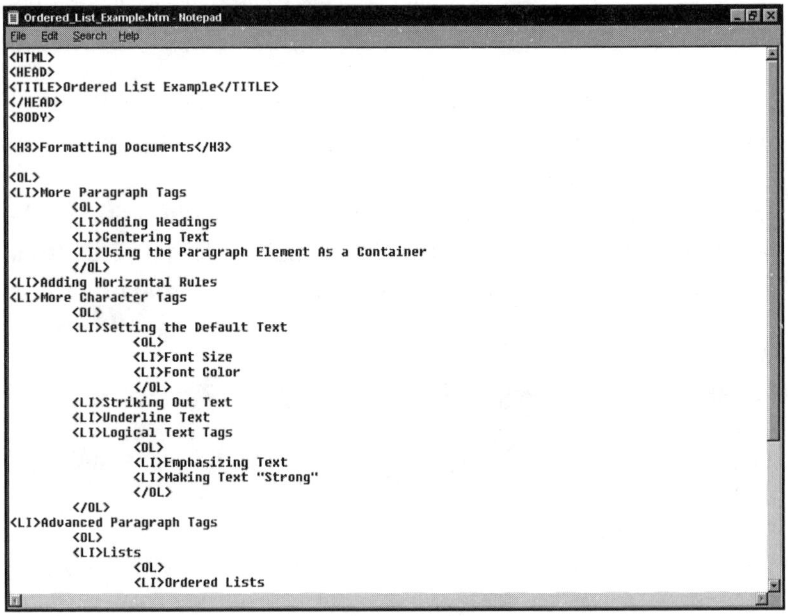

Fig. 3.11
This code was used to create the ordered list shown in figure 3.10.

```
Ordered_List_Example.htm - Notepad
File  Edit  Search  Help
<HTML>
<HEAD>
<TITLE>Ordered List Example</TITLE>
</HEAD>
<BODY>

<H3>Formatting Documents</H3>

<OL>
<LI>More Paragraph Tags
        <OL>
        <LI>Adding Headings
        <LI>Centering Text
        <LI>Using the Paragraph Element As a Container
        </OL>
<LI>Adding Horizontal Rules
<LI>More Character Tags
        <OL>
        <LI>Setting the Default Text
                <OL>
                <LI>Font Size
                <LI>Font Color
                </OL>
        <LI>Striking Out Text
        <LI>Underline Text
        <LI>Logical Text Tags
                <OL>
                <LI>Emphasizing Text
                <LI>Making Text "Strong"
                </OL>
        </OL>
<LI>Advanced Paragraph Tags
        <OL>
        <LI>Lists
                <OL>
                <LI>Ordered Lists
```

By default, ordered lists are numbered with a period after each prefix number. You can change the style of the list prefix using the TYPE="*a*" extension. Table 3.2 lists the types of prefixes you may use with an ordered list.

TABLE 3.2   Ordered List Prefixes

Modifier	Description
1	Prefix is numbers (default)
I	Prefix is roman numerals
i	Prefix is lowercase roman numerals
A	Prefix is uppercase letters
a	Prefix is lowercase letters

You may find that you need to interrupt an ordered list to include some explanatory information or a graphic. In this case, you will have broken the numbering scheme. You may get things back on track using the START="#" modifier.

For example, say your list has gone from 1. to 6. and then you have a graphic. If you want to start the list up again and continue from number 7., instead of simply using <OL>, start the list with <OL START="7">. Use a number no matter what type of prefix you want your list to use.

The following code illustrates the use of the start modifier:

```
<OL>
<LI>Medical Forms
    <OL START="6">
    <LI>Mark 47 Claims
    <LI>Alternate Dispersement
    <LI>Coverage Change
    </OL>
<LI>Employment Forms…
```

TIP

An important thing to keep in mind when your list includes the start modifier is that you must reset the number if you change the list before the break.

You may also interrupt the numbering of your list using the value modifier in the <LI> tag. For example, to skip from 3. to 6. in a list, replace the fourth item's <LI> tag with the tag <LI VALUE="6">. Again, use a number no matter what type of prefix you want your list to use.

The following code illustrates the use of the value modifier:

```
<OL>
<LI>Medical Forms
  <OL>
  <LI>Mark 47 Claims
  <LI VALUE="8">Alternate Dispersement
  <LI>Coverage Change
  </OL>
<LI>Employment Forms…
```

Unordered Lists

The unordered list tag creates a list similar to an ordered list except that the list is bulleted. You may have hierarchic lists the same as you would with an ordered list (see figs. 3.12 and 3.13).

Start and end an unordered list using the <UL> and </UL> tags, respectively. Each item in the list must begin with the list tag, <LI>. The viewer's browser program automatically inserts line feeds for each new list item as well as at the end of the list.

By default, the bullet used at the beginning of an unordered list is set by the browser program. To override the automatic bulleting, add the TYPE="*b*" modifier to the <UL> tag. This modifier may also be added to individual <LI> tags to change the bullet for an individual list item. Table 3.3 lists the types of bullets that may be manually set.

TIP

Note that not all browsers recognize the TYPE="*b*" modifier. Netscape does, while Microsoft Internet Explorer does not.

NOTE

Among the browsers that display manual bullet types, the actual shape and fill may be different. Don't count on what you see on a single browser as being what is seen on others.

Fig. 3.12
An unordered list may have many levels of hierarchy.

Fig. 3.13
Note that not all browsers display manual bullet types.

Default bullet ———

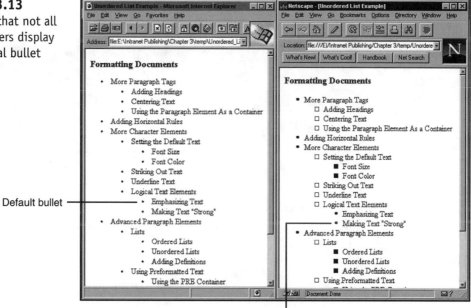

Manual bullet type

TABLE 3.3   Unordered List Manual Bullet Types

TYPE=	Bullet Description
DISC	Circle outline
CIRCLE	Filled circle
SQUARE	Filled square

Definition Lists

Definitions are another multi-part tag that automatically format a word or phrase and its definition. This can be especially useful if you are creating an employee manual that includes a glossary of terms (overtime, tardy, coffee break, and so on).

A definition is easy to implement. Within the <DL>…</DL> container (definition list) each term to be defined is headed by the <DT> tag (definition term) and its definition by the <DD> tag (definition definition). The definitions are indented to set them apart from the terms and other text and may contain any standard HTML codes. The <DL> container can surround many different terms and definitions (see figs. 3.14 and 3.15).

Fig. 3.14
A definition list may incorporate many defined words and each word may have more than one definition.

3 definitions under one word

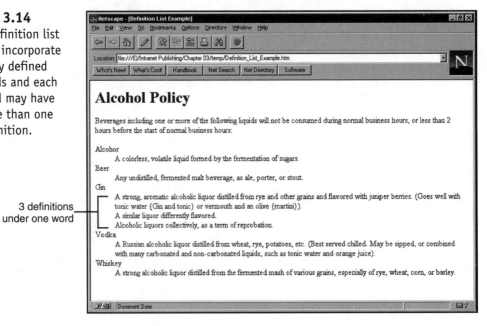

Fig. 3.15
Indenting the
definitions makes
a definition list
easier to read
while coding.

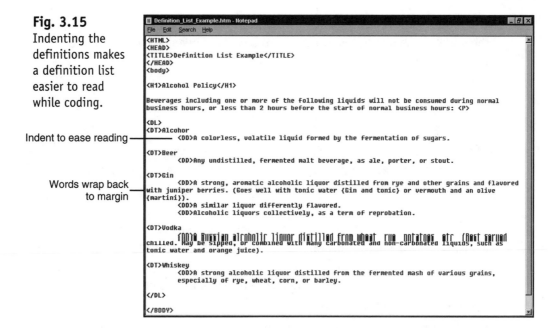

Indent to ease reading ──

Words wrap back ──
to margin

TIP
Since text in Notepad wraps back to the left margin, to see your definition list structure more clearly while editing, occasionally turn off word wrap (choose Edit, Word Wrap). This will let text flow off the right hand side of the screen.

Using Preformatted Text

Preformatted text uses a fixed-width typeface to display text in a browser exactly the way you want it. All line breaks and character spacings remain intact, just as you enter them. Preformatted text is especially useful when you need to copy large portions of a document from another electronic file.

▶ **See** "HTML Limitations," **p. 26**

Using the PRE Container

The <PRE>…</PRE> container defines text that you don't want a browser to make any changes to. The text retains all the line feeds you add to it without having to add <P> or <BR> at the end of a paragraph, but it also will not wrap to remain within the browser window; you have to hit the Enter key at the end of each line to insert a *hard return*. A blank space is automatically inserted at the beginning and end of the block of text within a <PRE> container.

T I P

If you are including a large portion of text in a <PRE> container, preview it in a browser to make sure you've included line feeds where you want them.

Text included in the <PRE>…</PRE> container is displayed in a fixed font instead of the usual proportional font. This can make creating small tables much easier and faster than using the <TABLE> container (see fig. 3.16 and 3.17). You can use any HTML codes within the <PRE> container to modify text attributes or created links.

Note that if you are creating your HTML code in an editor that uses a proportional typeface (Notepad, for example) you will find that text that lines up in the editor does not line up when viewed by a browser. Whenever possible, edit text to be used with the <PRE> container in an editor that supports fixed width typefaces, such as Word.

T I P

You can create a break in an ordered list by adding a line containing the code **<PRE>…</PRE>**. Place two spaces between the tags.

▶ **See** "HTML Limitations," **p. 26**

▶ **See** "Formatting Your Table," **p. 156**

Fig. 3.16
Text contained in the <PRE> container is displayed in a fixed width typeface. This makes it easy to create simple tables.

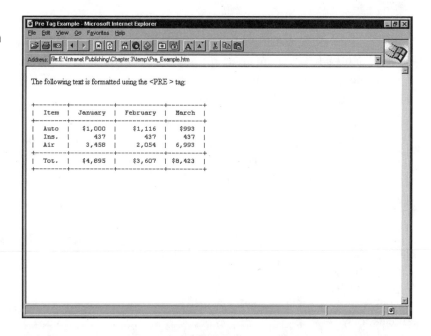

Fig. 3.17
The code used to create the <PRE> container text shown in figure 3.16.

These codes create the < and > symbols

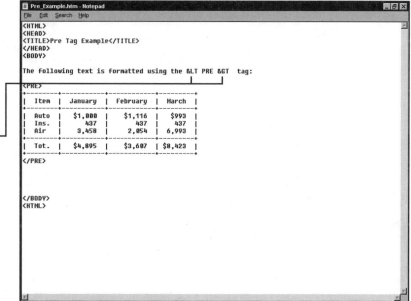

Using Block Quotes

When long passages of another document are quoted, they are often indented to set them apart from the rest of the text. HTML provides an easy way to implement this formatting using the <BLOCKQUOTE>... </BLOCKQUOTE> container.

Unlike the <PRE> container, <BLOCKQUOTE> displays in the default-viewer typeface (usually proportional) and it automatically wraps at the edge of the browser display. You also must include <BR> or <P> line feeds. You may use any HTML codes you like within a <BLOCKQUOTE> container.

Figure 3.18 shows an implementation of the <BLOCKQUOTE> container.

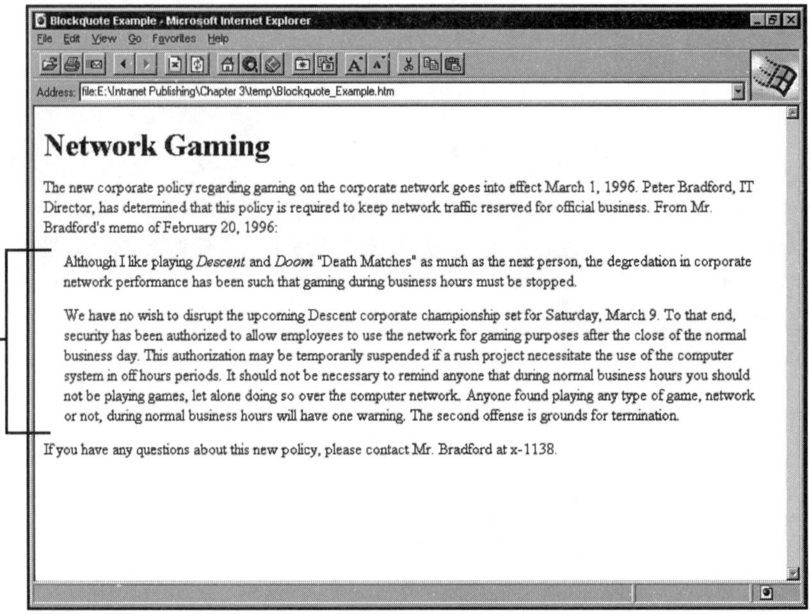

Fig. 3.18
Text within the
<BLOCKQUOTE>...
</BLOCKQUOTE>
container is
automatically
indented to set it
apart from other
text.

Block quote ─

Creating Columns

Although multiple columns of text are not supported directly in HTML, intranet tables provide an easy back door to let you create them. This is the simplest implementation of tables which are explained in more detail in Chapter 7, "Creating Intranet Tables."

A table exists within the <TABLE>...</TABLE> container. Individual rows within the table begin and end with the tags <TR> and </TR> respectively, while each cell is in the <TD>...</TD> container (see figs. 3.19 and 3.20).

To create three columns of text in your page, use the following code:

```
<TABLE>
<TR>

<TD>add first column text here</TD>

<TD>add second column text here</TD>

<TD>add third column text here</TD>
</TR>
</TABLE>
```

Each <TD>...</TD> container creates a new column. If you only want two columns, omit the third <TD>...</TD> container, or if you want a fourth column, add a fourth container.

Fig. 3.19
Although HTML does not directly support multiple columns of text, tables make an effective work-around.

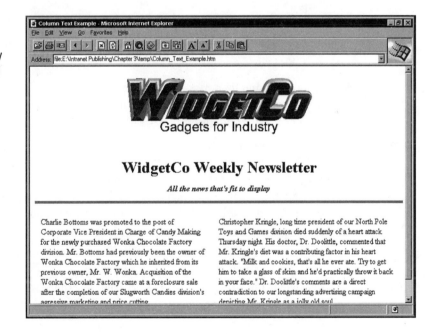

Fig. 3.20
Use the
CELLPADDING
modifier in the
<TABLE> tag to
add some space
between the
columns.

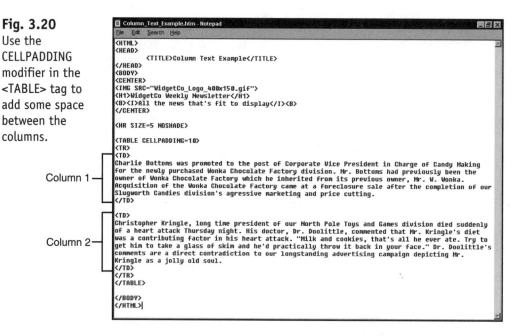

Column 1

Column 2

NOTE

If you are using long passages in your columns of text, it may be difficult to format your HTML code to make it obvious where each column begins and ends. This is because there is no way to indent an entire passage in the code.

One workaround for this is to indent each line of your code a few spaces. Start at the top of the passage and work your way down. Browsers will ignore all the spaces except for one (so there is space between words) so you have neatly written code that is easy to understand.

The one drawback to this workaround is that it makes the code much more difficult to change, and the HTML file can really only be viewed at one window size without being more confusing than it would have otherwise been. The first problem can't be fixed, but the second is easy to deal with if you remember to always edit your code in a maximized window (see fig. 3.21).

TIP

To keep your columns looking even, try to keep about the same amount of text in each table cell.

Fig. 3.21
Although browsers ignore spaces you add at the beginning of lines, resizing the editor window makes the text difficult to read.

Space makes text easy to read

Spaces don't wrap properly in a smaller window

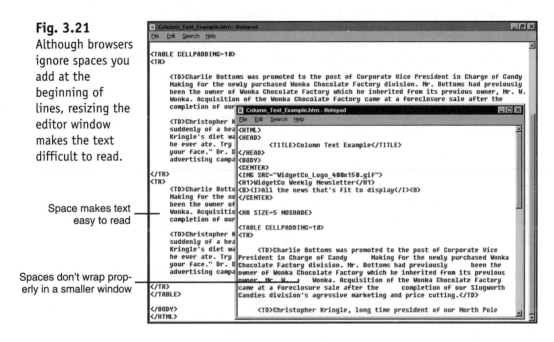

▶ **See** "Basic Table Elements," **p. 149**

Basic Graphics Use

Everything discussed thus far has been concerned with text—how it is entered and how it is formatted. Graphics have not been touched upon at all.

This section introduces you to the image <IMG> container so that you may begin to include graphics in your pages. For a more in-depth discussion of graphics, image maps, and video, see Chapter 6, "Adding Inline Graphics and Animation." Graphics displayed as part of your intranet page are called *inline graphics* because they are transferred in line with the rest of your HTML code.

Two graphics formats are supported by HTML: GIF and JPEG files. These are both compressed image files so they take less time to transfer through your network. While GIF files are limited to 256 total colors (8 bit), JPEG files may be in any format up to 16 million simultaneous colors (32 bit). GIF files are preferable for small, relatively uncomplicated graphics, and JPEG files are better for large, detailed images.

You add images to your intranet pages using the <IMG SRC="imagefile"> tag. For this discussion, we will assume that all image files are included in the same folder as the HTML file. For example, to include an image called LOGO.GIF to your page, you would add the following line to your HTML code:

```
<IMG SRC="LOGO.GIF">
```

An image file may be included on the same line as other text, or it may have its own area on the page. To isolate a graphic from other portions of the page, include line feed tags <P> or <BR> in any text before the graphic and at the end of the graphic tag (see figs. 3.22 and 3.23).

Fig. 3.22
A graphic may be placed within a line of text, or it may have its own page area.

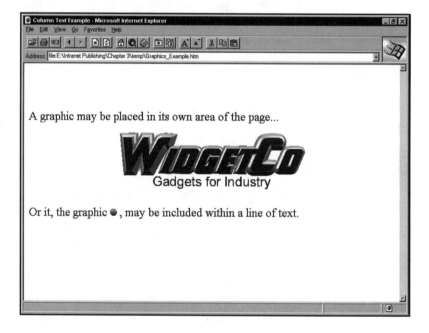

Fig. 3.23
To add a graphic to your page, use the <IMG SRC="imagefile"> tag.

```
Graphics_Example.htm - Notepad
File  Edit  Search  Help
<HTML>
<HEAD>
          <TITLE>Column Text Example</TITLE>
</HEAD>
<BODY>

<FONT SIZE=5>

A graphic may be placed in its own area of the page...<P>

<CENTER>
<IMG SRC="WidgetCo_Logo_400x150.gif">
</CENTER>

Or it, the graphic <IMG SRC="SPHERE1.gif">, may be included within a line of text.

</FONT>

</BODY>
</HTML>
```

▶ **See** "Using Inline Graphics Files," **p. 127**

HTML Reference

Tables 3.3 through 3.7 contain every tag and modifier that has been discussed in Chapters 2 and 3. For your convenience, each is cross-referenced so you can quickly look up the complete description of the tag.

Unless otherwise noted, each tag requires a closing tag.

TABLE 3.4   Character Tags

Tag	Name	See Page...	Description
<B>	Bold	33	Makes text within the container bold.
<EM>	Emphasize	60	Emphasizes text within the container. Usually displayed as italic.

continues

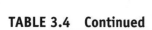

TABLE 3.4 Continued

Tag	Name	See Page...	Description
<I>	Italic	34	Makes text within the container italic.
<S>	Strikeout	58	Adds a horizontal line through text within the container.
<STRONG>	Strong	60	Makes text within the container "strong." Usually displayed as bold.
<U>	Underline	59	Underlines text within the container.
<BASEFONT>	Base font	57	Specifies default text size for all text in page. Use with SIZE="#" modifier. Does not require closing tag.
<FONT>	Font	34	Specifies size and color characteristics for text within container. Use with SIZE="#" and COLOR="#" modifiers.
SIZE="#"	Modifier	35	Specifies text size within the <FONT> or <BASEFONT> tag. # may range from 1 to 7.
COLOR="#"	Modifier	38	Specifies text color within the <FONT> tag. # is a six digit hexadecimal number.

TABLE 3.5 Paragraph Tags

Tag	Name	See Page...	Description
<BLOCKQUOTE>	Block Quote	70	Defines text within the container as a quotation and indents it.
 	Break	42	Adds a line break between two sections of text. Does not require a closing tag.

Tag	Name	See Page...	Description
<CENTER>	Center	52	Makes text within the container centered.
<H#>	Heading	50	Formats text in the container as a heading. # ranges from 1 to 6.
<P>	Paragraph	42, 52	Adds a line break and form feed between two sections of text. When used without modifier, does not require a closing tag. If used with ALIGN="a" modifier, requires closing tag.
<PRE>	Preformat	67	Makes text within the container fixed width. Preserves all line breaks and spacing.
<HR>	Rule	53	Adds a horizontal rule (line) between page sections. May be used with ALIGN="a", WIDTH="#", SIZE="#" and/or NOSHADE modifiers.
ALIGN="a"	Modifier	56	Aligns text or horizontal rule to left, right or center when a is replaced by LEFT, RIGHT, or CENTER, respectively.
WIDTH="#"	Modifier	56	Specifies the width of a horizontal rule. If # is replaced by a number (i.e., 50) the rule is a specific number of pixels wide. If # is replaced by a percentage (i.e., 50%) the rule is a percentage of the browser screen width.
SIZE="#"	Modifier	56	Specifies the thickness of a horizontal rule in pixels.
NOSHADE	Modifier	56	Removes engraved look from horizontal rule.

TABLE 3.6 List Tags

Tag	Name	See Page...	Description
<OL>	Ordered List	61	Creates an ordered list. May use TYPE="a", START=# modifiers.
<UL>	Unordered List	64	Creates an unordered (bulleted) list. May use TYPE="b" modifier.
<LI>	List Item	62	Creates an individual item in a list. May use VALUE="#" modifier in an ordered list. Does not require a closing tag.
TYPE="a"	Modifier	62	Determines the prefix type for an ordered list.
TYPE="b"	Modifier	64	Determines the bullet type for an unordered list.
START=#	Modifier	63	Specifies the starting value for an ordered list. Always use a number no matter what the prefix type is.
VALUE=#	Modifier	63	Specifies a new starting value within an ordered list. Always use a number no matter what the prefix type is.

▶ **See** "Basic Table Elements," **p. 149**

▶ **See** "Using Inline Graphics Files," **p. 127**

TABLE 3.7 Miscellaneous Tags

Tag	Name	See Page...	Description
<TABLE>	Table	71	Defines a table.
<TR>	Table Row	71	Defines a single row within a table.
<TD>	Table Cell	71	Defines a cell within a table row.

Tag	Name	See Page...	Description
<IMG SRC="x">	Inline Image	73	Specifies an image to be displayed on the page.

From Here...

You have now completed all the basic training in HTML you need. With the techniques learned in the last two chapters you can begin to create some fairly sophisticated intranet pages. Future chapters teach you how to include more intricate graphics, larger tables including headers, and how to link data from all your desktop applications into a cohesive intranet site.

- Chapter 4, "Creating Content with Your Desktop Applications," teaches you to use almost any application currently on your computer to create intranet content. Also introduced are programs specifically designed to make working with HTML code easier.

- Chapter 5, "Integrating Content from All Your Desktop Applications," shows you how to combine content from almost any application into your intranet site using hypertext links and OLE. HTML editors are discussed as a means of automating code integration.

- Chapter 6, "Adding Inline Graphics and Animation," enlarges your knowledge of inline graphics. Learn about image maps, the difference between GIF and JPEG files, and server push animation.

- Chapter 7, "Creating Intranet Tables," provides a more in-depth discussion of the table container introduced in this chapter.

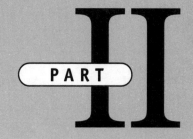

PART II

Creating Intranet Content

4

Creating Content with Your Desktop Applications

By Paul Bodensiek

Part I, "Getting Started," introduced you to the basic concepts of HTML and intranet pages. You also created your first intranet page using Notepad. It's a rather slow process and not terribly useful if you are planning on converting documents from your existing applications for posting on your site, but the examples you went through were useful in gaining a full understanding of how HTML works.

In this chapter, we begin the process of using your desktop applications to create content.

In this chapter, you learn

- To create text files from your applications
- The word processor commands that correspond to HTML codes
- To update text files with HTML commands
- The graphics files that work on an intranet
- To convert graphics files
- About HTML-specific editors

Working with Text Files

The most basic way to work with HTML is by directly editing a text file. You type in the text that you want displayed by a browser program and the formatting tags that tell the browser how to display it.

As we saw in Chapters 1 and 2, intranet pages are simply text files with tags that browsers interpret as formatting commands. These text files are easy to create and edit using any text editor, such as Notepad (see fig. 4.1).

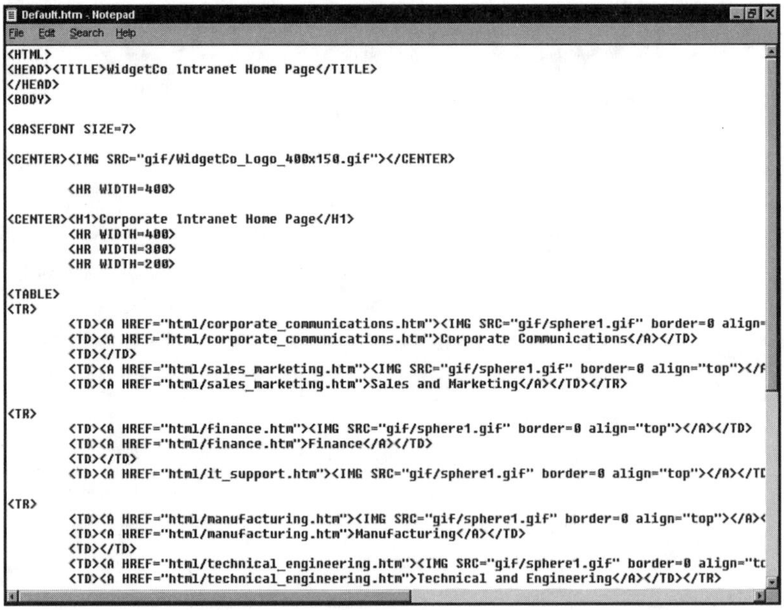

Fig. 4.1
Intranet pages begin as text files that include elements defining how they should be displayed.

```
Default.htm - Notepad                                                    _ □ ×
File  Edit  Search  Help
<HTML>
<HEAD><TITLE>WidgetCo Intranet Home Page</TITLE>
</HEAD>
<BODY>

<BASEFONT SIZE=7>

<CENTER><IMG SRC="gif/WidgetCo_Logo_400x150.gif"></CENTER>

        <HR WIDTH=400>

<CENTER><H1>Corporate Intranet Home Page</H1>
        <HR WIDTH=400>
        <HR WIDTH=300>
        <HR WIDTH=200>

<TABLE>
<TR>
        <TD><A HREF="html/corporate_communications.htm"><IMG SRC="gif/sphere1.gif" border=0 align-
        <TD><A HREF="html/corporate_communications.htm">Corporate Communications</A></TD>
        <TD></TD>
        <TD><A HREF="html/sales_marketing.htm"><IMG SRC="gif/sphere1.gif" border=0 align="top"></f
        <TD><A HREF="html/sales_marketing.htm">Sales and Marketing</A></TD></TR>

<TR>
        <TD><A HREF="html/finance.htm"><IMG SRC="gif/sphere1.gif" border=0 align="top"></A></TD>
        <TD><A HREF="html/finance.htm">Finance</A></TD>
        <TD></TD>
        <TD><A HREF="html/it_support.htm"><IMG SRC="gif/sphere1.gif" border=0 align="top"></A></TD

<TR>
        <TD><A HREF="html/manufacturing.htm"><IMG SRC="gif/sphere1.gif" border=0 align="top"></A><
        <TD><A HREF="html/manufacturing.htm">Manufacturing</A></TD>
        <TD></TD>
        <TD><A HREF="html/technical_engineering.htm"><IMG SRC="gif/sphere1.gif" border=0 align="to
        <TD><A HREF="html/technical_engineering.htm">Technical and Engineering</A></TD></TR>
```

But what do you do when you have word processing, spreadsheet, or database files that you would like to publish as an intranet page? Without purchasing any additional software, you can convert these files into straight text files that can be updated to include any HTML codes you like.

Working with Word Processing Files

While a word processor file is just a text file, it includes a lot more information than just the words that you type. A typical word processor file includes information about the printer you're using, the formatting you've added to the page, and even your name and the last date you edited the file (see fig. 4.2).

Fig. 4.2
This Word file, displayed in Notepad, shows that even though word processors deal with text, their files are not "text only" but also contain control characters.

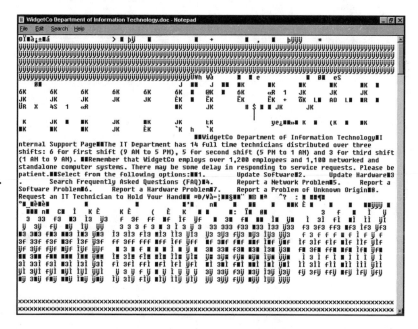

Word processors do give you a way to strip away all the extraneous bits of information from the data file (see fig. 4.2) and get right down to the actual text you originally typed in. Unfortunately, it also takes away all the formatting (like bold and italic characters) that you may have added.

Typically, all you need to do to create a text-only version of your document is save it and select Text Only (*.txt) or Text Only with Line Breaks (*.txt) from the Save as Type box.

The Text Only option creates a file exactly like your original file (without the formatting commands, of course). Line breaks are inserted only where you originally created them (see fig. 4.3 and 4.4). Use the Text Only option if the text will be included in the main body of your intranet page and formatted with HTML codes like bold and italic.

Fig. 4.3
A word processing file displayed in its native program. See figures 4.4 and 4.5 for text-only versions.

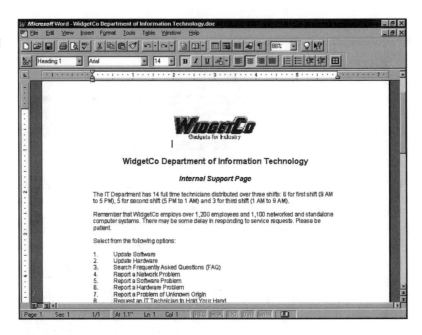

Line feed marker

Fig. 4.4
A text-only version of the same word processing document as shown in figure 4.3. Non-printing characters have been turned on to show more detail.

Space marker

Tab marker

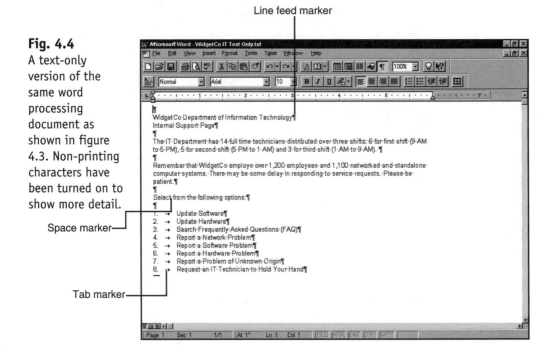

The Text Only with Line Breaks option automatically adds a carriage return at the end of each line of text, whether there was a paragraph break in your original file or not (see fig. 4.5). This is useful if you will be putting your text into a preformatted text container in your HTML page.

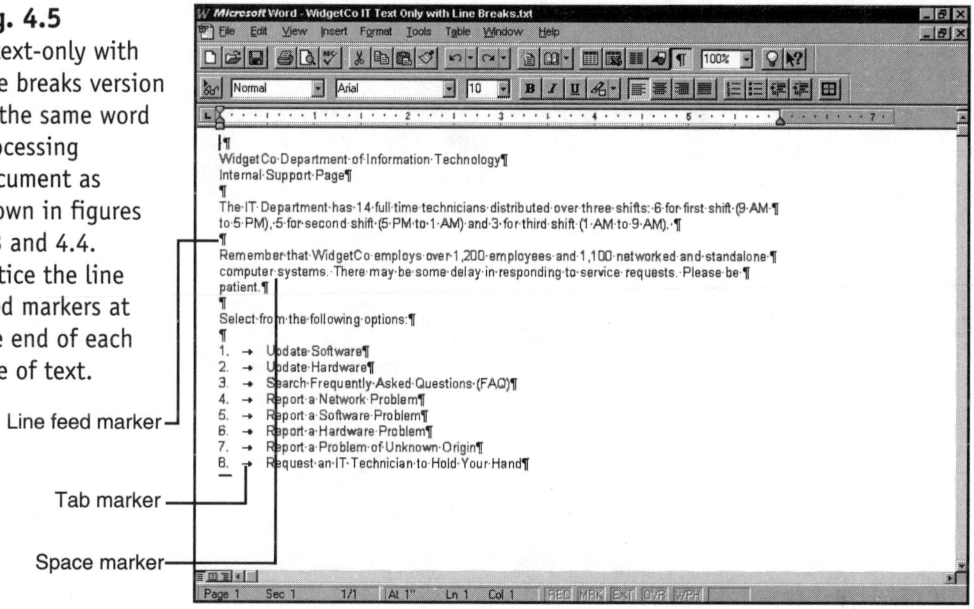

Fig. 4.5
A text-only with line breaks version of the same word processing document as shown in figures 4.3 and 4.4. Notice the line feed markers at the end of each line of text.

Line feed marker

Tab marker

Space marker

Both file formats include tabs in their files. As was discussed in Chapters 2 and 3, browsers ignore tabs, so these must be replaced with spaces. There are drawbacks to using spaces as well. Remember that browsers read only the first space in a file and ignore any others so that you can create an HTML file that is easy to read while editing without affecting what the browser displays. This means you'll have to use HTML formatting to make your page look appropriate to a browser.

TIP

Don't remove numbers and bullets from lists before you export a word processing document to a text file. Having these markers will help you locate areas that need to be turned into ordered and unordered lists later. Remember to remove the original numbering and bullets when you add the list tags.

To save a Word file in text-only format:

1. Start Word and load the desired document.

2. Choose File, Save As. The Save As dialog box appears.

3. Select Text Only (*.txt) or Text Only with Line Breaks (*.txt) from the Save as Type box. The file name automatically changes from *filename.doc* to *filename.txt* (see fig. 4.6).

Fig. 4.6
Select one of the two types of text-only files from the Save as Type box.

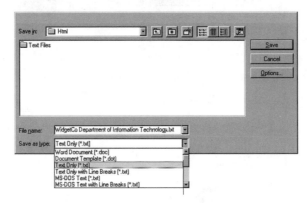

4. Optional: Type in a new name for the file in the File Name box.

5. Click Save to save the file.

Although the above directions are specifically for Word, the procedure is virtually identical for any Windows-based word processor. Note that you may want to save the file to a different folder, or even hard drive. Part III, "Managing Content," provides many suggestions for file locations to make working with your pages easier.

Working with Spreadsheet Files

Spreadsheet files are a whole different animal from word processor documents. This stems from the way in which a spreadsheet organizes its data. You see only the results of calculations in a spreadsheet even though there may be large, complex calculations used to create those numbers. The standard data file contains every bit of information needed to calculate every cell (see figs. 4.7 and 4.8).

Fig. 4.7
The same spread-sheet file is opened twice to show the "Standard," result-based view and the Formula view.

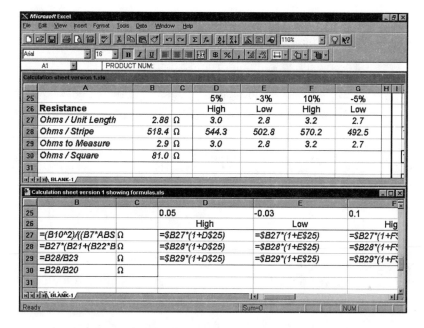

Fig. 4.8
The spreadsheet shown in figure 4.7 opened in Notepad shows how incomprehensible the raw data file can be.

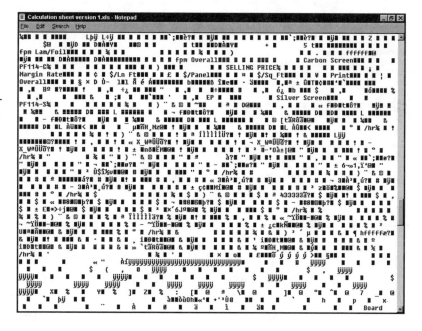

Because an HTML document won't calculate the values listed in the cells, spreadsheet files must be saved in the final, calculated form.

To save a text-only file from Excel:

1. Start Excel and load the desired spreadsheet or workbook.

2. Choose File, Save As. The Save As dialog box appears.

3. Select Formatted Text (Space Delimited)(*.prn) from the Save as Type box. The name automatically changes from FILENAME.XLS to FILENAME.PRN.

4. Optional: Type in a new name for the file in the File Name box. Make sure that you type in the extension as **.TXT**.

5. Choose the Save button to save the file.

6. Change the file's name from FILENAME.PRN to FILENAME.TXT using Windows Explorer to alert other programs (such as the one you'll be using to add the HTML code) that this is a text file.

Although the preceding directions are specifically for Excel, the procedure is virtually identical for any Windows-based spreadsheet program. Step 6 may be unnecessary for other spreadsheet programs.

Note that you may want to save the file to a different folder, or even hard drive to make editing your HTML document easier.

▶ **See** "Use Folders and File Names To Your Advantage," **p. 216**

Working with Database Files

Databases can generally be viewed in one of two different ways: Tabular view or Page view (see figs. 4.9 and 4.10).

Many database programs have an Export command listed under the File menu. This command usually lets you choose how you want the fields separated. The simplest way to deal with a database file is to export it using spaces as the separator, then format the text with the <PRE> tag to retain the resulting columns. Unfortunately, as of this writing there are no programs available that let you export a text version of a Form view. Microsoft and other vendors are reportedly working on programs that will export these views directly to formatted HTML and they may be available by the time this book is published.

Fig. 4.9
When viewed in Tabular view, a database can display a great deal of information.

Page view

Tabular view

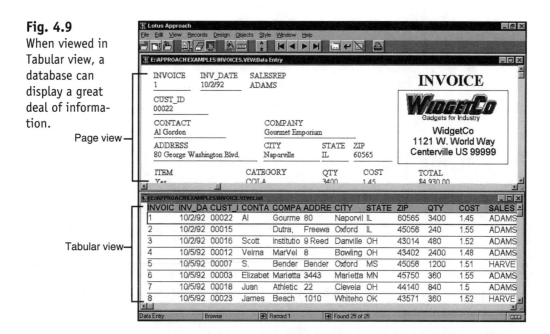

Fig. 4.10
A database output as a text file will generally work best when fields are separated by spaces. This example will require a lot of reformatting.

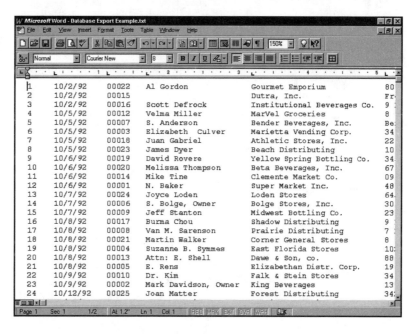

TIP

Most of the higher-end intranet publishers introduced in Part V, "Exploring Publishing Tools," make working directly with database files much easier than dealing with text-file output.

Formatting Text Files

As noted in the preceding sections on creating text files, all formatting has been removed from the original material. To return to a formatted form you need to manually enter tags to tell a browser how you want your text displayed.

An important point to keep in mind is that text files from spreadsheet and database files are often formatted to have a particular structure. In most cases, this structure is imposed on the text file by adding an appropriate number of spaces between words and numbers to make them line up when using a fixed-width typeface. Because browsers usually ignore more than one space, it's necessary to format spreadsheet and database text files using the <PRE>...</PRE> container. (Remember that the <PRE> container tells a browser to display text in a fixed-width font using all spaces and line feeds.)

When you have placed spreadsheet or database text in a <PRE> container, remember that the tags won't change the spacing of your text. This may make the original text hard to read while you are editing it, but don't use any extra spaces or line breaks to try to make it more readable. Extra line breaks and spaces will be used by a browser for any text that has been formatted with a <PRE> tag.

TIP

As an alternative to the <PRE> container, you may want to put spreadsheet and database text into tables as outlined in Chapter 7, "Creating Intranet Tables." Though useful for small jobs, intranet tables can become unwieldy when you have a lot of columns and rows.

Adding Tags

The most important tags you'll add to your text file are those that structure your document: the <HTML>, <HEAD>, and <BODY> containers. Without these containers, your document won't display properly on a browser. You should make it a habit to add these tags first so that you don't forget them.

Using a word processing program (such as Word or WordPerfect) can make adding and changing tags much easier than using Notepad. This is because "real" word processors allow you to view characters that don't normally print, like spaces, tabs, and line breaks (see fig. 4.11).

Fig. 4.11
Set your word processor to view all non-printing characters to better understand your text file's structure.

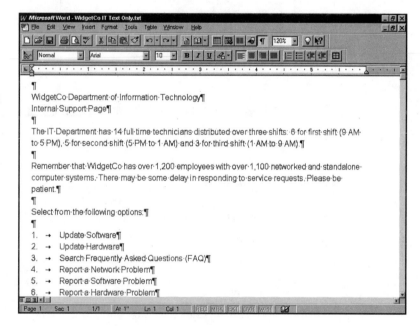

Word processors also allow you to use the Ctrl+down-arrow (↓) key combination to move automatically from the beginning of one paragraph to the next. This can greatly simplify adding <P> and <BR> line break tags to each paragraph. To make your code easier to read and more logical, add the line break tags to the end of the previous paragraph as shown in figure 4.12. Once you have moved to the beginning of a new paragraph, press the left-arrow key to move to the end of the previous paragraph and add the appropriate tag.

Fig. 4.12
Adding line break tags at the beginning of a paragraph or line of text can make your code difficult to understand.

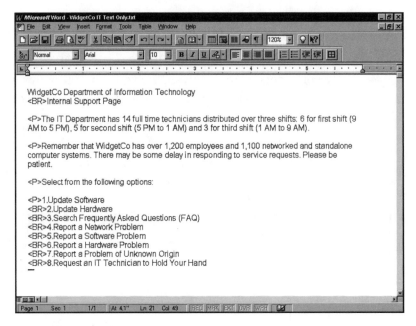

WidgetCo Department of Information Technology

Internal Support Page

<P>The IT Department has 14 full time technicians distributed over three shifts: 6 for first shift (9 AM to 5 PM), 5 for second shift (5 PM to 1 AM) and 3 for third shift (1 AM to 9 AM).

<P>Remember that WidgetCo has over 1,200 employees and 1,100 networked and standalone computer systems. There may be some delay in responding to service requests. Please be patient.

<P>Select from the following options:

<P>1.Update Software

2.Update Hardware

3.Search Frequently Asked Questions (FAQ)

4.Report a Network Problem

5.Report a Software Problem

6.Report a Hardware Problem

7.Report a Problem of Unknown Origin

8.Request an IT Technician to Hold Your Hand

Any other tags can be added at any point.

Universal Search and Replace

Perhaps the most important use of universal search and replace is getting rid of tabs. A word processing program leaves tabs in place when you save a document that has them in the original file.

To remove tabs from a text file in Word:

1. Open the text file.

2. Turn on nonprinting characters by choosing Tools, Options. This displays the Options dialog box.

3. Select the View tab (see fig. 4.13).

4. Select the All checkbox under Nonprinting Characters.

5. Choose OK. Nonprinting characters will be represented by dots (spaces), arrows (tabs), and paragraph symbols (line feeds).

6. Choose Edit, Replace and the Replace dialog box opens.

7. Choose the Special button and select Tab Character from the list. The text ^t is placed in the Find What box (see fig. 4.14).

Fig. 4.13
The Options
dialog box lets
you select many
different viewing
options for your
text file.

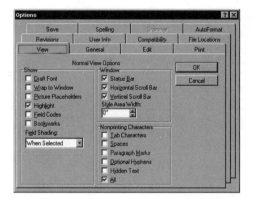

 TIP

You may want to replace a tab with a series of spaces to make your code
easier to read or add spaces to text that will be coded with the <PRE>
container.

Fig. 4.14
A tab is repre-
sented in the
Replace dialog
box by ^t, not the
arrow as displayed
in the text.

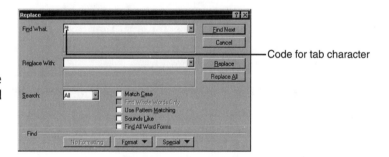

Code for tab character

8. If you want to eliminate tabs completely, leave the Replace With box
   empty. (If there is text in the Replace With box, highlight the text and
   press the Delete key.)

   If you want to replace tabs with a series of spaces, place the number of
   spaces you want in the Replace With box.

9. To replace all tabs in your document choose the Replace All button.

   To choose which tabs to replace, choose the Find Next button until the
   tab you want to replace is highlighted and choose the Replace button.
   Repeat for each tab you want to replace.

10. When you have replaced all the tabs you want, choose the Close or Can-
    cel button or press the Esc key. Note that this does not undo any of the
    changes you have made (see fig. 4.15).

Fig. 4.15
All tabs have been removed. Leave the numbers in place to aid later editing.

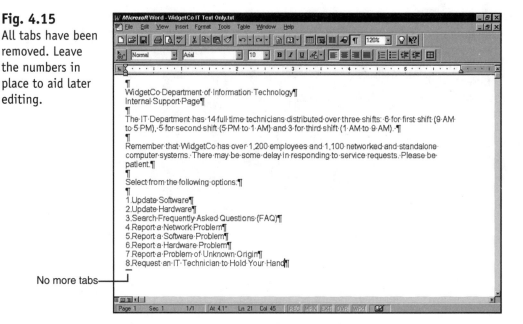

No more tabs—

The above procedure also works for any other text you want to replace. Enter the text you want replaced in the Find What box and the text you want it replaced with in the Replace With box.

Although the procedure is written specifically for Word, universal search and replace works the same way in most other word processors.

Saving Your File

When you have added all your tags to the text file and completed any editing, you need to save your document. Remember that browsers are looking for HTM, not TXT, files. To save your document as an HTML file:

1. Choose File, Save As. The Save As dialog box opens.

2. Enter a name for your file in the File Name box, remembering to name the file *filename*.**htm**.

3. Select the folder that you want to save the file to (if different from the one shown in the file display area).

4. Make sure the Save as Type box is set to Text Only (*.TXT).

5. Choose the Save button to save your file.

TIP

Use your browser to check out your page. Remember, it's a good idea to preview your HTML frequently while you create it to make sure it looks the way you want.

Working with Graphics Files

One of the great appeals of an intranet is its ability to use graphics to present information (either as the information itself or an enhancement to the text) or to make a page look more interesting (see fig. 4.16).

Fig. 4.16
Graphics can enhance the content of an intranet by providing informa-tion in a way that text can't.

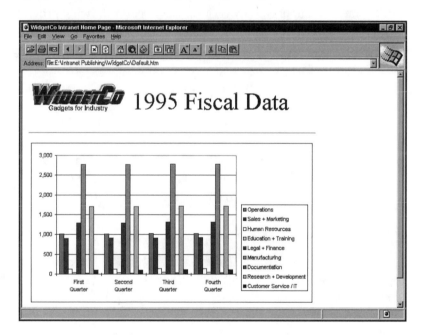

The following sections provide a quick introduction to creating graphics for your intranet pages. For a more in-depth discussion of graphics, see Chapter 6, "Adding Inline Graphics and Animation."

▶ **See** "Basic Graphics Use," **p. 73**

Supported Formats

Intranet pages support two graphics formats: GIF and JPEG. Both of these formats are compressed to make them easier to transmit over a network. GIF files support up to 256 simultaneous colors, while a JPEG file may incorporate millions of colors.

Both of these graphics formats are *raster images*, also called *bitmaps*. This means that they are made up of dots, or *pixels*, of various colors that make up the picture. Paint programs edit these pictures, either by "touching up" an existing picture or creating a picture from scratch.

The other type of computer graphic is called a *vector image*, which describes a picture as a series of colored geometric shapes. While vector images are not supported by HTML, many vector drawing programs, such as CorelDRAW! (a graphic arts program) and AutoCAD (a computer-aided design and drafting program) can export raster images that you can use in your intranet page.

JPEG and GIF files each have their own advantages and disadvantages.

GIF files, while limited to a maximum of 256 colors, are generally small files that transmit quickly across the network. They may also be created to have one color designated as "transparent." Although the color is visible while editing the image, when displayed by a browser this color disappears, allowing any background to show through (see fig. 4.17).

Fig. 4.17
GIF files may have a "transparent" color that keeps a portion of the image from being displayed by a browser.

This image contains transparency data.

This image has no transparency.

While JPEG files can display photographic images, they are compressed using a technique that can result in degradation of picture quality. To keep a high level of fidelity in the displayed image, a lower compression rate must be used, which makes the image file larger and slows down its transmission across your network. For certain images, high resolution photographs, for example, this is an acceptable problem.

TIP

If possible, avoid repeatedly opening and saving JPG files in an editing program. Each time you save a JPG file, its image degrades a bit more from the compression process.

NOTE

Other graphics files may be referenced by your intranet documents even though they cannot be displayed by a browser. If you create a link to an unsupported file format, the browser viewing the intranet page will either save the image to the user's hard drive or automatically launch a program that does support the file. See Chapter 5, "Integrating Content from All Your Desktop Applications," and Appendix B, "Using an Intranet," for more information.

NOTE

Although Microsoft Paint, included with Windows 95, can read GIF and JPEG files, it can only save BMP and PCX files that are not supported by browsers. If you are limited to creating bitmap images using Microsoft Paint, you must convert them to GIF or JPG files before including them in your pages.

Converting Graphics

If you have a file that isn't in either GIF or JPG format that you want to include in your intranet page, it must be converted into one of these two formats.

There are a number of utilities available that can convert image files from one format to another. Commercially available programs include HiJaak 95. The CD-ROM accompanying this book contains the shareware program LView PRO. (Additionally, many paint programs will allow you to convert images from one format to another.) Both of these programs convert just about any bitmap image to GIF or JPG format. While LView PRO has the advantage of being able to set any color in your image as a GIF file's transparent color, HiJaak 95 is limited to black and white.

Typically, the process for converting a graphic from one file format to another is the same no matter what program you use:

1. Start the program that will do the converting (HiJaak 95, LView PRO, or another similar program).

2. Choose File, Open and the Open dialog box appears.

3. Select the type of file you want to open from the Files of Type box. Alternatively, you may be able to choose All Files (*.*), depending on the program.

4. Navigate your drive(s) and select the file you want to open.

5. Choose the Open or OK button (depending on your program) to load the file.

6. After the image has loaded, choose File, Save As. The Save As dialog box opens.

7. Select either CompuServe GIF (*.GIF) or JPEG (*.JPG) from the Files of Type box. Note that the names might be slightly different, depending on your program, but you want to choose the option that says GIF or JPG.

8. You may also want to give your file a new file name. If so, enter the new name in the File Name box.

9. Choose the Save or OK button (depending on your program) to save the file in the new format.

Note that some programs open an Options dialog box asking you for specifics concerning the file you are saving. Other programs may have an option button in the Save As dialog box. If you are saving in GIF format, you may be asked whether you would like the file to be interlaced and/or what color you would like to be transparent. If you are saving in JPG format, you may be asked for the amount of compression you want applied to the file. Remember that the higher the compression rate, the worse the picture will look when it is displayed (see fig. 4.18).

Once the file has been saved in its new format, you may include it in any intranet document.

Fig. 4.18
If you set the compression level too high for a JPG file, the image can be severely degraded.

 — The original file

 — This image shows high compression JPG degradation

▶ **See** "Basic Graphics Use," **p. 73**

▶ **See** "Using Inline Graphics Files," **p. 127**

HTML Editing Programs

While writing HTML code in Notepad isn't terribly difficult, it can be time-consuming, and you've got to remember the different tags for every piece of formatting. With HTML editing programs you don't have to remember all the code elements and a certain amount of automation is added to your intranet page creation.

The following sections introduce a broad range of HTML editing programs, from a basic text editor to an almost-WYSIWYG (what you see is what you get) editor to tools that automatically create pages from your Microsoft Office applications. Part V, "Exploring Publishing Tools," introduces a number of high-end publishing tools that help you create an entire, integrated web site.

N O T E

All of these programs are powerful. They each have their own strengths and weaknesses. You may find it useful to start a project in one program and use another to add a specific type of formatting.

For example, Microsoft Word Internet Assistant is excellent at converting existing Word documents into HTML, but it doesn't currently support forms. You might use Word Internet Assistant to create your basic HTML page and then use Hot Dog or HoTMetaL to add and manipulate forms.

Text Based

Text-based editors, like Hot Dog, are the most basic type of HTML program (see fig. 4.19). Other than the button bar at the top of the screen, you could just as easily be looking at Notepad because all the HTML tags are visible in your text.

To view your final page, you must start a browser and load the image. Most text-based editors make this easy by allowing you to specify your browser so that you can view your page with a touch of the Preview button (see fig. 4.19).

Fig. 4.19
A complete set of menu commands and formatting buttons makes Hot Dog much easier to use than Notepad.

Preview button—

Relative link—

```
HotDog Pro - [E:\INTRAN~1\WIDGETCO\WIDGETCO.HTM]
File  Edit  View  Insert  Tags  Format  Tools  Window  Help

Preview  Tags  Charset  FileMgr  Upload  External  Internal  Target  Image  Table  Form  Internet  Quit  Publish  Font  Docmnt

<HTML>
<HEAD>

<TITLE>WidgetCo Intranet Home Page</TITLE>

</HEAD>
<BODY>

<CENTER><IMG SRC="gif/lgo4x150.gif" ALT="WidgetCo" ALIGN="BOTTOM"></CENTER>
  <HR WIDTH="400">
<CENTER><H1>Corporate Intranet Home Page</H1>
</CENTER>
  <HR WIDTH="400">
  <HR WIDTH="300">
  <HR WIDTH="200">

<TABLE>

<TR>
  <TD COLSTART="1"><A HREF="html/corporate_communications.htm"><IMG
    SRC="gif/sphere1.gif" BORDER="0" ALIGN="top"></A></TD>
  <TD COLSTART="2"><A HREF="html/corporate_communications.htm">Corporate
    Communications</A></TD>
  <TD COLSTART="3"></TD>
  <TD COLSTART="4"><A HREF="html/sales_marketing.htm"><IMG
    SRC="gif/sphere1.gif" BORDER="0" ALIGN="top"></A></TD>
  <TD COLSTART="5"><A HREF="html/sales_marketing.htm">Sales and
    Marketing</A></TD></TR>

<TR>
  <TD COLSTART="1"><A HREF="html/finance.htm"><IMG
    SRC="gif/sphere1.gif" BORDER="0" ALIGN="top"></A></TD>
  <TD COLSTART="2"><A HREF="html/finance.htm">Finance</A></TD>
  <TD COLSTART="3"></TD>

WIDGETCO.HTM
```

To add, say, the bold container, <B>...</B>, to a word, just highlight the word and click the B button (or press Ctrl+B). The two tags are automatically inserted before and after the word. Using other elements is just as easy.

Advantages

Hot Dog has a robust system for dealing with just about any aspect of your intranet page. Options in the menus and on the button bar make it very easy to insert graphics, make links, and format text.

For ease of publishing, Hot Dog recognizes relative links. This means that if you move an intranet site from one hard drive to another, or even to a totally different computer, all links between part of a page remain intact as long as the files are in the same relative position (see fig. 4.20). A complete explanation of relative and absolute links is provided in the "Relative Versus Absolute Path" section of Chapter 5.

Fig. 4.20
Links between files that are referenced relatively will remain intact if all folders containing content are moved.

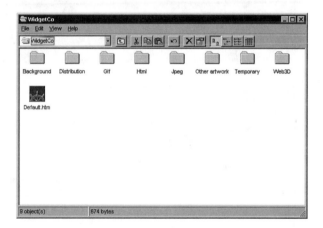

▶ See "Linking Documents," **p. 113**

▶ See "Use Folders And File Names To Your Advantage," **p. 216**

Disadvantages

On the downside, Hot Dog shows every tag in standard text. This can make your code very difficult to read and update if you do not format it as discussed in Chapter 3. (If you are updating an existing HTML page, however, this can be very handy.)

▶ See "Make the Code Easier To Read," **p. 45**

Also, Hot Dog is written by Sausage Software, which is based in Australia. Nothing against the Australians, but because of a 13- to 15-hour time difference (and the cost), phone technical support is impractical and e-mail replies effectively take two days minimum. This can be a real problem if you run into difficulty while on a deadline.

Extended Text Based

Extended text-based editors go regular text-based one better. While still working in a basically text screen, HTML tags are represented as icons. This makes reading text and differentiating elements much easier.

SoftQuad's HoTMetaL is an excellent example of an extended text-based HTML editor (see fig. 4.21).

Fig. 4.21
SoftQuad's
HoTMetaL uses
icons to represent
HTML tags.

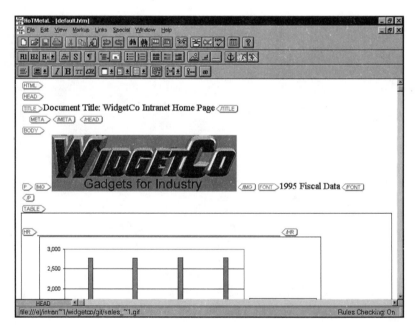

Advantages

With each tag being represented by an icon, viewing, editing, and formatting HTML code is much easier than with a straight text-based editor. HoTMetaL displays all graphics on the page so making changes to them is also easier. Error checking makes it very difficult to write bad code; if you forget to include a closing tag, HoTMetaL reminds you and helps you fix the problem.

Perhaps HoTMetaL's best feature is its table display, which shows tables on-screen, making them easier to work with (see fig. 4.22).

Fig. 4.22
HoTMetaL displays tables in an editable form. This is an excellent feature, making tables much more intuitive.

Long file name graphic—

Table display—

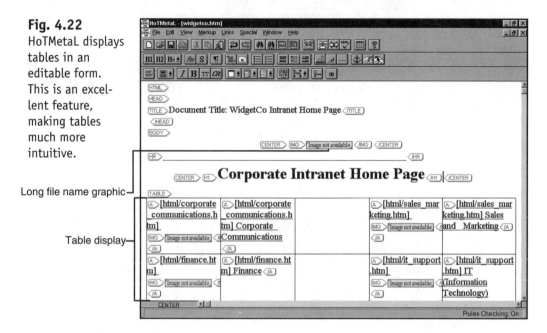

Disadvantages

HoTMetaL's biggest drawback is its lack of long file name support. Opening any existing HTML page that includes graphics saved with long file names results in an error box replacing the graphic on-screen (see fig. 4.22). This does not affect the final file, but makes it more difficult to work on some files.

Also, you must preview any page you design in a browser to find out what it will actually look like.

Almost WYSIWYG

Finally WYSIWYG editors are becoming available. Actually, that should read *almost* WYSIWYG. While text is shown in the right size and graphics show up properly on-screen, some of the formatting doesn't quite correspond to the way that a browser will display it. A new entrant to this genre, Netscape Navigator 2.0 Gold, comes with an almost-WYSIWYG editor that gets high marks for ease of use and power (see fig. 4.23).

Fig. 4.23
Netscape Navigator 2.0 Gold's integrated editor makes creating attractive intranet pages easy.

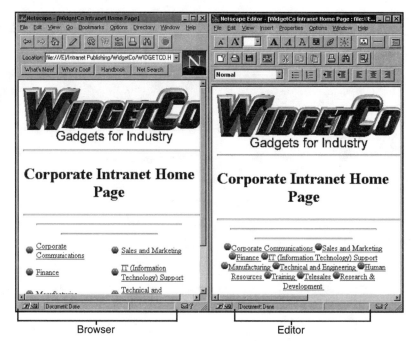

Browser   Editor

Advantages

Tightly integrated with Netscape Navigator 2.0, Gold's editor may be invoked at any time when previewing a page. This makes updating and tweaking page layout extremely easy. Editing and creating new pages is intuitive.

Disadvantages

Navigator 2.0 Gold's biggest problem is its lack of table support. While the browser portion of 2.0 shows tables and other advanced HTML features, there is currently no way to create them in the editor. Because Netscape helped pioneer the use of tables in HTML documents, this feature will probably be implemented in future releases.

Microsoft Office Internet Assistants

The Microsoft Office Internet Assistants use your existing Microsoft Office applications to create intranet content easily and efficiently. The three currently available Assistants work with Word, Excel, and PowerPoint, and make updating your existing documents for your intranet very easy.

Word Internet Assistant

Microsoft's original HTML editor, Word Internet Assistant, was released for Word version 6. Now updated for version 7 (Word for 95), Word Internet Assistant automatically converts your existing documents when you save them.

To save an existing Word file as an intranet page:

1. Open your existing Word file.

2. Choose File, Save As and the Save As dialog box appears.

3. Select HTML Document (*.htm) from the Save as Type box. The file name is automatically changed to include the HTM extension.

4. Choose the Save button to save your file. Word Internet Assistant automatically inserts all tags to format your document as closely as possible to the original.

Word Internet Assistant changes any styles it already knows to the appropriate HTML tags and you can manually create HTML equivalents for your own styles. The conversion is not perfect, however, mostly from the limitations of HTML (see fig. 4.24).

Fig. 4.24
Word Internet Assistant does a good, but not perfect, job of converting Word documents to HTML.

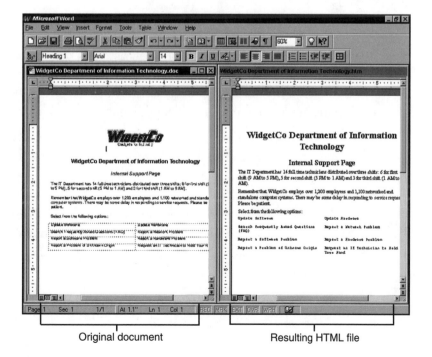

Original document   Resulting HTML file

Word Internet Assistant does have some limitations of its own. For example, it does not have any support for tables, so any tables in your Word documents are converted to preformatted text, which may be all right for your purposes.

In addition to simple conversions, Word Internet Assistant also is an almost-WYSIWYG HTML editor. The add-on makes creating simple intranet pages easy. Since it's based on Word, all the skills you've already developed for entering text and adding graphics can still be used.

When editing or creating an HTML document, Word Internet Assistant adds a new toolbar to Word (see fig. 4.25). This toolbar holds most of the new commands for the Internet Assistant. It would be nice to have some of the styles, such as headings, on the toolbar, but accessing them from the Styles drop-down list is not difficult.

Fig. 4.25
Word Internet Assistant loads a new toolbar when you are working on HTML documents.

A very nice addition to Word Internet Assistant is that it removes the GIF and JPG graphics limitation. Any graphics you import (or are present when you convert a document) are automatically converted to GIF format. This is a real convenience and cuts a number of steps out of the creation process.

Though not a great editor, for quick and easy conversion of your existing documents, it's hard to beat this add-on.

Excel Internet Assistant

The Microsoft Excel Internet Assistant's greatest claim to fame is the easy creation of tables. It is designed to quickly transform your Excel spreadsheets into intranet pages, and it does this efficiently with only two mouse clicks.

Excel Internet Assistant doesn't allow you to include links to other pages, so its use is limited to the initial conversion of a spreadsheet. After the spreadsheet is converted to HTML, it can be loaded into any of the other editors to include additional text, annotation, and links. (You may want to avoid using Word Internet Assistant to edit Excel Internet Assistant documents because the Word add-on does not support tables.)

TIP

Use Excel Internet Assistant to create complex tables that would be difficult to format in other editors.

To convert all or part of a spreadsheet to HTML:

1. Open Excel and load or create your spreadsheet.

2. Choose Tools, HTML Wizard.

TIP

When prompted, choose Create an Independent, Ready to View HTML Document so that you can quickly preview your work in a browser. Later you can cut and paste the table into another HTML document if you want.

3. Follow the instructions to select cells to be converted to HTML and to select where to save the file (see figs. 4.26 and 4.27).

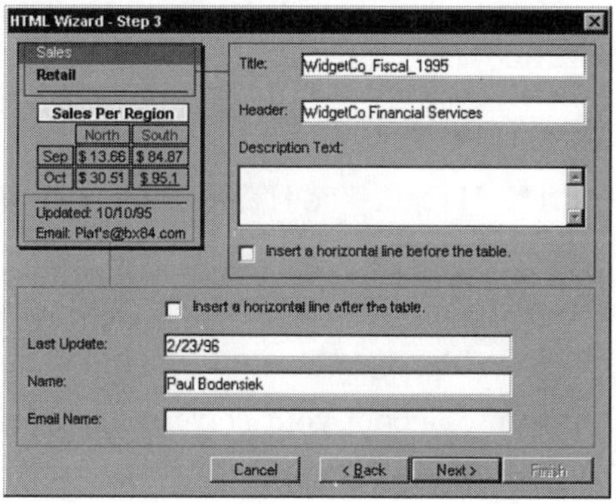

Fig. 4.26
The HTML Wizard walks you through the steps to convert your spreadsheet to an HTML document.

Fig. 4.27
Make sure to
preview your new
HTML table in a
browser before
publishing it on
your intranet.

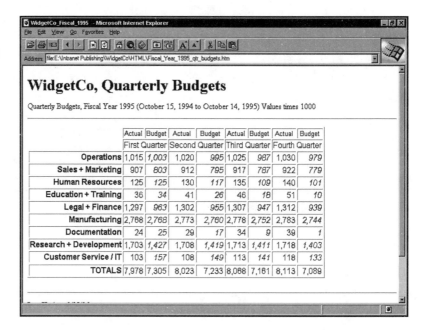

PowerPoint Internet Assistant

This is perhaps the most amazing of Microsoft's Internet Assistants. With
PowerPoint Internet Assistant you can instantly convert any presentation
into an intranet site. Even buttons placed on your slides are converted into
active *hotspots* that let your users interact with the intranet pages the same
way they would with the original presentation.

Each slide is translated to either a GIF or JPG file and placed in its own page.
Each page also includes a series of navigation buttons that link your presentation together (see fig. 4.28).

To create a series of HTML pages:

1. Choose File, Export as HTML. The HTML Export Options dialog box
   opens.

2. Select the graphic file format you want each page to contain and the
   folder where you want the pages located (each page is a separate file).

3. Choose the OK button to accept your settings. PowerPoint Internet
   Assistant converts your document.

Note that it may take several minutes for a complex presentation to be converted.

Fig. 4.28
Each PowerPoint slide is converted into an HTML page, complete with a graphic representing the slide and navigation buttons.

Slide⌐

Navigation buttons─

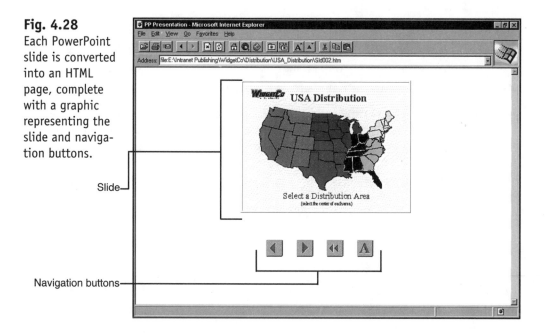

From Here...

In this chapter, you learned many different ways to create intranet content. Starting from many different types of programs, you can export information to text files to be updated later or, if you are using word processing programs, you may add HTML tags before exporting.

You also had an introduction to some of the types of HTML editing programs and content creation programs currently available. Part V, "Exploring Publishing Tools," builds on these relatively low-end products by introducing complete publishing packages. If you are involved in creating complex, corporate-wide web sites, one of these products may fill your needs better than the ones shown in this chapter.

You now have all the basic knowledge you need to begin taking content from all your desktop applications and building a complete intranet site. See the following chapters for further intranet building information:

- Chapter 5, "Integrating Content from All Your Desktop Applications," shows you how to link multiple pages into an integrated intranet site. Including files not directly supported by browsers is introduced, greatly expanding the power of your site.

- ● Chapter 6, "Adding Inline Graphics and Animation," teaches you how to include graphics and video in your intranet pages for maximum impact.

- ● Chapter 10, "Managing Pages," gives you tips and techniques to make multiple-page intranet sites easier to create and maintain.

- ● Part V, "Exploring Publishing Tools," contains four chapters that each focus on a different high-end intranet publishing program. These tools are specifically designed to make creating large intranet sites possible.

Integrating Content from All Your Desktop Applications

By Paul Bodensiek

Creating individual pages based on materials from your current desktop applications is only half the battle of creating your full intranet site. Each page is static, alone, and limited in its usefulness if it is unable to "communicate" with other pages, sites, and files throughout your intranet.

In this chapter, we explore the various ways to combine content from different applications into a coherent intranet site. With the knowledge you have gained from previous chapters, combined with the techniques in the following pages, you will be able to create a complete site that is linked to as much or as little of your network as you would like.

In this chapter, you learn

- What links are
- How to link to different files
- The differences between UNIX and DOS/Windows paths
- How to create relative links
- How to share data between applications

Linking Documents

When you are browsing an intranet document you can navigate between documents, or within the same document, using links. Links also allow you to access files that are not intranet documents. These links are called external, internal, and non-HTML links. Clicking the link sends a request to the computer containing the referenced document, in the case of an external link, to send it to the user's computer. The browser program then displays the document. Usually, a text link is underlined and in a different color to differentiate it from regular text. Graphics used as links are often surrounded by a border (see fig. 5.1).

TIP

A non-HTML link is really just an external link to a non-HTML document, but it is sometimes easier to think of as a third type.

Fig. 5.1
A link may be represented in a browser by text or a graphic.

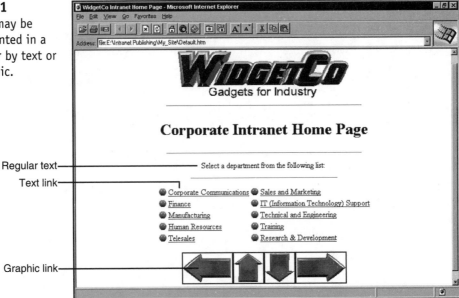

It's also possible to reference non-HTML files (see fig. 5.2). If a link leads to a non-HTML file, the user's browser asks for a location to save the file to. If the browser has been told ahead of time what program works with the type of file being downloaded, it automatically launches that program and loads the document into it. For example, if a user clicks a link to a Microsoft Excel spreadsheet, the user's browser would automatically start Excel and load the file into it.

Fig. 5.2
A browser gener-
ally tells the user
the location of
the file being
referenced. In this
case the file is a
non-HTML Excel
spreadsheet.

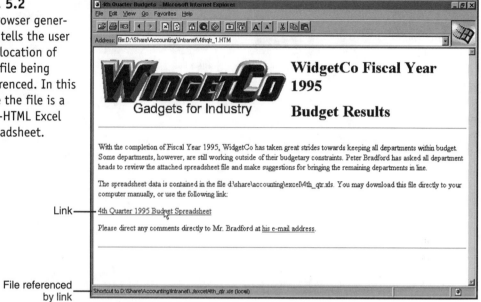

Link —

File referenced
by link

The third type of link is an internal link to a new location within a document. If you have created a long page, you can make it easier for readers to move around by adding bookmarks that are referenced in various locations throughout the page.

▶ **See** "Using an Intranet," **p. 485**

Creating a Link

A link uses the anchor container, <A>...</A>. There are two uses for the anchor container: it defines a link to a file or location and it can define a location within a document to be linked to.

External Links

An external link creates a reference in one document to another document or file. All you need to know about a file that you want to link to is its name and location. For example, files may reside on your network or intranet server under a folder named Share. There may be additional folders within the Share folder for each content provider, department, or project (see fig. 5.3).

Fig. 5.3
The main HTML documents folder may contain folders dedicated to each department, which then hold intranet and/or other documents.

Share folder

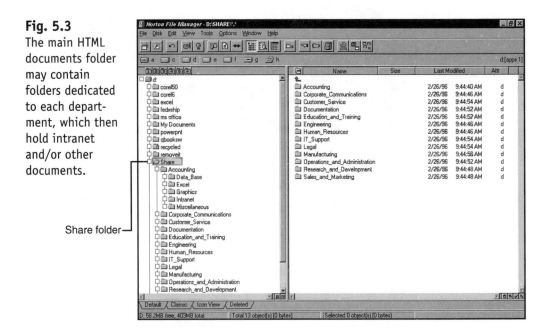

To add a link to a file, add the following command:

```
<A HREF="file://///server/share/.../filename"> description </A>
```

The portion HREF="file://///server/share/.../filename" tells the browser to make a hypertext reference (HREF), or link, to a file named *filename* that resides on a network drive named *Server*, in a folder named *Share* (see fig. 5.4). The ellipsis (...) just means that there may be other folders in Share holding the file. In place of *description* enter any text that describes the linked file to your reader. As noted above, the file may be any type, though most links reference other HTML files.

Internal Links

In many cases, you may wish to make an intranet page that is long and has distinct sections. This could be for a description of a budget where some readers would like to read it from start to finish while others want to skip around, reading only those sections that interest them. By making links within the page you can accommodate both types of readers.

Fig. 5.4
The two links
shown here
reference another
HTML file and a
database file.

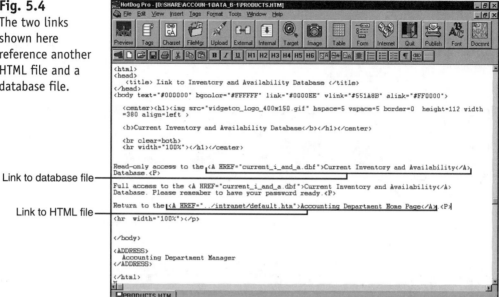

Link to database file ————

Link to HTML file ————

TIP

If you are creating a very long page, try to keep the number of graphic elements to a minimum. Long pages with a lot of graphics can take a long time to display and will be difficult for readers to use.

An internal link needs two tags to operate: the link tag and the bookmark tag. The bookmark tag provides a place for the link tag to attach to. The link tag operates the same way as it does for an external link. As noted previously, these two tags are just different uses of the anchor container.

A minor difference in the link element is the addition of "#bookmark". This tells the browser to look in the document for the tag <A NAME="bookmark">...</A> (see fig. 5.5). The word *bookmark* may be replaced with any name. Remember to give each bookmark a unique name. Although the reference description is highlighted in the browser window, there is no visible highlighting for the bookmark (see fig. 5.6).

CAUTION

Some browsers call their list of saved locations "bookmarks" (see "Storing Locations," in Appendix A). These are not the same as the bookmarks we are discussing here.

Fig. 5.5

An internal link contains two elements: the reference and the bookmark.

As a shortcut, you may omit the file name portion of an internal reference, so that the reference just reads

```
<A HREF="#bookmark">...</A>
```

If you include the file name in the reference, the reader's browser reloads the entire document when the reference is used, while leaving out the file name allows the browser to jump directly to the bookmark. Although this is how the HTML specification says you should write internal references, you don't need to. By dropping the file name from the reference, you can save yourself a lot of typing and your readers a lot of reloading time.

You may also make a link to a bookmark in an external document by including the name of the document and a valid bookmark inside that document in the link's reference. In this case, the tag will read

```
<A HREF=HREF="file://///server/share/.../filename#bookmark">...</A>
```

Fig. 5.6
The reference for an internal link is usually indicated by underlined text. The referenced bookmark is not.

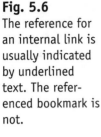

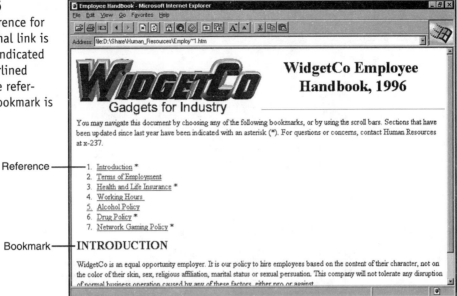

Reference ——

Bookmark ——

Specifying the Path

The path statement tells a browser where to find a file. The path indicates which folders and subfolders in a hard drive contain a file. For example, in standard DOS/Windows notation, a path statement might read

```
d:\share\accounting\excel\4th_qtr.xls
```

This corresponds to the file shown in figure 5.7.

UNIX Directory Notation

All browsers read path statements based on UNIX notation. You may have noticed that the previous examples use a forward-slash (/) to mark subfolders instead of the backslash (\) used in DOS and Windows applications. This is because the Internet, on which intranets are based, were originally built around UNIX computers. Now, almost every type of computer is connected to the Internet and intranets, but this notation has become the standard.

The path noted for figure 5.7 is written in UNIX notation as

```
d|/share/accounting/excel/4th_qtr.xls
```

Fig. 5.7
A path statement tells the computer what path to follow to find a file.

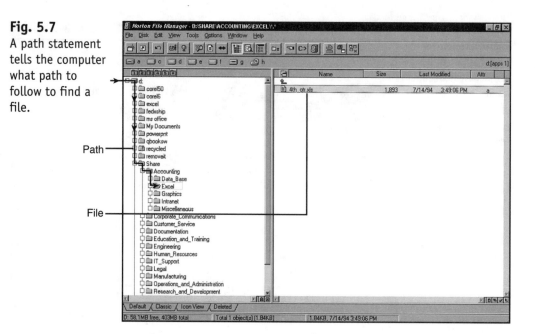

Path —

File —

The vertical line after "d" is typically made by pressing Shift+\ (check your keyboard).

TIP

Although Microsoft Internet Explorer reads "normal" DOS/Windows path statements, most other browsers do not. Never assume that a page will be read only by Microsoft Internet Explorer and always use the UNIX (/) notation in path names.

Relative versus Absolute Path

There are two ways to reference a file's path: absolute and relative. As their names imply, an absolute path provides the complete path statement leading to the file, while a relative path gives the file's location *relative* to the current intranet page. The previous examples have all given absolute paths.

Using the example shown in figure 5.7, suppose that the Accounting department keeps all of its HTML files in the folder d:\Share\Accounting\Intranet\ (or in UNIX notation: d/Share/Accounting/Intranet/). A relative path from an HTML page in this folder to the same Excel file would read ../excel/4th_qtr.xls (see fig. 5.8).

Fig. 5.8
This figure shows the relative path between an HTML document in the Intranet folder and an Excel file in the Excel folder.

Relative path

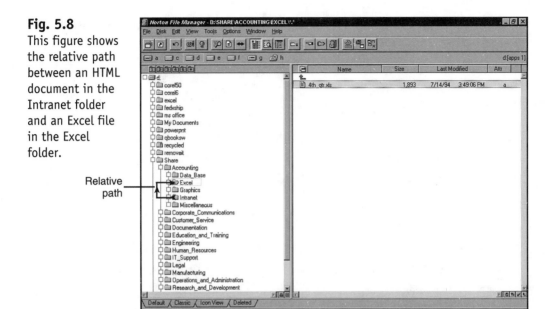

Each time you move up the folder tree to a higher level folder, you insert another ../ at the beginning of the relative path statement. In other words, if the full path to HTML files was d\/Share/Accounting/Intranet/Html/ then the relative path to the Excel file would read ../../excel/4th_qtr.xls.

Information from Many Sources in One Document

As you write your intranet pages, you'll probably find passages or graphics from other documents that you would like to include directly in your pages, rather than making links to the other documents. While you could retype all the other document's text into your page, there are a number of alternatives that generally make this unnecessary.

Copy and Paste

The most straightforward option for including material from other documents is the Copy/Paste command combination. You probably use this all the time to move text from one part of a document to another. You can also use it to copy and paste between documents and even programs.

To copy a passage of text from one document to your intranet page:

1. Start your HTML editor (Notepad, HotDog, Microsoft Word Internet Assistant, or the like) and open your intranet page file.

2. Start the appropriate program and open the file containing the passage you want to copy.

3. Highlight the text you want to copy to your intranet page.

4. Choose Edit, Copy or press Ctrl+C.

5. Switch to your HTML editor.

6. Position the insertion point where you want to insert the text.

7. Choose Edit, Paste or press Ctrl+V. The entire passage is inserted into your page.

Depending on which HTML editor you are using, you may have to manually add line and paragraph breaks (
 and <P>) for the text to display properly. If you copied a table or other text requiring exact formatting, you may have to use the preformatted text container, <P>...</P>.

Some editors, specifically Word Internet Assistant and there may be others, allow you to copy and paste graphics as well. Word Internet Assistant lets you paste any graphic into your page. When the page is saved in HTML format, the graphic is automatically converted to a GIF file that is placed in the same directory as the HTML file.

Drag and Drop

Drag-and-drop editing works in virtually the same way as copy and paste, except you don't have to use the Copy and Paste commands. Note that not all applications support drag-and-drop editing. If you try to use drag and drop and one (or both) of your programs doesn't support it, you can easily switch to copy and paste as outlined in the previous section.

To copy text between files using drag and drop:

1. Start your HTML editor and open your intranet page file.

2. Start the appropriate program and open the file containing the passage you want to copy.

3. Arrange the programs on your screen so that both programs and files are visible (see fig. 5.9). Use scroll bars so that the destination for the text is visible in the HTML editor.

Fig. 5.9
Arrange the programs on your screen so that the text you want to copy and its destination are visible.

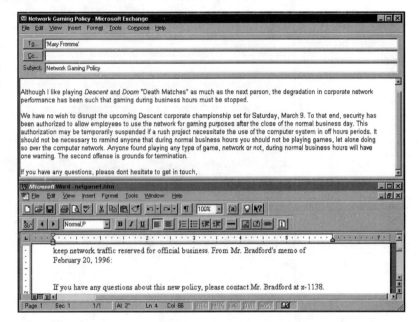

4. Highlight the text you want to use in your intranet page.

5. Place the mouse pointer over the highlighted material. Press and hold the primary mouse button (usually the left button) and drag the pointer to the destination (see fig. 5.10). The mouse pointer will change shape to indicate that you are dragging information.

6. When the pointer is directly over the destination, release the mouse button. The text is copied into place.

Note that not all programs allow you to perform drag-and-drop editing.

Object Linking and Embedding (OLE)

If you want to include text or graphics that are often updated in an intranet page, object linking and embedding (OLE, pronounced *olay*) may be a good option. OLE makes a connection between the file being edited and the original file containing the referenced text. When the referenced text is up-dated, the edited file is automatically updated.

Fig. 5.10
Drag the high-lighted text from the source file to its destination without releasing the mouse button.

Text to be copied —

Destination —

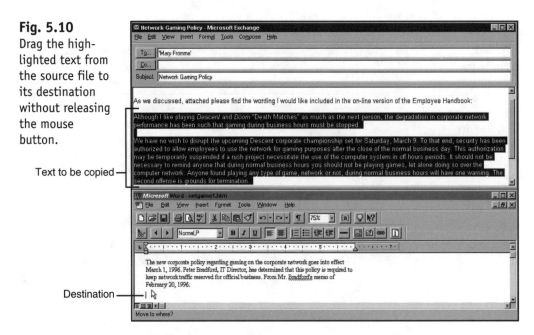

Only one of the editors discussed in Chapter 4 is OLE-ready: the Microsoft Word Internet Assistant. Some of the higher-end publishing packages out-lined in Part V, "Exploring Publishing Tools," are OLE-capable. The program that edits the source file must also be OLE-capable.

Since HTML files do not contain any commands for dealing with OLE, any page containing linked text must be saved as a Word document before it is saved as an HTML file.

To add linked information to a Word Internet Assistant file:

1. Start Word and either load an existing HTML file or start a new one from scratch.

2. Start the program containing the text or graphic you want to link to.

3. Open the file you want to use as the source.

4. Highlight the text or graphic you want to use in your intranet page.

5. Choose <u>E</u>dit, <u>C</u>opy or press Ctrl+C.

6. Switch to Word.

7. Place the insertion point where you want the linked text to be located.

8. Choose <u>E</u>dit, Paste <u>S</u>pecial. The Paste Special dialog box opens (see fig. 5.11).

Fig. 5.11
The Paste Special dialog box provides options for linking portions of one document within another.

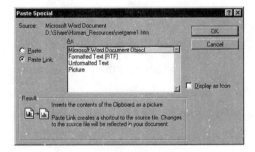

9. Click the Paste <u>L</u>ink radio button.

10. Select any of the available options as appropriate. For example, if the source is another Word document, you would want to select Microsoft Word Document Object. This option allows you to double-click the linked text to automatically load the source document for editing.

11. Click OK to insert the text into your document.

12. Choose <u>F</u>ile, Save <u>A</u>s. The Save As dialog box opens.

13. Select Word Document (*.doc) from the Save as <u>T</u>ype box.

14. Choose the <u>S</u>ave button to save the file in Word format.

15. Choose <u>F</u>ile, Save <u>A</u>s again. The Save As dialog box opens.

16. Select HTML Document (*.htm) from the Save as <u>T</u>ype box.

17. Choose the <u>S</u>ave button to save the file in HTML format.

Note that if you want to do further editing, the Word document must be used so that the OLE referenced text may remain updated. After editing, save the file in Word format then as an HTML file again (use the same name as the original to preserve any links to the page).

If the OLE source file is changed, you must start Word, load the Word document to automatically update the reference to the source, and save it again as a Word document. Then save the file in HTML format again using the same name as the original. Note that the OLE referenced document and the Word file must not remain in their original locations or the OLE link will be broken.

To update OLE linked information:

1. Start Word and open the Word document version of the intranet page. Any linked text or graphic is automatically updated.

2. Open the File menu and select Save As. The Save As dialog box opens.

3. Select Word Document (*.doc) from the Save as Type box.

4. Choose the Save button to save the file in Word format.

5. Choose File, Save As again. The Save As dialog box opens.

6. Select HTML Document (*.htm) from the Save as Type box.

7. Choose the Save button to save the file in HTML format.

From Here...

In this chapter, you learned how to use information from many different sources to enhance your intranet pages. You also learned how to link pages together to create an intranet site and to make reference to pages in other sites.

In future chapters, you will learn how to add advanced graphics, animation, and tables to your pages.

● Chapter 6, "Adding Inline Graphics and Animation," shows you how to include graphics and video in your intranet pages for maximum impact.

● Chapter 7, "Creating Intranet Tables," shows you how to use tables to organize data and format your pages efficiently.

● Chapter 10, "Managing Pages," gives you tips and techniques to make multiple-page intranet sites easier to create and maintain.

● Part V, "Exploring Publishing Tools," lets you build on your knowledge of HTML editors with these four chapters devoted to high-end publishing programs.

6

Adding Inline Graphics and Animation

By Paul Bodensiek

Chapter 3, "Formatting Documents," and Chapter 4, "Creating Content with Your Desktop Applications," introduced you to the image container used to place graphics within an intranet page. Even with the basic information presented there, you are able to make interesting and useful pages that have some graphic style.

In this chapter, we explore the different options available for the image container and also briefly look at two methods of transmitting animation over your network.

In this chapter, you learn to

- Add inline graphics
- Use graphics as links
- Add simple animation to a page
- Use offline animation

Using Inline Graphics Files

Inline graphics, the images that display in an intranet page, can be used to make the page look better or convey information in a way that text can't.

For example, adding a company logo to an intranet page doesn't add any new information, while using a graph provides your reader with a great deal of actual data (see fig. 6.1).

Fig. 6.1
Each of the graphics on this page serves a different purpose: aesthetics and information.

Picture provides aesthetics

Picture provides information

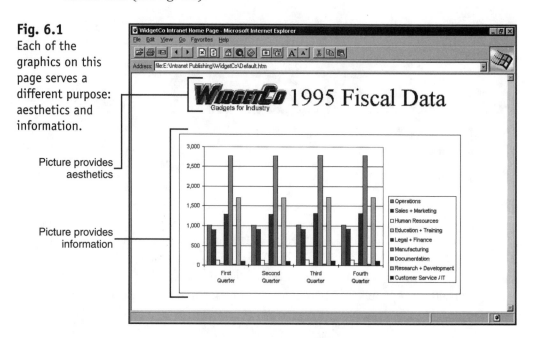

Other graphic accents, such as buttons and image maps, can help your reader navigate your intranet site by giving them visual cues (see fig. 6.2).

▶ **See** "Converting Graphics," **p. 99**

Intranet browsers generally support two types, or formats, of graphics: GIF and JPEG (or JPG). These two formats are compressed so that they take less time to be transmitted over the network. There are many other types of graphics formats, such as PCX and Microsoft Windows BMP files. To use these as inline images in your intranet page, you must convert them to either GIF or JPEG.

T I P

Though some browsers may work with other graphics formats, limit yourself to GIF and JPEG files for inline graphics so you don't ignore portions of your audience.

Fig. 6.2
Buttons provide
quick access to
different portions
of an intranet
site.

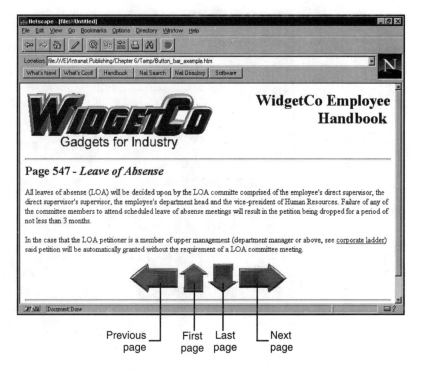

Both of these formats are known as bitmaps, or *raster*, graphics. They are
made up of individual picture elements (pixels) of different colors arranged
in a rectangular pattern. When put together, these pixels form a picture (see
fig. 6.3).

▶ **See** "Working with Graphics Files," **p. 97**

GIF Files

The Graphics Interchange Format (GIF) was developed by the online service
CompuServe and has become a de facto standard in the online world. After
public outcry when CompuServe set a policy of only allowing the format to be
used with their service (after seven years of it being, for all intents and purposes, in the public domain) CompuServe reversed its decision. This format
may now be used in any application, though software developers must pay a
licensing fee to incorporate support in their products. This will not affect you
or your pages' readers except by possibly making browsers and image editing
programs a little more expensive.

Fig. 6.3
When placed together, all the individual pixels in a file create a picture.

Area of detail

Close-up

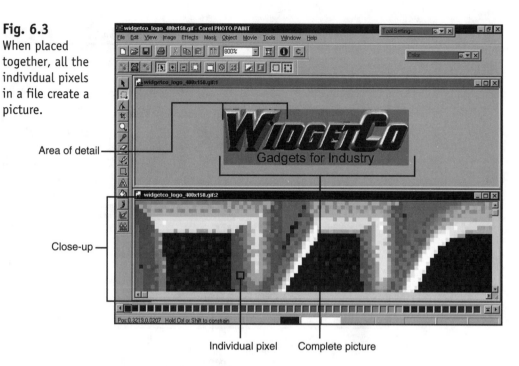

Individual pixel   Complete picture

GIF images are limited to a maximum of 256 simultaneous colors. If an image with a greater number of colors is converted to GIF, it's automatically reduced to 256 colors, with the additional colors being represented by *dithering* (placing dots of two or more colors close together to simulate a third color). Each of the graphics included in this book were shot from computer screens displaying 256 colors while the book uses far fewer (actually, only one). If you look closely, you'll notice that the pictures are made up of various sized black dots that have been dithered to simulate grays.

N O T E

The GIF format includes many advanced features that are not currently supported by graphics editing programs or browsers such as direct animation and sound. It's safe to assume that as interactive and animated intranet pages become more commonplace these features will be added to these programs.

Transparent

One of the most used features of GIF files is the ability to set one color "transparent." While editing the file in a paint program, the transparent color is still visible. When displayed by a browser, however, the color is dropped from the image so that the graphic or button appears to float on the page (see fig. 6.4).

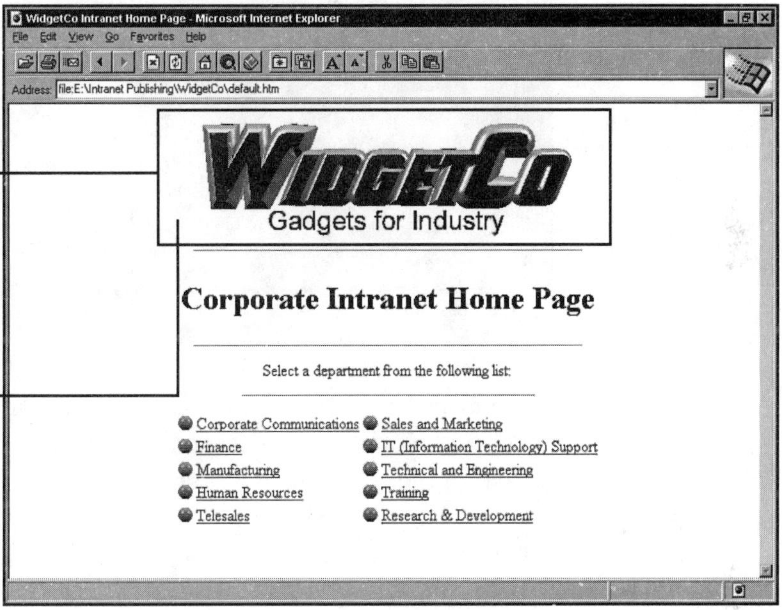

Fig. 6.4
Using a transparent color helps add impact to the logo and bullets in this page. The page's background color doesn't matter.

Outline of complete graphic
Transparent area

Most paint programs support transparent GIFs, though some have very limited support. LView Pro, available on the CD-ROM, lets you specify any color as transparent simply by clicking the pointer on that shade. HiJaak 95 and Corel PhotoPaint have very poor support for transparent GIFs. HiJaak only allows the transparent color to be black or white, which can be very limiting. Corel PhotoPaint lets any color be transparent, but selecting that color is made difficult because you have to do it from a dialog box when saving the file (see fig. 6.5). It's interesting that a shareware program provides more advanced and user friendly features than some expensive "professional" programs.

Fig. 6.5
Picking a transparent color in Corel PhotoPaint is difficult because the match must be exact.

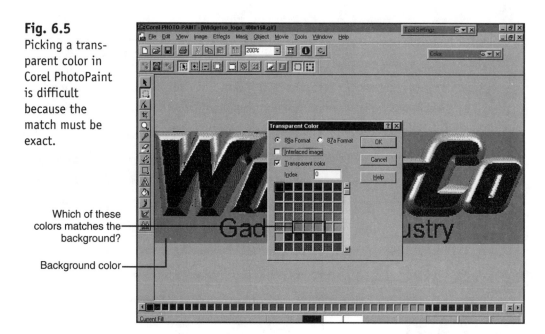

Which of these colors matches the background?

Background color

When creating transparent GIFs make sure there is a sharp transition between the transparent color and the portion of the image that you want to keep (see fig. 6.6). If the transition is not sharp, you may see a halo around your image (see fig. 6.7). This muddiness will occur if you have graphics whose edges have been anti-aliased. (If you have Microsoft Plus! for Windows 95, this is the same effect that makes large fonts look "smoother.")

Interlaced

Most GIF files are saved as a series of four incomplete images, broken up by rows of pixels. The first image is made up of rows 1, 5, 9..., the second of rows 2, 6, 10..., the third of rows 3, 7, 11... and the fourth from rows 4, 8, 12... (see fig. 6.8). When displayed by a browser, these four images are placed together to form one complete picture.

The advantage to an interlaced image is that you can usually figure out what the picture is when only 1/4 or 1/2 of the image has been downloaded to your browser. This is far more important when you are accessing your intranet by modem from a remote location. In most cases, your network will transmit the picture so fast that you won't even notice that it's been interlaced.

Fig. 6.6
This closeup shows the difference between a sharp and muddy transition between the transparent color and the image.

Muddy transition —

Sharp transition —

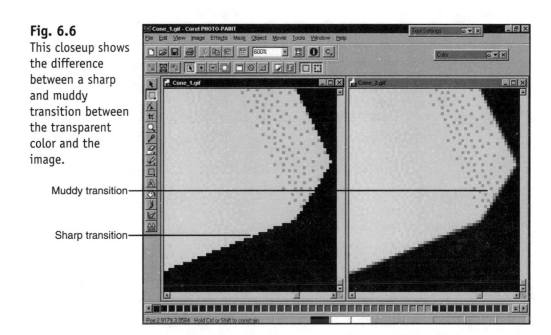

Fig. 6.7
If the transition from the transparent color to the image is not sharp, you may notice a halo.

Clean edge —

— "Halo"

Fig. 6.8
Each portion contains only 1/4 of the information in the complete image.

— Complete image

Interlaced portions

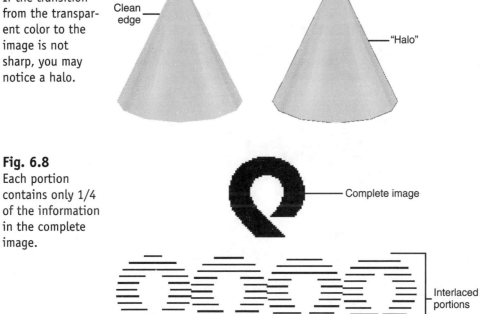

NOTE

Some browsers have a problem with GIF images that are both interlaced and have a transparent color. This is because of the way that they piece the picture together on-screen. Occasionally, an interlaced-transparent GIF will have a serrated edge instead of a nice clean one. To avoid this problem, if your image uses a transparent color, save it as non-interlaced.

JPEG Files

The JPEG format was developed by an industry group called the Joint Photographic Experts Group (JPEG). Mostly used for high resolution, high color depth images, JPEG files incorporate a unique method of compression that lets the artist determine how small to make the final file. JPEG is termed a *lossy* compression scheme because the smaller (the more it is compressed) the saved file is, the more information about the picture is lost (see fig. 6.9). Depending on what the image is being used for, this loss of quality may be acceptable. Generally, over an intranet the speed of image transmission is high enough that JPEG images don't need to be compressed too much.

Fig. 6.9
Notice the solid color area in the original has a nice, even tone, while this area is muddy in the JPEG compressed file.

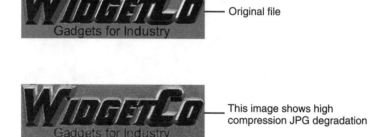

— Original file

— This image shows high compression JPG degradation

Every time a JPEG image is loaded into a paint program and saved again, it loses a bit more of its fidelity to the original file. It's a good idea to keep a master copy of any JPEG file you publish in some other format such as TIF (Tagged Image File format). This ensures that you have a copy free from the ravages of lossy compression if you need to edit it later.

JPEG files are excellent for transmitting photographs over your intranet because they support using millions of simultaneous colors. (Remember that a browser only displays an image with as many colors as the user's computer and video card allow.) Applications for this range from product database images to snapshots in an employee yearbook.

Adding Inline Graphics

As you learned in Chapter 3, "Formattting Documents," graphics are added to an intranet page using the image tag (`<IMG SRC="file">`). This is the most basic use of an inline image and provides no formatting options. The image tag supports a number of modifiers that help you display graphics exactly the way you want.

▶ See "Basic Graphics Use," **p. 73**

Aligning Text with Graphics

How text is aligned with graphics can have a great impact on how your page is laid out. Without any modifiers, text placed on the same line as a graphic starts at the bottom edge of the image and wraps underneath the image at the end of a line. Table 6.1 lists the align modifiers that determine how text wraps with a graphic (see figs. 6.10 and 6.11 for examples). The terms in table 6.1 are included in the image tag by adding **ALIGN=modifier**.

TABLE 6.1   Image Alignment Modifiers

Modifier	Description
TOP	Aligns top of first letter of text to the top of the image. Text wraps below the image.
TEXTTOP	Aligns tallest text to the top of the image. Text wraps below the image.
CENTER	Bottom of text (bottom of "g" not "a") aligns to the middle of the image. Text wraps below the image.

continues

TABLE 6.1   Continued

Modifier	Description
ABSCENTER	Baseline of text (bottom of "regular" letters, bottom of "a" not "g") aligns to the middle of the image. Text wraps below the image.
MIDDLE	Aligns the middle of the first letter with the middle of the image. Text wraps below the image.
ABSMIDDLE	Aligns the middle of the tallest text with the middle of the image. Text wraps below the image.
BOTTOM	Baseline of text aligns to the bottom of the image. Text wraps below the image.
LEFT	Aligns text to the top of the image. Image remains to the left of text which wraps alongside the image.
RIGHT	Aligns text to the top of the image. Image remains to the right of text which wraps alongside the image.

Fig. 6.10
This image shows examples of how text and graphics work together when the ALIGN modifier is used with the image tag.

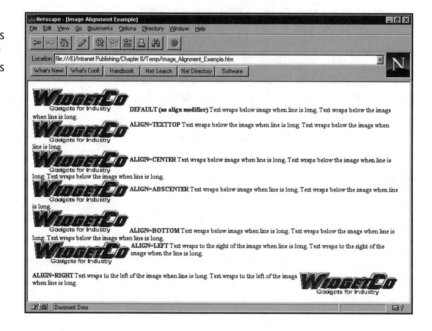

Fig. 6.11
The code used to create figure 6.10 shows the proper use of the ALIGN modifier.

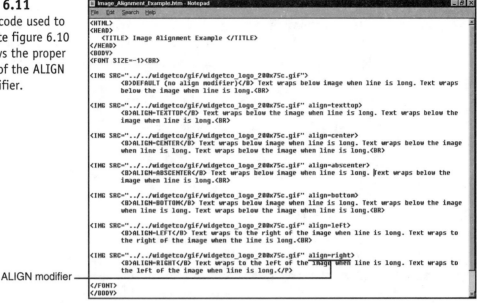

ALIGN modifier

In addition to just specifying the alignment between text and graphics, you can also state how much distance you want between them. By default, text begins at the edge of a graphic. This can make it difficult to read. Adding the HSPACE and VSPACE modifiers to the image tag allows you to place some space between text and graphics.

Each of these modifiers specifies a distance in pixels. In general, a distance of five pixels between text and graphics provides good readability, though you may want to add more space for certain applications.

To add a vertical and horizontal space of five pixels around a graphic, add **HSPACE=5** and **VSPACE=5** to the image tag

```
<IMG SRC="widgetco_logo.gif" HSPACE=5 VSPACE=5>
```

Specifying Alternative Text

Alternative text supplies a written description of an image that is displayed if, for some reason, the image can't be found or displayed. If some of your readers are using browsers that don't support graphics or if they have turned graphics support off (to speed up viewing), you should consider including alternative text in your image statements. Also, if your images are stored separately from the HTML files and there is a possibility that the images will occasionally be unavailable, include alternative text so your pages will make sense to your readers.

To add alternative text, add the modifier **ALT="description"** to your <IMG SRC="filename"> tag. For example, an image tag for the WidgetCo logo including alternative text looks like

```
<IMG SRC="widgetco_logo.gif" ALT="WidgetCo Logo">
```

Specifying Graphic Size

If you've already used your company's intranet (or gone surfing on the World Wide Web) you may have noticed that some pages with graphics take a long time to begin displaying. This is because each image must be downloaded to your computer so your browser knows how big it is before it can lay out the page on your screen.

If you tell the browser how big the image is ahead of time, the browser will display the page right away. To do this, add the **HEIGHT=#** and **WIDTH=#** modifiers to your image tag, where the pound signs are replaced with the image's height and width, respectively, in pixels. If your image is 200 pixels wide by 76 pixels high, the image tag would read

```
<IMG SRC="filename" WIDTH=200 HEIGHT=76>
```

T I P

Most image editing programs provide an easy way to find out the image's size. LView Pro, for example, displays this information in the program's header bar.

What happens if you make a mistake and enter the wrong numbers? Well, you aren't going to damage anything by doing this, but you may get some odd results (see fig. 6.12).

Fig. 6.12
In addition to telling a browser how big an image is, the HEIGHT and WIDTH modifiers can also be used to scale an image.

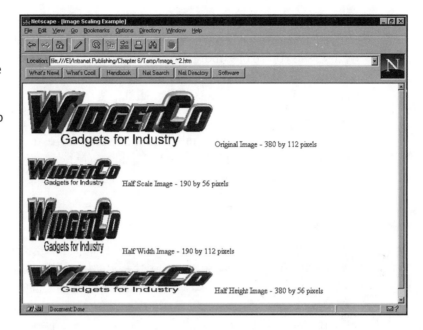

However, you can use the scaling to your advantage. If you want to include a half-scale image in your page (say the logo file you have looks too big), simply input the size you want the logo to appear on-screen in the HEIGHT=# and WIDTH=# modifiers. In the case of the example above, the image is 200×76 pixels so half of that is 100×38. Modify your image tag to read

```
<IMG SRC="filename" WIDTH=100 HEIGHT=38>
```

TIP

If you just want to scale an object, you only need to put in one of the size modifiers. The browser displaying the image assumes that the other modifier changes in the same proportion.

Using Low Resolution "Quick Load" Images

Although networks are generally quite fast, occasionally an image is so big that it takes a long time to download and display (up to several minutes for a really big, relatively uncompressed JPEG file). Alternatively, you may have a network that sometimes gets bogged down or there are a lot of users who access the corporate intranet via modem from remote locations. To help readers see your pages more quickly, you may want to have their browsers download a low resolution version of an image and display it quickly while the larger file takes its time to download.

The LOWSRC="filename" modifier provides this second, low resolution image. Actually, low resolution is a misnomer. You are not restricted to using a smaller size image at all. Your second image may be black and white, a JPEG file that has a high compression rate, or an actual low resolution version.

TIP

If you use a scaled-down copy of your original image as the low resolution version, make sure you use the HEIGHT=# and WIDTH=# modifiers in your image statement so the low resolution version displays properly.

To add a low resolution image, your image statement should look like

```
<IMG SRC="imagefile" LOWSRC="lowresfile">
```

where "*imagefile*" and "*lowresfile*" are the original image file name and low resolution file name.

Using Inline Graphics as Links

In Chapter 5, you learned how to make text link different pages together. You also learned how to create links within a single document. You can also make graphic images perform as links. This is especially useful for providing visual cues to your readers about what a link is for. In addition, readers find it helpful to have a consistent set of icons representing, say, links to Help pages and comment forms. Talk to your webmaster about setting up a folder full of such icons that can be referenced by any page in the intranet.

▶ **See** "Linking Documents," **p. 113**

Buttons and Images

For example, most pages in the WidgetCo intranet site contain a copy of the company logo. If a reader clicks the image, the browser displays the corporate home page (see fig. 6.13).

Fig. 6.13
A company logo can be used to automatically link the current page to the corporate home page.

Image used as link

Link to this file

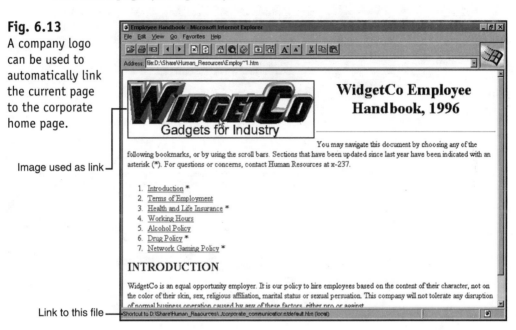

▶ **See** "Creating a Link," **p. 115**

To use a graphic as a link, include the image tag between the link anchor tags

```
<A HREF="linked file"> <IMG SRC="graphic file"> </A>
```

The image tag can employ any of the modifiers listed in the previous section to help you format your page. When an image is used as a link, a border is drawn around it to let users know that the image is "clickable." Some graphics are either obviously a link or look bad with the border. To remove the border, add the modifier **BORDER=0** to the image tag

```
<A HREF="linked file"> <IMG SRC="graphic file" BORDER=0> </A>
```

Graphics can also be used to make a virtual control panel to make navigating an intranet site easier. When using graphics this way, it's a good idea to make them look and work in ways familiar to your reader. For example, you may want to provide buttons that look like those found on a VCR. This helps your reader know, for example, that the right button takes him or her to the next page and the left goes to the previous page (see fig. 6.14).

Fig. 6.14
VCR style buttons are small graphics, used as links, that help a reader navigate your site.

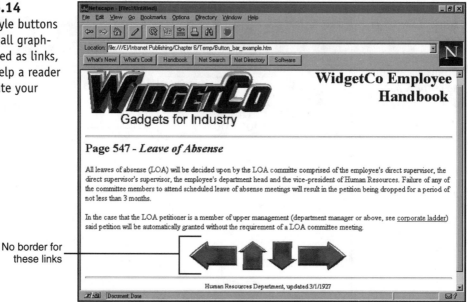

No border for these links

 The CD-ROM contains a collection of graphic elements that can be used as buttons.

Image maps

An *image map* is a specialized type of graphic link. An image map works with one image and allows different parts of it to link to different places. Figure 6.15 shows an alternative WidgetCo home page that employs an image map. Clicking the location of any department links to that department's home page.

Fig. 6.15
An image map
makes parts of an
image link to a
different location.

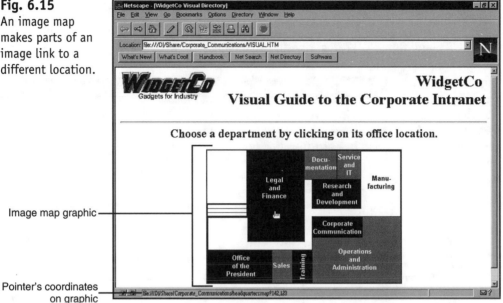

Image map graphic

Pointer's coordinates
on graphic

You have a lot of control over how each location on an image reacts. Not every location has to be active. In figure 6.15, only the locations of the actual department perform as links. The hallways and entrance do not perform any function.

Like an HTML file, an image map is simply a text file that tells a browser something about your graphic. The file can be named anything, but should have the extension MAP to distinguish it as an image map.

You define a clickable location by saying what shape you want it (circle, rectangle, or polygon), where it is located, and where you want to link to if that portion is clicked. You can also specify a default link that is accessed if a location outside any defined area is clicked.

Each clickable area in an image map requires a definition line. A definition line in an image map file is pretty straightforward and always follows this format:

(shape) (file to link to) (coordinates defining the shape)

You can also include remarks in the file by starting a line with a pound symbol (#). Figure 6.16 shows the image map file used for figure 6.15, while table 6.2 and figure 6.17 describe the shapes used.

Fig. 6.16
The image map
file used to make
certain areas of
figure 6.15
clickable.

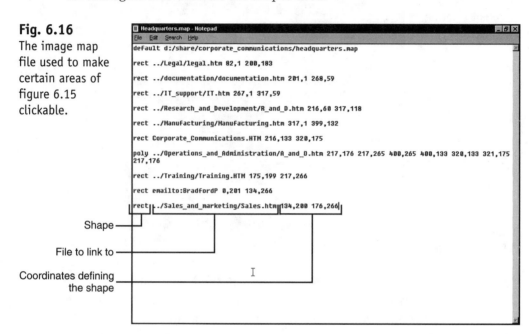

TABLE 6.2   Imagemap Shapes

Name	Coordinates
Circle	One at the center, the other along the circumference
Rect (rectangle)	One at the upper-left corner, the other at the lower-right (for a square, make the width the same as the height)
Poly (polygon)	One coordinate at each vertex
Oval	One at the upper-left corner, the other at the lower-right
Point	A single coordinate (a browser will pick the nearest area to link to if the pointer is not directly on the point)

TIP

You may find it easier to specify a circle using the oval shape. Just make sure that the height and width are equal.

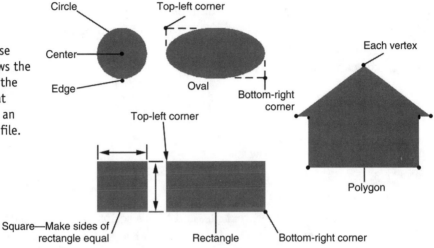

Fig. 6.17
Each of these shapes shows the location of the vertices that define it in an image map file.

Working with an image map can be difficult because you must determine what coordinates should be entered on each line. Most graphics programs display the mouse pointer coordinates, so you have to write them down and keep track of them while writing the map file. Luckily, there are a number of programs available that create imagemaps for you when you click certain parts of an image.

The HTML statement to use an image map is almost identical to that for creating a standard link except that the file noted by the hypertext reference (HREF) is the map file and the image tag includes the modifier ISMAP.

```
<A HREF="mapfile"> <IMG SRC="imagefile" ISMAP> </A>
```

The reference to the imagemap used in figure 6.15 reads

```
<A HREF="homepage.map"> <IMG SRC="office_layout.gif" ISMAP> </A>
```

Using Server Push Animation

One way to include moving pictures in your intranet pages is through *server push animation*. A series of individual images are sent from the server to the browser and displayed in the same location. In other words, the server pushes the images into the browser, hence the name.

Adding Server Push Animation

Server push animation can be difficult to implement since you have to write a script (program) that tells the server to keep sending the new images. Luckily, Nick Bicanic, a World Wide Web author, has supplied us with a script that takes care of this problem. To use the script:

1. Create a series of GIF files that contain the animation that you want. Make sure that all the files are the same size (for example, x × y pixels).

2. Write a text file that lists all the GIF files, in the order you want them played by the browser.

3. Save the text file, giving it a descriptive name. Note that it must have the extension .TXT.

4. Copy the GIF files, text file, and Nick's script to a single folder. If you want to rename the script, you may do so, but make sure that the first four characters are NPH- and the extension is .CGI.

5. Add the tag

   ```
   <IMG SRC="path/nph-script.cgi?textfile.txt">
   ```

   to your HTML file, where *path* is the path to the files in step 4 and *textfile.txt* is the name you gave your text file in step 2.

You may use any of the formatting modifiers that you would if the image were static. You can also use transparent and interlaced GIFs.

▶ **See** "Specifying the Path," **p. 119**

If you have trouble making this script work, check with your system administrator to make sure that you have scripting rights. You may also need to have your administrator put the script in the CGI-bin, in which case, you have to use absolute path names to the animation and text file.

Limitations

The biggest limitation to server push animation is that it's slow, since every image has to be downloaded from the server before it is displayed. There are also no controls in our script to have the animation *loop* (play over and over again).

To increase the paying speed of an animation, keep the images small.

Making GIF Animation Files

Making GIF animation files can be very time consuming if you do it by hand. Unfortunately, there are not a lot of resources for automatically making the series of images needed for server push GIF animation. One program that does a nice job is Web 3D from Asymetrix. This low-end 3D modeling program also creates animations which can be saved as a series of GIF files, just right for including in your intranet pages.

You may also be able to use a higher-end animation program to create an AVI or MOV file (see the next section, "Using Offline Animation Formats"). Then load this animation file into a paint program that supports animation, such as Corel PhotoPaint, and save the individual frames as GIF files.

NOTE

GIFCon (GIF Construction Kit) provides full support for the GIF 89A format, which includes multiple pages that the Netscape 2.0 browser can display sequentially as animation. Using this program, you can load your individual GIF images and compile them into one file. No server push animation scripts required. Note that most browsers do not support this feature, however.

If you are forced to work by hand, you might want to consider borrowing a book on traditional animation from your local library. This will help you get a feel for simulating motion and drawing the individual pictures.

Using Offline Animation Formats

There are a number of standard animation formats that are available for most any type of computer. Among the more common are Microsoft's Audio Video Interleaf (AVI), Apple Computer's Quicktime (MOV), and the Motion Picture Expert Group's format(MPEG).

All these formats support simultaneous motion and audio with high resolution images. None, however, are directly supported by browsers.

▶ **See** "Creating a Link," **p. 115**

Because of this lack of support, you may not include them directly in your pages. You must make links to the animation files which can then be activated by your readers. When a reader activates a link to one of these files, it's either downloaded to his or her computer for later viewing, or a helper application is started to display the animation immediately.

Appendix B, "Using an Intranet," has instructions for configuring browsers to automatically load helper applications.

From Here...

In this chapter, you have learned how to include graphics and animation in your intranet pages. By adding image maps and buttons, you can make your pages easier to navigate. You have learned how to incorporate a transparent color in your images.

- ● Chapter 7, "Creating Intranet Tables," shows you how to use tables to structure data in your intranet pages. Also, you'll learn to use them to provide formatting to your page as a whole.
- ● Chapter 10, "Managing Pages," teaches tips and techniques to make multiple page intranet sites easier to create and maintain.
- ● Chapter 11, "Making Content Available on the Server," provides complete instructions for compiling and publishing your intranet content.

7

Creating Intranet Tables

By Paul Bodensiek

Intranet tables were introduced in Chapter 3 as a way to create multiple columns in an intranet page. The example shown there, two columns with no modifiers, is the most basic example of a table's power. Though originally created to allow formatting of tabular information (like spreadsheet data), the extensive controls available in the table container give it a life far beyond just numbers.

You can use tables to present your financial data in an organized way, create a neat and clean button bar, and format your text. Tables' uses are limited only by your imagination.

In this chapter, you learn to

- Create intranet tables
- Add column and row headings
- Format the entire column and individual cells
- Add a border
- Use tables to layout entire pages

Basic Table Elements

A table is composed of individual cells arranged in rows and columns like a grid. You can fill each cell with any text or graphic (or combination) and format it using any standard HTML tag.

In addition, you may add row and column headings and captions to help identify tables.

The Table, Row, and Cell Tags

All the cells, headings, and captions in a table are placed within the table container (<TABLE>...</TABLE>). Each row starts and ends with the table row container (<TR>...</TR>), while individual cells are defined by the table cell container (<TD>...</TD>) (see figs. 7.1 and 7.2).

TIP

All of these nested containers, plus their text, graphics, modifiers, headings and captions, can get to look pretty messy in your HTML file. Make sure you organize your table text to make writing and editing easier.

Fig. 7.1
A basic table is composed of cells arranged in rows using the <TD> and <TR> containers.

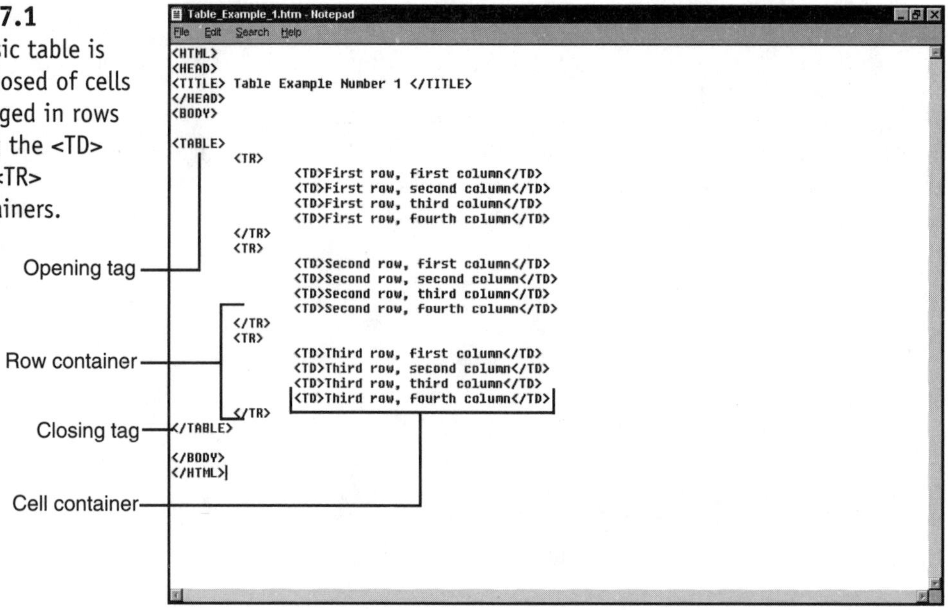

Opening tag

Row container

Closing tag

Cell container

```
Table_Example_1.htm - Notepad
File  Edit  Search  Help

<HTML>
<HEAD>
<TITLE> Table Example Number 1 </TITLE>
</HEAD>
<BODY>

<TABLE>
        <TR>
                <TD>First row, first column</TD>
                <TD>First row, second column</TD>
                <TD>First row, third column</TD>
                <TD>First row, fourth column</TD>
        </TR>
        <TR>
                <TD>Second row, first column</TD>
                <TD>Second row, second column</TD>
                <TD>Second row, third column</TD>
                <TD>Second row, fourth column</TD>
        </TR>
        <TR>
                <TD>Third row, first column</TD>
                <TD>Third row, second column</TD>
                <TD>Third row, third column</TD>
                <TD>Third row, fourth column</TD>
        </TR>
</TABLE>

</BODY>
</HTML>
```

Fig. 7.2
The table defined
in figure 7.1
shows how the
cells and rows
interact.

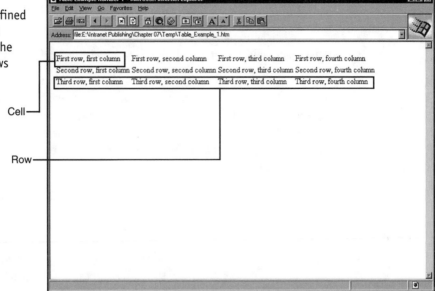

Cell—

Row—

To construct a table:

1. Open an existing HTML document or start a new one using Notepad or your favorite HTML editor.

2. Start your table by entering the **<TABLE>** tag.

3. Begin your first row by entering the **<TR>** tag.

4. Begin a cell by entering the **<TD>** tag.

5. Enter the text or graphic you want included in the cell.

6. Close the cell by entering the **</TD>** tag.

7. Enter any additional cells you want in this row by repeating steps 4 through 6.

8. Close the row by entering the **</TR>** tag.

9. Enter any additional rows you want by repeating steps 3 through 8.

10. Close the table by entering the **</TABLE>** tag.

> **NOTE**
>
> Text in cells is automatically formatted as the default text size. You can, however, add any HTML formatting you want within a cell.
>
> If you want to add specific formatting to all the text in a table, you have to do it on a cell-by-cell basis. (For example, if you want all cells to be bold, each individual cell must contain the bold container.) There is no way to format all the text in a table at once. Although this may seem like a major problem, you probably won't be doing overall text formatting in a table very often.
>
> ▶ **See** "Working With Text Files," **p. 84**
>
> ▶ **See** "Using Preformatted Text," **p. 67**

Creating tables from existing text (such as files from a word processor or a spreadsheet) sometimes can be a daunting task. If you save word processor or spreadsheet text in a text only file, typically the table text will have spaces added to create the columns and rows. In this case, it is generally easier to place this text within a preformatted text container. The Microsoft Excel Internet Assistant makes quick work of converting spreadsheet data directly to intranet table form and is the best alternative when you want to retain your formatting.

Row and Column Headings

When using a table to present data, you generally want to have row and column headings so your readers know what they are viewing. In an intranet table, these headings are automatically centered and boldfaced so that they stand out.

To add a row or column heading, replace the cell container(s) (<TD>... </TD>) that you want used as headings with the heading container (<TH>...</TH>) (see figs. 7.3 and 7.4).

Fig. 7.3
This table layout,
first shown in
figure 7.1, now
has row and
column headings.

Column headers

Row header

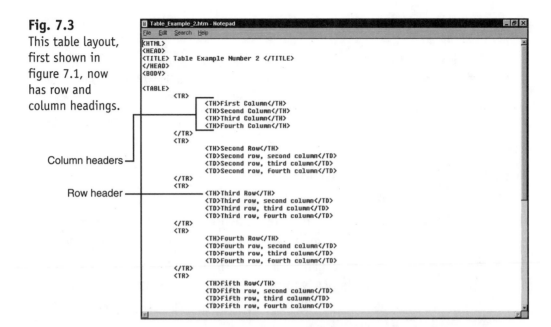

Fig. 7.4
The table layout
from figure 7.1
with the new
column and row
headings.

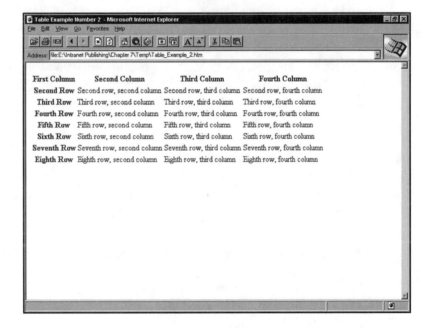

TIP

Note that, unlike "normal" cells, you can't use any HTML text modifiers (bold, italic, font size, and so on) with table headings. If you want to use specific formatting in table heads, leave them as normal cells and format them by hand.

Adding Table Captions

A caption is a quick reference for your reader to tell him or her what the point of your table is. For example, each figure in this book has a caption that tells you what number it is and a synopsis of what the figure is all about.

An intranet table's caption can be at either the top or bottom of the table (not both) and is automatically formatted using the default text size. You can have as many caption lines as you like and format them individually using any standard HTML tags.

Add a caption by including the <CAPTION>...</CAPTION> container between the opening table tag and the first row tag. The caption tag has only one modifier which determines whether the caption appears at the top or bottom of your table. By default, the caption appears at the top of your table. To specify the location of the caption, add either ALIGN=TOP or ALIGN=BOTTOM to the opening caption tag.

CAUTION

If you have two caption tags, one set for the top and the other set for the bottom, some browsers will display both captions at the top of your table, or provide unpredictable results.

Figures 7.5 and 7.6 show tables with either a caption at the top of the table or at the bottom.

Fig. 7.5
The two caption containers place the individual captions either above or below the tables they are with.

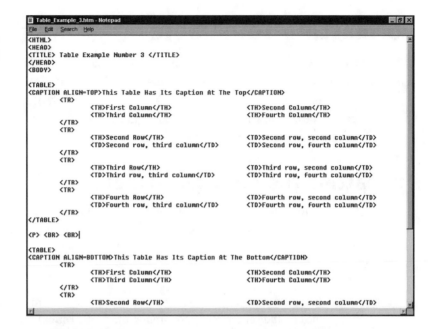

Fig. 7.6
These two tables are identical except for the placement of their captions.

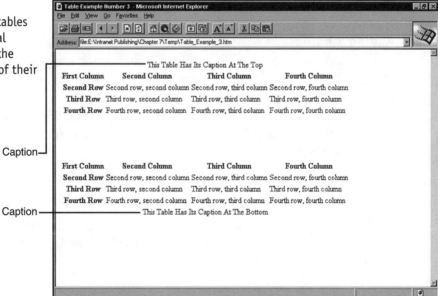

Formatting Your Table

Tables have a number of formatting options that can be applied on a cell-by-cell basis or to the table as a whole. You can specify the size of your table (either as an exact size or as a percentage of the width of the browser screen), how much space there is around the text in each cell, how far apart the individual cells are, and many text specific formats.

Formatting the Table as a Whole

You can affect the overall look of your table by adding a border, adding spacing between cells, and specifying an exact or relative overall width.

TIP

If you want your table centered in the width of the browser window, include the center container around the table. For example, <CENTER><TABLE>...</TABLE></CENTER>.

Adding a Border

You add a border to your table simply by including the BORDER=# modifier in the table tag. Replace the pound sign (#) with any whole number to specify the width of the border in pixels (individual dots on the computer screen). Figure 7.7 shows the effect of adding a border to the table we've been using throughout this chapter. The BORDER modifier adds an outline to the table and between individual cells.

TIP

Microsoft Internet Explorer does not support table border widths. If a border width has been specified, it will simply be displayed as a border of width 1.

Note that if you have blank cells, they won't have an outline when you add the BORDER modifier. If you want a blank cell to have an outline, add a non-breaking space within the cell container: <TD>   </TD>.

Fig. 7.7
These two tables
show the effect of
different border
widths. Note that
the lines between
cells remains the
same.

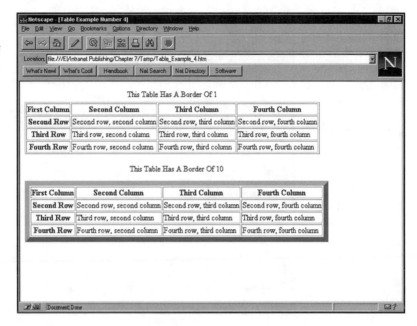

Changing the Table Width

By default, a table sizes itself based on the width of the text or graphics you have included in it. Sometimes, though, you want to specify an exact width for your table, either because you don't have much text in the table and the automatic setting makes it look too skinny or the default layout for your table looks too wide in comparison to the rest of your page.

Like the table border, the width is specified by including the WIDTH=# modifier within the opening table tag. In this case, however, the pound sign (#) can be replaced either with a plain number (for example, 700) which specifies an exact width for the table (in pixels) or with a percentage (for example, 50%) which sets the width as a percentage of the browser window's width (see fig. 7.8).

TIP

If you want your table to always be exactly as wide as the browser window's, include the modifier WIDTH=100% in the opening table tag.

Fig. 7.8
These three tables show the differ-ence between the default and an absolute and a relative table width setting.

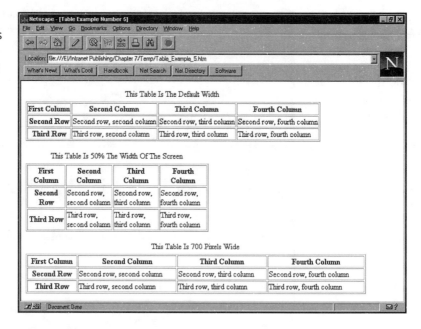

Controlling the Cell Spacing

You may notice that the text in your cells seems crowded together or that there isn't enough space in between individual cells. The table container has two modifiers that let you specify these attributes individually.

The CELLPADDING modifier specifies the distance between the text in a cell and the border of the cell. By default CELLPADDING is set to 1, though any number may be used. To specify a particular amount of padding, include the modifier CELLPADDING=#, where the pound sign (#) is any whole number, in the opening table tag (see fig. 7.9).

The CELLSPACING modifier specifies the space between the borders of indi-vidual cells. By default, cellspacing is set to 1, though any number may be used. To specify a particular spacing, include the modifier CELLSPACING=#, where # is any whole number, in the opening table tag (see fig. 7.10).

Both the CELLPADDING and CELLSPACING modifiers may be included in the opening table tag.

Fig. 7.9
These tables show the effect of specifying different cellpadding.

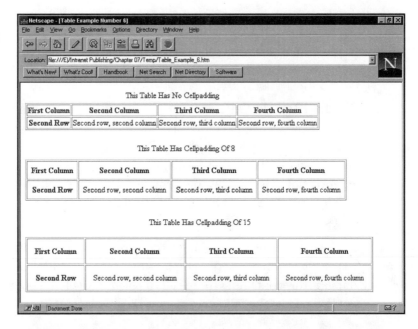

Fig. 7.10
Each of these tables has been formatted with a different amount of cellspacing.

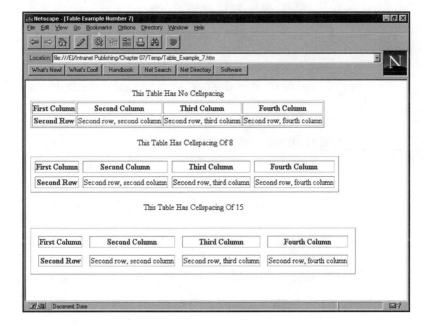

Formatting Individual Rows and Cells

In addition to the overall formatting you can apply to a table, individual cells and rows can be formatted to greatly enhance your tables' readability.

Aligning Text in Cells

Cell text can be aligned either horizontally or vertically (or both) using the ALIGN=x or VALIGN=y modifiers. These modifiers can be used in the opening cell tag (<TD>), to set the alignment for an individual cell, or in the opening row tag (<TR>) to set the alignment for all the cells within a row. Text in a table header may also be aligned by adding these tags to the table header tag (<TH>).

You have the option of aligning text horizontally to the left, right, or center. To set the alignment option, replace the x in the ALIGN=x modifier. For example, a row containing three cells aligned to the left, center, and right would read like the following in your HTML file:

```
<TR>
<TD ALIGN=LEFT> cell text </TD>
<TD ALIGN=CENTER> cell text </TD>
<TD ALIGN=RIGHT> cell text </TD>
</TR>
```

When aligning text vertically, you have the option of aligning it to the top, middle, and bottom of the cell(s). To use the vertical alignment option, replace the y in the VALIGN=y modifier. For example, a row containing three cells aligned to the top, middle, and bottom would read like the following in your HTML file:

```
<TR>
<TD VALIGN=TOP> cell text </TD>
<TD VALIGN=MIDDLE> cell text </TD>
<TD VALIGN=BOTTOM> cell text </TD>
</TR>
```

Note that the short cell text used above will display on one line (unless the browser window is really small). To see the effect of these modifiers, replace *cell text* with longer passages. These options may be mixed and matched to align your text in any way that you need.

Specifying Cell Width

Like the width of the overall table, the width of individual cells may be set using the WIDTH=# modifier. Again, the width may be specified either absolutely (as a specific number of pixels) or relatively. In the case of individual cells, however, the relative width is in proportion to the width of the table, not the width of the browser window. The width set in one cell is used by all the cells in its column (see figs. 7.11 and 7.12). If the width is specified in more than one cell in a column, the width will be set by the first tag indicating width.

The WIDTH modifier is available in row and column headings (set by the <TH> tag) but not in complete rows (set by the <TR> tag).

Fig. 7.11
The width of individual cells, and therefore columns, may be specified using the WIDTH=# modifier. The width may be set in any cell of the column.

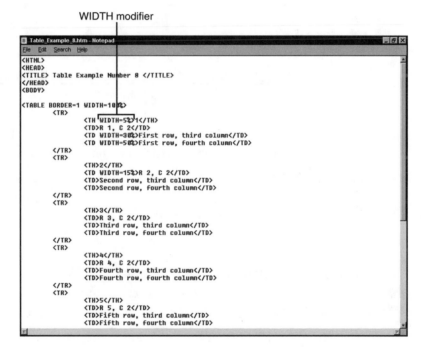

Specifying Row Height

The height of an individual row is specified using the HEIGHT=# modifier in a cell tag (<TD>). Logically, you would think that this modifier should be in the row tag (<TR>) since it automatically affects the entire row, but someone must have figured that it would work better this way.

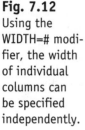

Fig. 7.12
Using the
WIDTH=# modi-
fier, the width
of individual
columns can
be specified
independently.

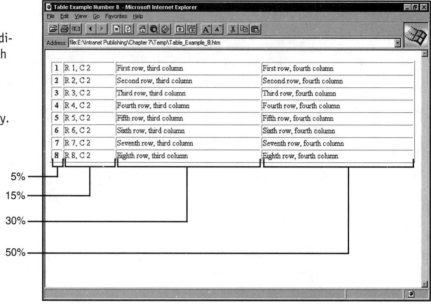

Row height is specified in pixels and is entered in place of the pound sign (#) in the HEIGHT=# modifier. There is no way to specify the height for every cell in a table except by adding the HEIGHT modifier in one cell of every row.

Row height differs from cellpadding in that the entire space of the expanded cell is able to accept text, whereas when the CELLPADDING modifier is used the size of the cell is expanded so that it's a certain amount larger than the text it surrounds.

Making Cells Span Rows and Columns

Many times you want a cell to span a certain number of columns or rows. This can be especially useful for creating headings (see fig. 7.13).

To instruct a cell to span a column, enter the COLSPAN=# modifier in the cell tag (<TD>). Replace the pound sign with the number of columns you want the cell to span. Remember to place fewer cells in that row since the spanned cell is taking the place of two or more cells.

Fig. 7.13
Headings that span rows and columns can make tables easier to read.

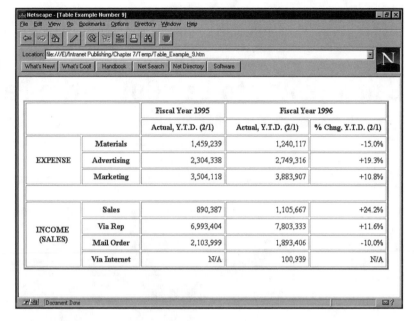

		Fiscal Year 1995	Fiscal Year 1996	
		Actual, Y.T.D. (2/1)	Actual, Y.T.D. (2/1)	% Chng. Y.T.D. (2/1)
EXPENSE	Materials	1,459,239	1,240,117	-15.0%
	Advertising	2,304,338	2,749,316	+19.3%
	Marketing	3,504,118	3,883,907	+10.8%
INCOME (SALES)	Sales	890,387	1,105,667	+24.2%
	Via Rep	6,993,404	7,803,333	+11.6%
	Mail Order	2,103,999	1,893,406	-10.0%
	Via Internet	N/A	100,939	N/A

To instruct a cell to span a row, enter the ROWSPAN=# modifier in the cell tag (<TD>). Replace the pound sign with the number of rows you want the cell to span. Remember to place fewer cells in the column since the spanned cell is taking the place of two or more cells.

Keeping Text on a Single Line

If text is too long to fit within the width of one cell, it is automatically wrapped down to the next line. You can keep this from happening, however.

TIP

Be careful when using the NOWRAP modifier in combination with the WIDTH modifier. If a line of text is too long, NOWRAP overrides specific width settings and may cause unpredictable results.

To specify that text won't wrap within a cell, include the NOWRAP modifier in the cell tag (for example, <TD NOWRAP> cell text </TD>).

Using Tables to Lay Out Entire Pages

You can create visually pleasing intranet pages by using tables in place of the guides employed by many desktop publishing programs. Figures 7.14 and 7.15 show examples of using tables to create an online newsletter. Your use of tables for page layout is limited only by your imagination.

Fig. 7.14
A simple table can help create columns, a feature not directly supported by HTML.

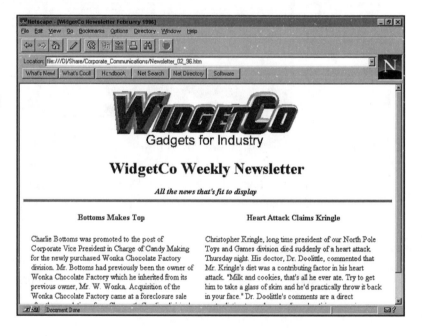

Fig. 7.15
Using column and
row spanning can
help you create
documents with
real flare.

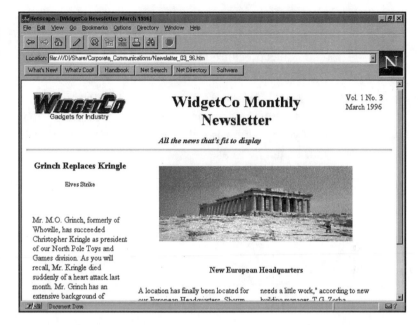

From Here...

Tables are an extremely valuable tool for organizing your data in intranet
pages. Their ability to lay out text and images also helps you create pages
with visual appeal that is impossible to do any other way. From here, you
may want to go to the following chapters:

- Chapter 8, "Planning and Using Intranet Forms," teaches you how
  to create interactive forms for transmitting and receiving data and
  information.

- Chapter 9, "Creating Interactive Databases," shows you how to create
  interactive pages that search databases based on information input in
  forms.

● Chapter 10, "Managing Pages," shows you how to keep your pages organized and easy to update as they become more sophisticated. Use the techniques presented in this chapter to make working with your files easier.

● Chapter 11, "Making Content Available on the Server," gives you complete instructions for uploading your content to the intranet server once all of your content is finished, and it's time to publish it for others in your company to use.

8

Planning and Using Intranet Forms

By Paul Bodensiek

So far, everything we've discussed has had you placing static information and graphics on a page for your readers to view. Nothing has been interactive; there's no direct way for your readers to view exactly what they need or to get in touch with you if they need more information.

Using forms in your page is the first step toward adding that interactivity. A *form* allows your readers to answer questions, create questions of their own, give feedback, and make your page as useful to them as possible.

▶ **See** "Creating Interactive Databases," **p. 189**

The form itself is only half the battle. Once the form is created, you need a way to retrieve information and use it. This is done by a program called a Common Gateway Interface (CGI) script. Don't worry if you aren't a programmer; CGI scripts are easy to write and relatively straightforward. In this chapter, we start with a basic CGI script to create an e-mail message. In Chapter 9, "Creating Interactive Databases," you'll learn how to use Microsoft's Internet Information Server to access a database and return information to your readers.

In this chapter, you learn to

- 🔘 Create a form container
- 🔘 Add text input and buttons to your form
- 🔘 Provide multiple-choice, pull-down menus

● Submit information to a CGI script

● Write a CGI script to deal with form data

The Components of a Form

There are three basic components that make up a form. These parts determine how a reader adds information to it. The first component, the *textarea container*, allows your reader to input an unlimited amount of text and is good for entering messages and other long passages. The *select container*, the second component, creates a drop down list that gives your readers a series of specific options to choose from. The *input container* is the third type of component. The input container differs from the other two in that it has many options allowing you to tailor it to short text entries or radio buttons and check lists, depending on your form's requirements. From a basic textarea to a series of radio buttons and checkboxes, you have complete control over what information is entered by your readers.

Everything that appears in your form must be contained within the form tag (<FORM>...</FORM>). If you include any form elements outside of the form container, they will either be ignored by the browser, or they will yield some odd results. There are some modifiers that must be included within the opening form tag, but these will be explained at the end of the chapter when CGI scripts are introduced.

All of the following containers require at least one modifier. This is the <NAME> tag which tells any scripts accessing the form what data is what.

The Textarea Container

The textarea container provides a space for "freeform" text. This allows your reader to enter as much text as he or she needs (unfortunately, it also paves the way for messages rivaling *War and Peace* in length). See figures 8.1 and 8.2 for examples of textareas.

To add a textarea, include the following code within the form container:

```
<TEXTAREA NAME="name"></TEXTAREA>
```

Your reader's browser picks a size for this text box. To provide more control over how the textarea is displayed, use the COLS=# and ROWS=# modifiers to specify the width and height, respectively.

To place sample text inside the textarea, add text between the opening and closing textarea tags.

Fig. 8.1
These three examples show the proper use of the textarea tag.

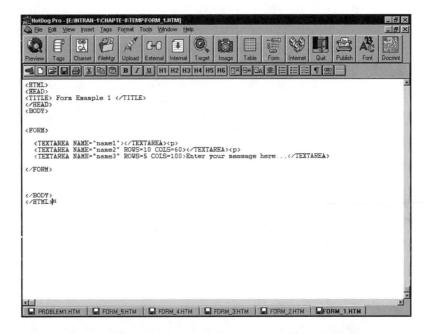

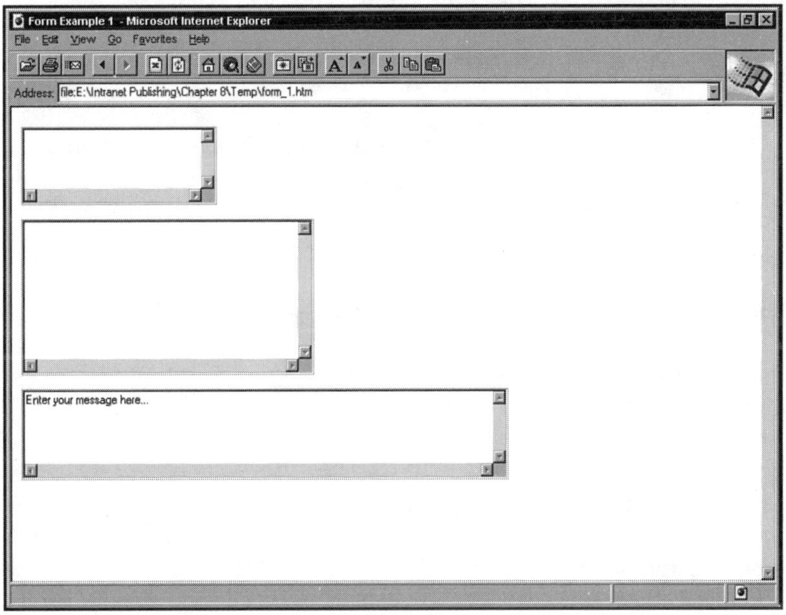

Fig. 8.2
The screen display of the three textarea examples shown in figure 8.1 shows the effect of the different options.

NOTE

If you are simply creating a form that will include one large textarea container that will be e-mailed to a specific person, you might want to use the mailto link instead. This will save you from having to create a form and CGI script to interpret it.

The mailto link is just a hypertext link that automatically loads the browser's e-mail application and fills in the appropriate e-mail address for you. For example, to include an e-mail reference to the author, you would enter the line **<A HREF="mailto:Paul@ParaGrafix.com">Paul</A>.**

The Select Container

This form tag differs from the textarea container in that it supplies your readers with a series of options to select from. The selection list can be displayed either as a drop-down list, like the font size list in most word processors, or as a scrollable list.

There are two parts to the select container, the select container itself, defined by the <SELECT>...</SELECT> tags; and the options tags, which tell the browser what the reader can select from (see fig. 8.3).

TIP

Different browsers display select containers differently (different sized text, and so on), so don't rely on these containers to do double duty as input devices and formatting options. Use tables and preformatted text to help lay out forms.

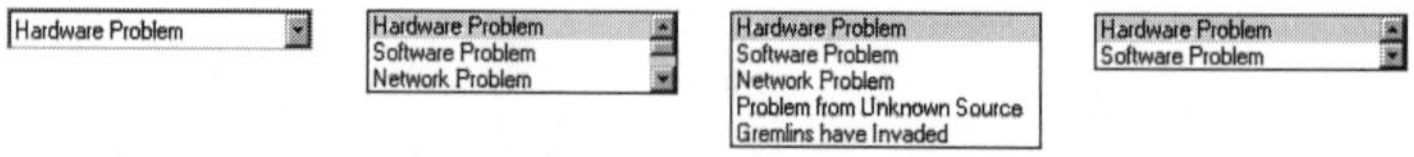

Fig. 8.3
Select elements can vary greatly in their appearance, depending on the options and browser used. This output is from Microsoft Internet Explorer.

The first example shown in figure 8.3 is the default select list. It was created using the following HTML code:

```
<SELECT NAME="problem_area_1">
    <OPTION VALUE="hardware">Hardware Problem
    <OPTION VALUE="software">Software Problem
    <OPTION VALUE="network">Network Problem
    <OPTION VALUE="unknown">Problem from Unknown Source
    <OPTION VALUE="gremlins">Gremlins have Invaded
</SELECT>
```

Note that only the first option, Hardware Problem, is visible. The rest are accessed by clicking the down arrow on the right-hand side of the box (see fig. 8.4).

Fig. 8.4

To access selections in a drop-down, menu style select box, click the down arrow on the right side of the box.

Click here to drop down list

Each of the option tags is divided into three parts: the initial OPTION, which tells the browser that this is part of the select list; the VALUE modifier, which tells the information that the form will output; and the text after the tag, which is displayed on the browser screen.

The second example list shown in figure 8.3 uses the MULTIPLE modifier to tell the browser to create a scrollable list. The scroll bar on the right-hand side lets the viewer move forward and backward through the list at will. The code used to produce this example is

```
<SELECT NAME="problem_area_2" MULTIPLE>
    <OPTION VALUE="hardware">Hardware Problem
    <OPTION VALUE="software">Software Problem
    <OPTION VALUE="network">Network Problem
    <OPTION VALUE="unknown">Problem from Unknown Source
    <OPTION VALUE="gremlins">Gremlins have Invaded
</SELECT>
```

The third example shows a selection box that does not have a scroll bar. This is done by adding the SIZE=# modifier to the select tag. In this case, the

pound sign (#) is replaced by 6 (one more than the number of items) as
shown below:

```
<SELECT NAME="problem_area_3" SIZE=6>
    <OPTION VALUE="hardware">Hardware Problem
    <OPTION VALUE="software">Software Problem
    <OPTION VALUE="network">Network Problem
    <OPTION VALUE="unknown">Problem from Unknown Source
    <OPTION VALUE="gremlins">Gremlins have Invaded
</SELECT>
```

NOTE

Microsoft Internet Explorer requires a size number one greater than the
number of selections to display a box without scroll bars. Netscape Navigator, on the other hand, always displays scroll bars and will display a
blank line if SIZE=# is set greater than the number of items.

The fourth example shows a select list with the SIZE=# modifier set to a
number lower than the number of items. Though there doesn't seem to be
much difference between this example and the second, using the SIZE=
modifier judiciously can help make your lists easier to work with.

The final modifier to the option tag is the SELECTED modifier. This allows
you to set a default value to a select list. If no value is chosen by your reader,
the form returns the value you entered with the SELECTED modifier.

The Input Tag

While all the form containers allow users to input information, the input tag
gives the form designer a broad range of tools to help readers make easy
choices and even enter confidential information.

Using the input tag, you can create small textareas, radio buttons,
checkboxes and the buttons to submit or clear your form. In fact, unless you
want to give your readers the option of inputting large volumes of text, you
could write a form that is composed of nothing but input tags.

Text and Password

Although the textarea container already provides your users with a way to
input text data, it has a big drawback in that it cannot limit the amount of

text your readers can send you. This makes it possible for them to return the first 12 volumes of an encyclopedia. Of course, there are times when this much text is necessary, but if you want to limit the length of reader responses, use the alternative text modifier in the input tag.

Password is a variation on the text modifier. The only difference between the two is that password echoes (displays on-screen) a series of bullets instead of the letters typed in by your reader. Note that this information is not automatically encrypted when the form is submitted; it is only hidden from prying eyes when entered. Chapter 12, "Security Issues," provides details on the use of encryption and other forms of intranet security.

The following listing produces the output shown in figure 8.5:

```
<FORM>
    Describe your problem: <INPUT TYPE="text" NAME="problem" SIZE=45
MAXLENGTH=45 VALUE="temp"><P>
    Enter your password: <INPUT TYPE="password" NAME="problem" SIZE=50
MAXLENGTH=30 VALUE="no password">
</FORM>
```

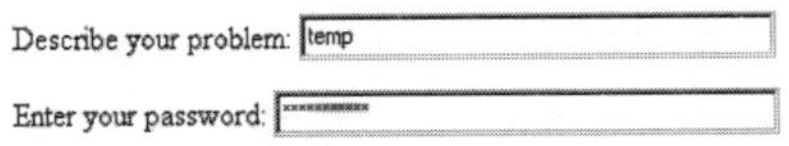

Fig. 8.5

The text and password input boxes are virtually identical except that the password box displays bullets to protect sensitive information.

Describe your problem: [temp   ]

Enter your password: [**********   ]

There are five modifiers used in the above example. As with all form elements, the NAME= modifier is required; the others are optional:

- *TYPE=*. Identifies what type of input element to display.
- *SIZE=*. Specifies the horizontal width of the box.
- *MAXLENGTH=*. Sets an upper limit on the number of characters that can be typed in.
- *VALUE=*. Provides default text to be entered in the box.

Checkboxes and Radio Buttons

Checkboxes and radio buttons provide two ways to give your readers easy access to choices. The main difference between the two, from a reader's point of view, is that any number of checkboxes may be checked, while only one radio button in a group may be checked.

For example, if asking a reader to describe a problem with a computer, you might use checkboxes to tell when the problem occurs and radio boxes to ask what hardware they are running (see fig. 8.6).

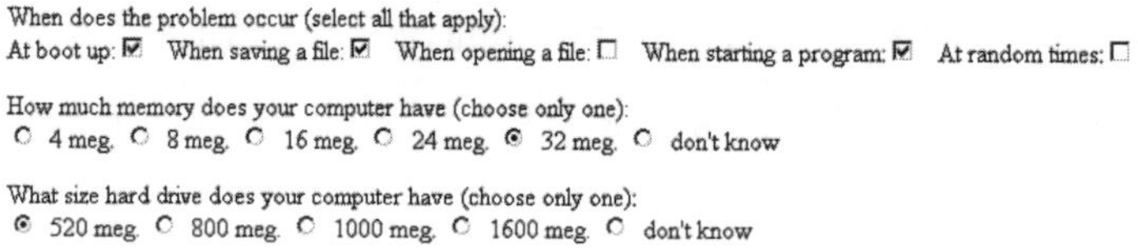

Fig. 8.6
While any number of checkboxes may be selected at one time, only one radio button may be active.

When does the problem occur (select all that apply):
At boot up: ☑ When saving a file: ☑ When opening a file: ☐ When starting a program: ☑ At random times: ☐

How much memory does your computer have (choose only one):
○ 4 meg. ○ 8 meg. ○ 16 meg. ○ 24 meg. ⦿ 32 meg. ○ don't know

What size hard drive does your computer have (choose only one):
⦿ 520 meg. ○ 800 meg. ○ 1000 meg. ○ 1600 meg. ○ don't know

From a content producer's point of view, however, the HTML code is rather different. Each checkbox must have its own name and value combination, while a series of radio buttons all have the same name but different values. You may also specify that a single radio button or multiple checkboxes are already checked to provide default choices.

TIP

If you don't specify a value as checked, you may receive no answer for a set of checkboxes or radio buttons. If one of your options is "unknown," you may want to set that as the default.

The following code (refer to fig. 8.6) demonstrates the use of checkboxes and radio buttons:

```
<FORM>
    When does the problem occur (select all that apply):<BR>
    At boot up:<INPUT TYPE="checkbox" NAME="when1" VALUE="on_boot">
    When saving a file:<INPUT TYPE="checkbox" NAME="when2"
VALUE="when_saving">
```

```
        When opening a file:<INPUT TYPE="checkbox" NAME="when3" VALUE="when_
opening">
        When starting a program:<INPUT TYPE="checkbox" NAME="when4"_
VALUE="program start">
        At random times:<INPUT TYPE="checkbox" NAME="when5" VALUE="random">
    <P>
        How much memory does your computer have (choose only one):<BR>
        <INPUT TYPE="radio" NAME="memory" VALUE="4mb">4 meg.
        <INPUT TYPE="radio" NAME="memory" VALUE="8mb">8 meg.
        <INPUT TYPE="radio" NAME="memory" VALUE="16mb">16 meg.
        <INPUT TYPE="radio" NAME="memory" VALUE="24mb">24 meg.
        <INPUT TYPE="radio" NAME="memory" VALUE="32mb">32 meg.
        <INPUT TYPE="radio" NAME="memory" VALUE="unknown" CHECKED>don't know
    <P>
What size hard drive does your computer have (choose only one):<BR>
        <INPUT TYPE="radio" NAME="drive" VALUE="520mb" CHECKED>520 meg.
        <INPUT TYPE="radio" NAME="drive" VALUE="800mb">800 meg.
        <INPUT TYPE="radio" NAME="drive" VALUE="1gb">1000 meg.
        <INPUT TYPE="radio" NAME="drive" VALUE="1.6gb">1600 meg.
        <INPUT TYPE="radio" NAME="drive" VALUE="unknown">don't know
    </FORM>
```

Reset and Submit Buttons

The purpose of the reset and submit buttons is pretty straightforward, considering their names. The reset button returns all textareas, select boxes, and input sections to their original values while the submit button transmits the data to your CGI script. To add a reset button, set the TYPE= modifier to reset. For a submit button, set TYPE= to submit.

Reset and submit each display a button in the form. By default, each button says reset or submit. You can change the displayed text by including the VALUE= modifier, and adding the text you want in quotation marks (see fig. 8.7).

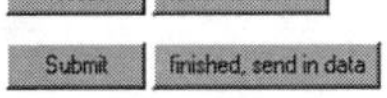

Fig. 8.7
The reset and submit buttons clear the contents of a form or send the data to a script for processing.

The following code creates the buttons shown in figure 8.7:

```
<INPUT TYPE="reset">
<INPUT TYPE="reset" VALUE=" return to default ">
<P>
<INPUT TYPE="submit">
<INPUT TYPE="submit" VALUE=" finished, send in data ">
```

TIP

To add extra space around the custom text in a reset or submit button, include blank spaces before and after the text within the quotation marks.

A Complete Form Example

The following example uses all of the form elements we have just discussed. Although it's specifically related to IT problems, the basic setup can be used for almost any inquiry.

TIP

You can have as many forms as you want in a single intranet page, but each form must be within its own form container and incorporate its own submit button.

First, write the basic page containers, <HTML>, <HEAD>, <BODY> (see fig. 8.8), and any text and graphics you want included on the page

```
<HTML>
<HEAD>
<TITLE> IT Support Form </TITLE>
</HEAD>
<BODY>
<IMG SRC="../gif/widgetco_logo_200x75.gif" ALIGN="left">
<CENTER><H1>IT Support Request Form</H1></CENTER>
<HR>


</BODY>
</HTML>
```

Fig. 8.8
The preliminary
layout is ready to
have form
elements added.

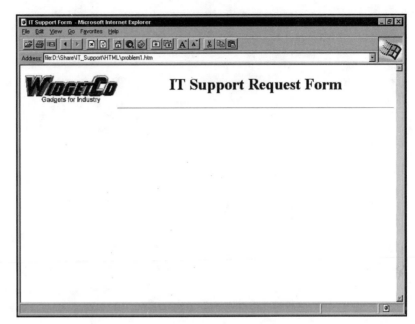

 Now we'll add the form container (between the <HR> and </BODY> tags)
and begin the form by adding some input text boxes (see fig. 8.9) to collect
information about the person making the request

```
<FORM>
      Your Name: <INPUT TYPE="text" NAME="user" SIZE="25" MAXLENGTH="25">
                   
      Job Title: <INPUT TYPE="text" NAME="title" SIZE="40"
MAXLENGTH="40"><P>
</FORM>
```

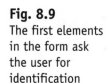

Fig. 8.9
The first elements
in the form ask
the user for
identification
information.

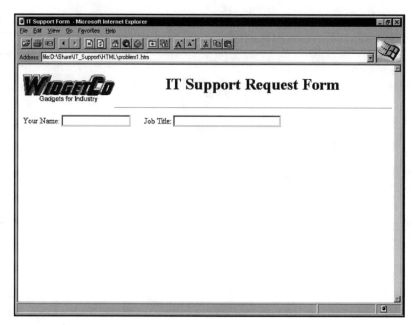

The user's department and location (see fig. 8.10) can be filled in using radio
buttons

```
Department (pick one only):<BR>
     <INPUT TYPE="radio" NAME="department"
        VALUE="Corporate_Communications">Corporate Communications
     <INPUT TYPE="radio" NAME="department" VALUE="Sales_Marketing">Sales
     and Marketing
     <INPUT TYPE="radio" NAME="department" VALUE="Human_Resources">Human
     Resources
     <INPUT TYPE="radio" NAME="department" VALUE="Education">Education
     and Training
     <INPUT TYPE="radio" NAME="department" VALUE="Operations">Operations
     and Administration
     <INPUT TYPE="radio" NAME="department" VALUE="Legal_Finance">Legal
     and Finance
     <INPUT TYPE="radio" NAME="department"
     VALUE="Manufacturing">Manufacturing
     <INPUT TYPE="radio" NAME="department"
        VALUE="Documentation">Documentation
     <INPUT TYPE="radio" NAME="department" VALUE="R_and_D">Research and
     Development
<INPUT TYPE="radio" NAME="department" VALUE="Customer_Service">Customer
Service
```

Fig. 8.10
Radio buttons can
sometimes
become confusing
if nothing is done
to format them.

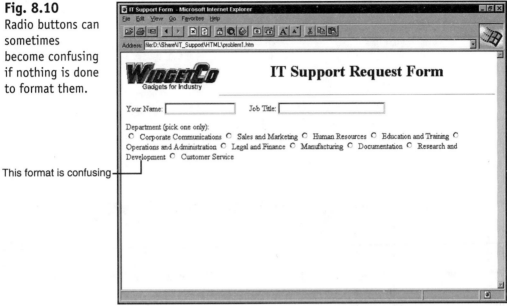

This format is confusing

This is a little messy, but if we add a table (see fig. 8.11) to format this list, it will be more readable

```
Department (pick one only):
<TABLE WIDTH=100%>
<TR>
<TD WIDTH=33%><INPUT TYPE="radio" NAME="department"
     VALUE="Corporate_Communications">Corporate Communications</TD>
<TD WIDTH=33%><INPUT TYPE="radio" NAME="department"
     VALUE="Sales_Marketing">Sales and Marketing</TD>
<TD WIDTH=33%><INPUT TYPE="radio" NAME="department"
     VALUE="Human_Resources">Human Resources</TD>
</TR>
<TR>
<TD><INPUT TYPE="radio" NAME="department" VALUE="Education">Education
and
     Training</TD>
<TD><INPUT TYPE="radio" NAME="department" VALUE="Operations">Operations
and
     Administration</TD>
<TD><INPUT TYPE="radio" NAME="department" VALUE="Legal_Finance">Legal
and
     Finance</TD>
</TR>
<TR>
```

```
<TD><INPUT TYPE="radio" NAME="department"
    VALUE="Manufacturing">Manufacturing</TD>
<TD><INPUT TYPE="radio" NAME="department"
    VALUE="Documentation">Documentation</TD>
<TD><INPUT TYPE="radio" NAME="department" VALUE="R_and_D">Research and
    Development</TD>
</TR>
<TR>
<TD><INPUT TYPE="radio" NAME="department"
VALUE="Customer_Service">Customer
    Service</TD>
</TR>
</TABLE>
</FORM>
```

Fig. 8.11
Using a table to format radio buttons and their text can improve a form's useful-ness.

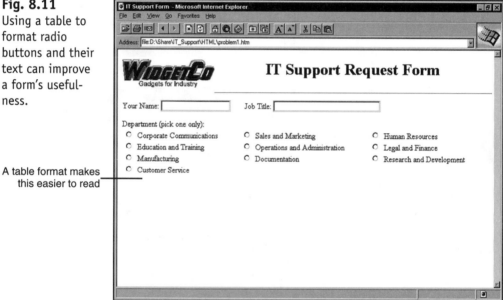

A table format makes this easier to read

 Routing a support technician is easier if you know exactly where the user is located (see fig. 8.12).

```
I am located in:
    <SELECT NAME="building">
        <OPTION VALUE="building_A"> Building A
        <OPTION VALUE="building_B"> Building B
        <OPTION VALUE="building_C"> Building C
        <OPTION VALUE="building_D"> Building D
        <OPTION VALUE="building_E"> Building E
        <OPTION VALUE="building_F"> Building F
    </SELECT>
My cubicle is number:
    <INPUT TYPE="text" NAME="cubicle" SIZE="4" MAXSIZE="3">
```

Fig. 8.12
A drop-down menu can make multiple options available without taking up a lot of space.

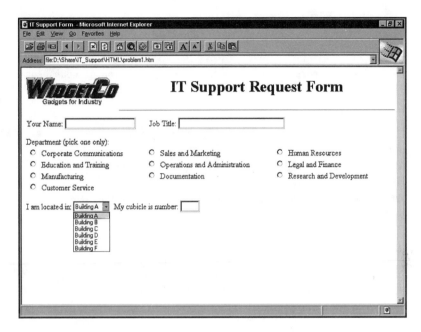

 Finally, we can find out what the problem is (see fig. 8.13).

```
<P>
The problem happens:
     When booting computer:<INPUT TYPE="checkbox" NAME="when1"
VALUE="on_boot">
     When saving a file:<INPUT TYPE="checkbox" NAME="when2"
VALUE="when_saving">
     When opening a file:<INPUT TYPE="checkbox" NAME="when3"
VALUE="when_opening">
     Randomly:<INPUT TYPE="checkbox" NAME="when4" VALUE="random">

<P>
How much memory does your computer have:
     <SELECT NAME="memory">
     <OPTION VALUE="4mb">4 meg.
     <OPTION VALUE="8mb">8 meg.
     <OPTION VALUE="16mb">16 meg.
     <OPTION VALUE="24mb">24 meg.
     <OPTION VALUE="32mb">32 meg.
     <OPTION VALUE="unknown">don't know
</SELECT>

Hard drive size:
<SELECT NAME="drive">
     <OPTION VALUE="520mb">520 meg.
     <OPTION VALUE="800mb">800 meg.
     <OPTION VALUE="1gb">1000 meg.
```

```
      <OPTION VALUE="1.6gb">1600 meg.
      <OPTION VALUE="unknown">don't know
</SELECT>
<P>
Please enter a <I>brief</I> description of your problem:
      <TEXTAREA NAME="description" ROWS="3" COLS="75">My problem is...</
TEXTAREA>
```

Fig. 8.13
Unfortunately,
with a textarea
box, you can only
suggest that users
keep their
comments brief.

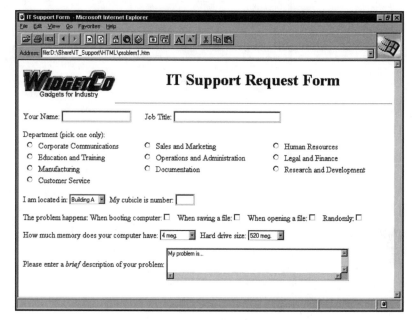

 A submit button is needed to send the form to the server. A reset button is not needed, but can make the form easier to use. The following code adds the reset and submit buttons (see fig. 8.14):

```
<INPUT TYPE="submit" VALUE="  Request Service Technician  ">
<INPUT TYPE="reset" VALUE="  Reset Form Values  ">
```

Fig. 8.14
The form is now complete and almost ready to be filled out by your readers.

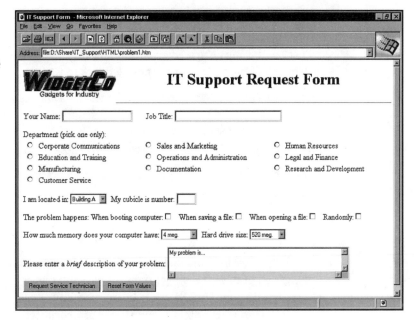

Dealing with Form Input

The form created in the previous section is complete except for one minor problem. There is nothing indicating what should be done with any of the information input by the user.

The job of routing and working with information from a form is handled by a Common Gateway Interface (CGI) script. CGI scripts are adept at handling other functions as well, but that is beyond the scope of this book.

Though a CGI script isn't technically a program, it's helpful to think of it that way. You write commands in the script, and software on the server carries them out.

Using the form we just wrote, let's create a CGI script to take the information and write an e-mail message to the IT department manager requesting action. (The following script is written assuming that your server incorporates PERL and the NCSA PERL library.) The form loads the library functions, sends a reply to the user, writes a temporary file containing the mail message, and finally sends the message to the IT manager.

NOTE

Check with your system administrator and/or corporate webmaster to determine whether you have network rights to write scripts.

If you do, find out what scripting utilities are available to users. A good set of utilities can save hours in writing scripts. If your system uses PERL and is UNIX-based, suggest that they get the CGI-LIB.PL library from **ftp://ftp.ncsa.uiuc.edu/Web/httpd/UNIX/ncsa_httpd/cgi/cgi-lib.pl.Z.**

Other scripting libraries are available for other systems.

CAUTION

The sample script contained on the CD-ROM may not work on your system if you do not have the proper rights or your intranet is not set up to deal directly with your CD-ROM drive. If you run into trouble running this script, talk to your system administrator or webmaster.

NOTE

If you want to learn about in-depth CGI scripting, there are a number of excellent sources listed in Appendix C, "For Further Reading."

Writing a simple CGI script is fairly straightforward and can be accomplished in a few short steps. First you have to tell the system to load the CGI library. This library takes care of a lot of drudgery, such as separating data from its name

```
#!/usr/local/bin/perl
#the following line load the CGI library file and returns an
#error if it can't be found
do "cgi-lib.pl" || die "Fatal Error: library can't be found";
#the following line calls a subroutine in the library
#that does the decoding of the form for you
&ReadParse;
```

TIP

Pound signs (#) at the beginning of a line indicate remarks in a CGI script. They are ignored by the server, but can help you revise code later. Always document your code. Also, note the semicolons (;) at the end of each non-remarked line.

Now we want to quickly write back to the user and let him or her know that the script has received the form data and is dealing with it

```
#alert server that what follows is HTML
print "Content-type: text/html\n\n;
#the next lines send the HTML message back to the user
print "<B>Your service request has been received.</B>\n";
print "A technician will be dispatched to correct your problem as soon
as
     possible.\n";
#the following line provides a link back to the form
print "<A HREF=/share/file/IT_Support/HTML/problem1.htm>";
print "Return to Support Request Form </A>";
```

To make sure two scripts don't try to create the same file, request a process id number (pid) to save the temporary file to (this number is automatically generated)

```
#request process id number, $pid
$pid=$$;
```

The script creates a temporary file using the pid number to make it unique

```
#create and open the mail message file
open (ITREQUEST,">/tmp/it_request.$pid";
#enter the contents of the form into the request file
print ITREQUEST @in;
#close and save the request file
close ITREQUEST;
```

Finally, the script mails the IT Support Request to the IT manager at his or her mail address (itmgr@server)

```
#sends request to IT manager
$command="mail itmgr@server ,/tmp/it_request.$pid";
```

To make sure the server does not fill up with old temporary files, the script erases the ITREQUEST

```
system($command);
#erase ITREQUEST file
unlink("/tmp/it_request.$pid");
```

> **C A U T I O N**
>
> The last section of the script invokes UNIX system commands. This can be very dangerous if you include user input in your file names and other portions of your code. A little malicious data entry by a user (or even carelessness) can result in system security problems. Always have your web master or system administrator review your scripts before he or she posts them on the server. See Chapter 12, "Security Issues," for more information on system security.

The final step involves updating your form so that it calls the CGI script to handle its output. The <FORM> tag needs to be updated to include two new modifiers that tell the server how to transmit your form data and where to send it. These operations are handled by the METHOD= and ACTION= modifiers.

There are two ways for the METHOD= modifier to send information to your script: POST and GET. POST is more commonly used. It sends all the information from the form separately from the form's URL, while GET creates a long text string that starts with the form's URL and adds the form data on the end of it. GET's length can get very long and potentially exceed the maximum URL length, resulting in lost form data. It's a good idea to stick with POST as your form submission method.

The ACTION= modifier provides the server with the name and path of your script file.

Assuming you've saved the script file as ITREQUEST.PL in the folder noted at the beginning of the file, (/Usr/Local/Bin/Perl) the <FORM> tag should be updated to read

```
<FORM METHOD="post" ACTION="/usr/local/bin/perl/itrequest.pl">
```

From Here...

You can now write forms to allow interaction between your users and your intranet pages; however, your knowledge of scripting is just beginning. For more information on scripting and scripting utilities, see the following chapters:

- Chapter 9, "Creating Interactive Databases," builds on your knowledge of forms and scripts to teach you to create intranet pages that interact with existing corporate databases.
- Chapter 11, "Making Content Available on the Server," provides techniques to help you make your pages available for use by other members of your intranet.

9

Creating Interactive Databases

By Michael Marchuk

The Internet has become one of the fastest-growing areas of technology since the introduction of the PC. The growth of the Internet has changed basic concepts of how people can share information. The ability to easily publish a database on the Internet is an offshoot of that growth. Without a significant amount of effort, you can allow people to view the database created as a result of a desktop application. Today, you can publish data using the Microsoft Internet Information Server on Windows NT.

Information such as internal policy documents, telephone extension databases, and customer service logs can all be created on an intranet server. Even more focused departmental databases are good candidates for an intranet server, since it's possible to allow others to see data that may be helpful in making decisions you did not know about. Databases such as internal product numbers, departmental policy documents, product pricing guides, and others may be useful to other departments which may not have known that the information was at hand.

In this chapter, you learn to

- Use intranet-enabled applications, client/server technology, and Visual Basic 4.0 to access data
- Understand why World Wide Web servers are the method of choice for accessing intranet and Internet data
- Use the Microsoft Internet Information Server to publish a database on your intranet

Interactivity with Intranet Databases

When discussing an interactive intranet database, remember that the same philosophy applies to both Internet and intranet publishing. Because many companies are spread out across the globe, an intranet database application may actually be used by people who are on the other side of a slow wide area network connection. With this in mind, the interactivity will be very similar to that of the Internet, which has speed and reliability issues. So when this chapter discusses database access on an intranet, it is in the context of a national or international enterprise.

T I P

Any design issues that will improve the performance on a relatively slow wide area network connection will also improve the access via a fast local area network connection.

The Internet has caused a shift in how people perceive the value of sharing information. Because the Internet is a worldwide network connecting any two points with a reliable connection, the boundaries of the office and city have been broken wide open. The change has come upon us so quickly that application vendors are scrambling to upgrade their software packages to take advantage of this tremendous opportunity for sharing information.

The intranet applications you see today are the browsers like Microsoft Internet Explorer and Netscape Navigator. But the connectivity offered by the intranet will extend to the everyday applications you use.

One technology enabling this interactivity is Visual Basic for Applications (VBA). With VBA, your Word documents, Excel spreadsheets, and other Office documents can perform tasks interactively with the user. For instance, you can use a VBA application within a Word document to enter information into a form used to create a new document. Legal forms can be filled out and printed by entering a few pieces of information.

This VBA application technology can also be applied to the databases created within Microsoft Access. With a VBA-enabled database application, you can extend the functionality of the database by using tools such as Microsoft's Internet Information Server to publish the data on the intranet. In addition, Microsoft's new Access Internet Assistant allows you to publish specific information on your intranet, or even a complete, interactive database.

Applications Become Intranet-Enabled

Many of the applications you use today may take advantage of the intranet in the near future. Which applications will do so isn't clear at this point in time, but Microsoft announced that the applications in Office 97 will become intranet-enabled. WordPerfect also provides an intranet-ready publishing environment which makes document creation for the intranet a much easier task.

One change in today's applications to become intranet savvy is the capability to read and write information in HTML format, which is used on the World Wide Web. As a result, you are able to create and edit content to be published on HTML pages. In the case of Microsoft, Internet Assistant for Word, Internet Assistant for Excel, Internet Assistant for PowerPoint, and Internet Assistant for Access can already be downloaded from their Web sites free of charge. Que has made accessing these assistants even easier by including them on the CD-ROM which accompanies this book. Microsoft has also committed to adding this capability to the rest of the Office applications. Unfortunately, these Assistants currently don't retain any VBA code that may have been included as part of the document. It is unclear whether or not this will be an option in the future.

> You can obtain the latest versions of the Internet Assistants from Microsoft at the following WWW page:
>
> **http://www.microsoft.com/IntDev/AUTOOLS.HTM**

A second change is for application vendors to produce viewers for the documents created by their software. In this way, you can publish your documents and display the data in its native format. By doing this, you let users take advantage of the special display capabilities of the application which extend beyond the basic HTML formatted text. For example, Microsoft has already created viewers for Microsoft Word, Excel, and PowerPoint. They are available free on its Web site and on the CD-ROM which accompanies this book. Unfortunately, the viewers available today don't interact with the VBA code associated with the documents. It is unclear whether or not this will be an option in the future.

> You can obtain the latest versions of the Office viewers from Microsoft at the following WWW page:
>
> **http://www.microsoft.com/Internet/PRODUCTS.HTM**

Third, today's applications could be enhanced by giving them the capability to include references to, or the actual content of, an intranet site. For example, when you read a word processor document, you'll be able to click a hot link to access information. This will start your Internet browser and point you at the new location. Or, you can import a page of an Internet or intranet site to be embedded in the report or presentation you created.

Last, the search functions in applications could be enhanced to encompass the content of the Internet. Just as search engines like Lycos, Excite, and Alta Vista index the content of the Internet, the applications' search engines could send a request off to one of the Internet indexes and return the results. You will then be able to include a reference to, or the contents of, the search results right in your documents. Again, Microsoft states that the Find Fast search engine, which currently ships with Office 95, will enable you to search HTML files locally or out on the World Wide Web. Microsoft hasn't stated whether VBA will be able to control these searches. But the likelihood is much greater than any of the other Internet-enabling features being added to software.

Client/Server Architecture Is the Rule

The very nature of the Internet implies client/server technology. Every implementation of client/server can be summarized in the following description. The client sends a specific request to a server. The server puts forth the effort to find, process, and format the data being requested. The server then sends that data back to the client. As client/server relates to the intranet, every Internet browser is a client.

Each WWW, ftp, or gopher site you visit is a server. For example, to view the Microsoft home page, you enter **http://www.microsoft.com** in the browser. As seen in figure 9.1, the Web browser sends a request out over the Internet. The request is sent over the Internet to Microsoft's WWW server. After the server sees the request, it knows it should get the home page from its files and send the HTML text and graphics back to you. Your browser then receives the data, interprets the HTML format, and displays the home page for you.

Fig. 9.1
Web browsers and World Wide Web servers communicate using a client/server methodology.

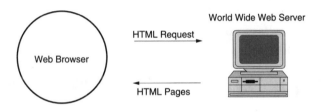

In contrast, the manner in which VBA data access is implemented in today's applications won't work over the Internet. As discussed earlier, VBA can control the current application, access the special functions offered by a program, or access other OLE objects on a network. Because of the methods used by the applications to transfer data over networks, VBA needs to rely on a high-speed connection to the data being accessed.

A typical LAN connection is an EtherNet capable of carrying 10 megabits per second. Connection speeds across the Internet can vary from 9,600 bits per second to 1.5 megabits per second. According to a recent survey, most companies have a connection to the Internet that can handle 56 kilobits per second, but some are upgrading to 1.5 megabit-per-second connections to handle the increased traffic.

By its very nature, accessing databases is communications-intensive. If you have a slow link to the database, your performance will suffer greatly. The users of your database will quickly find other ways to store the information that are much faster. Therefore, if you want to provide data access over the Internet, you have to go with a client/server solution.

Network OLE

On the horizon is a new technology called Network OLE. Network OLE will give VBA programmers the ability to have two OLE objects communicate with each other over a low-speed network connection. In fact, the very existence of the Internet implies Network OLE.

Although pure Network OLE isn't quite here, Distributed OLE is offered in Microsoft's Visual Basic 4.0. Distributed OLE has a Communication Manager to assist the connection between the client and the OLE object over a WAN or the Internet. Distributed OLE is programmatically complicated, however, and doesn't give you the true connectivity that Network OLE will provide. It would be better to wait for Network OLE. Or, you could publish your database today using Microsoft's Internet Information Server without any more VBA or Visual Basic code.

Choosing a Data Access Method for the Intranet

Selecting a method to access your database created with VBA is complicated by the rapid pace of change in the intranet. The rise of Netscape Corporation from a research project to a $250 million publicly traded company is a prime example of this skyrocketing market. Therefore, it isn't surprising to discover that the options available today to publish a database on the intranet are few and far between. Companies are beginning to develop add-ons, but they are for large-scale products like Oracle and Sybase. For a simple VBA implementation, the cost and hardware required for these choices doesn't make good business sense. Microsoft has met the need with a scalable (and free) database access option in the Microsoft Internet Information Server.

It is important to pause and take a look at what the future holds for data access using Office applications and VBA.

Future Intranet Data Access Choices

As this book was being published, Microsoft announced several new exciting technologies that will enable Office VBA programmers to continue using their skills in the intranet realm. These technologies include Visual Basic Script for Internet browsers, a Win32 Internet API for programmatic Internet services, and JDBC (ODBC for the Java language). Although some Office users will not want to extend themselves this far into programming, others may find that these new technologies will provide additional opportunities to publish their data interactively over the intranet.

Visual Basic Script

Visual Basic Script is being developed by Microsoft as a stripped-down version of VBA. Visual Basic Script will allow you to insert VBA-like code into an intranet page and script actions that occur when the user first views your page, presses a button, leaves your page, and so on. Everything you've learned under VBA will transfer directly over to Visual Basic Script.

Due to security issues and potential misuse, Visual Basic Script has left out some VBA commands which could have been potentially dangerous when used maliciously. If you would like to see the current command set being proposed for Visual Basic Script, check out Microsoft's World Wide Web page.

> Check out the Microsoft Visual Basic Script home page at:
> **http://www.microsoft.com/VBASIC/vbscript/vbscript.htm**

Win32 Internet API

The Microsoft Win32 Internet API (sometimes known as the Sweeper SDK) will provide an easy way to access typical Internet functions and features without having to learn or understand the complicated protocols or standards of the Internet. The Win32 API will provide all programming languages with the capability to access HTTP, ftp, and Gopher services from a task point of view.

By providing these services on a task level, Microsoft eliminates the need for a programmer (even VBA programming) to understand TCP/IP, Windows Sockets, HTTP protocols, ftp protocols, and gopher protocols. This will give the VBA programmer the ability to focus on the features required instead of learning and debugging problems associated with Internet protocols. Additionally, the end users will benefit by seeing a consistent user interface. For example, when all the different ftp applications use these standard functions, they will be differentiated by features instead of how the directory listings look.

> To see the latest progress and information on Microsoft's Sweeper SDK, point your Internet browser at:
>
> **http://www.microsoft.com/intdev/sweeper/sweeper.htm**

When this technology is available, you'll be able to programmatically update data on remote ftp servers. You'll also be able to retrieve HTML content and place it into your documents. Until the technology development is complete and released to the public, the actual possibilities won't be known.

JDBC

JDBC stands for Java Database Connectivity. Sun Microsystems, Inc. recently announced a new API for Java developers who want to access data from within their Java applets. Java applets are similar to Visual Basic Script in that they are self-contained applications. Java applets are cross-platform and stored on a server until a Web page requests the functionality provided by them. By including the ability to access data from within the applet, the possibilities for interactive content increase dramatically.

Unless you know the Java language (similar to C++), you won't be able to use JDBC as part of your VBA programming.

At the time of publication, the JDBC was under public review to become a standard. The current JDBC specification is available on Sun's World Wide Web site.

> More information on JDBC is available at
>
> **http://java.sun.com/JDBC/**

Today's Intranet Data Access Choices

The future looks bright for intranet services from within VBA. If you want to publish your database today, the choices are limited. You can use Visual Basic 4.0 and distributed OLE components, but the cost and configuration management of the choice is not advantageous.

You can set up NetBIOS computer names in your HOSTS file for TCP/IP. Then, by using the NetBIOS computer name when opening database files using the Jet database engine, you can remotely access the database over the Internet. Unfortunately, the performance of this implementation is woefully slow.

Fortunately, an ingenious solution to the problem exists to combine a standard World Wide Web server with a database source. This way, a user makes a request to the Web server using a standard data entry HTML page—the kind used when you fill out a survey at a site. The Web server performs the intensive communication with a local database. Then, by placing the results in a template Web page, only the results are sent back to you.

The benefits of a Web server database are tremendous. In regard to security, the intranet users have access to only the Web server, never direct access to the data. The Web server acts as a firewall to your data.

Second, the performance of accessing the database is greatly increased. Instead of the remote client trying to send all the data back and forth over a slow Internet link (averaging 56 kilobits per second), the Web server accesses the database for the user over a fast network (typically, 10 megabits per second).

To maintain the user interface to the database, the person responsible for the intranet access has to change only the template file stored on the Web server. In contrast, if VBA is used, each user has to install a new version of the code on his or her installation of the Office applications. Because each user's computer is different, you would probably end up with special configuration problems that would be better solved if someone was doing it for them. But because it's the Internet, the users of the database can be anywhere in the world.

By providing your database access through a Web server, you immediately gain the ability to publish your data cross-platform. You can publish your data to anyone who has a Web browser. Today, Web browsers are supported on UNIX, Windows, and Macintosh.

Several products are available to publish your data on a Web server. Some companies included are Allaire, Apple, DataRamp, dbWeb, WebBase, Microrim, Microsoft, Oracle, and Sybase. Trial versions of Allaire's Cold Fusion and Microrim's R:Web are available on the CD-ROM which accompanies this book.

> For a complete interactive list of companies providing Web access to databases, check out Yahoo's list at:
>
> **http://www.yahoo.com/Business_and_Economy/Companies/Computers/Internet/ Databases_and_Searching/**

Publishing Your Data with the Microsoft Internet Information Server

Publishing your data using a Web server is one of the best methods available for intranet distribution. Although several companies offer Web access to databases, Microsoft offers a low-cost alternative to those who already have a Windows NT Server and want to focus on the user interface to the database rather than managing database connections. You can obtain a completely free copy of Microsoft's Internet Information Server over the Internet at Microsoft's home page or on the CD-ROM which accompanies this book.

> To get the latest version of the Internet Information Server, point your browser at:
>
> **http://www.microsoft.com/infoserv/iisinfo.htm**

After installing the Internet Information Server under Windows NT, the process of publishing your database using the Internet Information Server includes configuring ODBC for your database, creating a query into your database, and then creating an HTML template to display the results of the query. In this section, the database, queries, and HTML templates could be used to publicize houses for sale from a real estate office. With some minor changes to the query structures and the HTML graphics, these could be used with any database.

TIP

The Internet Information Server requires Windows NT Server 3.51 with Service Pack 3 installed and ODBC v2.5 drivers.

Configuring ODBC

After you install the Microsoft Internet Information Server (IIS), your task is to make the Windows NT Server aware of your database via ODBC. You can do this via the ODBC Control Panel on the Windows NT Server. The database can be located on any computer (not necessarily a Windows NT Server), as long as it is accessible via the standard Universal Naming Convention (UNC). For example, if the database called RC.MDB is stored on a computer named JACKDATA in the PRIMARY folder, it could be accessed by the Internet Information Server via the UNC location \\JACKDATA\PRIMARY\RC.MDB.

TIP

The Internet Information Server only comes with the Microsoft SQL Server ODBC driver. You can obtain the ODBC drivers for the other major database formats from Microsoft. The Desktop Driver Pack v3.0 is available on Microsoft's home page.

To configure ODBC to point at your database, use the following steps:

1. Open the Control Panels. Double-click the ODBC Control Panel to access the ODBC configuration of the Windows NT Server, as shown in figure 9.2.

2. Choose System DSN to set up the database as a System Data Source.

Fig. 9.2
Configure your
ODBC data source
using the ODBC
Control Panel.

CAUTION

Because the Internet Information Server runs as a Windows NT service,
you must set up ODBC access to the database via a System Data Source.
Windows NT services cannot access regular ODBC database sources as they
would be listed in figure 9.2.

3. Select to Add a new ODBC System Data Source (see fig. 9.3).

Fig. 9.3
A new System
Data Source is
attached by
selecting Add.

4. From the Installed ODBC Drivers list in the Add Data Source dialog box
(see fig. 9.4), select the database type matching your database and
choose OK.

TIP

If you don't see your database type in the list, contact the database
vendor for the latest ODBC driver.

5. An ODBC Setup dialog box appears that is specific to the database type
selected from figure 9.4. Because you're using VBA, the Microsoft Jet
database engine is a good choice. To use the Jet engine, choose the
Microsoft Access option. Figure 9.5 shows the Microsoft Access ODBC
Setup. Enter a Data Source Name and a short Description.

Fig. 9.4
Select the correct
database type
from the Installed
ODBC Drivers list.

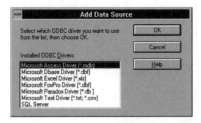

Fig. 9.5
The ODBC Setup
dialog box
specific to your
database type
must be filled out.

6. If your database type is Microsoft Access, the database is identified
using a standard File Open dialog box when you choose Select in the
Database group box (see fig. 9.5). Choose OK when complete.

7. To complete the configuration, close the ODBC Control Panel by selecting Close on both the System Data Sources dialog box and the Data
Sources dialog box.

You're now ready to create the query to specify the records and fields to
be displayed on the HTML page. The next section takes you through the
process.

Creating a Query

The Internet Information Server uses a small Internet Database Connector
configuration file (IDC) to define how the data should be retrieved and re-
ported back to the user. Using HTML form tags, the Web browser can define
values to be used as part of the query.

The input field names defined in the HTML document become the names of
the variables used in the Internet Database Connector file. For example, if
the user wants to limit a search to the price of a house and other house quali-
ties, the search form HTML source looks like this:

```
<FORM method="POST" action="rclist.idc">
<input type="hidden" name="State" value="IL">
<TABLE WIDTH=75% ALIGN=CENTER><TR><TD WIDTH="25"></TD><TD  VALIGN=TOP>
County<br><SELECT NAME="County" SIZE=8>
        <OPTION VALUE="" SELECTED>-None-
        <OPTION VALUE="Boon">Boon
        <OPTION VALUE="Cook">Cook
        <OPTION VALUE="DeKalb">DeKalb
        <OPTION VALUE="Kane">Kane
        <OPTION VALUE="Lake">Lake
        <OPTION VALUE="McHenry">McHenry
    </SELECT>
<TD  VALIGN=TOP><br>
<TD>Maximum Price<br><Input NAME="MaxPrice" SIZE=8 Value="200000"><br>
Minimum Price<br><INPUT NAME="MinPrice" size=8 Value="0">
<TD>At least<BR><INPUT TYPE="text" NAME="Beds" VALUE="0" size=3
MAXLENGTH=2  _
_MIN=0 MAX=99>Bedrooms<br>
<INPUT TYPE="text" NAME="Baths" VALUE="0" size=3 MAXLENGTH=3  _
_MIN=0 MAX=99>Bathrooms<br>
<INPUT TYPE="text" NAME="Garage" VALUE="0" size=3 MAXLENGTH=3 _
_ MIN=0 MAX=99>Car Garage<br></TR>
</TABLE>
<TABLE WIDTH=75% ALIGN=CENTER>
<TR ALIGN=CENTER><TD ALIGN=CENTER><INPUT TYPE="submit" size=10  _
_VALUE="  Search     "> <INPUT TYPE="reset"  _
_size=10 VALUE = "Clear form"></TD></TR>
</TABLE>
</FORM>
```

Presented to the user, this HTML language looks much nicer in figure 9.6.

Fig. 9.6
The user is presented with form fields to narrow the SQL query to be used in the IDC file.

The input fields from the preceding code example would be State (as a hidden field), County, MinPrice, MaxPrice, Beds, Baths, and Garage. The IDC file uses these values to define the SQL formatted ODBC query. The IDC file must contain the ODBC Datasource name, the name of the HTML template to format the returned data, and the SQL statement to select the data to be returned. The SQL statement can be any standard SQL string, as long as each new line of the query begins with a plus (+) sign. In the real estate example, the IDC file might look like this:

```
Datasource: Estate
Username: Admin
Password:
Template: RCList.htx
SQLStatement:
+SELECT Listings.* FROM Listings
+ WHERE Price BETWEEN %MinPrice% AND %MaxPrice%
+ AND Bedrooms >= %Beds%
+ AND Bathrooms >= %Baths%
+ AND Garage >= %Garage% AND State = '%State%'
+ AND County IN ('%County%')
ODBCOptions: SQL_LOGIN_TIMEOUT=10, SQL_ACCESS_MODE=1,
SQL_QUERY_TIMEOUT=10
```

The Datasource is Estate, which matches the ODBC System Data Source created in the ODBC Control Panel. The Username is the default name used to read Microsoft Access databases. The Template is the HTML template (described in the next section). Some additional standard ODBC options are specified to increase the performance of the search. These options aren't required, but should work for most instances.

 The source database and template files are included on the CD-ROM which accompanies this book.

After the user submits his or her choices to the Internet Information Server (by clicking the Search button), the IDC file is passed to the Internet Database Connector DLL for processing. This DLL (HTTPODBC.DLL) combines the results of the database query into the HTML template specified.

In a database that queries employee information or a departmental database, the same type of query could be applied using variables that identify last name, first name, document ID's, or the like. Any field within the database can be used within a query statement for intranet access.

Creating HTML Templates

The most difficult part about creating an HTML template is authoring the HTML page to display the results of the SQL-formatted ODBC query. The new HTML tags associated with presenting your data are a few simple commands. You can intermix these commands throughout the HTML template with other standard HTML tags.

<%FIELDNAME%>

The <%FIELDNAME%> tag is the generic form for any column name returned by the SQL formatted ODBC query. For example, if the query returned columns for Address, City, and State, then the data for each record for each field could be referenced in any part of the HTX document as <%ADDRESS%>, <%CITY%>, or <%STATE%>.

<%BEGINDETAIL%>, <%ENDDETAIL%>

The <%BEGINDETAIL%> and <%ENDDETAIL%> tags surround HTML tags in your template file that will repeat for each record returned as part of the ODBC query. As shown in the following code, in its simplest form you can display a line of data for each record returned:

```
<%begindetail%>
<%AddressLine1%><BR>
<%AddressLine2%><BR>
<%city%>, <%state%><BR>
<BR>
<%enddetail%>
```

If no records are returned by the ODBC query, then everything between these two tags is skipped.

Your detail section can be as complicated or as simple as you'd like to make it. The more data fields you have to show, the more coding you will have to do.

NOTE

You may want to use complex HTML codes such as tables, or frames to return your data. Keep in mind that while this may make the data more easily accessible, it may also complicate any changes you need to make to the display templates.

<%IF%>, <%ELSE%>, <%ENDIF%>

The <%IF CONDITION%>, <%ELSE%>, and <%ENDIF%> tags enable you to conditionally include different HTML sources. The condition portion of the <%IF CONDITION%> tag is a regular comparison expression. Its format is

```
value1 operator value2
```

The operator can be one of four values:

EQ	Value1 equals value2
LT	Value1 is less than value2
GT	Value1 is greater than value2
CONTAINS	Any part of value1 contains the string value2

Value1 and value2 can be column names (for example, Address), built-in variables, HTTP variable names, or constants.

For example, if you want to skip the second address line when it doesn't contain any data, insert the <%IF%>, <%ELSE%>, and <%ENDIF%> tags as such:

```
<%begindetail%>
<%AddressLine1%><BR>
<%if AddressLine2 EQ ""%>
<%else%>
<%AddressLine2%><BR>
<%endif%>
<%city%>, <%state%><BR>
<BR>
<%enddetail%>
```

NOTE

Notice that when a column name is used as one of the variables, it isn't surrounded by <% %>.

The <%IF CONDITION%>, <%ELSE%>, and <%ENDIF%> tags can be used to evaluate mathematical expressions as well as other query responses to provide you with a dynamic display capability. This feature is an important one for you to understand, so try using <%IF CONDITION%>, <%ELSE%>, and <%ENDIF%> tags in some sample queries on your database to see how they work.

Built-in Variables

The HTML template file supports two built-in variables: CurrentRecord and MaxRecords. These two variables can be used only in the condition portion of an <%IF%> tag.

The CurrentRecord variable contains the count of how many times the <%BEGINDETAIL%> <%ENDDETAIL%> section has been fully processed. The MaxRecords variable contains the number of records returned by the ODBC query defined in the IDC file.

In the real estate example, if no records were found as a result of the user's choices for a house the following code would be executed:

```
<%begindetail%>
<%AddressLine1%><BR>
<%if AddressLine2 EQ ""%>
<%else%>
<%AddressLine2%><BR>
<%endif%>
<%city%>, <%state%><BR>
<BR>
<%enddetail%>
<%if CurrentRecord EQ 0%>
<TABLE CELLPADDING=30 ALIGN=RIGHT><TR><TD ALIGN=RIGHT><FONT=6> _
 _There are no properties matching your request. _
 _Try broadening your search or searching by county instead.</FONT> _
 _</TR></TABLE><BR CLEAR=RIGHT>
<%endif%>
```

Advanced Techniques

You can take the display of your data one step further. By placing in each record a hot link in the result of the first query, you can provide a detailed display of the record. This detail can show more information than room allowed on the initial list of records from the first search.

In the HTML template file, create a hot link by using the standard <A HREF="link_location">TEXT</A> notation. But instead of pointing to a fixed HTML file in the link location, insert another IDC file.

For the real estate example, the picture of the house can be the link to query the database for a detailed record display of the house:

```
<%begindetail%>
<A HREF="RCHit.idc?ListingCode=<%ListingCode%>">
<%if PictureCode EQ ""%>
<IMG ALIGN=left WIDTH=120 HEIGHT=90 BORDER=1 SRC="/rc/graphics/
```

```
notavail.jpg">
<%else%>
<IMG ALIGN=left WIDTH=120 HEIGHT=90 BORDER=1 _
 _SRC="/rc/images/listings/thumb/<%PictureCode%>.jpg">
<%endif%></A>
<%AddressLine1%><BR>
<%if AddressLine2 EQ ""%>
<%else%>
<%AddressLine2%><BR>
<%endif%>
<%city%>, <%state%><BR>
<BR>
<%enddetail%>
<%if CurrentRecord EQ 0%>
<TABLE CELLPADDING=30 ALIGN=RIGHT><TR><TD ALIGN=RIGHT><FONT=6> _
 _There are no properties matching your request. _
 _Try broadening your search or searching by county instead.</FONT> _
 _</TR></TABLE><BR CLEAR=RIGHT>
<%endif%>
```

This type of query would also be appropriate in an employee database that could pull up phone extension information, cubical location, home telephone, or other personal information.

From Here...

In this chapter, you've learned about what it takes for your Office VBA applications to cross into the intranet realm. You've also studied the options to publish the data on the rapidly expanding Internet. A few options exist today, with the promise of many more choices to come. Some of the promising technologies include Visual Basic Script, the Win32 Internet API, and JDBC. If you want to get your data on the Internet today, the best choice is via a Web server—specifically, Microsoft's Internet Database Connector—as part of the free Internet Information Server.

From here, you may want to explore this chapter:

- Chapter 11, "Making Content Available on the Server." With all of your HTML and scripting skills in place, it is now time to make your pages available for use by other members of your intranet. This chapter provides techniques to make this process run smoothly.

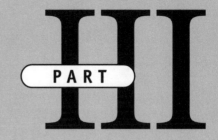

PART

III

Managing Content

10

Managing Pages

By Paul Bodensiek

With the knowledge you've gained from the preceding nine chapters, you can create intricate, interactive intranet sites. However, the more intricate your sites become, the more you need to plan ahead before the first line of HTML code is written.

In this chapter, you'll learn techniques to make your intranet sites easier to create and manage. By working logically, you can save yourself a lot of headaches both during the initial writing of your site and also when the inevitable changes and updates have to be made.

In this chapter, you learn to

- Flowchart your links
- Make use of existing content
- Develop your pages "offline"
- Use absolute and relative paths to your advantage
- Test your site before publishing it

Before You Start Writing

If you're an accountant, you'd never dream of writing a chart of accounts without planning it in advance. If you're an engineer, you only design a widget after you've thoroughly studied what you want it to do and where it is to be used. If you're in sales, you wouldn't contact a customer before you had anything to sell.

Creating an intranet site is no different from anything else you do in your job. Planning and forethought can make a vast difference in the amount of time and energy you have to expend on your site.

Find Out Where Your Site Will Be Published

Will your site be placed on the corporate server or on a departmental server? Do you have write access to the folder where your site will ultimately be located? What files and folders are located on the same server?

These may seem like obvious questions, but it can be invaluable knowledge when you're planning your site.

Will your site be placed on the corporate server or on a departmental server?

Say your site is being placed on the corporate server instead of your departmental server. This may be because your departmental server does not incorporate the intranet server software. (Remember that HTML code can only reference files that are located on a computer that is running the intranet server software.) In this case, you probably won't be able to access files on your departmental server via HTML and will have to have synchronized folders on the corporate server. Synchronized folders store the exact same information and each is automatically updated if there is a change in the other. The briefcase in Windows 95 is an example of a synchronized folder.

Do you have write access to the folder where your site will ultimately be located?

If you don't have direct access to your site's location, posting new pages and changes may be delayed because your system administrator (or one of his or her assistants) must manually copy your files. See Chapter 11, "Making Content Available on the Server," for more information.

What files and folders are located on the same server?

Knowing the structure of the server around your site can help you make quick links to other pages using relative paths and also allows you to reuse existing graphics and other resources. Using graphics located on other servers can slow down transmission of your pages.

Make sure you also know which of these resources are subject to periodic change. If you lay out a beautiful page based on the size of a particular photograph located in the Human Resources area of the server, be aware that HR may decide to move, delete, or change that photograph at any time. If in doubt about the permanence of any resource on your server, check with the author and/or copy it to your site. (You don't want to copy every resource to your site because they are generally updated for a good reason and your links would not be up-to-date. You also probably have limits on the amount of hard drive space you can take up on the server.)

▶ **See** "Updating Files Locally," **p. 256**

Plan Your Site

Most people hate to flowchart. Getting down to the nitpicky details of how your site will interact with other sites and pages may seem like a lot of wasted time, but it's invaluable when your site grows to more than one or two pages.

Flowcharting a site can get messy. When you think about it, every page can potentially link to every other page and you could have a total zoo of hypertext references (see fig. 10.1).

Fig. 10.1
An intranet site with no underlying structure can become a nightmare of hypertext links.

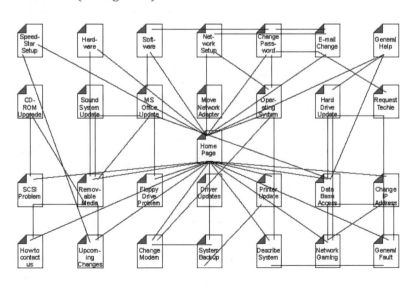

Use flowcharts to help you develop an underlying structure and provide a logical order for your readers (see fig. 10.2). You don't need to have a link from every page to every other page: make your site work like a tree, with your basic information at the top, working your way out to more and more in-depth data.

Fig. 10.2
With planning, your site is easier to create and maintain, and easier for your readers to navigate.

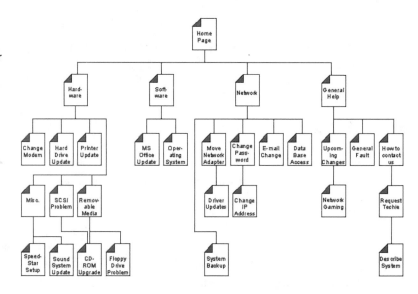

TIP

If you place a link to your home page on every page in your site, don't show them all on your flowchart. Just make a note to yourself that you will include this link in every page and your flowchart will be much more readable.

If you are creating a huge intranet site (say for your whole department), break your flowchart up into sections. For example, you are creating an intranet site for the Human Resources department. One flowchart might have the department home page and show links to the primary areas (see fig. 10.3). Other flowcharts would then be written for each of these areas (see fig. 10.4).

TIP

Place links to pages above and below the tree to help readers who reach the page directly.

Fig. 10.3
For large intranet sites, create a master flowchart that shows the overall structure of the site.

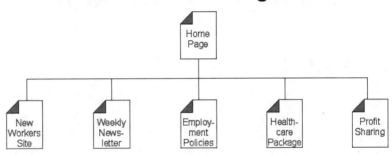

WidgetCo
Human Resources Department
Overall Intranet Site Organization

Fig. 10.4
Create detailed flowcharts that reference back to the master flowchart.

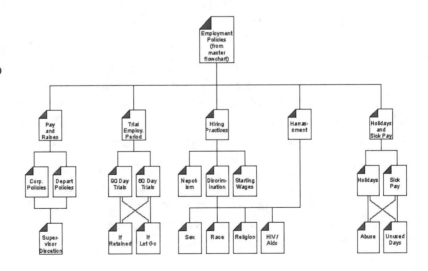

TIP

If, while you are writing your HTML code, you feel you must deviate from your flowchart, update the chart to show the deviations. An up-to-date flowchart is invaluable when updating your content.

Remember that an intranet site is multilayered. There can be links crossing various levels of your flowchart, so anything you do to make the flowchart more readable is an advantage.

Writing Your HTML Code

Once your site has been designed, it's time to get down to actually writing the code. This is where all of your planning shows its worth.

▶ **See** "HTML Editing Programs," **p. 101**

Use an HTML Editor

Even though you can write HTML by hand using a text editor like Notepad and entering all of the tags manually, you should use an HTML editor. These programs take care of dealing with your links, adding required tags, changing colors, and so on. You will find that the HTML-specific nature of these programs will make organizing and publishing your pages much simpler. Let the programs do the work, so you don't have to.

You may find that no single editor does everything you want. Some editors are excellent at dealing with tables and forms (HotDog, for example), while others may automatically take care of converting graphics to GIF or JPEG format (Microsoft Word Internet Assistant). Feel free to use more than one editor. You might set up your basic page using Word Internet Assistant or Netscape Navigator 2.0 Gold, then open the document in HoTMetaL to add tables, then use HotDog to create your forms.

If you are creating extremely large sites, consider investing in one of the publishing systems outlined in Part V, "Exploring Publishing Tools." Though some of them are expensive, the cost savings in time may more than make up for the initial monetary cost.

Use Folders and File Names to Your Advantage

There are no hard-and-fast rules about what HTML and graphics files must be named (except for their file name extensions). Use this to your advantage when writing your site.

One way to keep all your files organized is to make a logical folder structure for your site. Keep files of a certain type together and keep individual projects separate. If you mash everything together in one folder, keeping track of your files and updating them later can become a full time job in-and-of itself.

TIP

Name your site's home page DEFAULT.HTM or INDEX.HTM. To find your home page, all a reader has to do is point his or her browser at your folder, and either of these files will automatically be loaded. (If you have a file with one of these names, don't place another file with the other name in the same folder.)

One good way to organize the files for a site is to have a central folder containing your home page and additional folders containing individual projects and resources (see fig. 10.5). Keep HTML files in their own folders, graphic files in their own folders, spreadsheets in their own folders...you get the picture. By segregating files in this way, you can instantly get a picture of what files you have.

Fig. 10.5
Keep separate projects separate, and similar files together.

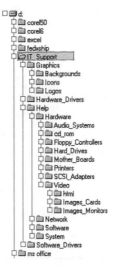

Write Your Site Locally

Earlier it was said that a browser can only view pages that are contained on a computer that runs server software. This is not entirely true.

Actually, the intranet server software is only required for transmitting pages over the network and running CGI scripts. You may view pages located on your *own* computer and even make links to files on any intranet server in your corporation (at which time the server software will take over).

By creating your content locally, on your own hard drive, you can write code, make changes, and perfect your site before it's ever available for anyone else to see. Here are some tips for creating your pages on your computer:

- *Use relative links between the pages in your site.* If you use absolute links, they won't work on the server if your site is placed several layers down in the folder structure.

- *Make sure you use the exact folder structure you want your site to have on the server.* Any relative links won't work if you change the folders around.

- *Use absolute links to other resources in the network.* This ensures that if you want the corporate logo on your page it will always be linked, no matter where your site is placed. (Note that you have to include the name of the server where the resources can be found in the beginning of all links.)

  ▶ **See** "Using Links," **p. 487**

- *Make the home page for your browser the home page file that you have on your own hard drive.* This saves you from manually having to open the file every time you want to work on your site.

- *Set up your HTML editor program so that it starts your browser when you click the preview button (if available).* Most editors give you this option and it makes checking your work much easier. See your editor's documentation or help file to find out how to do this.

Reuse, Reuse, Reuse

This can't be said often enough. Reuse any graphics, HTML, or other resource to save yourself from having to recreate it every time it's needed.

If your pages are all set up the same way, save a copy to use as a template
that includes the basic containers (<HTML>, <TITLE>, <BODY>) and any
common graphics and links. Note that you may have to update any relative
links in your page based on its final location in your folder structure.

To get around this problem of relative links, use the <BASE HREF="path">
tag. In place of "path," insert the drive and path of your home page and base
all of your relative paths on the location of your home page.

For example, using the folders shown in figure 10.5, assume your home page
is on your own hard drive in the folder d\IT_Support/Help, you have an
intranet page in the folder d\IT_Support/Help/Hardware/Video/HTML, and all
of your icons are in the folder d\IT_Support/Graphics/Icons. By having the
tag <BASE HREF="d\IT_Support/Help"> in all of your pages, your relative
path to the bullets for both of these pages would be "../Graphics/Icons."

This means that any time you wanted to use a bullet, you would use the tag
<IMG SRC="../Graphics/Icons/bulletname.gif"> instead of having to figure
out a new relative path for each page. Note, however, that when you publish
your content on the server you have to update the base href tag in all your
pages to the absolute path of your home page on the server. (Only update
the files on the server so that your copies on your hard drive still interact
with themselves.)

N O T E

If you are using the base href tag, make your local folder structure mimic
the structure on the server. For example, if your files on the server will
reside in the folder /IT_Support/Help/ (and some folders within Help)
then create the folders IT_Support and Help on your local hard drive even
though your local IT_Support folder may be empty. This will make it
easier to update the base href tag when you move your files to the server.

Test Every Page

This is another rule that bears repeating. Test every page.

No matter how much care you take in writing your HTML code, there will always be mistakes. When your pages are published on the server, it gets more difficult to make changes to your code, so the time to test is while they are still on your own hard drive.

After you have viewed every page and used every form, grab a coworker and have him or her sit at your computer and test your site again. Remember, you know how your site is laid out and what is supposed to happen when you select a particular link—other people don't and they are much more likely to find errors than you.

Don't get offended when they find something that doesn't work or that they don't like. If it's a problem, fix it. If there's a difference of opinion over how an option should work, debate it and either convince the other person that your page is right or take the opinion as constructive criticism and use it to make your site better.

There are problems that are going to make it through, no matter how much testing you do. Look at the major software companies. They spend millions in testing *after* they have finished a product, then they go back and fix problems, and the software that makes it to your desktop still has bugs. While you can't eliminate them all, it's your job to make your site as error-free as possible.

TIP

If your site is essentially error-free and presents the information you want it to, publish it. Don't keep trying to make it perfectly polished before placing it on the server—that's what updates are for. As the saying goes, "If Henry Ford had waited to sell a car until he could make the Lincoln Continental, he wouldn't have made the Model T *or* the Lincoln."

From Here...

You now know how to plan your intranet site, manage individual pages, combine them into a useful whole, and test your finished site. Now comes the moment of truth, placing your site on the intranet and letting it perform its function—communication. For more information, see the following chapters:

- Chapter 11, "Making Content Available on the Server," shows you how to compile your site for publication on the corporate web server.
- Chapter 12, "Security Issues," teaches techniques to keep your pages safe from tampering, both intended and accidental.
- Chapter 13, "Updating Intranet Content," shows you that no matter how perfect your site may seem, there will come a time when it has to be updated. Use the techniques in this chapter to make the process as painless as possible.

Making Content Available on the Server

By Paul Bodensiek

You've finished writing your copy, laying out your pages, and editing all your HTML code and graphics files. Now you want to make your work available to others in your company. To do this you must copy your files from your local hard drive to your corporate or departmental server.

How you copy your files depends on your network privileges. If you have been given write access (or rights) to your site's location, you can copy or ftp your files directly. If you don't have these rights, you have to go through the system administrator or webmaster. Either way, the process is not difficult, and both are detailed in the following pages.

Before you put your site on the intranet, make sure you read Chapter 10, "Managing Pages." It gives many tips and techniques to help make your transfer as painless as possible.

The instructions presented in this chapter assume you created your content on your local hard drive and need to transfer your files to the intranet server. As outlined in Chapter 10, this is definitely the preferred way to work on a site since it gives you complete control.

In this chapter you learn to

● Copy your pages directly to the server using Explorer

● Place your pages on the server using File Transfer Protocol (ftp)

● Work with the system administrator if you don't have write rights on the server

● Compress your files including their directories

Copying Your Files Directly to the Server

The easiest way to place your site on the server is to simply copy your files there. This assumes you have write rights to the corporate or departmental server.

▶ **See** "Reuse, Reuse, Reuse," **p. 219**

NOTE

If you use the <BASE HREF="..."> tag in your pages, it's extremely important to make sure the folder structure you included corresponds to the location of your site's home page.

For example, if you built your intranet site assuming your home page is in the folder /Intranet/ (using UNIX notation) while its location on the server is /your_department/your_group/your_name/, you will have to change all your BASE HREF statements. This can be time-consuming, depending on the number of pages in your site. As outlined in Chapter 10, it's easier to build your site locally if you have duplicated the folder structure on your own hard drive.

There are two ways to copy files to the server: using Explorer and via File Transfer Protocol (ftp). Both methods allow you to move your files and folder structure intact, thus eliminating a lot of manual work on the server.

Copy Files Directly

To copy files directly to the server using Explorer, use exactly the same procedure as if you were copying the files on your local hard drive.

Using Copy and Paste

To copy your entire intranet site from your local drive to the network server using copy and paste:

1. Open Explorer by double-clicking the My Computer icon on your desktop.

2. Navigate your local hard drive until you display your local copy of your intranet site.

3. Select all the folders and files included in your site (see fig. 11.1).

Fig. 11.1
Using Explorer, you can copy your entire intranet site, including its folder structure, to the server in one step.

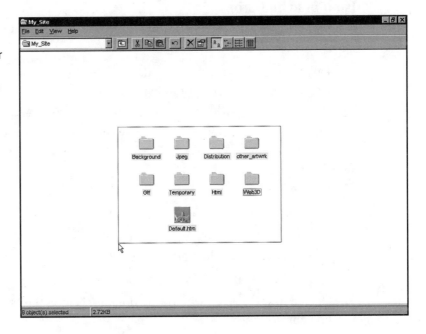

4. Choose Edit, Copy (or press Ctrl+C).

5. Change the Explorer view so it shows the folder in which you'll be placing your site. Note that you may have to create a new folder. If you do:

   Change the Explorer view so it shows the folder that will contain your folder.

   Choose File, New, Folder.

   Enter the name corresponding to your home page folder (see the note at the beginning of this section regarding the base href tag).

   Double-click your new folder to open it.

6. Choose Edit, Paste (or press Ctrl+V).

Your entire site is now located on the server, ready to be viewed by anyone in your company.

Using Drag and Drop

To copy your entire intranet site from your local drive to the network server using drag and drop:

1. Open the Explorer window by double-clicking the Network Neighborhood icon on your desktop.

2. Change the Explorer view so it shows the folder in which you will be placing your site. Note that you may have to create a new folder. If you do:

   Change the Explorer view so it shows the folder that will contain your folder.

   Choose File, New, Folder.

   Enter the name corresponding to your home page folder (see the note at the beginning of this section regarding the base href tag).

   Double-click your new folder to open it.

3. Open a new Explorer window by double-clicking the My Computer icon on your desktop.

4. Navigate your local hard drive until you display your local copy of your intranet site.

5. Select all the folders and files included in your site.

6. Drag the files from your local hard drive to your new folder on the server (see fig. 11.2).

Fig. 11.2
An easy way to copy your intranet files and folders directly to the server is to drag them from one Explorer window to another and drop them in place.

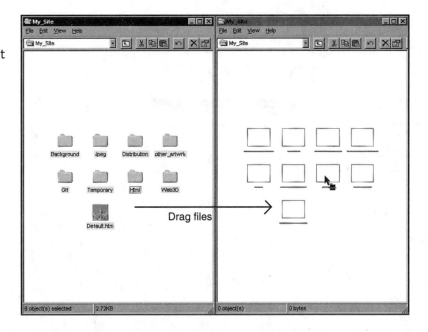

Drag files

Your entire site is now located on the server, ready to be viewed by anyone in your company.

Using File Transfer Protocol

You may need to use File Transfer Protocol (ftp) if your network is designed to be identical to the Internet. In this case, Explorer may not let you access folders not located on your local drive(s).

 Unless you have an ftp program, transferring files to the server can be a very arduous process because you must enter the commands to create each folder, and copy each file separately. The CD-ROM accompanying this book has a number of excellent programs that help automate the task of transmitting files via ftp. For this exercise we will be using CuteFTP, though the steps used for the other programs will be similar.

TIP

If you value your time and sanity, don't try to do ftp manually, at least not for a large number of files.

To copy your site to the server using CuteFTP:

1. Launch CuteFTP from the Start menu. The FTP Site Manager dialog box opens (see fig. 11.3).

Fig. 11.3
CuteFTP allows you to quickly connect to an ftp site by maintaining a group of frequently used locations.

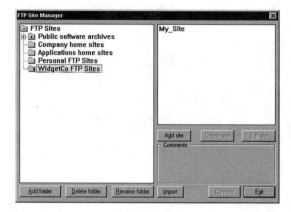

2. Select your home page location shown in the ftp Site Manager dialog box and click the Connect button.

   Note that you have to configure your ftp program so it can access your site's location. Your system administrator or webmaster can provide the necessary information (see fig. 11.4).

Fig. 11.4
The information contained in the ftp Site Edit dialog box must be provided by your system administrator or webmaster.

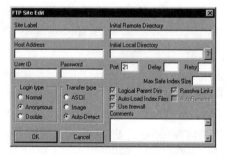

3. Create your site's folder structure by first clicking in the right-hand screen to highlight the right-hand folder path (see fig. 11.5).

Fig. 11.5
CuteFTP displays
your local drive
and the server
drive in the left-
and right-hand
windows.

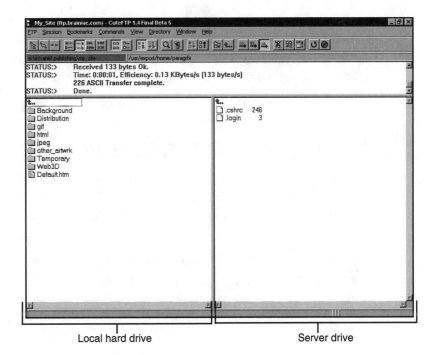

Local hard drive   Server drive

 4. Click the Make New Dir button on the button bar.

5. You are prompted to enter a folder (directory) name. Enter one of the names of the folders in your site structure and click OK.

6. Repeat steps 4 and 5 to create all the folders needed for your site. Note that you may have to navigate between folders if you are using nested folders.

 7. In the left-hand window, highlight all the files you wish to copy to the server, then click the Upload button.

8. Repeat step 7 for each folder in your site. Note that you must change folders in both the right- and left-hand windows to keep your file/folder structure intact.

9. Quit CuteFTP by choosing FTP, Exit (or by pressing Ctrl+Q).

Your entire site is now located on the server, ready to be viewed by anyone in your company.

TIP

When using ftp, ensure that your folder structure is correct by testing your entire site before telling anyone it's up and running.

Working Through the Webmaster

Even if you don't have write rights to the server, you can still get your intranet site up and running with a minimum of work. You just have to go through the system administrator or the webmaster (depending on your company).

There are two basic steps to this: transmitting your files to the webmaster, and having the webmaster put them in the correct location on the server. If you take some care before you transmit the files to the webmaster, you can greatly reduce the chance of error.

Compress Files and Folder Structure

While it isn't necessary to compress your files before sending them to the webmaster, this step reduces the chance of error. This is because most compression programs allow you to store all the files in your site and their relative path within the compressed file (also called *recursive directories*). When the files are expanded again by the webmaster, they are also in the proper relative positions (this is important whether you're using relative or absolute paths).

WinZip, a program included on the CD-ROM that accompanies this book, makes creating compression files with folder structure easy. If you are using one of the other programs on the CD (or from another source), see the Help file or documentation for that program to find out how to include folder structure.

To compress your intranet site using WinZip, follow these steps:

1. Start the WinZip program.
2. Choose File, New Archive (or press Ctrl+N). The New Archive dialog box opens (see fig. 11.6).

TIP

The most common compressed file format is ZIP. Unless your webmaster tells you otherwise, compress your files in ZIP format.

Fig. 11.6
The New Archive dialog box allows you to specify the name and location of your new ZIP file.

3. Enter a name and location for your compressed file and click OK. (You may want to navigate your hard drive to find a particular location to place the file before you click OK.)

4. Choose Action, Add (or press Ctrl+A). The Add dialog box opens (see fig. 11.7).

Fig. 11.7
Setting the File Name box to *.* automatically includes all files when you click the Add or Add With Wildcards button.

5. Navigate your hard drive until the home page folder of your intranet site is displayed (as shown previously in fig. 11.7).

6. Make sure the File Name text box reads *.*, the Recurse Subdirectories checkbox is filled, and the action box says "Add (and Replace) Files." Then click the Add With Wildcards button to add all displayed files and folders to the compressed file (see fig. 11.8).

Fig. 11.8
Here are the files contained in your ZIP file. Note that the DEFAULT.HTM file has no directory information, while all the other files do.

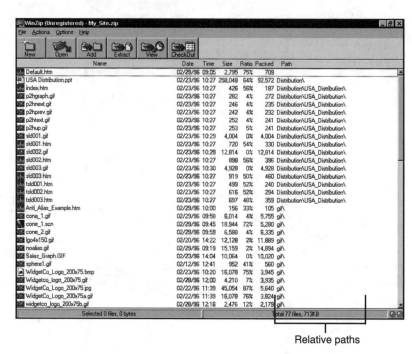

Relative paths

7. Exit WinZip by choosing File, Exit (or press Alt+F4).

Your files are now ready to transmit to your webmaster.

Transfer Files to Webmaster or System Administrator

One of the easiest ways to transmit your compressed intranet site to your webmaster or system administrator is to add it as an attachment to an e-mail message. The following instructions are based on Microsoft Exchange, which is included with Windows 95, but the procedure is similar no matter what e-mail program your company uses.

To send your site to the webmaster as an attachment:

1. Start Microsoft Exchange (if it isn't automatically started when you turn on your system) by double-clicking its icon on your desktop.

2. Choose Compose, New Message (or press Ctrl+N). The New Message window opens.

3. Enter the e-mail address of your webmaster or system administrator in the To text box (or click the To button and select from your address book, if applicable).

4. Enter a brief description such as **intranet site upload** in the Subject text box. You can press Alt+J to place the cursor in the Subject text box.

TIP

Make sure you tell your webmaster exactly where your intranet site should be located on the server. Don't rely on him or her to remember a conversation you had three weeks ago when your space was assigned.

---

5. Enter a description of your intranet site and the full path location of the home folder in the message box.

6. Choose Insert, File. The Insert File dialog box opens.

7. Navigate your hard drive to locate the compressed file you created in the previous section.

8. Highlight the file and click OK. An icon representing your file is placed in your e-mail message (see fig. 11.9).

9. To send the message, choose File, Send (or press Ctrl+Enter). The message window closes, and your message is automatically sent to the webmaster or system administrator.

Your webmaster or system administrator may have set up a folder on the share drive specifically for receiving new materials for inclusion on the corporate intranet. If this is the case, he or she will tell you where this directory is.

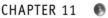

You can then use Explorer or an ftp program, as instructed by the webmaster, to transfer files to this folder. The instructions given earlier in this chapter still hold true when going through the webmaster; you just have to change the destination of the files to whatever the webmaster instructed.

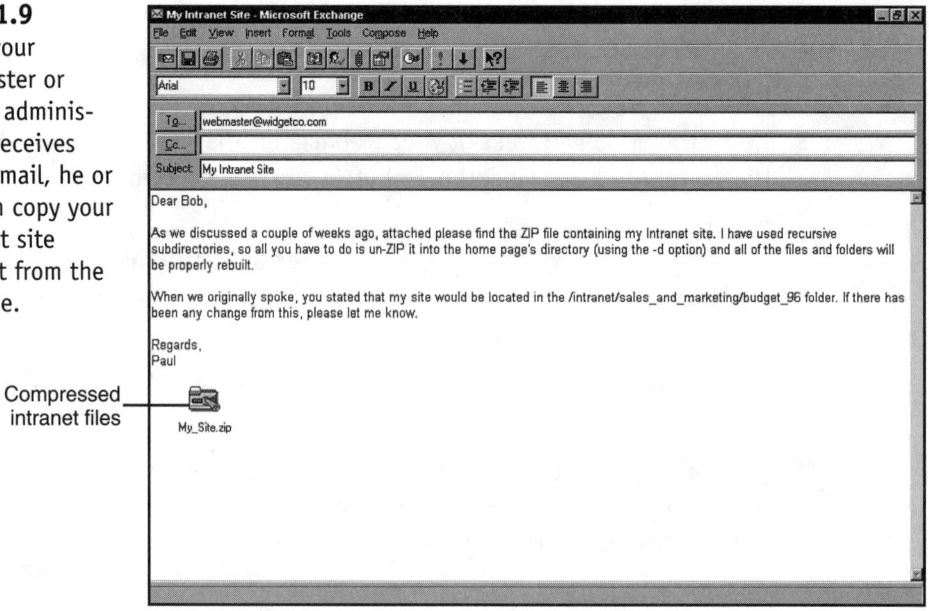

Fig. 11.9
When your webmaster or system adminis-trator receives your e-mail, he or she can copy your intranet site straight from the message.

Compressed intranet files

From Here...

You've done it! By copying your intranet files, either directly or in conjunc-tion with the webmaster or system administrator, to the intranet server you have made your intranet site available for everyone in the company to use.

In this chapter you learned to copy your complete intranet site from your local hard drive to the intranet server's hard drive, to use CuteFTP to copy files when Explorer isn't available, and to compress your intranet site into a single file for transmission to the system administrator or webmaster when you don't have write rights on the intranet server.

The following chapters present further information about keeping your site secure, making changes to the site, and using the corporate intranet:

- Chapter 12, "Security Issues," teaches you about security from both the content provider and intranet browser points of view. Particular attention is given to controlling access to intranet files.

- Chapter 13, "Updating Intranet Content," shows how to update content offline with a minimum of effort and frustration, using many of the techniques introduced in Chapter 10.

- Appendix B, "Using an Intranet," shows you how to begin exploring the other sites available on your company's network.

Security Issues

By Gordon Benett

By now, you probably need no convincing that intranets bring unprecedented value to information sharing, workgroup automation, and corporate data access. There's no free lunch, however, and the price of easy access via intranet is the greater risk of data theft, loss, or corruption. To keep these risks in check you need to pay attention to intranet security.

In this chapter, you learn to

- Protect information assets in a client/server computing environment
- Control access to your intranet resources
- Choose and implement an encryption standard for confidentiality
- Practice more secure web server administration

Network security is a large and complex subject that changes as fast as computing technology itself. Consider this chapter a solid introduction, but be prepared to investigate further. You'll find some excellent sources, in print and on the Web, listed in Appendix C, "For Further Reading."

Aspects of Security

Everyone knows it's a jungle out there, but isn't security a much smaller concern on webs entirely within company walls? Smaller, perhaps, but not by much. One reason is that the employees of any company are drawn from the general population, with its small but significant fraction of hackers, vandals, and opportunists. Another is that a large organization's intranet may span offices around the country or the globe, using the public Internet as a wide area network to keep costs low. Finally, an intranet without proper access controls invites accidental erasure or overwriting of documents.

Intranets make many aspects of computing simpler, but security policy isn't one of them. This section presents a basic approach to protecting your company's information assets in a web-based network environment.

Protecting Information Assets

There are three types of hazards to consider when planning your secure intranet:

- *Exposure of confidential or private data to unauthorized personnel.* Unauthorized personnel might be employees without a legitimate need to know, temporary workers with login privileges, or outside agents, if your intranet connects to the Internet or other public network.

- *Corruption or deletion of valuable files.* This hazard exists whenever multiple users have the ability to update shared information.

- *Illegitimate access to shared resources.* This includes files, applications, and network peripherals such as printers or modems.

NOTE

When deciding which documents and data on your intranet need protecting, remember that well-meaning users with inappropriate access privileges can do almost as much damage as the bad guys. Each of the hazards listed above can be caused by accident, as well as by purposeful intrusion. For example, salary data stored in a publicly accessible area might be viewed by an unauthorized user during a legitimate hunt for sales data. As a rule, it's better to limit access initially and loosen it on demand than to leave the vault door open.

Protecting your company's information from these hazards is a matter of controlling *who* can do *what* with *which* resources and services on the network.

The process of verifying that a user is who she says she is, is called *user authentication*. Most networks, including intranets, can be set up to authenticate the user through a challenge/response dialog. Often this takes the form of a username/password exchange. Stronger authentication is possible with "public key" technology, which is the basis for securing commercial transactions on the World Wide Web. User authentication techniques are discussed further in the section "Controlling Access to Intranet Resources."

Once the server trusts the client, it grants or denies access to given resources based on each resource's *Access Control List (ACL)*. How you set up access control depends on your choice of server and network operating system. For instance, on a UNIX-based intranet, access control is mostly a matter of file permissions. Web pages in a NetWare shared directory can be accessed according to *trustee rights*. See the following sidebar "File Permissions and Security," for more information.

▶ **See** "Controlling Access to Intranet Resources," **p. 241**

Client/Server Security

As the phrase suggests, there are two sides to any client/server story. Often there is a third element as well: the network connecting clients to servers. Security is an issue at each of these locations.

File Permissions and Security

The first line of defense in every network comes from file permissions. Network operating systems enable administrators to assign access rights for a specific resource—file, printer, or Internet service—on a user-by-user basis.

If you're running a UNIX-based web server, for instance, you can assign read, write, and execute permissions by owner (the user who created the file), group (the group to which the owner belongs),

or world (everyone). A world-readable file is visible to everyone, while a world-writeable file can be changed—or deleted—by anyone. Furthermore, since in UNIX everything is a file, intranet services such as ftp and script execution can be similarly controlled.

Windows NT, Novell NetWare, and Banyan Vines each have their own capabilities and nomenclature for controlling access.

Server security protects the back-end resources of your network, including web servers and databases. It's mainly of concern to system administrators. *Network security* is concerned with the secure transport of data from point A to point B, for which encryption is the technology of record. Network and server security are discussed at greater length in the following sections. Important *client security* issues are mentioned in this section.

The number one security risk for clients on an intranet is careless setup of so-called Helper Applications, also called *viewers*. (Netscape 2.0 "plug-ins" are in this category, as well.) Viewers pose a risk by associating downloaded file types with client-resident applications—tantamount to inviting strangers to run code on your computer. When setting up browsers on your intranet, don't assign viewer associations that can launch applications before you've had a chance to virus scan any downloaded files.

Three additional steps required to secure clients on an intranet are listed in the table that follows.

What You Should Do	Reason
Always log off before leaving a client computer unattended.	Anyone can masquerade as the active user once login has been completed.
Be conservative when sharing disk drives over the network.	Clients can easily expose more than intended when sharing directories via file://localhost/.
Consider encrypting sensitive files, including copies on tape backup and floppy disk.	Even when your computer is turned off, tapes and floppy disks can compromise security if openly readable.

Legal Considerations

The ease with which web servers can be set up heightens the risk that confidential data will be casually replicated across an organization. A corollary is that some of this material may be legally protected by the Privacy Act or other entitlements. Distributing protected material on an intranet could carry severe legal penalties for a business.

As an example, consider the value of making a central repository of personnel data available to managers via internal web. With a form allowing keyword searches as a front end, such a repository would doubtless be a powerful staffing tool. But the allowable search criteria would have to be restricted by design, to preclude queries specifying discriminatory attributes such as age or sex. Not doing so would invite lawsuits.

This is equally true of traditional databases, of course. The difference is that setting up a database server typically involves IS professionals and perhaps auditors in addition to users, while an intranet application can be assembled by a lone power user in a weekend, without IS knowledge. Moreover, if the Human Resources department runs Windows 95, users can launch the application on a homegrown 32-bit web server, as well.

The point of this cautionary tale is not to say that user empowerment is dangerous. On the contrary, lowering barriers to information flow is what intranets are all about. But as our hypothetical situation makes clear, security awareness has a crucial role to play in the way intranets are deployed and operated.

Controlling Access to Intranet Resources

You can restrict access to documents or whole directories on a web server in three ways:

- *By IP address or domain name.* This is the weakest form of restriction, since it takes on faith that the visitor's IP address is accurate.

- *By user authentication (name and password).* This method provides moderate security and is recommended for most applications.

  The setup procedure for user authentication access control varies by server type. In this section, you'll learn how to grant access selectively to resources on the UNIX-based NCSA server.

- *Using public key cryptography.* This, the strongest method, is recommended for applications where absolute confidentiality must be assured.

Controlling access using public keys requires digital certification of the server and issuance of public and private keys by a certification authority. These topics are discussed later in this chapter in "Encryption: The 'Key' to Secure Communications."

Controlling Access by IP Address, Segment, or Domain Name

The NCSA HTTPD server offers a global access control mechanism for administrators and a local, directory-level mechanism for users. Global access is configured in the file ACCESS.CONF, which is usually writeable only by superusers. This configuration file determines default authorizations and whether users can set up their own local access files. Assuming the webmaster at your site allows directory-level control, here's how you manage it:

1. Decide which resources you want to protect. For instance, you might grant everyone access to the directory tree starting at /Home/Web, but restrict /Home/Web2 and its subdirectories to a narrower group.

2. In the directory containing the resources you want to protect, create a file called **.htaccess**. Lines in this file explicitly deny or allow access by hostname.

3. Depending on how your intranet is set up, you may want to grant access to users from a certain subdomain only, denying access to everyone else. The following lines do just that for the Sales department:

```
<LIMIT GET, POST>
     deny from all
     allow from sales.yourcompany.com
</LIMIT>
```

The LIMIT directive (which, despite its appearance, has nothing to do with HTML) specifies which server actions are allowed or prohibited.

You can use other commands in your .htaccess files:

- order tells the server whether to process deny first, then allow (the default), or vice versa. For example:

```
<LIMIT GET>
      order allow, deny
```

```
        allow from friendly.com
        deny from un.friendly.com
    </LIMIT>
```

- You can specify allowed/denied hosts in several ways. For example:

```
allow 204.167.104.208    full ip address
allow 204.167.104        partial ip address (inclusive)
deny .playboy.com        partial domain (leading dot required)
```

- You can turn on or off selected NCSA options, such as CGI script execution and server-side includes, by adding an Option line as follows:

```
Options ExecCGI Includes
```

Most options contain security holes; the conservative setting is `Options None`.

Controlling Access by User/Group Authentication

The NCSA HTTPD server comes with a utility called *htpasswd* for creating and editing password files. There can be one or more global password files specified in ACCESS.CONF, as well as directory-level password files named .HTPASSWD by default.

To set up directory-level password protection, follow these steps:

1. Run the program htpasswd with the -c option to create new user/password pairs. For example:

   ```
   htpasswd  -c  /home/web2/.HTPASSWD julie
   ```

   You will be prompted for Julie's password. Upon entering it (twice), julie will be added to the .HTPASSWD file (Note: password is DES encrypted).

   ```
   julie:fad2jjAdk3k3Q
   ```

   Existing users' passwords can be changed with the htpasswd command, *without* the -c option.

2. To create groups of users, first create a file called **.htgroup** in the directory to be protected. Then define each group by entering lines consisting of the group name, a colon, and a comma-delimited list of users belonging to the group. For example:

```
Sales:      julie, art, trogers, melinda
webmaster:  gbenett, trogers
incentpay:  amy, Sales
```

NOTE

User groups can themselves contain groups.

3. To control access by user or group, edit the .HTACCESS file. You need to set the following directives:

Directive	Action
AuthType	Defines type of authentication used. Only Basic is implemented in production servers. NCSA beta v1.5 supports KerberosV4 and KerberosV5 in this field. Others are planned. For more information, see CERN's Access Authorization reference at **<http://www.w3.org/hypertext/WWW/AccessAuthorization/Basic.html>**, and Adam Cain's FAQ, *Kerberizing the Web*, at **<http://snapple.ncsa.uiuc.edu/adam/khttp/intro.html>**
AuthName	Set this field to the name of the resource being protected; for instance, "Sales Data." Don't leave it blank, or password dialogs will refer mysteriously to "UNKNOWN."
AuthUserFile	The full path name (not URL!)of the .HTPASSWD file controlling this resource.
AuthGroupFile	The full path name (not URL!)of the .HTGROUP file, if any, controlling this resource.

Here is a sample .htaccess file:

```
AuthType       Basic
AuthName       Proprietary Info
AuthUserFile   /home/web2/.htpasswd
AuthGroupFile  /home/web2/.htgroup
<LIMIT GET>
```

```
        require user julie
        require group webmasters
        deny from all
        allow from sales.yourcompany.com
</LIMIT>
```

By following these steps, you've established access control for a set of resources on your intranet.

> **NOTE**
>
> Often, an intranet acts as a presentation layer for data gathered from many sources, such as web servers, databases, and legacy systems. Each of these servers may repeat the user authentication process, in fulfillment of its own security plan.
>
> It's possible to pass authentication data securely from server to server, making multiple logins unnecessary. In practice, however, few networks have implemented "single login" designs, because doing so requires resource coordination at the enterprise level. Secure frameworks like Open Software Foundation's Distributed Computing Environment address this problem.
>
> For now, try not to get too frustrated if you're challenged more than once on the way to crucial information.

Firewalls and Proxies

Intranets put corporate data within reach of your web browser, but what happens when you need to access information outside the company? Standard security practice is to isolate internal systems from the Internet with a firewall.

A *firewall* is a system that enforces an access control policy between two networks, such as your intranet and the global Internet. Network-level firewalls are routers that either pass or block packets, depending on their source and destination addresses. Application-level firewalls block all traffic, inspect it against a set of access rules, and forward legitimate packets.

A *proxy* is a server that allows intranet users to access the World Wide Web and other Internet services through a firewall. It's like a one-way mirror: you can see out through it, but the bad guys can't see in. Proxies enable administrators to set up fine-grained access rules, such as allowing inbound ftp but blocking outbound transfers.

Ask your network administrator if your organization offers one or more proxy services, If it does, you'll need to configure your web browser accordingly. Here's how to do it for Netscape Navigator:

1. Choose Options, Preferences.

2. Select the Proxies tab (see fig. 12.1).

3. Enter the names and port numbers of the various proxies on your network. Often, one proxy will provide all the services shown (for example, WWW-Relay:8080).

4. Enter the host names or IP addresses of servers within your firewall in the No Proxy For text box.

5. Choose OK to save your settings.

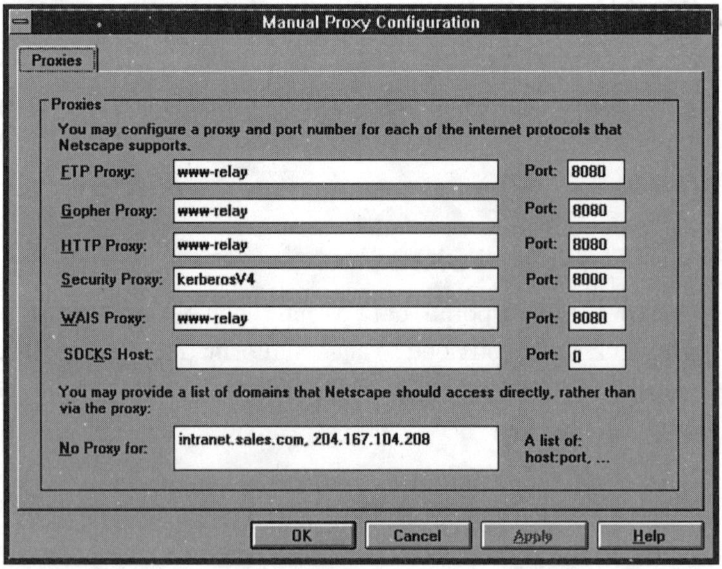

Fig. 12.1
Netscape Navigator 2.0 for Windows lets you configure different proxy servers for each Internet protocol.

Remote Intranet Access

Connecting mobile users to an internal web poses special security problems. There are two fundamentally different approaches. One is to provide authenticated dialup access to the intranet via a modem pool. In effect, the company acts as an ISP (Internet Service Provider) for its own employees, but provides access to the company intranet, rather than the WWW. This method is about as secure as the public telephone network (good enough to carry credit card and automatic teller machine transactions). If additional security is wanted, the channel can be encrypted.

The other approach is to leverage the Internet as a *wide area intranet*. While less secure on its face than dialup, this method offers other advantages. Where remote users have access to high speed Internet connections—for instance, at a client's site—they can access the headquarter's intranet at speeds much greater than the dialup maximum of 28.8 Kbps. Moreover, Internet access costs are flat. Mobile users can connect locally to the Internet in the city where they're staying via any of several thousand points of presence. The savings in line charges (or 800 numbers) can be great for business travelers accessing the intranet from across the globe.

In either scheme, authentication can be strengthened by using one-time passwords (such as Bellcore's S/KEY system)or a password generator such as the CRYPTOCard.

The two approaches are compared in the table that follows.

Remote Access Method	Pros/Cons
Direct dialup	*Pros*—inherently as secure as the public telephone network; easy to administer
	Cons—data rates limited to 28.8 Kbps; long-distance access costly
Via Internet	*Pros*—can support higher data rates than dialup; access charges aren't usage-based
	Cons—less secure than dialup

Encryption: The "Key" to Secure Communications

According to RSA Laboratories (*FAQ About Today's Cryptography*, **<http://www.rsa.com/rsalabs/faq/faq_gnrl.html>**):

> "Encryption is the transformation of data into a form unreadable by anyone without a secret decryption key. Its purpose is to ensure privacy by keeping the information hidden from anyone for whom it is not intended. In a multi-user setting, encryption allows secure communication over an insecure channel."

In this section, cryptographic technology is discussed as it pertains to intranets.

Encryption works by encoding the text of a message with a *key*, which is just a very long number. Typical keys are 40, 64, 80, or 128 digits long, with the longer keys affording stronger encryption.

Secure web servers like Netscape Commerce Server, use public key technology to provide encryption, authentication, and digital signature services. In a public key system, everyone owns a unique pair of keys. One is called the *public key*, and is widely distributed to anyone who wants a copy. The other, called the *private key*, is kept secret

Under this system, a person who needs to send a message to a recipient encrypts the message with the recipient's *public* key. So encrypted, the message can only be read by decrypting it with—you guessed it—the recipient's *private* key. This way, anyone can send a secure message, but only the intended party can read it.

In order to set up a server capable of secure communications, you need a *digital certificate*. Certificates attest that the person holding a public key is who he claims to be. The details of obtaining a public key and certificate depend on the particular server you run. For both the Netscape Commerce Server and Microsoft Internet Information Server, for instance, the Certifying Authority is VeriSign, Inc. VeriSign's web site, at **<http://www.verisign.com/netscape/>**, gives a six-step procedure for obtaining a certificate.

Once you have your certificate and key pair, you'll be able to use Secure Sockets Layer (SSL) technology to add security to your intranet. To do this you will need special web server software that supports Netscape's HTTP-over-SSL (or HTTPS) standard. Both Netscape's Commerce Server and the Microsoft Internet Information Server, among others, support this enhancement. Documents, forms and e-mail sent via HTTPS are fully encrypted.

TIP

There may be no free lunch, but you can set up HTTP and HTTPS on the same server! The two protocols are independent and use different ports (80 and 443, respectively). Hence, you can design a single server to handle secure and non-secure information. The Netscape and Microsoft browsers accommodate both protocols gracefully.

Administrative Concerns

Creating a secure network requires planning, and maintaining it demands vigilance. In this section, you learn the basics of secure server administration.

To learn more about the ins and outs of intranet security, check out Lincoln D. Stein's , available on the Web at

<http://www-genome.wi.mit.edu/WWW/faqs/www-security-faq.html>.

Setting and Enforcing a Security Policy

One of the simplest guidelines for securing a server is also one of the most effective: "Less is More." Here are some steps you can take to put this into practice.

- Limit the number of login accounts on the host, and periodically scan for, and delete, inactive users.
- Don't activate TCP/IP services you don't intend to use. Common culprits include ftp (physically remove the ftp server program if possible), tftp, NFS, and finger. On a UNIX host, check the file /ETC/INETD.CONF for daemons you don't need and comment them out.

● Use the password option in web fields to mask sensitive entries like your password as you type.

● Make sure user passwords are strong enough to withstand at least cursory attempts at cracking. User education is your best hope here, followed by password-testing programs like crack (for UNIX, available at **<ftp://info.cert.org/pub/tools/crack>**).

CGI Scripting Risks

CGI scripting and the easy programming interface it provides are among intranetting's most attractive features. Unfortunately, they're also the greatest contributors of security risk in a web-based network.

The problem lies not with the Common Gateway Interface itself, but with the power it gives to CGI script authors and, potentially, to users. The burden of establishing secure CGI guidelines falls on the server administrator. This section tells you what to look out for.

TIP

Remove shells and interpreters from the server that you don't intend to use. For example, if you don't run Perl-based CGI scripts, remove the Perl interpreter.

Passwords to Pass On

They may seem obvious, but the following list of passwords to avoid bears repeating, especially to your users. When choosing a password, NEVER use:

- Words found in the dictionary of any language (for example, gesundheit)

- Proper nouns, including names of real or fictitious characters (for example, Bullwinkle)

- Acronyms commonly used by computer professionals (for example, WYSIWYG)

- Simple variations of first, last, or login names, pets' names, your birthday, and so on (for example, Snookums)

There are two types of risk associated with scripts. One is inadvertent disclosure of server information, such as password or registry files, that could be used to further subvert security measures. The other is the potential that users can spoof the script into doing something perverse, like executing system commands.

You can take several precautions to lower the risk of running CGI scripts on your web server:

- Keep all CGI scripts in a single directory (for instance, /cgi-bin) that only the web administrator can write to.

- If possible, use compiled executables rather than Perl scripts, and avoid shell scripts altogether for CGI processing. (This includes *.BAT programs on NT-based servers.)

- Never trust input data. In Perl, for instance, use the following routine to "untaint" insecure user-input data:

```
$SCARY =~ /^([\w.]*)$/;          # pattern prunes non-alphanumeric
  characters
$COOL =~ $1;              # untainted version
```

If you must allow non-alphanumeric characters (which could be used to run unauthorized programs on the web server), here's a Perl command that renders them harmless:

```
$RISKY_VAR =~ s/([;<>\*\|'&\$!#\(\)\[\]\{\}:'"])/\\$1/g
```

TIP

If you're using Perl 5, test your scripts using

```
perl -T
```

to invoke the "taint" checking option.

Check out the following web sites for additional detail on safe scripting:

Safe CGI Programming   <http://www.cerf.net/~paulp/cgi-security/safe-cgi.txt>

CGI Security Tutorial   <http://csclub.uwaterloo.ca/u/mlvanbie/cgisec/>

CGI is the most common means of adding functionality to a web page, but there are others.

● *Server-Side Includes* are directives embedded in HTML code itself, making possible in-line execution of scripts or operating system commands. Quite a few web servers support SSI. Some, such as WebQuest NT™ by Questar Microsystems Inc., offer an extended set of directives (for example, ODBC database access).

● *Proprietary APIs* have begun to appear in commercial servers such as Netscape. These trade the portability of CGI for enhanced performance and functionality.

N O T E

The pros and cons of these methods are also discussed in Que's primer, "Introducing Intranets."

The caveats given in this section concerning CGI administration apply to SSIs and APIs as well, as they must to any means of launching processes remotely on network computers.

Using Server Access Logs

Over and above their value for market research and server capacity planning, access logs can alert you to certain types of security violation.

Check your server access and error logs periodically for suspicious activity. On UNIX systems, look for accesses involving system commands such as "rm," "login," "/bin/sh," or "perl." On NT servers, look for "cmd," "ntperl," or "del." These may indicate an attempt to trick a CGI script into invoking a system command. Also look for very long lines (>256 characters) in URL requests. This could be an attempt to overrun a program's input buffer and sneak commands to the server. Look as well for multiple unsuccessful attempts to access password-protected documents, particularly configuration files like /ETC/PASSWD (UNIX) or the Windows Registry (NT).

CAUTION

While server logs can be a powerful tool for enhancing security, distributing them casually can be a security risk. The reason is simple: access logs reveal a lot about the usage patterns and interests of your users. Outside the firewall, this gives rise to privacy concerns that have led many Internet providers to restrict the visibility of logs.

On an intranet, privacy may still be a concern, particularly if the intranet has a social dimension that includes things like the AA meeting schedule. Another concern is that analysis of logs can indicate the location of confidential data. The files most accessed by Payroll personnel, for instance, might contain sensitive salary or budgetary data.

As with other files on the web server, take a conservative approach to access and error logs. Make them available on a need-to-know basis.

From Here...

This chapter has just scratched the surface of the large and complex topic of intranet security. From here, you may want to explore these sections of the book:

- Chapter 13, "Updating Intranet Content," shows how, using many of the techniques introduced in Chapter 10, content can be updated offline with a minimum of effort.
- Appendix B, "Using An Intranet," gives instructions on setting up helper applications.
- Appendix C, "For Further Reading," suggests some additional sources in print and on the Web.

13

Updating Intranet Content

By Paul Bodensiek

As with everything else in the business and computer worlds, change is the only constant. This is one of the great advantages of an intranet, the ability to update content on an almost continuous basis so that the latest information is always available. This fluidity is why you have set up an intranet site in the first place. Look on changes as an opportunity, not a chore.

Whatever the reason, your pages need to be revised. There's no getting around it. If you prepared your site using the techniques outlined in Chapter 10, "Managing Pages," updating your site can simply be a matter of editing your local files and replacing the ones the server. Sometimes you aren't so lucky and you are updating a site produced by someone else and the files aren't immediately available locally.

This chapter provides methods to help you add and update intranet content in an already existing site.

In this chapter, you learn to

- Update local copies of intranet files
- Upload revised intranet files to the server
- Edit intranet files directly on the server
- Download files from the server for local editing

Updating Files Locally

If you're working on a site that you created locally and you retained copies on your hard drive (as outlined in Chapter 10), you are already three-quarters of the way through your updating battle. If it's been a while since you created your site, you may want to skim Chapter 10 to refresh your memory on the techniques introduced there. Everything in that chapter is still applicable when updating your intranet site: finding out where your site is located on the server, using folders and file names to your advantage, and reusing existing HTML and other files.

Updating your files locally is just an extension of your original editing process. The four main steps involved in updating your intranet site are the following:

1. Open your existing HTML file(s) in your favorite editor.

2. Make any necessary changes to the HTML code.

3. Save the file and exit the editor.

4. Transmit your file(s) to the server either directly or via the webmaster.

TIP

You only need to update *changed* files on the server. Since everything else remains the same, you can transmit only an updated HTML text file without sending all of the linked pages and graphics.

That's all there is to it. Of course, in addition to just the changes you are making in your existing HTML code, you may be adding additional pages and graphics to your site. These changes are done exactly the same as if you were building your site from scratch. Just create your pages and graphics as outlined in Part II, "Creating Intranet Content," and transmit them as you normally would. See Chapter 11, "Making Content Available on the Server," for more information on transmitting files to the server.

TIP

To make transmitting the changed files to the server easier, view your files in Explorer by their date (choose View, Arrange Icons, By Date then choose View, Details). This will place the most recently edited files at the top of the list (see fig. 13.1).

Updated files

Fig. 13.1
The two HTML files edited today are easy to pick out of this list because they are at the top.

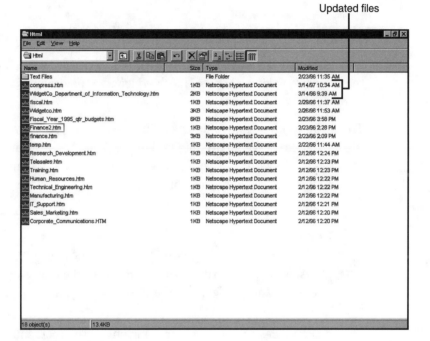

If Files Aren't Local

The above procedure is great if you created the content and retained copies of the original files on your local hard drive. But what if you are updating someone else's site or you had to delete your copy of the site because your hard drive was getting full and the only copies of the files are on the server?

You have two choices, either download the files to your local hard drive for editing or edit them directly on the server. Each of these methods has its advantages and disadvantages.

TIP

If your IT department takes care of backing up local hard drives and retains old backups, you may be able to obtain the complete site. This may
be a lot of trouble and you will have to be careful to check file dates in
case content was updated since the local backup.

Downloading Files to Your Local Hard Drive

The advantage to downloading files to your local hard drive for editing is
that you are making a copy of files and leaving the originals in place so the
intranet site continues to work.

The main disadvantage to downloading files is that, unless you copy the entire site, any relative links contained in the pages are lost until you replace
the original file with your edited one. This means that testing the page(s) can
be virtually impossible before uploading.

TIP

Make a backup copy of the original file before editing. If you make a
mistake in your updating, you can reference the copy even if you have
overwritten the original on the server.

You can copy files from the server using any of the techniques outlined in
Chapter 11 (except e-mail), just reverse the direction of your copy or ftp
procedures. In addition, most browsers also let you copy HTML and graphics
files back to your hard drive.

To copy HTML files to your hard drive using Netscape Navigator:

1. Start Netscape Navigator and move to the page that you want to copy.
2. Choose File, Save As. The Save As dialog box opens, displaying your
   local drive (see fig. 13.2).
3. Enter the folder where you want to save the file and click the Save button. A copy of the HTML file is now on your local hard drive.

Fig. 13.2
Netscape
Navigator's Save
As dialog box
allows you to save
HTML files to your
local hard drive.

To copy HTML files to your hard drive using Microsoft Internet Explorer:

1. Start Microsoft Internet Explorer and move to the page that you want to copy.

2. Choose File, Save As. The Save As dialog box opens, displaying your local drive (see fig. 13.3).

3. Enter the folder where you want to save the file using the standard dialog box navigation tools.

4. Enter the name of the file in the File Name text box and click the Save button. A copy of the HTML file is now on your local hard drive. Make sure you use the same name as the original file to make updating easier later.

To copy graphic files to your hard drive using Netscape Navigator:

1. Start Navigator and move to a page containing the image you want to copy.

2. Click the image using your secondary mouse button (usually the right button). A pop-up menu appears (see fig. 13.4).

Fig. 13.3
Internet Explorer's
Save As dialog
box allows you to
save HTML files to
your local hard
drive.

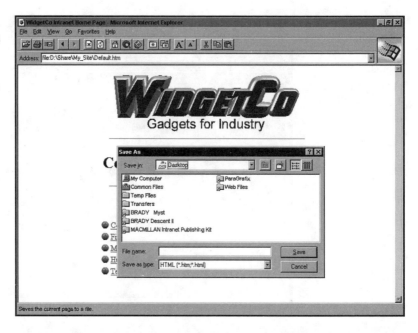

Fig. 13.4
Right-clicking an
image opens a
pop-up menu,
giving you
options for saving
and viewing the
image.

3. Select Save This Image As. The Save As dialog box opens.

4. Enter the folder where you want to save the file and click the Save button. A copy of the graphic file is now on your local hard drive.

To copy graphic files to your hard drive using Microsoft Internet Explorer:

1. Start Internet Explorer and move to a page containing the image you want to copy.

2. Click the image using your secondary mouse button (usually the right button). A pop-up menu opens (see fig. 13.5).

Fig. 13.5
Right-clicking an image opens a pop-up menu giving you options for saving and viewing the image.

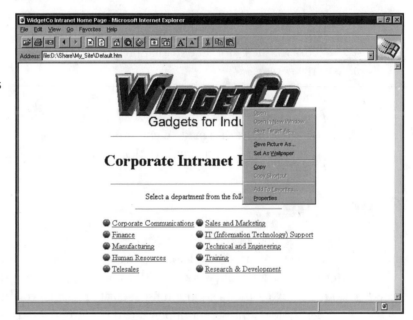

3. Select Save Picture As. The Save As dialog box opens.

4. Enter the folder where you want to save the file and click the Save button. A copy of the graphic file is now on your local hard drive. Make sure you use the same name as the original file to make updating easier later.

Editing Files on the Server

This is a risky proposition at best. Aside from the security and privileges aspects, what happens if you make a mistake and trash the page or other file you are working on? True, there should be backups of the files, but you don't want to count on it. Also, while you are editing the file, your intermediate versions are available on the server for everyone to use (errors, incomplete links and text, and all).

If you have privileges on the server and you decide that you want to edit the files in place, you can do so in generally the same manner as you would on your local hard drive: open the HTML or other file in your favorite editing program, make the necessary changes, and save the file again. See Chapter 12, "Security Issues," for an explanation of the different types of access available to the server.

You should consider editing directly on the server only when your changes are minor. If you begin making large-scale changes and make a mistake, the integrity of the entire site may be compromised. Fixing a site after a major editing problem can be extremely difficult and time consuming.

From Here...

Using the techniques learned in Chapter 10, "Managing Pages," and Chapter 11, "Making Content Available on the Server," you can update intranet sites with relative ease. While working with a copy of your complete site on your local hard drive is the best option for security reasons, you may directly edit the original file on the server depending on your network privileges.

You now have all the skills necessary to create, modify, and maintain an intranet site on your company's computer network. If you've only created one site, there are still hundreds of other applications that you can use the intranet for.

● Part IV, "Putting Intranets to Work," shows real life examples of how other intranet authors are using their computer networks to enhance communications throughout their companies. Learn new techniques for every aspect of your site(s) by viewing screen shots and exploring examples of intranets being used at a variety of corporations.

- Part V, "Exploring Publishing Tools," enhances your ability to turn around complete intranet sites in a minimum of time and with greater flexibility. One or more of these programs may be just what your company needs to expand its intranet system.

Putting Intranets to Work

14

Corporate Communications

By Paula Jacobs

Corporate Communications may be the first department within your organization to implement an intranet. As such, your intranet site may serve as a model for other groups. Therefore, it's important to develop high-quality content, with appropriate text and graphics.

At the same time, like any new program, expect your intranet implementation to be an evolutionary, multi-phase process. It's unrealistic to accomplish everything instantaneously. Don't aim for an award-winning Corporate Communications home page. Instead, set realistic objectives.

Planning Your Intranet Content

As you plan the content for your department's intranet site, use these questions to help get organized:

- What information will you provide initially?
- How will you organize the Corporate Communications home page?
- Who will be responsible for managing and updating content?
- What process will you implement to ensure up-to-date content?
- Is it necessary to provide hyperlinks to the external company home page?

● What will be an easy-to-understand and accessible format?

● Will the initial contents include text only or also graphics?

● Who will be the primary liaison between Corporate Communications and other departments that need to provide intranet content?

● How will you communicate initial implementation plans, policies, and procedures?

● How often will you update content?

● Will you phase out printed materials? If so, which ones and what will be the time frame?

Sample Uses in Corporate Communications

Intranetting offers an efficient, cost-effective way to enhance internal communications, disseminate information, respond to new business directions, and increase productivity. An intranet will help you communicate more effectively with employees at worldwide locations, providing on-demand communications for improved informational flow. You'll find your intranet is a convenient tool to update employees on the latest corporate and product strategies, while saving time and money. Since internal corporate LANs function at high speeds, an intranet enables you to incorporate audio and video.

The following are representative uses for an intranet in Corporate Communications:

● Employee newsletters

● Press releases and press clippings

● Annual Reports, brochures, and data sheets

● Corporate presentations and overviews

● Frequently Asked Questions (FAQs)

● Contact and literature listings

● Forms

● Calendars

- Status updates
- News feeds and daily news bulletins
- Discussion forums

Employee Newsletters

Perhaps your Corporate Communications department publishes a weekly or monthly employee newsletter. The newsletter may contain the company bowling league schedule, "for sale" postings, recipes, and announcements of promotions, new employees, stock prices, and special company events.

An intranet is an excellent vehicle for employee newsletters and helps reduce traditional production, labor, and distribution costs. Newsletters can also be archived for handy reference. Another option is to supplement the printed newsletter—either on a temporary or permanent basis—with an intranet version.

One company that uses this practical approach is Teradyne Corporation, a multi-national electronics company in Boston, Massachusetts (see figs. 14.1 and 14.2). Since not all employees have computer access, Teradyne Corporation still produces a traditional printed version. However, because of space limitations, not all the submissions can be printed. The supplementary intranet newsletter allows use of these stories, together with scanned in color images (the printed version requires black-and-white photos). This approach enables Teradyne's employee communications to expand the scope of its communications efforts and produce a greater variety of creative materials than using traditional printed newsletters.

The newsletter represents a simple, first project for your intranet. To get started, your newsletter editor notifies employees (via e-mail and in a printed newsletter) that newsletters will be available on your intranet as of a certain date. Employees continue to e-mail their contributions to the newsletter editor who reviews and edits the appropriateness of submissions. Your newsletter editor (or the individual assigned to creating content) inserts the necessary HTML tags and places the newsletter on your intranet. For more on HTML, see Chapter 2, "HTML Primer: Planning a Document."

Fig. 14.1
An intranet newsletter can contain a wealth of information. This is the home page of Teradyne World, an electronic employee newsletter. (Screen shot courtesy of Teradyne, Inc.)

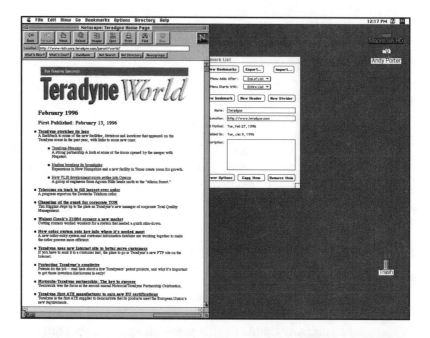

Fig. 14.2
Here's a feature article from the same Teradyne newsletter. (Screen shot courtesy of Teradyne, Inc.)

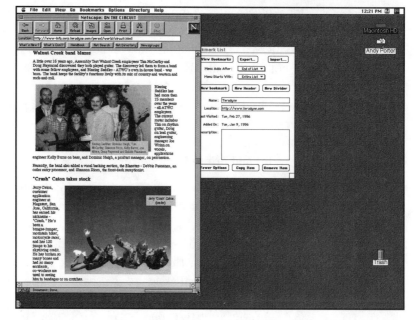

Press Releases and Press Clippings

An intranet can help you streamline an extensive press review cycle, requiring legal, marketing, and executive sign-off. The time-consuming task of tracking down mobile executives becomes a non-issue. Simply send an e-mail note to your distribution list. Executives from remote locations can access the press release via notebook computers, while reviewing comments of those on the distribution cycle. This approach is significantly easier and less time-consuming than faxing a press release to a vice president on a business trip in the Far East.

Press releases need to be archived for future reference. By archiving press releases on your intranet, you can provide easy access, while eliminating cumbersome paper storage. The beauty is that the press release is instantly accessible—for the corporate attorney who needs to check a date for legal purposes, the marketing manager who requires content information, or the sales representative who wants to give a copy to a customer.

Published press clippings can also be scanned into your intranet. It helps you publicize the results of your public relations efforts, while providing an easy tracking mechanism. Instead of distributing monthly press clippings to your corporate executives, simply use your intranet as an information repository. You'll find this approach a more effective way to track your public relations success rate than the traditional approach of leafing through photocopied clippings.

Frequently Asked Questions

By posting Frequently Asked Questions on the Corporate Communications intranet, you can save the inordinate amount of time devoted to routine e-mail or telephone requests for information. The use of FAQs can increase productivity, provide employees with instant information access, enhance intra-organizational communications, and improve employee satisfaction. Corporate Communications' staff will be pleased that they have more time to spend on assignments, and other organizational employees will be pleased to have a variety of information at their fingertips. While Frequently Asked Questions may vary by organization, the following are suitable for many Corporate Communications' intranet sites:

● Whom do I contact to initiate a direct mail campaign?

● What is the lead time for developing a new brochure?

● How do I order a product data sheet?

● What is the ordering part number for the corporate overview presentation?

● When will the new corporate brochure be available?

● Who is responsible for corporate advertising?

● Where can I find the latest company press releases?

Contact and Literature Listings

A highly practical use of an intranet is the posting of lists. Typical postings include new corporate communications material, literature part numbers, trade show schedules, department listings, and other general information.

Intranets offer an easy way to provide a regular updated list of new corporate brochures, data sheets, presentations, and so on with associated part numbers. Employees around the world can easily access this information at their convenience.

Post a department list of Corporate Communications personnel, including their function, telephone number, mailing location, and e-mail address. It's easier to update and certainly less expensive to post this information on your intranet rather than mailing out printed directories. By cross-referencing this list with your Frequently Asked Questions, you'll be able to give employees access to quick information.

Forms

By posting forms on your intranet, as shown in figure 14.3, you make it easier for your organization's employees to order brochures and product literature, presentations, business cards, and other material. Employees simply download the form they need and fill in the appropriate information. This process eliminates possible miscommunications or ordering errors. To further streamline communications, cross-reference forms with your Frequently Asked Questions.

Fig. 14.3
This IT Support
Request Form is
one of many such
forms that you
can house on your
intranet.

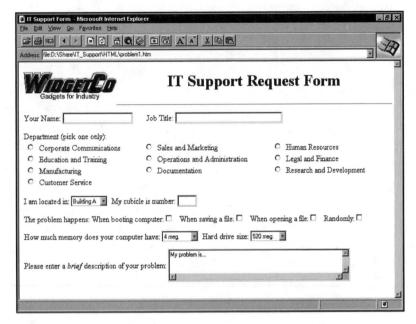

For example, an employee in Paris may need to order a corporate brochure
from your home office in Indianapolis. The employee simply downloads the
form, fills in the appropriate part number by checking the literature listing on
the intranet, and then mails the form to your Corporate Communications
literature fulfillment e-mail address.

NOTE

Depending on your application, you may need to add commercial form
creation software. One such package is net.Form from net.Genesis Corporation (**http://www.netgen.com/**). This software, for example, allows the
creation of interactive World Wide Web forms for applications that integrate with existing corporate databases. Another such package, JetForm's
Web Filler, allows users to fill out and route forms from their Web server
(**http://www.jetform.com**).

Annual Reports, Brochures, and Data Sheets

Annual Reports, brochures, data sheets, and other typical material can be stored on your intranet or on the public server with hyperlinks to the external WWW site. Your employees benefit from fingertip access to the latest information. By instructing employees to use glossy versions only for customers, Corporate Communications can save typesetting and printing costs. An intranet also provides a convenient mechanism to field-test corporate communications material before printing final versions.

When you start placing content on the Corporate Communications intranet, you improve communications with branch and office locations worldwide and across time zones. Both your New York and London staff can simultaneously access the latest company news, brochures, or strategy information. The advantage is especially significant in a competitive market economy with a tight window of opportunity.

Intranets represent a reliable, cost-effective alternative to first-class mail or bulk mail, and ensure that worldwide sales offices or distributors receive dated materials in a timely fashion. This approach eliminates the need to update internal mailing lists, saves mailing and production charges, allows timely receipt of critical information, and reduces paper clutter. Branch offices receive timely information on schedule, and you don't need to worry about mailing delays. Since employees print only the information they require, production costs are reduced, not to mention the paper for materials that go unread by employees who do not need access to specific information.

Intranets also enable you to produce more creative materials, without incurring additional costs. By adding audio and video capabilities, you can easily distribute high-quality slide and video presentations worldwide.

An intranet can help you reduce costs for materials with a limited shelf life or those that are revised frequently. New and emerging companies or those in transition will find an intranet especially useful to update employees on the latest corporate strategy. If your company is in a high-growth area where communications changes are frequent, you'll find that your intranet will let you plan print quantities more effectively, reducing excess literature inventory and storage charges.

Spyglass Inc., a web technology company in Naperville, Illinois uses its intranet to communicate the latest corporate strategy to employees. The latest corporate messages are posted on the president's personal WWW page. The company has also slashed production costs, by reducing print quantities of glossy product literature.

Most important, you are providing your employees easy access to a variety of information. This *intranetting* approach is important for many business situations.

Perhaps you are on a fundraising trip and require information from last year's Annual Report for an early morning breakfast meeting with prospective major contributors. Rather than disturbing your secretary at home in the middle of the night, you can simply log on to your notebook PC, connect with your organization's intranet, click Annual Report 1995, and check the required financial data for the presentation. The advantage is that information is instantly accessible, and you don't need to worry about time zones or whether someone at the home office will be available to help you locate the information.

Status Updates

By posting project status updates and rollout schedules on your Corporate Communications intranet, you can facilitate the planning process. This usage is especially handy if you must coordinate projects with numerous departments. For example, if a product announce date changes, corporate communications writers and designers will know to adapt their schedules accordingly.

Calendars

Intranets are a perfect place to store calendars, including corporate events and deadlines. For example, you can post newsletter deadlines, trade shows, user groups, special company events, and other schedules. It's easy to update this calendar monthly, quarterly, or as often as it makes practical sense.

Suppose your company has an annual user group meeting. Instead of sending e-mail reminders about deadlines for presentation proposals or booth requests, simply create a "User Group" section on your home page. Send employees an e-mail notification that their intranet will be the exclusive place to find user group registration and logistical information, including deadline milestones. This method is tremendously more efficient than sending out frequent e-mail or paper notice reminders.

Daily News Feeds and Daily News Bulletins

If your organization distributes daily news feeds to corporate executives or company employees, you will find your intranet more efficient than sending out e-mail messages. For example, post a section called "Daily Bulletins" on your intranet; this may include information such as company stock prices, major corporate wins, and competitive information provided by third-party news bureaus. Another advantage is that you are not using unnecessary computer disk space by replicating the same information in numerous e-mail inboxes.

Discussion Forums

Intranets are a perfect place to promote interactive discussions among project team members. For example, geographically dispersed groups can share and log comments.

NOTE

Special software, such as net.Thread (net.Genesis) can be used for topic-sorted discussion areas. You can find it at **http://www.netgen.com**.

Sales and Marketing

By Paula Jacobs

With appropriate planning and imagination, intranets can be invaluable sales and marketing resources and powerful, competitive weapons.

Intranets allow frequent input and updating of marketing and sales material in response to a competitive business environment. The advantage is a cost-effective way to distribute time-critical marketing and sales information that can be accessed from customer sites, telesales locations, remote offices, and corporate headquarters.

A well-organized Sales and Marketing intranet site can also help eliminate information overload or "marketing clutter." It lets you address the needs of busy sales representatives who need instant access to specific marketing and sales information, but don't have time to read lengthy printed materials.

Another advantage is enhanced information flow and consistent messaging. Sales representatives worldwide have access to the same presentations, product descriptions, corporate overviews, and so on. Meanwhile, productivity is increased because time isn't wasted trying to locate a specific data sheet or brochure, now instantly available with a single click.

NOTE

Don't forget to communicate the "http" path of your intranet server to the Sales and Marketing team. Make sure to give the address to your outside sales representatives so they can access the server while they are traveling or meeting with customers.

Content Implementation

It's best to implement a regular creating and updating schedule that involves close coordination with other groups. First, work with these groups to determine their intranet content requirements for the first phase. Next, determine how often they plan to submit content updates; for example, price lists may require monthly updating; customer testimonials, weekly revisions, and sales guides may only need to be revised quarterly. In any case, to ensure accurate intranet content, establish a detailed plan with groups responsible for contributing and updating material. The following issues need to be addressed up front:

- Who will be the primary liaison between each group and the intranet content developer?

- How will content be submitted? Will individual group liaisons furnish the latest documents (including HTML formats) or simply update specific sections?

- Can each group provide a preliminary set of new and updated requirements?

- What should the home page look like? Should there be hyperlinks to other locations?

- What is the estimated time frame between submissions and completion of content updates?

- How will last-minute submissions and exceptions to the rule be handled?

- What is the target date for the initial implementation phase?

- Who/how will the availability of the intranet site be communicated to Sales and Marketing?

- Who will assume responsibility for informing the field sales force about new content and/or updates?

Sample Sales and Marketing Uses

An intranet enables you to communicate timely information quickly to your sales and marketing staff. Easy access to accurate product and pricing descriptions can hasten the sales cycle, eliminating the need to verify information with corporate headquarters.

Key uses for sales and marketing include:

- Marketing bulletins
- Sales kits
- Presentations
- Sales guides
- Customer references
- Price lists
- Frequently Asked Questions
- Forms
- Product and configuration specifications
- Product updates
- Competitive information
- Proposals
- Telesales
- Contact lists
- Lead generation
- Forecasts
- Miscellaneous postings
- Distributor information

Marketing Bulletins

Once you implement your intranet, you'll find that you no longer need to distribute (electronically or manually) lengthy weekly, bi-weekly, or monthly marketing bulletins. Distribution is significantly easier, plus these bulletins can easily be archived for future reference.

Sales Kits

Intranets offer a more efficient, cost-effective way to distribute sales kits than using traditional mail. Intranets eliminate the problem of lost or misplaced packages. This capability is especially important for sales kits accompanying new product announcements which require worldwide distribution. And, unlike a shrink-wrapped traditional sales kit, last-minute changes can be easily made without financial impact; generally, it's just a matter of inserting new documents with embedded HTML codes. In any case, if you plan to substitute an intranet for traditional sales kit distribution, there are several preliminary steps you must take:

1. Obtain necessary buy-ins from key Sales and Marketing decision makers, including an agreement to provide users with the necessary hardware and software required, such as SLIP lines.

2. Establish an appropriate implementation schedule and rollout plan. Will traditional sales kits be totally eliminated, will they be phased out gradually, or will there be a combination of traditional and intranet sales kits?

3. Determine the content requirements of an intranet sales kit. How will it differ from the traditional kit? Will you include nifty graphics, audio, and video? Will you limit such creative uses to major product announcements or will they be included in all sales kits? Will the person responsible for creating and managing intranet content also develop the graphics or will this effort require collaboration with your in-house art department?

4. Decide if you will need to set up hyperlinks to different intranet sites.

5. Most importantly, make sure to communicate this information to Sales and Marketing, especially if they are accustomed to regular sales kit distribution. If e-mail is your organization's standard mode of communications, an e-mail memo is probably the easiest way to announce both the initial process as well as ongoing notification about the availability of new sales kits. Depending on your organization's communication style, face-to-face meetings, newsletters, paper memos, or a combination may serve as a more appropriate communication mechanism.

One company that has successfully implemented the intranet approach for distribution to its worldwide marketing and sales organization is Data General Corporation, a computer systems company in Westboro, Massachusetts.

Previously, the company distributed monthly "Sales Survival Kits," which included product literature, sales guides, demonstration disks, and other sales tools. This information is now housed on the company's "Information Libraries," as Data General's intranet is called, with links to the external web site. Notification about the availability of new material is sent electronically (see figs. 15.1 and 15.2). The beauty of this system is tremendous cost-savings, timely distribution, greater productivity, and the elimination of information overload. Like users of a public library who only check out the books they want, Data General sales representatives access the company's "Information Libraries" for selective information.

Fig. 15.1
Data General's Information Libraries gives its marketing and sales staff quick access to up-to-date product literature, sales guides, demonstration disks, and other sales tools. (Screen shot courtesy of Data General.)

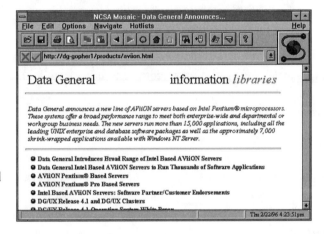

Fig. 15.2
For staff just getting used to the Information Libraries, Data General makes a Quick Start available that explains the Libraries system. (Screen shot courtesy of Data General.)

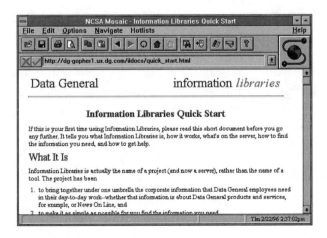

Product Updates

In addition to new product announcements, your intranet is the perfect vehicle to announce product updates or changes. These may range from announcements about product enhancements to notifications of recently obsolete models.

Presentations

Your intranet is a superb repository for overhead presentations. It gives your entire organization access to consistent presentations, saves significant production and distribution costs, and enables you to improve dramatically the quality of your presentations.

An intranet makes customizing and updating presentations a cinch. You can store an assortment of graphics, icons, and corporate logos or scan in photographs and other images. It's also easy to update presentations as business directions and organizational structures change or as new products are introduced.

The ability to customize a presentation for different sales situations offers tremendous advantages over the use of standard corporate hard copy presentations. For generic presentations, you simply download the standard presentation from the intranet site, insert an introductory overhead slide, eliminate unnecessary overheads, and add some colorful graphics.

Suppose you are making a sales call to a prospective customer in the healthcare industry. You don't have time to present the 80 standard corporate overheads, so you simply click the thirty that you want to use. As an initial overhead, you customize the presentation with the prospective customer's name, company, and relevant graphics. You further customize the slide with names of referenceable healthcare accounts. Since your competition is a larger and more established company, you also insert an overhead to show your company's solid financial history.

Sales Guides

Intranets greatly improve the usefulness of a typical sales guide, while reducing costs. Revisions are easier than with the conventional printed approach.

Sales representatives simply drill down to access the necessary information. And with better quality information, the sales guide becomes a more effective and more frequently used sales tool.

Additionally, you can improve the readability of a sales guide. To illustrate a product feature, add a pictorial representation, which can be changed as needed.

Consider the advantages from a sales perspective. Productivity is increased because it's unnecessary to read through a multi-page volume to locate key selling information. Meanwhile, accurate product descriptions and competitive data help the selling process.

Customer References

Consider storing customer references and testimonials on your intranet. By setting up hyperlinks to specific product areas, you can create an easy customer and product cross-reference tool. Assuming that your customer reference list expands regularly, you should plan on frequent updates.

Suppose one of your sales representatives is looking for a major-accounts customer in the insurance business. By clicking the "Customer References" section of the Sales and Marketing home page, he accesses the right location. Then, using a Web browser search engine, he can type "insurance and major-accounts customer" and find appropriate customer references for his sales call.

Price Lists

Price lists are easier to update than hard copy price books. They are available on demand, eliminate printing and distribution costs, and sales representatives need not lug heavy price books around.

A primary advantage is that a sales representative will not accidentally misquote a price by referring to an out-of-date price list. With on-demand access, the need to verify pricing with the home office is eliminated—a significant benefit for organizations with offices spanning different time zones.

Frequently Asked Questions

By including a set of Frequently Asked Questions on your intranet site, you can help streamline the sales process. FAQs are ideal for new sales representatives. Typical FAQs may include:

- How do I quote/book an order?
- What is the sales qualification process?
- What is the cutoff point for a dollar-volume discount?
- What are the procedures for requesting special customer discounts?
- Where is a list of qualified third-party software vendors?
- Where can I find boilerplate proposal descriptions?
- How do I locate the latest corporate slide shows?
- What is the schedule for new marketing bulletins?
- How do I order sales literature?

Forms

Consider placing commonly used forms on your intranet site. Typical uses include sales qualification, ordering procedures, equipment requisition, travel and expense, and conference room reservation forms.

Product and Configuration Specifications

Consider using the intranet to store product specifications and configuration information. This usage makes practical sense for situations where product revisions are frequent or where configurations are complex. It also increases productivity since information is readily accessible, and does not require staff time or resources.

In some sales situations, you may need to verify whether custom configurations are available or if other customers have requested similar unique requirements. One company that has used the intranet for this purpose is Interleaf, Inc., a supplier of document management and publishing software in Waltham, Massachusetts. The company's sales force remotely dials in to corporate headquarters to access marketing and sales information located on the company's intranet. Using Web browsers and Intellecte/Business Web (Interleaf's document management system), they can access and retrieve information contained in different repositories (see figs. 15.3 and 15.4). For example, by posting HTML forms, field staff can post queries against the corporate database to verify configuration information or to determine whether other sales representatives have encountered similar sales scenarios.

Fig. 15.3
The Intellecte/ Business Web sample application shows views of document repositories, document collections, and other web sites that are useful for a field sales force. (Screen shot courtesy of Interleaf, Inc.)

Fig. 15.4
The Intellecte/
Business Web can
deliver informa-
tion in a choice
of formats. This
screen shows one
file that has a
choice of rendi-
tions: Word,
Adobe Postscript,
and WorldView.
(Screen shot
courtesy of
Interleaf, Inc.)

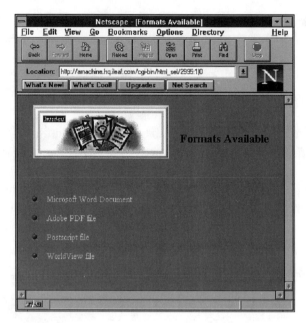

Competitive Data

Competitive market data can be easily updated on your intranet. This approach is more efficient than distributing hard copy competitive reports. In a competitive situation, sales representatives can also verify competitive information right from a customer site.

Proposals

Your intranet is extremely useful for storing sample proposals, including boilerplate materials. Such material may include mission and capability statements, corporate overviews, and product descriptions. The benefits for the sales representative working late hours to complete a lengthy proposal are incomparable.

Telesales

What can be a more efficient way of providing your telesales representatives with product and pricing information than via the intranet? Consider the advantages during a telephone sales call when it's necessary to check information stored on corporate databases, provide additional information not in the standard script, or to complete special comments forms and customer information.

NOTE

Forms and database capabilities may require special software. See Chapters 8 and 9 for details on planning and using intranet forms and creating interactive databases.

Assume you are a telesales representative for a large training company. During a telephone conversation with a prospective customer about a word processing course, you are able to quickly check schedules, course content, and prerequisites from your intranet. Even more important, when your customer inquires about Internet training, you simply point your Web browser to the right location, find the appropriate form, and immediately register the customer.

Contact Lists

Intranets are the perfect location for lists of marketing and sales personnel, including office locations, telephone numbers, and e-mail addresses. A directory of marketing staff by function and product area serves as a handy reference when you need to determine who is the marketing manager for a specific product suite. Having a sales office listing, including account responsibility, is much more convenient than placing calls to the sales office. By including photos, you can personalize the overall effect.

Companies who work with third-party distributors can list authorized distributors according to geographical location, phone number, and contact information. This is of particular advantage for total solution selling, where components from different sources may be required.

Sales Leads

Consider posting or distributing sales leads on your intranet. It's more efficient than traditional methods. Or you may combine leads generated from a variety of sales campaigns.

> **NOTE**
>
> Some usages, such as lead generation or forecasting, which use database retrieval techniques, may require special software. A growing number of companies offer software to address special requirements.

Forecasts

Assuming that you need to provide sales management and finance with monthly or quarterly sales forecasts for strategic business planning, the intranet offers you a more efficient approach than traditional e-mail or hard copy distribution. Additionally, using special database and project management software, you can integrate your forecasts for more efficient planning.

Miscellaneous Postings

Like a bulletin board, your intranet can be used to announce and display a variety of miscellaneous information. It lets you announce special promotions and discounts, sales contests or incentives, major wins, event calendars, and sales representative of the quarter. By scanning in graphics or photos, you can make your intranet bulletin board as eye-catching as you want. Lure sales representatives to win a sales trip with photos of Hawaii or post a picture of the sales representative of the month.

Distributors

You will also find the intranet an effective means of communicating with third-party distributors, resellers, and subsidiaries. As a timely, cost-effective alternative to traditional mailing distributions, consider setting up an intranet site accessible only by these channels. To ensure a successful implementation, the recommended approach is to survey the channels to address their specific concerns, including content, graphics, and other requirements.

16

Human Resources

By Paula Jacobs

Human Resources is a superb candidate for an intranet, given the scope of the HR charter and the amount of paperwork you must process. The intranet makes it easier to distribute benefits information, organizational charts, and policy and procedure manuals. The intranet can also help you respond to routine information requests, manage recruitment and staffing, and track employees' records or salaries. Once you implement your intranet, you'll discover how effortless some of these tasks become.

The intranet offers a more efficient and cost-effective way to answer typical HR requests than the conventional telephone or e-mail tag approach. It saves considerable Human Resource time and money, plus it gives your employees quick access to information such as stock purchase plans, health benefits, and vacation schedules.

Whether you work in a non-profit organization, professional firm, small company, or large corporation, the intranet is a win-win situation. The bottom line is that you and your organization's employees will become much more productive.

Sample Uses in Human Resources

The following represent some typical HR usages:

- Policy and procedure manuals
- Benefits programs

- Stock purchase plans
- Bonus and compensation programs
- Internal job postings
- Job descriptions
- Staffing and recruitment
- Résumés
- Organizational charts
- Contact lists
- Frequently Asked Questions
- Forms
- Holiday schedules
- Employee records

Policy and Procedure Manuals

As one of your first intranet projects, consider placing policy and procedure manuals on your internal web site. Assuming that much of the information is already available electronically, formatting and adding HTML tags should be a relatively easy task. The long-term benefits certainly outweigh the initial time required, which is much less than the traditional production process requires. See Chapter 3, "Formatting Documents," for instructions for formatting and adding HTML tags.

By storing policy and procedure manuals on your intranet, you can eliminate the hassle and expense of regularly updating and distributing material to reflect policy changes or new government regulations. It ensures that employees reference the latest version, makes it easier for employees to find specific information, and simplifies the training of new hires. This usage is especially ideal for worldwide organizations with a variety of handbooks that reflect different state or country regulations.

Perhaps your organization has recently changed its tuition reimbursement policy. Because of the potential impact on the large number of employees registered in evening courses, you need to communicate this across the organization. Simply send an e-mail message to all employees notifying them that a new tuition reimbursement policy is in place and that specifics are detailed in the employee handbook. Then, interested employees can simply link to the Human Resources home page, click the "Employee Handbook," and drill down to the appropriate location. This method is significantly less time-consuming than writing a long memo and it also avoids possible miscommunications.

Benefits Programs

The intranet can help alleviate the challenge of explaining the intricacies of Health Maintenance Organizations (HMOs), medical/dental benefits, 401K programs, and insurance plans. Employees can check this information at their convenience from their desktop or home office computer. This capability saves everyone considerable time and effort, and is especially useful for open enrollment registration.

By adding HTML tags to standard benefits forms, you can make this information available online. Employees can access this information via standard Web browsers.

There are several ways to implement benefits information on the intranet. You can supplement traditional paper benefits packets with online information access or totally eliminate the traditional information packets. When you get started, you should probably use the intranet to simply supplement paper distribution. You should also include benefits information in Frequently Asked Questions.

GTE Corporation, a Stamford,Connecticut-based communications provider and the largest U.S. regional local communications provider, has piloted a program that provides Boston-area employees with up-to-date information on company health insurance plans via the intranet and the use of Health Fair On-Line, an interactive Web resource from MedAccess Corporation in Lexington, Massachusetts (see figs. 16.1 and 16.2). The company has collected information from its seven Boston-area benefits providers, which employees can access using standard Web browsers. Although GTE Corporation does not plan to eliminate the traditional paper packets, this method enables employees to compare instantaneously the costs and benefits of the various programs. The advantage is that employees can use only the information they need and can drill down for additional details not provided in the hard copy.

Currently piloted in the Boston area, this program may also be expanded to 139 locations across the United States.

Fig 16.1
MedAccess provides Boston-area employees with up-to-date information on company health insurance plans via the intranet. (Screen shot courtesy of MedAccess Corporation.)

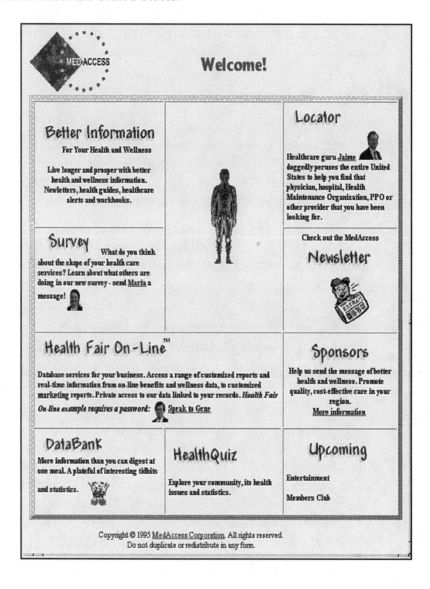

Fig 16.2
Health Fair On-Line, an interactive Web resource, offers information from seven New England-area benefits providers, which employees can access using standard Web browsers. (Screen shot courtesy of MedAccess Corporation.)

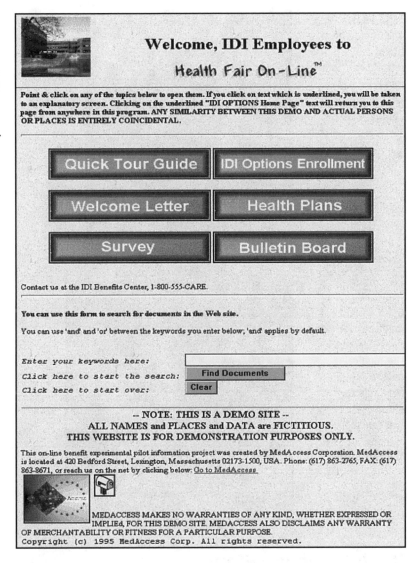

Another example is the Teradyne benefits and medical coverage home pages (see figs. 16.3 and 16.4). The online version of the enrollment process enables employees to review their medical and dental benefits online before choosing a plan for the coming year. The use of online descriptions enables employees to simply click for additional coverage details instead of leafing through paper booklets.

Fig. 16.3
The Teradyne benefits open enrollment home page. (Screen shot courtesy of Teradyne, Inc.)

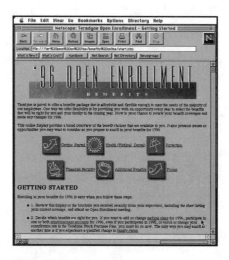

Fig. 16.4
The Teradyne open enrollment medical coverage page describes the medical coverage plans available to employees. (Screen shot courtesy of Teradyne, Inc.)

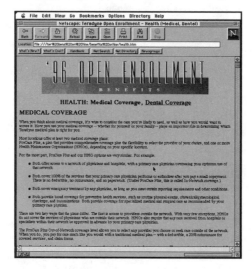

Stock Purchase Plans

If your organization has a company stock purchase program, why not post details on the intranet? Include information such as daily company Wall Street stock prices, how to buy and sell stocks, automatic selling programs, and daily stock prices.

Bonus and Compensation Programs

Communicate to company managers information about special bonus, compensation, and incentive plans. If only certain levels of management are authorized to review this information, set up special security controls to limit access privileges accordingly. See Chapter 12, "Security Issues," for details on security issues.

Internal Job Postings

The intranet is a great place to post internal job postings. It's more practical than using bulletin boards or sending e-mail notifications to internal staff and ensures that all employees receive the same timely notification. By posting internal jobs on the intranet, you don't need to print out and photocopy job announcements or distribute this information to worldwide locations. By setting up hyperlinks to "job descriptions" or "application forms," employees can click to locate more detailed job information or to apply for the specific position.

In some situations, however, you may still need to use bulletin board postings. For example, if not all your company's manufacturing personnel have computer access, you may continue to use bulletin boards at manufacturing plants.

Job Descriptions

Instead of using a hard copy job description manual, it's more efficient to post job descriptions on the intranet. You can include complete descriptions of all current (filled and unfilled) organizational positions, including job classification codes (and explanations), and other pertinent information. For an easy cross-reference, set up hyperlinks to other intranet web pages, such as internal job postings.

Staffing and Recruitment

For routine staffing and recruitment tasks, the intranet is a perfect solution. It's a convenient place to store processes and procedures for annual job reviews, job requisitions, employee grievances, promotions, and other information related to employee staffing and recruitment.

Résumés

Many companies scan résumés into their computer system, using an Optical Character Reader (OCR). Carry this process one step further and place résumés on your intranet site, adding appropriate HTML tags and formatting. Since this information is proprietary, you need to limit access privileges to authorized personnel. See Chapter 12, "Security Issues," for details on implementing security.

Pulse, Inc., a computer consulting firm in Beltsville, Maryland is using a Web-based resume database for its intranet (see fig. 16.5). It uses a custom search engine and WWW search forms. Prospective employees fax or e-mail their résumés to the company's server; an OCR then reads this information and inputs it into the company's database.

Fig. 16.5
This is a sample search engine and search results for Pulse, Inc., resume database. (Screen shot courtesy of Pulse, Inc.)

Organizational Charts

The dynamic nature of the intranet is ideal for organizational charts. They can be easily updated and changed to reflect new organizational structures or staff changes. You can even personalize your organization by adding staff photos. This setup is also useful for employees in other groups who need information about other company groups. Intranet organizational charts are especially helpful in large, multi-national organizations where sheer size impedes effective intra-group communications and where employees spend an inordinate amount of time trying to identify the appropriate internal group for information access or problem resolution.

Photos of all company employees can be found on the intranet site of Geffen Records, a Los Angeles music company. Benefits information, insurance forms, and a variety of other HR materials can also be found on its intranet.

Frequently Asked Questions

Frequently Asked Questions (FAQs) obviously vary across organizations. Listed below are some typical questions (with corresponding answers) that you can post on your intranet.

- Where do I find vacation request forms?
- How many vacation days do I receive after five years of employment?
- What is the sick leave policy?
- Where can I find out information about the company credit union?
- How do I arrange for direct deposit?
- How does my child apply for a corporate National Merit Scholarship?
- What is the procedure to apply for an internal job?
- What is the employee job referral program?
- Is the company an equal opportunity employer?

Forms

If you think about the amount of time spent processing requests for forms, you'll understand why the intranet is an ideal repository for HR forms, especially for organizations with many locations. It makes it easier for employees to locate the appropriate form, ensures use of the latest version, and saves everyone considerable time. Since you don't need to reproduce or reprint forms to accommodate slight policy changes, you also economize on typesetting and printing costs.

You can set up hyperlinks between a form and corresponding material. It's an efficient way to cross-reference forms described in the "FAQs" section. The following forms may be appropriate for your HR intranet:

- Direct deposit applications
- Credit union enrollment
- Employee stock purchase
- Tuition reimbursement
- Vacation requests
- Health and insurance benefits
- Maternity and sick leave
- Job requisitions
- Internal job transfers
- Evaluations
- Questionnaires

Contact Lists

Simply posting the names, functions, and phone numbers of HR personnel can be a tremendous time saver. It helps employees immediately locate the HR representative who can help them with their immediate situation or problem.

Holiday Schedules

Post annual company holidays or manufacturing shutdowns on your intranet. It enables employees to plan their vacation schedules accordingly.

Employee Records

By setting up special security privileges, you can give authorized HR personnel access to employee records. It represents a secure way of sharing confidential information. This capability is also useful for Human Resources Managers who need to analyze salary histories and hiring patterns for planning purposes.

NOTE

Special database query tools may be required. It's also necessary to set special access controls to assign access privileges. See Chapter 12, "Security Issues," for more information.

17

Education and Training

By Paula Jacobs

The intranet offers numerous creative possibilities for corporate training departments, universities, public and private schools, and other organizations that deliver training, especially in campus environments. It's the perfect storage repository for curricula and courseware, lesson plans, training manuals, catalogs, presentations and videos, bibliographies, registration forms and materials, student lists, and class schedules.

Use of the intranet enhances communications, promotes faculty collaboration, eliminates duplication of effort, and provides accurate, up-to-date information. The intranet allows last-minute changes and revisions to be made that were traditionally difficult to implement and communicate. Plus, with the use of hyperlinks, related materials can easily be cross-referenced.

Colleges and universities that are implementing long-distance learning over the Internet can combine this new educational medium with the intranet. For example, instructors and students can exchange e-mail over the Internet. Yet, course materials, lecture notes, and assignments can be posted on the school's intranet for access only by students registered in the specific course.

Finally, cash-strapped educational organizations will find that the intranet represents an extremely cost-effective solution. Since materials are available electronically, the intranet helps reduce printing costs.

Uses in Education and Training

While actual usage depends on the nature of your organization, the following are some representative uses:

- Curriculum materials and courseware
- Lesson plans
- Training manuals
- Catalogs
- Presentations
- Videos
- Reading lists
- Student and faculty lists
- Class schedules
- Frequently Asked Questions
- Forms and questionnaires
- Bulletin Boards
- UseNet news

Curriculum Materials and Courseware

The intranet enables you to streamline the time-consuming, ongoing process of developing and revising curriculum materials and courseware. It facilitates curriculum development by project teams, including those with team members at remote locations. For example, the intranet makes it easier for project members to share suggestions and comments, without spending time participating in face-to-face meetings or telephone conference calls.

Electronic distribution eliminates the tight production time frames of printed materials. Once you implement your intranet, you'll find it easier to distribute the latest curriculum materials to instructors at satellite campuses.

Another advantage is the opportunity to share materials with other instructors. Assume that you are teaching a Russian II language class. In order to plan your curriculum material, you want to review the Russian I curriculum.

Or as a European history instructor, as part of a cross-discipline approach, the ability to check the German literature curriculum may be handy for curriculum planning.

The University of Missouri School of Medicine uses the intranet for teaching and research. In addition to course material, it also houses an image bank helpful to medical students.

An intranet provides an ideal clearinghouse for research on a particular specialty. The University of Kansas Department of Special Education has a comprehensive set of research data, ranging from listings of textbooks to descriptions of appropriate technology for people with disabilities. By clicking a particular topic, such as learning disabilities, users can cross-reference related research, such as Handicap News Archives, disabilities educational resources, and examples of specific programs (see fig. 17.1).

Fig. 17.1
The University of Kansas has educational resources online. Shown here are some resources for research on disabilities.

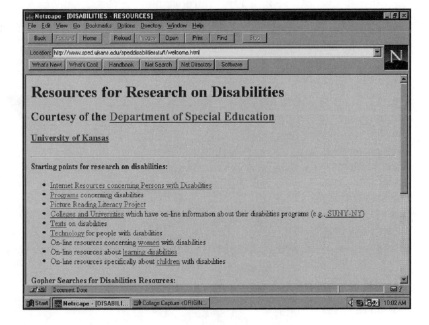

Lesson Plans

By placing lesson plans on the intranet, you can collaborate more effectively with other faculty members. This approach is especially well-suited to team teaching and situations where several faculty members are teaching the same topic and need to deliver consistency. And since you can access the intranet from your home PC, you can use this material when you are preparing lessons in the evening.

Perhaps you are teaching a unit on World War II. By using the intranet, you can liven up the quality of your teaching by sharing audio and graphics clips, in addition to textual lesson plans. For example, audio clips may include speeches by President Roosevelt and General Eisenhower, while there may be graphics clips showing the Battle of Normandy. Additionally, by drilling down and downloading the lesson plans, you'll find it easy to modify them from year to year or for different ability levels. In any case, the interactive nature of the intranet promotes teaching creativity and mutual cooperation.

The Owen Graduate School of Business at Vanderbilt University has placed a variety of course materials online (see figs. 17.2, 17.3, and 17.4).

Fig. 17.2
The title page for the course "Management 352—Economic, Social, and Legal Environment of Business" includes links to the Vanderbilt University and the Owen Graduate School of Business home pages.

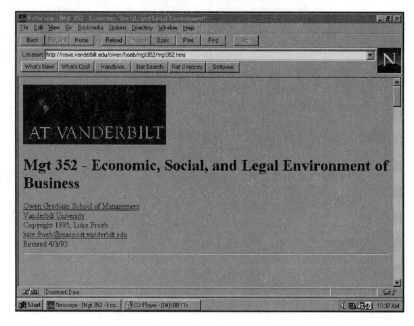

Fig. 17.3
Term papers,
evaluation
criteria, lecture
notes, and grades
are provided
online.

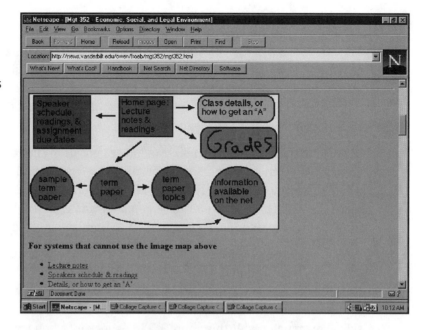

Fig. 17.4
Lecture Notes
including assign-
ments, discussion
questions, and
reference material
are also included
online.

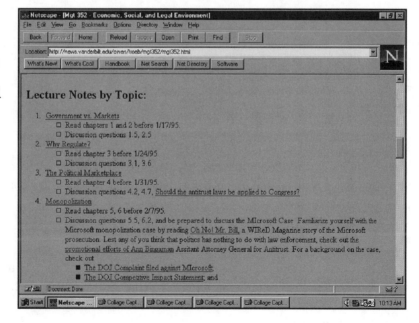

Training Manuals

The intranet eases the pain and expense of updating training manuals to reflect product and organizational changes. It is an especially handy tool for sales training manuals that need to be revised to accommodate company reorganizations, new product introductions, minor product enhancements, and shifts in corporate strategy.

The use of the intranet can help training organizations increase the effectiveness of formal training courses. For example, several months later, a student who has attended a word processing class may want to check how to format a table. It's much easier to refer to the online training manual than to sift through lengthy training documentation to find one specific paragraph.

Sales training organizations find that the intranet helps improve review and follow-up, while reducing information overload. After completing a crash one-week training course, a new sales hire can review relevant material by simply clicking the right manual and drilling down to product specifics. Consider how much easier this approach is, especially when you are still on an organizational learning curve.

By adding audio or video, you can increase the effectiveness of your training programs. For example, audio references may help you clarify difficult technical areas.

Catalogs

The intranet is a perfect fit for universities and corporations that produce and distribute course catalogs. It enables you to incorporate unanticipated, last-minute revisions that reflect instructor changes and course cancellations or additions.

The use of the intranet may also help you reduce the number of printed catalogs. For example, in a university setting where all students have computer access, you may choose to distribute printed catalogs only upon request. The result may be a tremendous cost-savings. Additionally, with on-demand access, students can browse through catalogs at their convenience from their dormitory rooms.

Consider creating hyperlinks between the catalog and related material. For example, when you click a university catalog description of a French translation course, you can access required textbooks, bibliographies, and instructors.

Adding images is a great way to promote a course or an extra-curricular educational experience. By clicking the course French Impressionism, the student can interactively view sample impressionist paintings to be discussed in the course. Similarly, the use of images can heighten interest for a study-abroad program.

Perhaps you are responsible for developing and distributing a semi-annual, internal company training catalog. Because not all employees have computer access, you may still choose to produce a printed version. However, the intranet provides you with the option of reducing the actual number of printed copies. Additionally, you can create hyperlinks to class schedules and other related company material.

Presentations

Presentations can be easily created, updated, and shared via the intranet for a considerable savings of time and effort. This capability is ideal for instructors in corporate training environments and academic institutions, and enables you to mix-and-match material from existing presentations. For example, suppose there is only time allotted for a 10-minute presentation; simply download the lengthy "Understanding Networking Technology" presentation and use the appropriate overheads.

An additional advantage is presentation consistency. Suppose your corporation has sales training facilities in Chicago, New York, Los Angeles, Dallas, and Atlanta. Don't you want your instructors to deliver the same training message to corporate customers in these different locations? This capability also saves your instructors time, since instead of spending time "re-inventing the wheel," they can concentrate on preparing an effective class or workshop.

Videos

By adding video clips to your presentations and courseware, you can greatly enhance the quality of the educational experience. Because of the speed of the Local Area Network, video can run quickly on your intranet, assuming you have the appropriate hardware and software.

Reading Lists

For environments where students have intranet access, consider placing reading lists on the intranet. For example, in a university environment, you may find this a more efficient distribution mechanism than the use of hard copy lists. With the intranet, reading lists are easier to revise, plus you can make them available before the semester begins for students who want to gain a head start on their reading. Other faculty members can check reading lists against their own class assignments.

Student and Faculty Lists

Why not put lists of students and faculty on your intranet site? It's simpler than reproducing and distributing these lists manually. This method certainly saves time and effort when there are last-minute revisions.

Additionally, consider supplementing faculty and student lists with online biographies and photos. Using the online course catalog, for example, students can click the instructor's name and view the faculty member's biography and picture. Similarly, by functioning as an online class yearbook, the intranet can help students in a particular class become better acquainted.

Class Schedules

By posting class schedules on your intranet, you can communicate dynamic information quickly to employees and students, especially those at different office or campus locations. This solution addresses situations where unpredictable enrollment and last-minute course cancellations or rescheduling are common. This method is a better form of communication than the standard bulletin, and allows students to revise their programs accordingly. When travel plans are involved, the intranet enables students to make revisions before unnecessary travel expenses have been incurred.

Frequently Asked Questions

When you post Frequently Asked Questions on the intranet, you'll find that staff and student time can be used more effectively. Another way to increase productivity is to create hyperlinks between Frequently Asked Questions, catalogs, and forms. Here are some common Frequently Asked Questions that you may want to use:

- How do I register for a class?
- What is the last date to register for a class?
- Is there a late registration fee?
- What is the procedure for dropping a class?
- What is the penalty for dropping a course?
- What is the cutoff date for adding or changing a course?
- Can I cross-register in another department?
- Does my manager need to approve each course?
- Can I cross-charge the course to my corporate department?

Forms and Questionnaires

Posting forms and questionnaires on the intranet is one way to increase productivity. It's more efficient than paper distribution for students, faculty, and staff, and certainly less expensive than printing hard copy forms.

Typical forms suitable for your intranet include:

- Course registration
- Course withdrawal
- Book ordering
- Questionnaires

Perhaps you need a course registration form. In the past, you would need to pick up a printed form from the office secretary. The intranet eliminates the need to make a special trip, place a phone call, and spend money printing a variety of forms.

By posting questionnaires on the intranet, you can solicit student feedback on instructors, course content, and other types of input. Typically, a student will use a Web browser to input answers to an HTML-generated form. You'll find this method quicker and more efficient than using traditional paper questionnaires.

The University of Edinburgh is piloting a web-based questionnaire program. Instructors submit a simple text template that is automatically converted into a forms-based questionnaire. Once results are collected, they can be returned in a choice of formats.

Bulletin Boards

The bulletin board—the staple of the educational and training environment—can still be used on your intranet, albeit in a different format. By adding an electronic bulletin board, your students and instructors can continue to enjoy this familiar educational tool and post the messages of their choice. For example, your intranet bulletin board can highlight "student of the month," or "teacher of the month," as well as special projects, sports events, and other items of interest to your school and community. Or consider a special bulletin board for teachers —a virtual teachers' lounge—where teachers can conduct discussions, make comments, or share their gripes.

UseNet News

Download Internet UseNet News discussions and other Internet educational resources that pertain to your organization's area or your faculty's interest. It will keep your faculty updated on current trends, while reducing web-cruising time required to locate educational materials relevant to a specific subject area. One way to implement this program is to poll faculty members about their resource requirements and preferred topics.

18

Operations and Administration

By Paula Jacobs

Whether you work in a non-profit setting or a corporate environment, an intranet can help streamline a variety of operations and administration functions. Businesses, healthcare providers, educational institutions, government agencies, and non-profit organizations can all realize significant benefits from an intranet site.

One way is to create a general Operations and Administration home page with links to functional departments and perhaps to other company intranet web servers. Each of these departments can use the intranet for organizational charts, contact lists, bulletin boards, Frequently Asked Questions, procedures, forms, calendaring, project discussions, and online approvals.

Obviously, you must adapt this setup to fit your organizational structure. Since Operations and Administration encompasses a number of functional areas, how you actually implement your intranet depends on the size and nature of your organization. In any case, it's important to develop a regular updating schedule and process, determine who in your group will be responsible for updating content, and how often updating will occur. You also need to determine the format for providing this material—for example, completely new documents or simply updates of existing material. To ensure consistency, these decisions should relate to your organization's intranet plan.

Uses in Operations and Administration

Using the above scheme, the Operations and Administration home page (an example is shown in fig. 18.1) may point to the following general areas:

- Company/organization information
- Employee information
- Policies and procedures
- Facilities
- Library
- Sales/ordering administration
- Purchasing
- Contract administration
- Traffic control

Fig. 18.1
A typical Operations and Administration home page. This Eli Lilly home page contains hyperlinks to other company departments. (Screen shot courtesy of Eli Lilly and Company.)

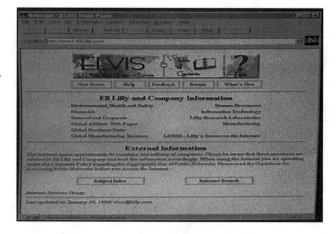

Company/Organization Information

Company/Organization Information is a way to provide general company background material, such as department listings, company or organization history, organizational charts, the corporate telephone book, a listing of corporate locations, and company news. You may also want to provide links to Corporate Communications, Human Resources, and other departmental web servers.

Publisher Simon & Schuster's internal company home page includes company and product information, company news, a site map, and a worldwide employee telephone directory (see figs. 18.2 and 18.3). Using their web browsers, employees can easily look up an employee name and telephone number. And they can easily modify and update incorrect information.

Fig. 18.2
An example of an intranet-based database is Simon & Schuster's Corporate Telephone Directory. In this case, employees are able to look up phone numbers online, and the numbers are kept much more current than in printed directories. (Screen shot courtesy of Simon and Schuster.)

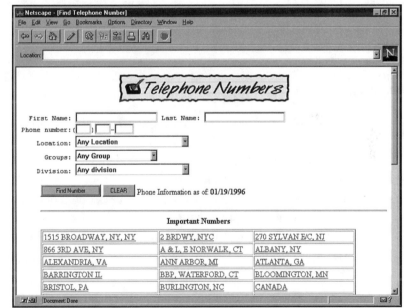

Fig. 18.3
Helper applications can be used to display documents that do not exist natively in HTML, or contain formatting that HTML does not support. Here, a desktop-published document (the company newsletter) can be viewed as it was originally designed. (Screen shot courtesy of Simon and Schuster.)

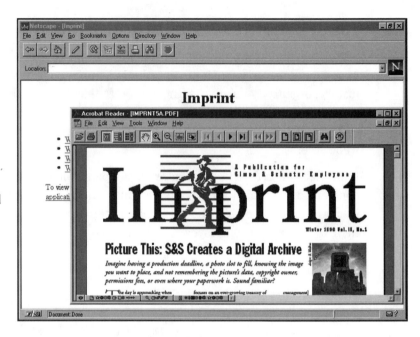

Employee Information

Employee Information is a handy way to provide general types of information. It can include everything from a listing of intranet resources and descriptions of corporate resources to "hot" news and corporate bulletins, blood drive notices, cafeteria lunch menus, profiles of the "employee of the month," Frequently Asked Questions, building maps, and a myriad of assorted information, including company merchandise. You may also want to provide links to Human Resources, Corporate Communications, and other key areas. To bring this information to life, simply add the appropriate graphics and images.

Perhaps corporate headquarters is resurfacing the main parking lot and employees need to change their parking patterns. Instead of distributing a detailed memo, just send a brief e-mail message and refer employees to the intranet.

If your company sells merchandise, such as sweatshirts and cups with company logos, consider using the intranet as an advertising and ordering vehicle. Use graphics to depict the merchandise, which your employees can order by completing the proper intranet form. You'll find this approach more efficient than a company store.

Geffen Records, a Los Angeles-based music company, maintains a list of its recording artists, works in progress, and schedules. The company's intranet also includes links to Internet sites describing musical bands and their performance schedules.

Facilities

Instead of distributing hard-copy inventory and equipment lists, status reports, facilities maps, and contact information, Facilities can maintain this material on an intranet. By simply drilling down to the appropriate spot, you can quickly locate the precise data you require. Since this information is subject to frequent change, updates and revisions are easy to implement.

If you are a large company, consider placing a detailed building map to show office locations. Similarly, companies with multiple locations can post travel directions, including maps showing access from major highways and airports.

A company might, for example, post a range of facilities information on its worldwide intranet. It could include maps with schematics of each company facility, contact names (for example, whom to contact for a lighting problem), and a facilities guide with information about the mail system, securities, and building facilities.

Policies and Procedures

Chances are your organization has a variety of policies and procedures in place, including security information, reporting security breaches, parking regulations, emergency evacuation procedures, travel arrangements and allowances/reimbursement, meeting rooms and video conference reservations, and other general procedures.

As an alternative to a printed employee procedures manual, provide this information via an intranet. This approach is more cost-effective, easier to update, and can help reduce potential miscommunications that occur when employees refer to out-of-date manuals.

Suppose you are a new employee scheduled to leave on your first company business trip. By checking the intranet, you can find out how to order airplane tickets, make hotel and rental car arrangements, and obtain a cash advance. You simply download the appropriate forms, fill in the information, and send the travel request to your company's travel coordinator. By completing this information yourself, you don't have to worry that hotel reservations were accidentally made for Springfield, Massachusetts instead of Springfield, Illinois. Since the intranet also includes a description of the travel allowance and reimbursement policy, you won't make accidental mistakes. And since reimbursement forms are also on the intranet, you can simply download them when you return—without bothering your administrative or managerial staff.

Library

The intranet is an excellent tool to promote greater use of your library. It can help you attract new patrons who previously have not had the time to make a physical trip to the library, while improving service to your current library customers.

Use the intranet as a vehicle to inform your employees about the latest library book or magazine acquisitions. Produce a list of new books and periodicals, which you can update on a monthly basis. Similarly, develop a master list of all library materials.

Other practical ways your library can use the intranet include:

● Database of resources downloaded from the Internet that pertain to your business

● Description of library databases available to your employees

● Summary of cooperative and inter-library relationships available to your employees

● Summary of recent magazine articles pertaining to your company's area

● List of available videos, audio tapes, CDs, and demonstration software

● Book reviews

● Summary of recent press releases by competitive vendors

● Summary of competitive information

Sales/Ordering Administration

Sales Administration can use the intranet to increase staff productivity. The intranet provides an efficient way to streamline model submission and ordering processing, including improving information flow across the organization. For example, by including project release dates, schedules, status reports, and other relevant information, internal miscommunication problems can be significantly reduced.

By storing forms and general information on the intranet, your staff can devote less time to answering routine requests for information. Depending on the nature of your organization, the following items may be appropriate:

- Price submission forms
- Model submission forms
- Ordering forms
- Questionnaires
- Booking/ordering/shipping procedures
- International ordering
- Shipping third-party materials
- Fulfillment procedures
- Frequently Asked Questions
- Key contacts

With the appropriate software, you may set up a link between your internal web server and corporate model/pricing/ordering databases. For example, assuming that the appropriate (commercial or in-house) software is on your web server, you can use your web browser to issue a query and access the appropriate data. This capability is useful for business planning, project management, and the sharing of data between finance and sales administration groups.

NOTE

You will probably want to limit database query access to authorized individuals in Operations and Administration.

Typical Frequently Asked Questions include:

- What is the price submission procedure?
- What is the lead time for submitting a price?
- What is the step-by-step model submission procedure?
- How do I change a price or obsolete a model number and associated pricing?
- How will I know when the order is booked/shipped?
- How does each group receive revenue credit?
- What is the ordering fulfillment process?
- How do I change/cancel an order?
- How will my customer know when the order will ship?
- What special steps need to be implemented for international orders?
- How do I notify a third-party vendor that an order has been booked?

Purchasing

Purchasing can use the intranet to streamline the requisition and ordering function for improved communications with other groups. For example, you may include lists of vendors, subcontractors, and contract agencies, requisition and ordering forms, purchasing contracts, status reports, and related information. To increase productivity and alleviate miscommunication, consider posting Frequently Asked Questions (and answers) such as the following:

- How do I order equipment and office supplies?
- How do I submit a purchasing request?
- What is the approval cycle for ordering office supplies?
- What are the rules for using a third-party contractor?
- What third-party contractors and agencies are on the approved vendor list?
- How can I use a contractor not on the approved list?
- What items/services are put out to bid?
- How long does the purchasing approval process take?
- Whom should I contact in purchasing to initiate a request?

Contract Administration

Third-party contracts, descriptions of the contract process, GSA Schedules and deadlines, and other materials that are needed can be placed on your intranet for easy access across the organization. The ability to "drill down" enables you to find precisely the information you need quickly, an especially handy feature when reviewing lengthy contracts. Another advantage is the ability to share information interactively among members of different groups and departments.

Traffic Control

Traffic Control can use the intranet to track your company's vehicles, schedules, and package deliveries. If this information is already in company databases, you can use your web browser to query the database for status updates.

19

Legal and Finance

By Paula Jacobs

An intranet can help Legal and Finance departments monitor the status of legal and financial projects, track key financial data and billing, and communicate processes and requirements across the organization. It's also a convenient repository to store electronic resources downloaded from the Internet or external database systems. Whether you work for a large corporation, a non-profit organization, or an independent law or accounting firm, you'll find that an intranet dramatically transforms your work habits, improving administrative efficiencies. An intranet is an especially effective tool if you have a number of affiliate offices at different locations.

However, because of the highly confidential nature of legal and financial material, appropriate security measures are essential. You may want to strongly consider implementing private web servers, protected by internal firewalls. See Chapter 12, "Security Issues," for details on implementing an intranet security program.

In any case, the first step is to review the purpose of your intranet. Is it to exchange information within your department? Will you share confidential data with other groups? Do you also need to provide general information to the entire organization?

Your objectives should determine how you implement your system. For example, if the system is exclusively for intra-department exchange, then a private intranet web server is probably the best approach. If you also need to provide answers to Frequently Asked Questions, consider also making this information available. Remember, from your user's perspective, it doesn't matter where the information resides, provided it is accessible.

Uses in Legal and Finance

The following are some representative uses for legal and finance:

● Contracts

● Legal briefs

● Electronic law library

● Approvals

● Accounting and billing procedures

● P&L reporting

● Project accounting and activity management

● Budgets and forecasts

● Reports

● Frequently Asked Questions

● Organizational charts

● Corporate databases

Contracts

Storing standard contract forms on your intranet site is one way to save time and money, while providing on-demand access. It's easier and less expensive to update electronic contract forms than paper versions, storage space is not required, and employees have convenient access to contracts. Additionally, by simply drilling down to the appropriate location, it's easier to find what you need than sifting through reams of paperwork.

Legal Briefs

Legal briefs and cases pending can be stored on an intranet as a way to share information with colleagues and engage in interactive discussions. If you use Lotus Notes as a discussion tool, consider integrating it within your intranet environment. For example, together with Lotus InterNotes Web Publisher, you can store these discussions for future reference (see Chapter 26, "InterNotes Web Publisher).

Electronic Law Library

Use your intranet to create an electronic law library tailored to your organization's requirements. For example, download public Internet legal resources, including UseNet newsgroups, key contact lists, and other information for a custom online library. Or, create a library that includes a comprehensive listing of legal resources, including phone numbers, e-mail addresses, and web site locations.

No matter whether you specialize in general, family, corporate, immigration, environmental, entertainment, or another specialty area of law, there are external Internet resources you can integrate into your electronic intranet library. A sample of such resources includes online resources on antitrust policies, legal journals, U.S. tax codes, and trademark information.

Vanderbilt University has a wealth of online information on antitrust policies. It includes information about antitrust cases, as well as links to related legal information. For example, it includes information about mergers, price-fixing, and vertical restraints, including lists of cases, news items, and research topics (see fig. 19.1).

Fig. 19.1
This online
resource is based
at Vanderbilt,
describing
research on
antitrust policies.

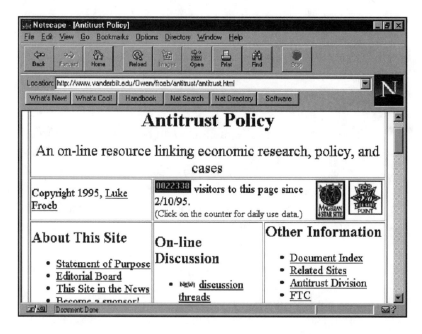

For example, Cornell University Law School has placed numerous legal
resources online on its web site (**http://www.law.cornell.edu**), such as
the Uniforum Commercial Code and Victim Compensation articles (see
fig. 19.2). Numerous special interest legal resources, academic journals, and
legal publications such as the *Harvard Journal of Law and Technology*
(**http:/www.studorg.law.harvard.edu/jolt**) and the *National Law Journal* (**http://www.ljextra.com/nlj**) can be downloaded into your electronic
library, according to your area of interest and expertise. You can also provide
a listing of articles in the latest journals, such as the *Intellectual Property*
magazine, which is available on the Internet (**http://www.portal/com/
recorder**).

Also available at the Cornell site is information about recent court decisions, as
well as a summary of decisions made during the past five years (see fig. 19.3).
Users can access this information by referencing the appropriate topic or date.

Fig. 19.2
The Uniforum
Commercial Code
(Articles 1-9
General Provision)
is available at
Cornell University
Law School's web
site.

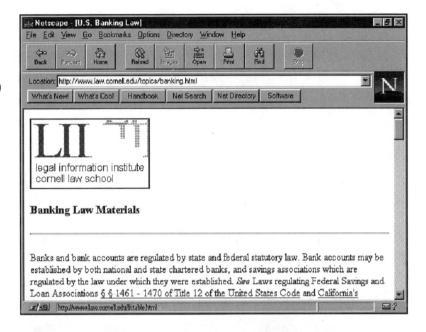

Fig. 19.3
The Cornell site
has resources for
exploring U.S.
Supreme Court
decisions—
searchable by
index and key-
words.

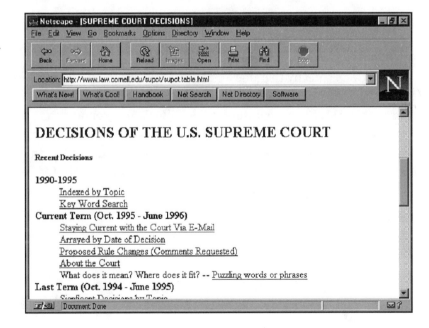

Approvals

An intranet can help streamline the approval process, while providing a centralized online repository. It provides an excellent tracking mechanism, is an efficient way to handle multiple levels of approval, and helps eliminate traditional paperwork drudgery.

Accounting and Billing Procedures

Improve information flow about the accounting and billing process by using your intranet as a key communications tool. It's a convenient place to post procedures about invoicing, third-party billing procedures, vendor royalty codes, and special vendor payment procedures, internal revenue credit assignments, and other operational matters.

P&L Reporting

For P&L reporting, you will find your intranet an efficient alternative to traditional e-mail or paper report distribution. With an intranet, you can be assured timely and successful delivery of P&L reports to the appropriate managers.

One company that delivers all its P&L and Book/Ship reports over the intranet is Lawson Software (see fig. 19.4). The Minneapolis-based company places all of its monthly P&L and Book/Ship reports on its intranet system, which department managers can access with a web browser for actual report views of P&L data. Since all authorized managers have on-demand access, there's no need to worry that e-mail files will be rejected because a file is too long or an e-mail inbox is too full.

Fig. 19.4
A sample Book/
Ship report that
is accessible via
Lawson Software's
intranet. (Screen
shot courtesy of
Lawson Software.)

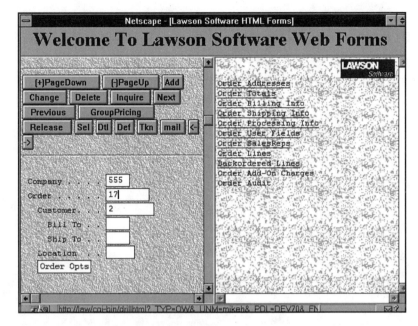

Project Accounting and Activity Management

An intranet also provides a solution for a full range of project accounting and activity management functions, assuming you have the appropriate financial software. Since you use a standard web browser instead of client financial software on every workstation, your cost of ownership will be lower in a client/server environment. Another advantage is that you don't need to install client financial software on every workstation, since the browser will be your only client software.

Whether it's reviewing cost models, monitoring overhead costs, or collecting financial data, an intranet can help streamline financial activity management for process-oriented businesses. Intranets simplify the review of detailed financial reports, providing a convenient viewing mechanism to analyze data according to different categories. For example, using your web browser, you can link to different financial screens and conduct "what-if" scenarios.

Lawson Software has successfully implemented an integrated accounts payable and receivables system on its intranet. It contains a completely integrated customer information database that includes everything from information about the customer implementation to contract renewal information. A set of financial modules also provides full financial activity management, collecting the financial and non-financial effects of executing a particular event. For example, Lawson Software is able to capture information such as overhead or installation costs. Using web browsers to access the financials on the company's intranet, Lawson Software's managers can easily analyze data from different perspectives, such as a financial calendar or units of labor cost. Web browsers enable company managers to access inquiry forms on their intranet for information required to make the proper budget and allocation decisions (see fig. 19.5).

Fig. 19.5
A sample purchase requisition form generated via Lawson Software's Open Enterprise Applications. (Screen shot courtesy of Lawson Software.)

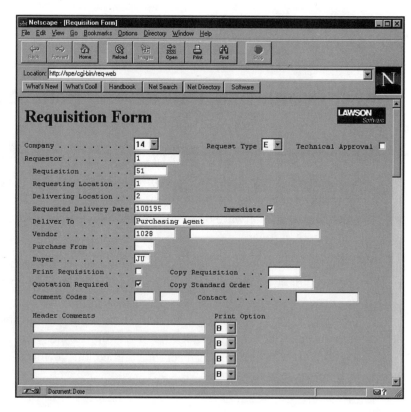

Budgets and Forecasts

An intranet allows your managers to post budget reports, information on spending against budget, and forecasts of future spending. It's also a convenient tool to notify managers where spending is exceeding budget. This enables you to keep managers up-to-date, and also allows managers within your department to have simultaneous access to the same information. Since it's easy to drill down to a specific location, it's easy to check certain information. In addition, by setting up hyperlinks between budgets and forecasts, you can easily measure whether you are spending according to plan.

Reports

Instead of processing and distributing routine paper reports, place this information on your intranet. For example, your managers will find their intranet a convenient way to review monthly phone usage bills.

Assuming that proper security measures have been implemented, an intranet offers an alternative to e-mail—an especially handy capability for organizations that rely on a variety of disparate e-mail systems. Use an intranet to disseminate confidential financial reports, financial research, and presentations to your key managers. Financial managers can scan or review specific information more quickly by drilling down to the appropriate location.

Set up hyperlinks between different areas to provide your managers with detailed financial information. For example, your corporate controller may need to check budget or expense reports for different company groups.

Frequently Asked Questions

By posting answers to Frequently Asked Questions on your intranet, you can reduce the time devoted to routine requests for information. Appropriate legal questions may include:

- How do I initiate a trademark search?
- What are the regulations for reproducing a company logo?
- What external documents require legal approval?

● How do I obtain legal approval for a marketing brochure?

● What is the process to initiate a legal agreement with a third-party strategic vendor?

● Where are standard legal contract forms stored?

● What is the company's non-disclosure policy?

● How do I amend a standard legal contract?

Appropriate Finance questions include:

● Where do I find a list of financial analysts assigned to different business units?

● What is the financial approval process?

● What are the procedures to pay royalties to third-party vendors?

● How does my group receive revenue credit?

● What is the company's project accounting process?

Organizational Charts

If you work in the Legal or Finance department of a large organization, place organizational charts, including staff photos, on your intranet. Modifications and updates are easier to perform than with traditional methods. The use of intranet organizational charts also streamlines communications across the organization.

Corporate Databases

With the appropriate application software, you can use your intranet to query financial or legal data stored in centralized databases. By simply clicking your web browser you can access the appropriate financial information.

20

Manufacturing

By Paula Jacobs

Whether your manufacturing organization consists of a single facility or plants dispersed across corners of the globe, an intranet can improve communications in ways never before imaginable. If your company has many different computer and e-mail systems, the intranet may represent the only common mechanism for exchanging information within the organization.

The intranet allows you to share everything from routine information to critical business data. Like a bulletin board, all sorts of local manufacturing announcements—cafeteria menus, work schedules, blood drives, and retirement parties—can be posted for quick and easy viewing. Share information about standardized processes and procedures to employees worldwide. Increase productivity by storing service and maintenance manuals online. Or communicate with the rest of your company by setting up hyperlinks between manufacturing and the corporate home page.

Planning Your Site

When planning your intranet site, it's important to set realistic expectations and clearly defined objectives (see Chapter 14, "Corporate Communications"). Don't expect the intranet to be the substitute for your existing Materials Resource Planning (MRP) or Enterprise Resource Planning (ERP) system. Instead, review some of the suggested intranet usages described later in this chapter and determine how you can apply them to help your organization enhance communications, increase productivity, and save money.

Similarly, it's important to develop a regular updating schedule, such as on a monthly basis. In a manufacturing area, this consistency is critical.

Additionally, define your specific, unique requirements. For example, consider these questions:

- Will there be a primary Manufacturing intranet web server with links to other Manufacturing web servers? Or will there be simply one centralized Manufacturing intranet web server?
- What will be the key elements on your home page?
- Does Manufacturing have a special logo? If so, will you include the image on your home page?
- What language(s) will be supported? Do you need to provide links between English and other languages?
- Will you give all employees intranet privileges? If so, how will you provide them with PC and intranet access?
- How often will you update material? What will be the update schedule?
- What provisions will you make for intranet training?
- Will you eventually establish links between the intranet and existing manufacturing databases?

Recognizing that not all manufacturing employees have universal computer access, it may be necessary to make some practical accommodations. In this situation, use the intranet selectively to supplement rather than replace traditional communications. Or, perhaps, if your secretarial staff has intranet privileges, assign them the responsibility of downloading and distributing specific material on a regular schedule.

The sample home page shown in figure 20.1 contains links to key Manufacturing areas, such as Product Design and Development, Suppliers, ISO Certification, Forms, Parts Lists, Project Schedules, Forecasts, and other information sources. By clicking Total-Quality Management buttons, users gain quick access to volumes of data.

Fig. 20.1
This is a sample
Manufacturing
home page for
Widget Company.

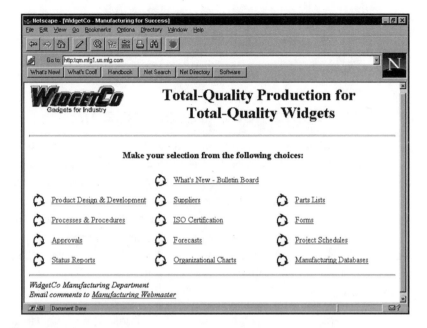

Manufacturing Usages

A typical Manufacturing intranet site provides links to an assortment of product design specifications, supplier information, parts lists, forms and schedules, ISO standards, and other information relevant to your Manufacturing organization.

- Product design and development
- Bulletin boards
- Supplier information
- Parts lists
- Processes and procedures
- ISO certification standards
- Forms
- Approvals
- Forecasts
- Project schedules
- Status reports

● Service and Maintenance Manuals
● Organizational charts
● Manufacturing databases

Product Design and Development

For organizations with geographically distributed manufacturing engineering groups, the intranet offers the perfect collaboration mechanism for manufacturing product design and development. By maintaining product design specifications, technology information, or CAD-CAM illustrations on your intranet, you can increase the productivity of your engineering staff. Additionally, the use of the intranet, together with the implementation of proper security procedures, is infinitely more secure than traditional methods of sharing data and files, such as the e-mail and/or file transfer protocol (ftp) transmission.

Lucent Technologies has successfully boosted manufacturing productivity by setting up an intranet behind its corporate firewall system. Engineers and scientists at the New Jersey-based company use the intranet to access the internal technical library that contains extensive reference material on the electronics industry. The intranet is also used to solve manufacturing problems. With images of microscopic silicon Integrated Circuit (IC) defects catalogued in a database with information on the defect and problem resolution; manufacturing engineers at different plant locations can scan the database for potential solutions when yield problems reach a production line. Finally, sales and application engineering staff use the intranet to access product and design-rule information, including the status of factory lots via the intranet. The home page for Delco Electronic's manufacturing department is shown in figure 20.2.

Bulletin Boards

The intranet can function as a bulletin board to provide a variety of communications. For example, the bulletin board at your Ohio plant may include announcements of employee promotions and retirements, birthdays, manufacturing training classes, and special calendar events. Bulletin boards can also be used to distribute software, manufacturing designs, and manufacturing product information. There may be similar intranet bulletin boards for your Michigan, California, and Ireland facilities. And despite the local information appeal, you'll find the intranet bulletin board a wonderful way to promote your programs worldwide.

Fig. 20.2
Manufacturing technology teams at Delco use the intranet to share information to assist in the manufacturing process. (Screen shot courtesy of Delco Electronics Company.)

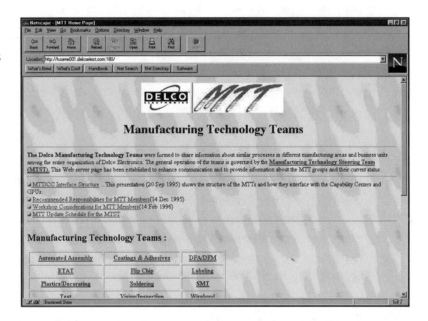

NOTE

If you are using your bulletin board to distribute board designs or other confidential material, it's important to set up appropriate security mechanisms, such as multiple layers of password protection. See Chapter 12, "Security Issues," for more information.

Supplier Information

If your organization has relationships with multiple suppliers, the intranet provides you with an efficient mechanism to maintain and update supplier status information. This capability is especially important for companies with numerous plant locations.

Similarly, you can use your intranet for one-way supplier communication. For example, by using the Internet, your suppliers can submit product and other specifications by ftping these files to your intranet site. However, since your intranet site is protected by a firewall security system, only authorized company personnel will be able to access this information.

Perhaps your Minnesota plant needs to order some electronic components. Your local purchasing agent in California checks the latest supplier list on your intranet and orders components from the approved supplier. If your intranet has an external Internet connection, you can also e-mail the ordering forms directly to your supplier.

Parts Lists

Use the intranet as an online parts list or catalog, including part numbers, descriptions, specifications, and photographs. This system makes it easier for your engineers to locate and order the correct part. It's also simpler to revise the material to reflect new or obsolete parts and you eliminate the time and expense of updating this material regularly. Meanwhile, on-demand access to accurate information eliminates the chance of ordering a wrong or obsolete part.

Suppose you are a manufacturing engineer for an automobile manufacturer. You need to reorder a certain engine part, and remember the supplier's name but not the part number. Call up the Parts List on your intranet. Using your web browser, click the supplier's name, then drill down to the appropriate location. And, since you can match the part description with the stored image, you can quickly verify that you have selected the right part.

Processes and Procedures

Instead of printing and distributing hard copy processes and procedures' regulations, place this information on your intranet site. It saves the time and expense of producing printed materials, is easier to update, and simplifies the distribution of consistent information to geographically dispersed manufacturing locations.

ISO Certification Standards

For organizations undergoing a time-consuming International Standards Organization (ISO) certification, the intranet can help streamline this rigorous process. Include ISO forms, procedures, status information, schedules, and project milestones on your intranet for easy employee access. The advantage is that your employees can easily download the necessary forms and drill down to review specific ISO procedures instead of reading lengthy paper documentation. You can also add groupware to facilitate interactive discussions.

If your company has already achieved ISO certification, the intranet is still a convenient tool. Take the case of Rockwell Automation's Allen-Bradley Company in Milwaukee, Wisconsin, which maintains ISO procedures on its intranet. This setup enables manufacturing personnel to verify correct ISO procedures. Additionally, there are links to ISO procedures maintained by other corporate groups. A major advantage is that this information is readily available and the need to output a variety of publication formats or print lengthy documents is eliminated.

Forms

Generally, any form that you now print and process manually, including ordering and requisition forms, can be placed on your intranet. Since your employees also need to access forms on other company home pages (HR, Training, Operations, and so on) you also need to create the necessary hyperlinks to this material. Employees can then use their web browsers to download and complete the forms.

Approvals

Once your intranet is in place, all approvals and sign-offs can occur electronically. After completing an online form, which you download from the intranet, you can easily e-mail it for approval. In addition to reducing printing costs, this method provides you with an efficient paper trail.

Service and Maintenance Manuals

As an alternative to distributing hard copy service and maintenance manuals, place them on your intranet, complete with graphics and charts. Since technicians can simply drill down to the right location, they can refer to these manuals quickly and interactively while repairing manufacturing equipment or checking diagnostics. This is a real advantage when repairing highly sophisticated equipment that requires lengthy, detailed documentation. Your technicians will find this method much simpler than leafing through cumbersome written documentation.

Forecasts

Manufacturing executives can share forecast information with your company's finance department and peers in other company manufacturing facilities. For example, each facility can post forecast, booking, shipping, and inventory information, that can be consolidated into a single manufacturing financial report or PowerPoint presentation.

NOTE

Because of the highly confidential nature of this material, it's important to develop stringent security procedures. One way is to set up private web servers with firewall protection and highly limited access privileges. Another alternative is to encrypt this information or perhaps to combine both approaches. The approach you adopt may ultimately depend on your computer network capacity and other technical factors.

Project Schedules

Posting project schedules on your intranet allows you to communicate effectively both within your manufacturing area and with other groups that need access to this information. For example, if there's a potential delivery slippage because of manufacturing backlog, it's important to communicate this information to your sales organization before it becomes a problematic customer issue. Similarly, if different manufacturing facilities are collaborating on a specific product, it is critical that everyone be similarly and simultaneously informed.

Status Reports

Instead of distributing hard copy or e-mail status reports, place your status reports on your intranet site. Whether you submit weekly, bi-weekly, monthly, or quarterly status reports, the intranet approach offers these advantages: First, it's easy to reference back status reports in order to check a specific item; second, because of greater readability, status reports become a more useful tool.

NOTE

If you do not already use a standard status report template, it is recommended that you develop a standardized format before placing such reports on your intranet.

Organizational Charts

Posting manufacturing organizational charts, complete with staff photos on the intranet, can help personalize large manufacturing environments. This capability is especially useful for companies with many plant locations worldwide. By having this information available at their fingertips, your employees will spend less time on the unproductive task of identifying the appropriate manufacturing contact.

Manufacturing Databases

The intranet won't replace your existing manufacturing database applications running on mainframe and/or UNIX computer systems. But with the appropriate software and querying capabilities, you can make it easier for your users to access information residing on these systems. Instead of using traditional mainframe query tools, your users can use standard web browsers to access this information. In addition to providing users with an easy-to-use interface, you save money and time normally required to distribute software and revision updates to many PCs and workstations across the enterprise.

21

Documentation

By Paula Jacobs

An intranet can significantly streamline the entire documentation and publications process, including planning, review, distribution, workflow management, and revision control. It offers a common mechanism for sharing text files, graphics and CAD/CAM illustrations, and specifications both within your department and with other groups, such as engineering and marketing.

With proper implementation and the right software tools, an intranet provides a single delivery mechanism to manage the entire documentation process more efficiently and cost-effectively. Finally, using the Internet, documentation stored behind your firewall security system can be sent to third-party suppliers, printers, and other vendors.

Planning Your Content

Since your intranet site must set an example for the rest of your organization, plan to devote the same careful attention as you would to an external company Web page, at least within budget constraints. Pay special attention to the look-and-feel of your home page, choice of graphics, and the organization of your contents.

Additionally, factor in the practical realities of managing and updating content on a regular basis. Determine who will be responsible for providing content update material, the updating schedule, and the submission/revision process. To streamline this effort, plan on a fixed schedule, develop procedures for submitting new/revised material, and assign a single point of contact. It's important to communicate this information to your department, including lead times and schedules for submissions.

In addition to managing your department's intranet server, you also need to coordinate efforts with other groups, such as marketing and engineering. While you'll probably be responsible for maintaining links from the documentation department, it's important to ensure consistency.

Another key consideration is your current documentation structure, especially when there are documentation standards and formats already in place. If documentation is stored on multiple systems across the organization, you need to give users easy access, no matter where the information is located. Commercial document management solutions such as Intellecte/BusinessWeb or Enterprise Management System can help you address these requirements.

> Interleaf Inc.'s Intellecte/BusinessWeb can be found at:
> **http://www.ileaf.com**
> Documentum Inc.'s Enterprise Management System can be found at:
> **http://www.documentum.com**

Proper implementation involves more than simply adding HTML tags to existing documents. Instead, view your intranet as an integral component of your entire documentation workflow management plan. And remember that, like documentation, development of your intranet is a dynamic, evolutionary process subject to changing business requirements.

Documentation Usages

One key advantage to using an intranet is the ability to produce online internal documentation. This is especially important for companies that publish large volumes of internal technical documentation that need to be updated regularly. For example, if you are an electronics equipment manufacturer, it's critical to provide field engineers with the latest revision of diagnostics manuals so they can repair equipment correctly.

Similarly, engineers from different development groups need to share illustrations and CAD/CAM specifications. Access to the same information improves workflow and ensures consistency, especially for organizations with geographically dispersed engineering workgroups.

The following are some ways an intranet can improve workflow and document management for documentation and publications departments:

- Documentation and image library
- Technical specifications
- Scripts and macros
- Inventory lists
- Review cycles
- Status reports and project schedules
- Supplier information
- Links to external sites
- Bulletin boards
- Organizational charts
- Conferencing

Documentation and Image Library

Use your intranet as an online documentation and image library. Post editorial standards, clip art, CAD/CAM illustrations, product terminology, policies and procedures, and reference materials. It offers one way to ensure consistency, while providing on-demand access to a variety of information. This approach is also convenient if your organization must adhere to CALS (Commerce at Light Speed) and other suites of standards.

Perhaps a new technical writer has just joined your staff and needs to check your company's editorial standards and product terminology. Posting your company's style guide on your intranet is a more practical approach than printing and distributing printed style guides. Your new staff member can check on print and format styles by simply clicking the online style guide to locate a particular topic.

Instead of distributing huge CALS-standards manuals to your documentation staff, publish the standards on your documentation library. Your staff will find it easier to review specifications online than leafing through cumbersome paper documentation.

In the examples shown in figures 21.1 and 21.2, Interleaf's Intellecte/Business software shows how a search mechanism can be used to allow employees to find documentation on an intranet. The first figure illustrates the use of multiple drop-down lists that allow employees to pose very specific queries to the database of documentation. The resulting list lets employees read a brief overview file about the material before downloading the entire file. The ability to view document relationships as tracked in the document management system eliminates the need to build and maintain explicit links among the documents.

Fig. 21.1
Specific queries to this database of documentation can be made by choosing from a series of drop-down lists and filling in text boxes. (Screen shot courtesy of Interleaf, Inc.)

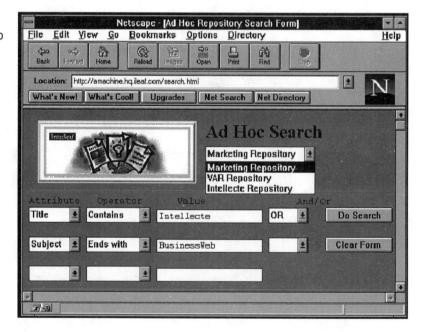

Fig. 21.2
These are the results of searches or browsing through repositories based on the query in figure 21.1. These HTML documents contain embedded URLs or links that can download files, view properties, or go deeper into the document hierarchy. (Screen shot courtesy of Interleaf, Inc.)

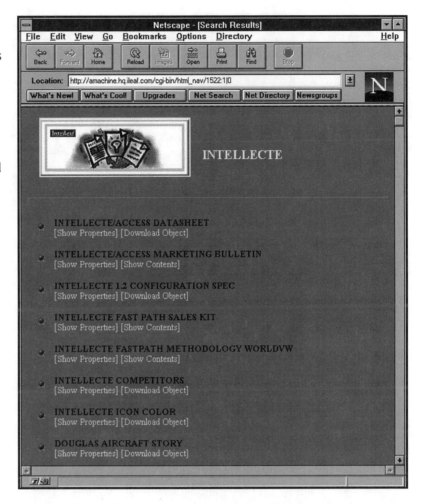

Including clip art, stock photos, and standard templates in your documentation library can help ensure consistency, while saving staff time. For example, you can include your company logo and photos of company products, which can be included in your documentation. Similarly, if every company manual requires boilerplate disclaimer and trademark information, the documentation library is the perfect repository.

In the intranet-based database on Simon & Schuster's intranet, shown in figure 21.3, employees are able to use a keyword-based search to browse images owned or licensed by the company.

Fig. 21.3
By clicking the appropriate image, the production staff has immediate access to Simon & Schuster's online library of stock photographs. (Screen shot courtesy of Simon & Schuster.)

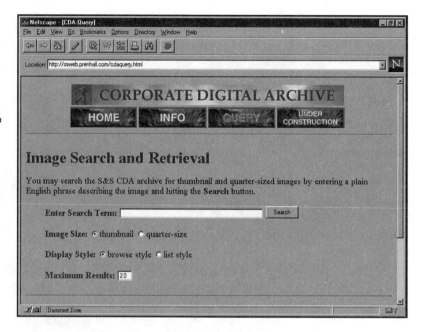

Technical Specifications

Your technical writers can use your intranet to access the technical functional specifications required for producing documentation. It's also important to communicate even the slightest specification changes to your customer support staff.

The documentation department of Pleasanton-California Documentum relies on its intranet for managing the complete workflow process. Technical writers are notified as soon as new specifications are made available, while customer support staff receive immediate notification when there is a new set of release notices. The company uses its Documentum Accelera product, together with the DocBase database, to manage the documentation process, including full text retrieval and appropriate routing.

Scripts and Macros

If your staff uses scripts and macros, your intranet represents a tremendous time-saver. Make your intranet a storage repository for scripts, such as Web applications, software macros, and technical examples. By eliminating the need to re-create frequently used standard materials, your staff can focus its efforts on producing new documentation. This capability is especially helpful for new project or staff members, as well as for organizations with geographically distributed documentation departments.

Inventory Lists

Maintain a list of available company documentation, including document description, part number, revision level, and inventory quantities on your intranet. This list enables company employees to find the appropriate manual quickly without bothering other staff members. If you are responsible for developing customer documentation, this list will also help you plan and schedule future revisions more appropriately. By reviewing documentation inventory over a specific calendar period, you can also make more informed "what if" decisions by tracking usage trends.

Create hyperlinks between your technical documentation and marketing/ sales literature. Perhaps a prospective customer has received a marketing brochure, but now wants more extensive technical details. Hyperlinks from the Sales and Marketing home page will link the sales representative to the Documentation home page for immediate access to technical specifications and product manuals.

Review Cycle

An intranet enables you to reduce the traditionally long documentation review and approval cycle. Instead of submitting review chapters via e-mail or ftp, a writer simply notifies the distribution cycle that the chapter is available on the intranet. Documentation is easier to review. And since you can access your intranet from remote locations, you can maintain schedules, even if illness or inclement weather keeps you at home.

You can also take advantage of commercially available tools designed to automate the review workflow process. Interleaf's RDM (Repository Document Manager) supports workflow management, which distributes documents to reviewers who can make notations in a read-only format. Documentum's Accelera product enables users to forward documents to the next reviewer for appropriate comments.

Status Reports and Project Schedules

Maintain online status reports and project schedules on your intranet. It's a convenient way to share information with engineering, marketing, and other groups involved in your projects. This approach will help improve communications, especially for large organizations with geographically distributed project teams. Your intranet helps monitor the status of current projects and deliverables and also provides a record for future reference.

TIP

If you don't already use a standard status report template, you should develop a standardized format before you place reports on your intranet.

Supplier Information

Use your intranet to maintain information about approved documentation suppliers, such as printing and mail houses. Include area of specialization, contact names, addresses, phone numbers, and other pertinent details.

Instead of supplying your printer with documentation disks, transmit the information directly from your intranet site via the Internet. This approach is quicker and more cost-effective than the use of mail or special delivery.

Links to External Sites

In addition to linking to internal home pages, set up links to relevant external Internet Web sites. For example, if your documentation department produces documentation on computer networking products, links to third-party networking vendors may help your staff keep up-to-date with the latest technology.

Bulletin Boards

Leverage the power of your intranet to improve general communications within your documentation department. Create an internal bulletin board that includes employee suggestions, announcements of professional society meetings, editing workshops, special employee achievements, department parties, online copies of professional publications, favorite recipes, or carpool requests.

An intranet is an excellent vehicle for exchanging ideas. Whether it's a suggestion on creating more effective presentations or a tip for using the Microsoft Windows style gallery, the bulletin board can help increase productivity.

Perhaps, one of your staff members has received a publication award from a local technical communications association. Publicize this achievement on your bulletin board.

Organizational Charts

Post your department's organizational charts on your intranet. Include staff photos, job function, office location and phone number, and reporting structure. An intranet organizational chart is a wonderful orientation tool for new employees, while keeping new staff members up-to-date with organizational changes.

For example, an engineering manager who is setting up a project team meeting simply checks your department's organizational chart to identify the appropriate documentation staff member responsible for a specific product. And since your organizational chart includes photos, you'll be able to associate names and faces much more easily.

Conferencing

An intranet is an excellent vehicle for workgroup collaboration and conferencing. If you have geographically distributed documentation groups or need to communicate with engineering groups at dispersed locations, you'll find this a tremendous bonus. A number of online software conferencing packages can help you implement conferencing.

22

Research and Development

By Paula Jacobs

The intranet is the natural collaborative tool for a Research and Development (R&D) environment, such as scientific and medical research, software development, and engineering. The intranet allows you to coordinate projects, share design specifications, and manage processes more efficiently.

You'll find the intranet a convenient way to share blueprints and mechanical designs, exchange research results, review meeting notes, schedule project reviews, and maintain status reports. It is an ideal solution for R&D groups spread across different locations. And unlike many workgroup solutions, minimal training is required.

Guidelines for an R&D Intranet

Because you probably have a fair amount of in-house technical savvy, it is critical to establish up-front some firm guidelines. First, determine within your group the scope of the content material and who will determine the accuracy of the technical submissions. Second, carefully coordinate efforts with other departments to set up pointers to their web sites. Third, specify the procedures for submitting content, designating one principal liaison from each group. Even though your web site is for internal use only, it is important to spell out guidelines for submissions to avoid the accidental publication of highly confidential material.

Finally, make sure to clearly communicate the process, schedules, and deadlines that you have defined. Although you will probably e-mail these guidelines initially to staff members, plan on publishing them on your web site once it is in operation.

Uses in Research and Development

The following list describes representative uses of the intranet for Research and Development environments. Actual applications will be tailored to your organization's needs.

- Technical specifications
- Configuration information
- Engineering change orders
- Electronic software distribution
- Software release notices and documentation
- Bug fixes and software patches
- Test results and benchmarks
- Blueprints and illustrations
- Standards organizations
- Technical presentations
- Technical library
- Policies and procedures
- Status reports and schedules
- Project discussions
- Links to internet sites
- Bulletin boards
- Organizational charts
- Personal home pages

The Engineering home page of Process Software Corporation in Framingham, Massachusetts contains a variety of technical resources, such as product information and documentation, project timesheets, online CD-ROMs, listings of available company reference books, and URLs to relevant external technical web sites, as well as a link to the Boston weather report (see fig. 22.1). The company's intranet also includes information about the Internet Engineering Task Force, technical standards bodies, and hot links to technical consortia—critical information for company engineers who develop a suite of TCP/IP networking software and the Purveyor web server.

Fig. 22.1
The Process Software Engineering home page provides links to technical products, engineering administration procedures, technical information, and even local weather reports. (Screen shot courtesy of Process Software Corporation.)

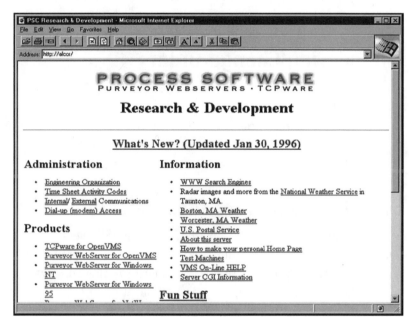

Technical Specifications

The intranet simplifies the sharing of technical specifications with your project team. Each specification can contain hyperlinks to related information. Insert a hyperlink to connect each technical term to its definition in a glossary. A mechanical engineering group can use hyperlinks to connect a specification to the blueprints for a part. Medical research environments can share test measurements with links to test results. Software development teams can insert a hyperlink for each subroutine described to link the discussion to the code that makes up the routine. Each time a data structure is mentioned, a hyperlink can be used to connect to the structure definition.

Configuration Information

Post equipment configuration information on your intranet home page. It is the ideal repository for instructions on configuring printers, workstations, research devices, and other laboratory and/or office equipment. Your R&D staff can access this information at their convenience, which is more productive than trying to locate the appropriate technical manual or support staff member.

Engineering Change Orders

Use the intranet to communicate Engineering Change Orders (ECOs) quickly to engineering, manufacturing, and documentation. Set up a mechanism where the appropriate departments check status information on a daily basis. Such a program helps reduce unnecessary errors due to accidental miscommunications.

Electronic Software Distribution

Software development environments can use the intranet to ensure consistent software development. For example, by placing object-oriented programs, program executables, standard routines, or Java applets on your intranet, you can help eliminate duplication of effort for standard programming tasks. Each time you develop a new software revision, simply place the software on your intranet so that programmers, technical writers, support staff, and other internal users can access this material.

Software Release Notices and Documentation

Reduce the costs of printing and distributing hard copy software release notices and technical documentation by placing this information on your intranet. Users can use their web browsers to quickly drill down and locate a specific reference, and, if necessary, print out specific pages. Although HTML format does not currently support advanced formatting features such as PostScript, this limitation is not an issue for internal documentation where format is not essential.

Bug Fixes and Software Patches

Provide information about bug fixes and software patches on your intranet. It gives a more efficient alternative to e-mail or telephone calls to software support staff. Similarly, publishing details about bugs that have been found helps reduce duplication of effort.

Test Results and Benchmarks

Publish product-quality testing, performance benchmarks, and the results of clinical research trials on your intranet. This information will be easily accessible to your research staff for measurement and future planning. For example, if you are conducting product-performance testing, it is easy to compare different parameters of previous and current releases by simply clicking the appropriate descriptions. This method is simpler than referring to hard copy documentation. Additionally, because you can publish results while in progress, other team members can analyze the data appropriate to their areas of responsibility.

Blueprints and Illustrations

CAD/CAM designs, architectural blueprints, medical illustrations, and other drawings can be stored easily on your intranet (see fig. 22.2). This provides easy access to R&D, documentation, marketing, and other staff members who require this information.

Fig. 22.2
An illustration of a new corporate airplane is only one example of the type of illustrations that can be stored on an intranet. Users can also click the appropriate icon to review financial data, check status reports, or surf the web. (Screen shot courtesy of Attachmate.)

Standards Organizations

Whether you work in an engineering, scientific, or medical R&D group, chances are your group must adhere to standards established by the relevant U.S. and/or international standards bodies. By publishing the latest reports of your standards organization on your intranet, you can help keep your staff abreast of the latest developments in your technical field.

Technical Presentations

Your intranet is the perfect repository for technical presentations. It gives your Research and Development organization access to the same presentations, while making them available to other departments that require this information, such as marketing. You can also store an assortment of graphics, icons, and corporate logos, or you can scan in photographs and images.

It's easy to customize a presentation to fit your audience. Simply download the standard presentation from the intranet site, insert an introductory overhead slide, eliminate unnecessary overheads, and add some colorful graphics. For example, a presentation to a highly technical engineering manager will probably have a different level of technical detail than a product plan overview to non-technical management.

By linking to other company web sites, you can add appropriate materials. If you're making a technical presentation to a customer, you may want to add general company overview information available on the Corporate Communications web site.

The intranet simplifies the task of updating presentations to reflect new product enhancements or revisions. Simply insert new pages with the appropriate HTML tags.

Technical Library

Create an online technical library for your department. List the books, technical trade journals, and freeware software, including a brief summary description that your R&D staff can borrow. Develop a What's New page to highlight new acquisitions or a Recommendations page to reference software recommended by other staff members. Mercury Sports uses its intranet to highlight new products (see fig. 22.3). Also consider downloading from the Internet freeware software and online journals that pertain to your specific area. If your group is part of a larger organization, you may also add links to the corporate library. This online library will save your staff considerable time by providing them with reference material at their fingertips.

Fig. 22.3
Product information, a nutrition Q&A, and profiles of famous athletes from Mercury Sports are included as handy reference material. (Screen shot courtesy of Lotus Development Corporation, a subsidiary of IBM Corporation.)

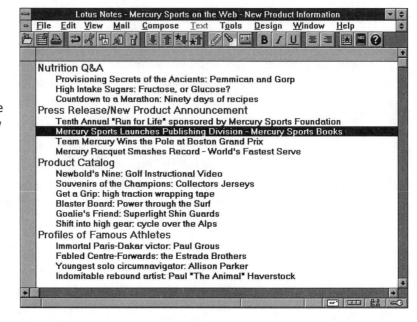

Policies and Procedures

By posting policies and procedures on your intranet, you can help improve communications and increase productivity. You probably will want to include information specific to your department, such as regulations for using equipment or hiring outside contractors. Additionally, you can set up hyperlinks to general company policies and procedures on the corporate home page.

Motorola Semiconductor Products in Austin, Texas uses its intranet as a common mechanism to share policy and procedure information. Previously, because of disparate in-house e-mail systems, document exchange was extremely difficult. The company has implemented Lotus Development Corporation's InterNotes for HTML conversion. The intranet has streamlined the ability to share technical specifications, obtain technical feedback, conduct technical discussions, report software "bug" fixes, and exchange new product ideas.

Status Reports

Instead of distributing hard copy or e-mail status reports describing trouble-shooting activity, place these status reports on your intranet site. They provide an excellent reference backlog and enable other members of your organization to review this information.

If your organization is "billable," you may need to track project hours carefully. The intranet is the perfect spot to place timesheets for each project and project member, providing a convenient way to quickly check and compare hours devoted to a specific project. You may also need to add links to other internal web sites, especially for projects that involve team members from different groups within your organization.

Project Discussions and Conferencing

Whether your project groups are located at one site or spread across the world, the intranet provides an excellent vehicle for discussions and conferencing. It also fosters discussions between R&D staff and other departments.

One company taking advantage of this capability is Attachmate Corporation in Bellevue, Washington. Using the company's OpenMind software, company engineers are able to collaborate over the intranet, both within their own group and with other departments, such as sales and marketing (see figs. 22.4 and 22.5). For example, a field salesperson can post a customer issue to a collaborative database accessible to support personnel and product engineers, who can see the incoming requests and make appropriate comments in a discussion forum. Both documents and comments are maintained in this discussion forum. Users can also maintain a personal area on the web server for online chat facilities.

Fig. 22.4
Attachmate uses their OpenMind software to allow employees to collaborate over the intranet. (Screen shot courtesy of Attachmate.)

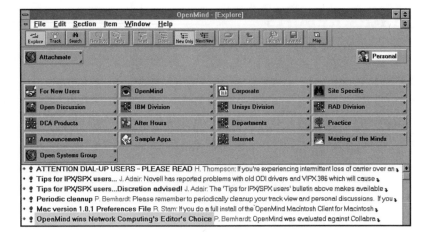

Figure 22.5 shows responses to a discussion conducted with OpenMind software. It also lists the number of people who responded to this particular discussion.

Fig. 22.5
A sample discussion that can occur over the intranet, using Attachmate's OpenMind software. Users simply click the appropriate icon to participate in the appropriate discussion area. (Screen shot courtesy of Attachmate.)

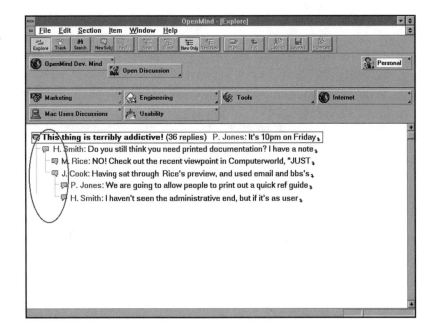

Links to Internet Sites

Create links between your intranet and those relevant to your R&D area. Pointers may link to Uniform Resource Locators (URLs) of pertinent online technical journals, research laboratories, industry news summaries, government alerts, UseNet news groups, and Web search tools, such as Yahoo.

Update this information on a regular basis, notifying users of new information either via a What's New page or e-mail to your user community. In any case, it is highly recommended that you review the appropriateness of material, especially UseNet newsgroups, before setting up links or downloading it to your site.

Bulletin Boards

An intranet bulletin board is a great way to communicate all sorts of general information. You can post notices of user group meetings, technical conferences, employee suggestions, announcements of professional society meetings, employee recognition awards, retirement lunches, and special employee life events.

Organizational Charts

Publish R&D organizational charts on the intranet. Include staff photos, job functions, office location and phone number, and reporting structure. An intranet organizational chart is a wonderful orientation tool for new employees, while keeping new staff members up to date with organizational changes. It is especially handy for large organizations with project groups in different locations. And if your organizational chart includes photos, employees can associate names and faces much more easily.

Imagine that you're making an important presentation to key managers from your company's facility in England. Consider the advantages of greeting them by name, although you have never met in person. This simple usage of the intranet can help business relationships get off to a great start.

Personal Home Pages

Perhaps members of your R&D staff want to create personal home pages. They can include personal data (birth date, marital status, hobbies, and so on), as well as descriptions of key company projects with which the staff member is involved. Create links between organizational charts and personal home pages.

23

Customer Service and IT Support

By Paula Jacobs

Whatever the size of your organization, you'll find that an intranet can greatly enhance the quality of customer service and Information Technology (IT) support. Whether your department supports internal users or external customers, the intranet can help you disseminate information more easily and track problems more effectively for greater user satisfaction. By providing an efficient alternative to traditional telephone or e-mail support, your organizational effectiveness will increase because users and IT staff can dedicate their energies to mission-critical business issues instead of routine support questions.

Planning Your Content

Like any new venture, success depends on careful planning and a multi-step implementation program, with a gradual rollout. First, define this multi-phase rollout plan, with your objectives for each phase.

Define the routine tasks in which you can easily make a transition to the intranet for the first phase. Develop a realistic implementation timetable. Assign staff to create content with HTML codes. Finally, announce the initial program, including procedures and usage, to your internal user community.

At the same time, develop measurements to gauge success, obtain user feedback, and revise your intranet as required. Assume that your intranet implementation will be a dynamic and continuously improving process in response to user and business requirements.

Uses in Customer Service and IT Support

The intranet is a perfect solution for customer service and IT support. It can complement your current support infrastructure and provide your support staff with a more efficient way to exchange information about customers. You will also find the intranet a more productive way to handle routine functions, ranging from user questions to software distribution. By adding commercial web tools or in-house developed solutions, you can use the intranet to automate your help desk and customer support.

While actual usage depends on the nature of your organization, the following are some representative applications:

- Policies and procedures
- Help desk assistance
- Problem tracking and resolution
- Documentation and software release notices
- Bug fixes and software patches
- Software distribution
- Statistical monitoring
- Links to external and internal sites
- Status reports
- Frequently Asked Questions
- Newsgroups
- Forms and questionnaires

Policies and Procedures

Use the intranet to communicate a variety of policies and procedures to your user community about your computer systems and networks. It's an efficient way to post information about the following areas:

- Network security
- PC virus alerts
- Computer bulletins
- Software distribution
- Help requests
- Remote dial-in privileges
- Network printing and faxing
- Internet usage

In sum, the intranet is well-suited to the posting of a variety of general IT-related information. You can also create hyperlinks to Documentation and Frequently Asked Questions to provide users with further detail on these areas.

Help Desk Assistance

As an alternative to traditional computer help desk setups, place online help on your intranet. This should include specific information about how to obtain system and network help, where to address PC questions, and so on.

Bechtel, a San-Francisco engineering procurement firm, uses its internal web server to provide employees with information about the company's external Internet site. The company's intranet includes information about configuring the Internet connection, how to use ftp, help assistance, and details about new Web technology.

Problem Tracking and Resolution

With the appropriate software, your users can resolve help desk problems themselves. They can submit new problems, check the status of the problems they have previously submitted, and perform self help. This end-user involvement, with a timely response, is critical to the success of your help desk and will improve service quality.

This capability provides a tremendous advantage over conventional problem tracking and resolution. Users no longer need to make a phone call and wait in the queue for telephone support, problem analysis, escalation to the appropriate staff member, and final resolution, including on-site dispatch. With an intranet help desk system, you can resolve problems seven days a week, 24 hours a day, 365 days a year. You simply point your web browser to the right place on your home page and interactively perform self-diagnosis.

One such system is available from Remedy Corporation, a software company in Mountain View, California. Using the Remedy Action Request System with ARWeb, a tool used to perform querying and submit requests, end users can directly resolve their own problems by accessing the same knowledge database used by help desk staffers. Using a web browser, the user points to the equivalent of a help desk home page, selects the application, and views a query form (see fig. 23.1). Then, selecting from a series of menus, the user runs a query and obtains a list of potential solutions. If the problem is still not resolved, the user submits a request to the help desk, based on problem description, to the appropriate help desk staff member.

Fig. 23.1
With Remedy Corporation's Action Request System, a user submits a request for help desk assistance via the intranet, using a web browser and special software. (Screen shot courtesy of Remedy™ Corporation.)

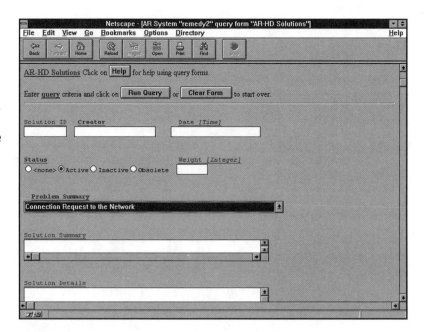

Documentation and Software Release Notices

Reduce the costs of printing and distributing hard copy user documentation by placing your internal user documentation on the intranet. Users can use their web browsers to quickly drill down and locate a specific reference, and, if necessary, print out specific pages. While HTML format does not currently support advanced formatting features, such as PostScript, this limitation is a non-issue for internal documentation, where format is not essential.

Bug Fixes and Software Patches

Place details about bug fixes and software patches on the intranet, including descriptions of workarounds. By referring to this information, your staff can eliminate duplication of effort.

The intranet has increased support staff productivity at DataBase Publishing Software in Woburn, Massachusetts. The company maintains a record of unique customer problems and software patches, which helps them quickly address and resolve similar types of issues.

Software Distribution

If you have a site license for certain software products or provide freeware to your users, use the intranet instead of using traditional software distribution methods. It is simpler than disk or CD-ROM distribution and alleviates the headache of providing updates for each new Microsoft Internet Explorer or Netscape Navigator Web browser software release.

Statistical Monitoring

The intranet can also help you collect data about customer problems and the average response time. You can use this information to improve your response time. Using ARWeb, you can log the time from report to closure of a problem. Also, with logs kept in a database or spreadsheet form, judging response time per general problem or help desk employee is a small feat.

Status Reports

Instead of distributing hard copy or e-mail status reports describing troubleshooting activity, place these status reports on your intranet site. They provide an excellent reference backlog, and enable other members of your organization to review this information.

Tyson Foods places bi-weekly status reports on its intranet. By drilling down to the appropriate section, computer support personnel can quickly view the status of different company sites, including equipment availability.

Links to External and Internal Sites

Create hyperlinks from your Customer Service and IT home page to internal and external locations. Internally, provide hyperlinks to other company home pages, such as documentation and operation. If you use Microsoft Windows 95 or Novell NetWare software products, perhaps you want a link to these vendors' external web pages. Or, if you have software support agreements with third-party vendors, set up hyperlinks from your intranet to their external web pages.

Newsgroups

Many organizations provide their users with access to newsgroups, either via internal online bulletin boards or by downloading relevant UseNet newsgroups from the Internet. However, it's highly recommended that your network manager review such information regularly to review the appropriateness of the material for your organization. If your company has its own news server or receives news feeds from an Internet Service Provider (ISP), your network manager can control individual groups that are viewable to employees. There is also special software to assist in this effort; for example, network managers can use CLEARweb from Clear Software in Newton, Massachusetts to draw a map to specific web sites.

Internal bulletin board-style newsgroups can be used for communications of all sorts, including general announcements and private announcements (see fig. 23.2).

Forms and Questionnaires

Use the intranet to store an assortment of forms and questionnaires. These can range from service and software ordering forms to questionnaires measuring user satisfaction with a new software package. For example, users can order new PC software upgrade packages through forms stored on the intranet.

Fig. 23.2
Publisher Simon &
Schuster updates
its users about PC
virus protection
via the intranet.
(Screen shot
courtesy of Simon
& Schuster.)

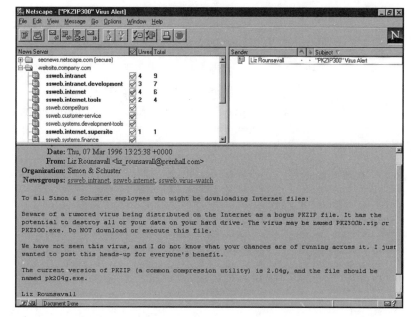

The intranet simplifies the time-consuming task of obtaining user feedback. Whether it's polling users about Windows 95 usage or obtaining input about a proposed network change, you can achieve a better response rate via the intranet than using conventional paper questionnaires, which are easily misplaced or discarded.

Frequently Asked Questions

By posting Frequently Asked Questions on the intranet, you can provide your user community with answers to routine support questions. Access to immediate feedback promotes user satisfaction, while enabling your support staff to use its time more productively.

The University of Michigan disseminates a variety of customer service and support information via the intranet. It includes answers to FAQs such as: How do I dial-in to the network from off-campus? What is the procedure for ordering an EtherNet connection? What kind of software do I need for certain requirements?

Common Frequently Asked Questions include:

- How do I find out system status information?
- What is the procedure for reporting system problems?
- How do I send messages externally via the Internet?
- What is the procedure for sending/receiving faxes from my computer system?
- Who do I contact for PC support problems?
- How do I order software upgrades?
- What printers are available on the network?

PART V

Exploring Publishing Tools

24

Web Publishing with WordPerfect

By Diane Koers

With WordPerfect—and its newest feature—the Internet Publisher—you can now create a document to publish on your company intranet. Your associates will be able to download catalogs, view video about your department, or just become acquainted with your staff through information available on your intranet. Your coworkers or employees can create electronic forms, fill out information surveys, order company manuals, or send you e-mail.

In this chapter, you learn to

- Use WordPerfect's Internet Publisher to design a basic web page
- Make your pages stand out by applying styles, colors, and other attributes
- View the document in your web browser to get the final results since what you see isn't necessarily what you'll get

WordPerfect's Internet Publisher

WordPerfect includes a built-in feature called the Internet Publisher. It's an easy-to-use tool that assists you in creating HTML documents.

The Internet Publisher uses the styles feature of WordPerfect. As you apply styles to the WordPerfect document, the Internet Publisher assigns the HTML tags to the text.

Tags can be used to apply attributes, such as bold, to text. You would see the text as bold in the browser; however, Internet Publisher assigns beginning and ending tags which appear as `<BOLD>text</BOLD>`. The advantage of using Internet Publisher is that you don't have to learn the exact HTML tag language. All you have to do is tell WordPerfect how you want certain text to look. Internet Publisher assigns the tags for you.

The Basics of Creating an HTML Document

An HTML document normally has several components to it: a title, headings, paragraphs of information, graphics, and the name and intranet address of the author. It also may contain lists or tables of information.

To create an HTML document, follow these steps:

1. Choose File, Internet Publisher. The Internet Publisher dialog box appears, as shown in figure 24.1.

2. Click New Web Document.

Fig. 24.1
WordPerfect's Internet Publisher feature enables you to start with a new document or convert an existing document.

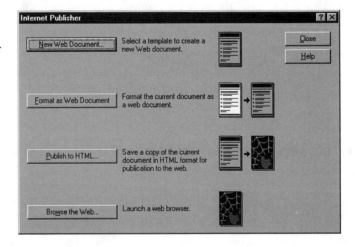

As seen in figure 24.2, you are prompted to Select a New Web Document template. There is only one web template that ships with WordPerfect 7, but you can create others, just like any other template.

N O T E

The Internet Publisher, like other WordPerfect features, has an "expert" to assist you. The Web Page Expert begins a web page for you, giving you basic elements to work with. I suggest that you start with the blank template and build from there. This gives you more flexibility in the design of the page and a great learning experience as to the concepts behind web page publishing.

3. Choose Create a Blank Web Document, then click Select.

   The new document appears on-screen, and the WordPerfect Internet

Fig. 24.2
You can create your web page from a blank template or use the Web Page Expert template.

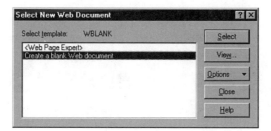

Publisher feature is now in effect. The dialog box shown in figure 24.3 appears.

4. Click OK to acknowledge the announcement.

   Although the dialog box announces that only web-compatible features are available, you will encounter a few choices on the menu that are not web-compatible.

Several things are going to look different, most noticeably the background of

Fig. 24.3
Many features
normally available
in WordPerfect
are unavailable
to the Internet
Publisher.

your screen; it's no longer white like a normal WordPerfect document, but gray. The other items to notice are your toolbar and Power Bar. Figure 24.4 shows the options on both the toolbar and Power Bar have changed to reveal only web document features. Also, many choices under the menu bar are grayed out and unavailable. Some menu selections even change. For example, take a look at the Format menu. The choices under this menu are totally different than in a regular WordPerfect document.

Fig. 24.4
A special toolbar
and Power Bar
with web publish-
ing features
appears.

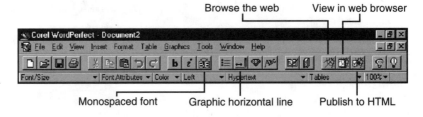

Converting Standard WordPerfect Documents into HTML Documents

Although you may find it easier to create a document from the beginning using the Internet Publisher, a WordPerfect document can often be converted to HTML format for use on your intranet.

C A U T I O N

If the document is complex and contains merge commands, columns, footnotes, or other WordPerfect features, it won't convert cleanly. Even something with a manual page break may give Internet Publisher problems in converting.

Only a document with plain text and some formatting can be converted. The only acceptable formatting codes are bold and italics. Underlining, fonts, sizes, text color, and other choices cannot be used. If the document contains margin settings, line spacing, and other such settings, they are ignored during the conversion.

Here are some troubleshooting tips that may help you solve some potential problems:

- *My original WordPerfect document had several graphic images in it. When I converted it, they weren't there.* The only graphics that are recognized during the conversion are horizontal graphic lines. Graphic images should be added after the conversion has taken place.

- *I converted a document to the Internet Publisher, but my formulas are not showing up in my tables.* Although the Internet Publisher converter recognizes tables, the actual formulas are not converted; only the results of the formula calculations appear. WordPerfect Internet Publisher also puts lines around each cell of the table and in your Internet Browser, and these lines appear as raised borders.

Figures 24.5, 24.6, and 24.7 illustrate how a document looks during the conversion from a WordPerfect standard document, to a WordPerfect HTML document, to viewing it in Netscape.

Fig. 24.5
This WordPerfect document is in its original format before conversion, including fonts and attributes.

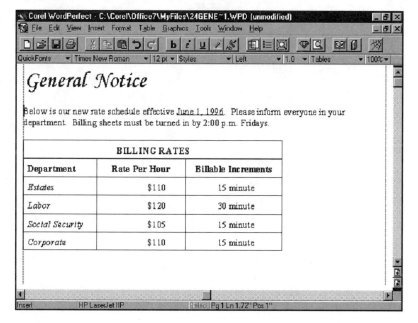

Fig. 24.6
After conversion, the WordPerfect document is displayed with the Internet Publisher feature. Notice that the original font choices are no longer displayed.

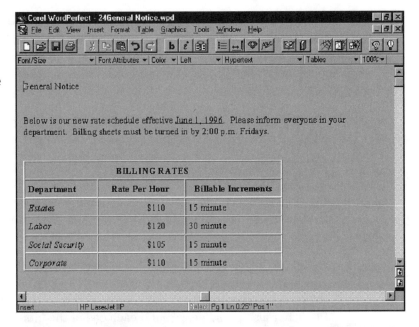

Fig. 24.7
The converted WordPerfect document is shown in a Netscape browser. Notice that the underlining attribute is no longer displayed.

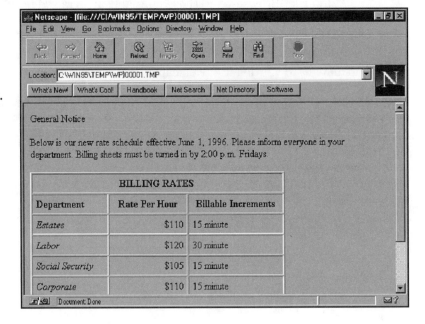

To convert an existing WordPerfect document to HTML:

1. Choose File, Internet Publisher.
2. Choose Format as Web Document.
3. Choose OK.

The existing WordPerfect file is converted using the Internet Publisher template to an HTML format. You can then continue to work on the document using HTML features.

CAUTION

You may want to save your original WordPerfect document under a different name before you convert it to HTML. Once a document has been converted, it can't be restored to the standard WordPerfect format.

Creating an HTML Document Title

HTML documents must have a title. The *title* is the text that appears in the title bar of your web browser when your web page appears. The title can be the first line of your web page text, or it can be a totally different line of text that does not appear directly on the body of the web page. If you do not assign a title, WordPerfect will use the first line of text in the document as the title. An example of when you would use a custom title is if you want your reader to see a graphic image first, instead of text.

To give the HTML document a title:

1. Choose Format, Title.
2. Be sure the Title tab is displayed (see fig. 24.8).
3. Click the Custom Title button, and then type the desired text in the box below it.

   Or, select First Heading to have WordPerfect enter the first line of text in your document as the title, also.
4. Click OK.

If you opted to use the Custom Title, you do not see this title in the HTML document. It appears when you are viewing the document in your Web browser.

Fig. 24.8
Unless you specify a custom title, WordPerfect uses the first heading as the title.

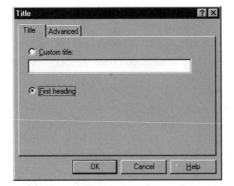

Creating Body Text

The next step is to type the contents or the body of the page. You could also create a table here. When typing the text, follow standard word processing rules of letting the text wrap to the next line until you have completed the paragraph. Then press Enter to complete the paragraph.

NOTE

I am a firm believer in a word processing practice called *type first, edit later*. Over the years, I have found this to be a tremendous time saver for me. It basically means to concentrate on what you want your document to say rather than how it looks. You don't have to stop and lose your train of thought while creating your document. After the text is typed, then you can select various portions of it and apply formatting as needed. (In the writing of this chapter, I am using this concept.)

There is no need to press Enter the second time for the standard blank line as you would in a normal word processing document. WordPerfect's Internet Publisher automatically places additional spacing between paragraphs. The

Internet Publisher is actually placing a paragraph tag every time you press Enter. That paragraph tag tells the Web browser program to separate the paragraphs by a small amount of extra spacing. It also ignores any extra Enter commands it encounters in the HTML document.

If, however, you do want to press Enter, and you don't want the extra spacing between these paragraphs, you can insert a *line break*, which produces separate lines of text, but without extra spacing. Figure 24.9 illustrates the difference between a paragraph break and a line break. To create a line break, choose Insert, Line Break.

Fig. 24.9
The shortcut key for a line break is Ctrl+Shift+L.

Paragraph break ———

Line break ———

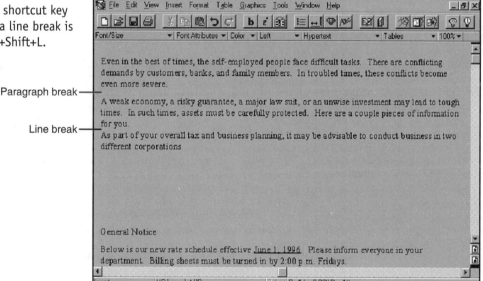

Adding Headings

HTML documents need headings to separate the topics of your web page. Just as this book has several types of headings, so should your HTML page. Headings are similar to an outline in that a Level 1 heading is larger than a Level 2 heading. You can't choose the actual font for the heading because this isn't determined by the HTML document; it's determined by the Web browser program. Netscape may show a Level 2 heading in a totally different font or size from a Level 2 heading in Mosaic. You may not have control over which Web browser your readers are using.

An HTML document is capable of supporting up to six different heading types. You should note that some Web browsers only support up to five different heading styles. If you have used all six styles in your HTML document, the browser ignores the sixth style and makes it look like the fifth style.

TIP

It's a good idea to use the heading levels in a sequential manner; that is, don't skip from Heading 1 to Heading 3. Go from Heading 1 to Heading 2, or from Heading 2 to Heading 3, and so on.

Although you can't apply fonts or point sizes to the headings, you can select extra appearance enhancements. These enhancements include bold, italic, monospaced, or blink. You can also change the size proportionally, such as Fine, Small, Large, Very Large, or Extra Large. The actual size of this font is going to vary with different Web browsers.

You are probably familiar with bold and italics. *Monospaced* text changes the text from a proportional typeface to a non-proportional typeface similar to the typewriter style `Courier`. Each character takes the same amount of space if you choose Monospaced. Monospaced is a good attribute to use to create the appearance of tabbed columns of text.

NOTE

The Monospaced tag is WordPerfect's term for the commonly used Typewriter Text tag.

Blink text flashes on and off when displayed on the Web browser. On the WordPerfect document, it looks similar to a shadow effect. Figure 24.10 illustrates these attributes and sizes.

Fig. 24.10
Blink text does
not flash in the
HTML document,
only in the Web
browser.

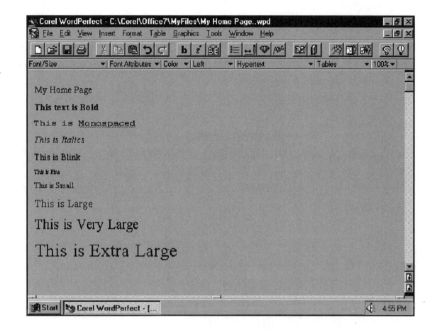

CAUTION

Use blink sparingly. It can be very distracting to the reader.

NOTE

Some Web browsers can't display these appearance enhancements. For
example, a character-based browser sometimes cannot display italics
or underlining. Some browsers are incapable of displaying the blink
attribute.

To add a heading:

1. In the document, type the text for the heading.
2. Select the line of text for the heading.
3. Choose Format, Font. The Font dialog box appears (see fig. 24.11).
4. In the Font/Size box, select from the list of available headings, such as
   Heading 2.

5. In the Appearance box, select an appearance attribute (Italic, Monospaced, or Blink).

 You cannot use the Bold attribute in a Heading. If you choose it, it will simply be ignored.

6. Choose OK.

FIG. 24.11
The Internet Publisher Font dialog box does not display actual fonts by name; it displays styles.

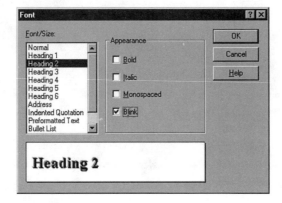

Adding Formatting

Character styles are used to change the appearance of a few words or characters in your HTML document. Character styles are the attributes discussed in the previous section: bold, italics, monospaced, and blink. The same information applies, in that many browsers can't display all attributes.

To apply character formatting:

1. Select the text to be formatted.

2. Choose Format, Font. The Font dialog box appears (refer to fig. 24.11).

3. Select the desired appearance attribute: Bold, Italics, Monospaced, or Blink.

4. Click OK. The text is now formatted.

Another type of formatting is applied to paragraphs of text. The text could be an indented quotation. Figure 24.12 shows an example of indented quotation text. With indented quotation, the left margin of the paragraph is moved in approximately 1/2 inch. Indented quotation is commonly used when you are quoting someone's words, or creating a subparagraph of a paragraph above it.

Fig. 24.12
Indented text is
set apart from
other body
paragraphs for
special attention.

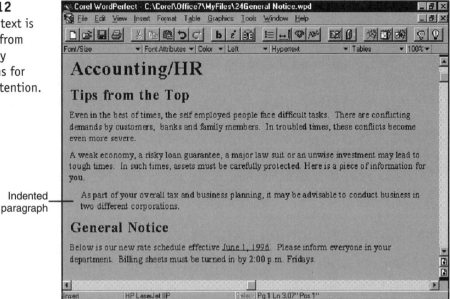

Indented paragraph

To created indented quotation text:

1. Place the insertion point in the first line of the paragraph to be indented.

2. Choose Format, Font.

3. Select Indented Quotation from the Font/Size box.

4. Click OK. The specified paragraph is indented.

Adding Address Blocks

Occasionally, you may want to allow your fellow employees to contact certain departments or people in your company, whether via e-mail or by a regular mailing address. To call attention to an address, WordPerfect's Internet Publisher provides an *address block*. In most Web browsers, it appears as italicized text.

> **TIP**
>
> Address block is a good style to use at the end of your document, where you should place the web page author's name and intranet address.

The typed address block can contain multiple lines of text; however, in most Web browsers, the text runs together in a single line.

To change text into an address block:

1. Place the insertion point in the text to be formatted as an address block.
2. Choose Format, Font.
3. Choose Address from the Font/Size selections.
4. Click OK. The text is then formatted as an address block.

Creating Bullets and Lists

Three types of lists are supported by WordPerfect's Internet Publisher:

- Bulleted list
- Numbered list
- Definition list

Lists can be created in several levels. The Tab key is normally ignored in an HTML document, but if you have defined a list, the Tab key creates the indentation for multi-levels.

Bullet list items are usually not in any particular order and are preceded with a bullet point. The style of the bullet varies according to the Net browser you are using. It could appear as a round circle (•) , a hollow square (☐), or one of several other styles.

This is an example of a multi-level bullet list:

- Day One
  - Opening Remarks
  - Guest Speaker #1
  - Round Table Discussions

• Day Two

    • Guest Speaker #2

    • Breakout Session

    • Closing Remarks

A numbered list could be used to show a sequence of steps to follow. If you are displaying a procedure, a numbered list would be very appropriate. A numbered list can also be multiple levels.

This is an example of a numbered list:

1. Select the program file for the application you want to run.
2. From the File menu, choose Run.
3. In the Run dialog box, specify the file you want to open.
4. Choose the OK button.

A definition list allows you to display items similar to a glossary. The heading item is left-aligned, and the item under it is indented. You must press the Tab key at the second level to tell WordPerfect to indent it. This does not work like a Tab in a normal WordPerfect document, it works like an indent.

N O T E

The Tab key indents text to the right, and Shift+Tab unindents, or moves text back to the left.

This is an example of a definition list:

Bookmark

    A location or selection of text that you name for reference purposes.

Procedure

    A procedure is a miniature program that is part of a main program. The procedure is executed when the main program calls for it.

Formula

    Calculates a number using a mathematical formula. With a formula, you can use numbers, bookmarks that reference numbers, or fields resulting in numbers, along with the available operators and functions.

To indent text in a list, place the insertion point at the beginning of any paragraph to be indented and press the Tab key.

To create a list:

1. Highlight the text to be modified into a list.
2. Choose Fo**r**mat, **F**ont.
3. From the **F**ont/Size selections, choose the type of list—bullet, numbered, or definition.
4. Click OK. The items appear with your selected choice.

TIP

You selected a numbered list, typed your text, and now find that every time you press Enter, the numbers are continuing. How can you turn the feature off? At the line where you want to discontinue the numbering, press the Backspace key. This deletes the numbering style and returns the text to normal. The same is true if you have selected bullet points.

Using Color

Even though you have no control over font selection or text size, you can choose the color of the text. You can also pick a background color and even a wallpaper for the background. The default background color for an HTML document is gray. The color of hypertext links (discussed later in this chapter) also can be selected.

CAUTION

Make it easy on your readers. You want to grab their attention, but you don't want to blind them with color choices that are too bright or text that is too hard to read.

When a text color is selected, it is consistent throughout the entire HTML document. WordPerfect does not allow you to make only a certain portion—say for example, a heading with your company name on it—red while the rest of the text is blue. If you choose to make the text red, it's red throughout your HTML document.

TIP

Corel has included some wonderful graphics that can be used as wall-paper. Look in the GRAPHICS folders for the folders called FABRICS, PAPER, STONE, or WOOD.

To assign a color:

1. Choose Format, Text/Background Colors and the Text/Background Colors dialog box appears (see fig. 24.13).

2. Make your selections from the drop-down boxes available.

   From this dialog box, you can choose the color for the regular text in your document as well as the hypertext links. The background color and background wallpaper is also available.

3. Click OK.

Fig. 24.13
You can specify a bitmap graphic file name to be used as wallpaper for your web page.

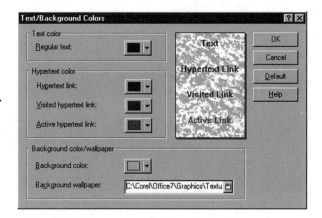

TIP

Did you select a wallpaper, but it doesn't show up? Wallpaper does not show in your HTML document, but it is available in the Web browser. Also, if you select a wallpaper, it appears on every page.

Setting Alignment

Alignment options in an HTML document are similar to a standard WordPerfect document. If you want only a portion of the text to be centered, you must first select the text to be centered. If you don't select the text first, the entire document (from the location of the insertion point down) is centered or realigned. The shortcut keys are the same ones used for a standard WordPerfect document:

- ● Ctrl+L to left justify
- ● Ctrl+R to right justify
- ● Ctrl+E to center justify

A selection is also available on the Power Bar. There is no full justification available in an HTML document.

To change the alignment of text:

1. Select the text to be aligned.
2. Choose Format, Justification.
3. Select Left, Right, or Center.
4. Choose OK.

Adding Graphics

It's one thing to write about your new invention, but what an advantage it is to have a picture to illustrate its usage as well. Graphics can be used to display your logo, a photograph, an illustration, or even to link to another web site.

NOTE

Graphics should be used in addition to your text, not in place of it. Some Web browsers are character-based, which means they can't display any type of graphic. If you tell your story in pictures only, these readers won't know what you are trying to say.

Understanding Graphic Formats

A document created for a web page is actually only plain text. A graphic that you see on a web page is really coming from a different document or file. The HTML document contains a tag that points to the graphic and its location. As an example, to insert a graphic called MYLOGO.GIF (located in the CLIPART folder) into your document, WordPerfect's Internet Publisher inserts the following tag:

```
<IMG SRC= "c:\clipart\mylogo.gif">
```

Dozens of types of graphic formats exist today, but there are only a few that can be used on a web page. The two most widely used formats are *GIF* (*Graphics Interchange Format*) and *JPEG* (*Joint Photographic Expert Group*).

The JPEG format is the better quality of the two—especially for photographs because of color depth—but have a tendency to be larger in size and therefore slower for your viewer to load. GIF formats are usually much smaller than JPEG and much faster to download. Sometimes the quality is not as good, however.

TIP

Suppose the picture you want to use is not in a GIF or JPEG format. You can convert it using most image processing programs such as Adobe Photoshop, LView PRO, or HiJaakPro. Corel's Presentations program can convert many graphic files to the JPEG format, but not the GIF format. The Microsoft Paint accessory program that comes with Windows 95 cannot convert these files at all. There are also many shareware programs available on the Internet that can convert these files for you.

▶ **See** "Converting Graphics," **p. 99**

Although the WordPerfect menu enables you to insert several types of graphics, including text boxes and equations, these graphics are not acknowledged in the browser programs. Only graphics inserted with the GIF or JPEG format can be displayed.

To insert a graphic image:

1. Choose <u>G</u>raphics, <u>I</u>mage.
2. Select the name of the desired graphic image.
3. Click Insert. The graphic comes into the HTML document.

The graphic might be quite large in size, but you can resize it like a normal WordPerfect graphic. To resize a graphic image, click the graphic to select it. Eight small handles appear. Place the mouse pointer over one of these handles and notice how the mouse pointer changes into a double-headed arrow. Drag these handles to resize the graphic image. Click anywhere else in your document to deselect the graphic.

If you change your mind and decide you don't want this graphic image on your web page, click the graphic to select it and press the Delete key.

Using Graphic Lines

An HTML document does not allow for page breaks in the way you would use them in a normal WordPerfect document. There are a couple of ways you can allow for a break in your topics on your page. You can use headings and/or create a horizonal line or *rule*. See figure 24.14 for an example of a web page with a horizonal rule. Effective use of a horizontal rule enables users to see a jump in the topics of your page and gives them a "breather" from their reading.

TIP

Don't overuse horizonal lines in your document. Too many lines makes a document look choppy and can confuse the reader.

To create a horizontal line:

1. Place the insertion point at the location for the line to appear.

2. Choose <u>G</u>raphics, <u>H</u>orizontal Line, or click the Image icon on the toolbar. A line appears at the insertion point.

FIG. 24.14
Rules allow for a
separation of
topics.

3D ruled line ──

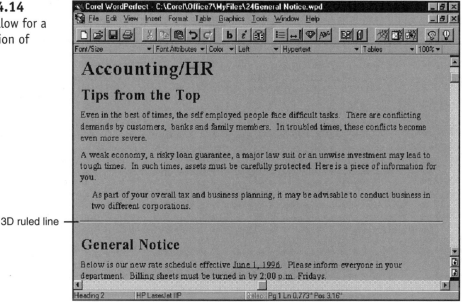

TIP

To delete a horizontal line, select it with your mouse and press the Delete key on the keyboard.

TIP

Make sure you are on a blank line before creating a line. If you have text on the line, the paragraph breaks at the point where the line is inserted.

In an HTML document, using a horizontal line also places extra spacing between the text and the horizontal line.

NOTE

Different browsers may display the horizontal rule differently. Some, such as Netscape, display it as a thin three-dimensional gray line. Others may display it as flat black line. You have little control over the appearance of the horizontal line.

<hr noshade>

Adding Special Characters

Occasionally, you need a special character in your HTML document that is not on your keyboard. Perhaps you want to display the registered trademark (™) or the copyright symbol (©). These characters and several multinational characters can be added to an HTML document (see fig 24.15).

FIG. 24.15
In the Typographic Character set, only characters 4,22 (Registered Trademark) and 4,23 (Copyright Symbol) are currently supported. In the Multinational Character set, numbers 23 to 89 are supported, excluding characters 2,24; 2,25; 2,74; 2,78; and 2,79.

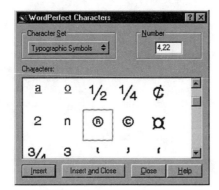

To insert special characters and symbols:

1. Place the insertion point where you want the character to appear.

2. Choose Insert, Character; or press Ctrl+W. The WordPerfect Characters dialog box appears.

3. From the Character Set pop-up list, choose Multinational or Typographic Symbols.

4. Click the desired character.

5. Click Insert And Close to close the dialog box. The character is inserted into your document.

NOTE

Certain characters and symbols might not be visible by all Web browsing programs. If possible, display your web page with several different browsers to see the effects of using these commands.

Creating Links

At this point, you have created a basic web page that could be placed on your intranet. Instructions for putting your page on your intranet can be found later in this chapter in the section "Publishing to HTML."

The page, however, is still a relatively simple one. It provides the reader with something to read, and that's it. Many web pages include hypertext links to allow the reader to quickly "jump" to another topic. That topic could be farther down in your page, on a different HTML document, or even to another page on your intranet.

When should you use a link? It's really your choice, but if your document is relatively small—say, one or two screens full—you might not need a link. If your document is lengthy or it's only the beginning of several other documents, linking becomes necessary.

TIP

If your document is long, you should put a link at the bottom that links back to the top of the document. Sometimes this is referred to as *Go Home* or *Return to Top*.

Creating Bookmarks

In order to link to another location, you must first create a bookmark at the location to jump to. A *bookmark* in a WordPerfect document is similar to a bookmark in a real book. It's a placeholder, and marks specific locations in your document with an English-sounding name. It's much easier to tell WordPerfect to Go To *Managing Your Finances* than it is to Go To *Section 2, Page 14, Paragraph 5.*

To create a bookmark:

1. Place the insertion point at the beginning of the location, or highlight the area to be specified as a bookmark.

2. Choose Insert, Bookmark and the Bookmark dialog box appears.

3. Click the Create button. The Create Bookmark dialog box appears (see fig 24.16).

4. Enter a name for the bookmark in the Bookmark Name box—for example, **Chapter Six** or **New Methods**.

5. Click OK and the bookmark is created.

Fig. 24.16
Bookmarks help
you find a desired
location in the
document quickly.

To quickly get to a specified bookmark, you can use any of the following methods:

● Choose Edit, Go To.

● Press Ctrl+G.

● Double-click the page number at the bottom of the screen on the status line.

The Go To dialog box appears, as shown in figure 24.17. You can then choose to go to a specified page, or in this example, to a named bookmark. The last bookmark created appears in the bookmark section of this dialog box. Choose the bookmark name, click the Bookmark radio button, and click OK.

Fig. 24.17
The Go To box
enables you to
move quickly to
the Last Position
your insertion
point was located.

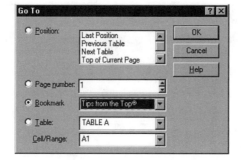

TIP

Save yourself a little frustration—don't forget to click the Bookmark button in the Go To dialog box. It's an easy mistake to not actually click this button because a bookmark name appears, but by default, the button is not selected.

Creating Hypertext Links

Bookmarks can get you around in a standard WordPerfect document, but when you are working with a web page, you might also want the reader to quickly move from one place in your page to another. This process makes the web page interactive for your reader. To do this you need a hypertext link.

HTML hypertext links can create a link from one place in your document to another place in the same document. They can also create a link from one place in your document to another HTML document, whether it's another of your HTML documents or an HTML document belonging to a different department in your company. If you are planning to link to someone else's web page, be sure to contact that person first for permission.

To create a hypertext link:

1. Highlight the text to be designated as the Jump Text. This is the location in the document where the reader may desire to "jump" to another location.

2. Choose Tools, Hypertext/Web Links. The Hypertext Feature Bar appears beneath the toolbar and Power Bar (see fig. 24.18).

Fig. 24.18
Bookmarks can
also be created or
edited from the
Hypertext Feature
Bar.

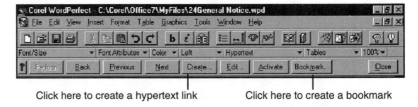

Click here to create a hypertext link   Click here to create a bookmark

3. Click Create from the Feature Bar. The Create Hypertext Link dialog box appears (see fig. 24.19).

Fig. 24.19
If you are online,
you can click the
Browse Web
button in this
dialog box to
access the
Internet.

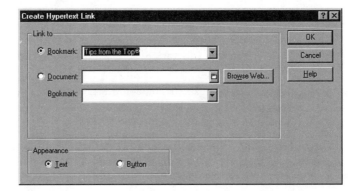

4. Enter the name of the Bookmark to jump to. Or select a different HTML Document and its Bookmark to jump to.

5. Select the appearance choice of either Text or Button.

6. Choose OK. The text selected as the hypertext link turns to a different color and is underlined, or it turns into a button.

N O T E

You should always create a link as text, and then optionally create a second link at the same location that appears as a button. Some Web browsers are character-based only and won't be able to display a graphic button.

TIP

Many web pages include a hypertext link to other web sites. You may want to create hypertext links to other divisions or branches of your company.

Editing a Hyperlink

After you have created your Hypertext link, you might find you need to change it. Perhaps you want it to jump to a different bookmark or document than originally chosen.

To edit a hypertext link:

1. By using the keyboard, move the insertion point to any part of the "jump" text. Be sure to use the arrow keys on the keyboard, and not the mouse.

2. Choose Tools, Hypertext/Web Links. The Hypertext Feature Bar appears.

3. Click the Edit button. The Edit Hypertext Link dialog box appears.

4. Make any desired editing changes, such as changing the bookmark or URL.

5. Choose OK. The Edit Hypertext Link dialog box closes, and the change you made is now in effect.

TIP

To make editing easier, if your Hypertext Link Feature Bar is on-screen, you can temporarily deactivate hypertext by clicking the Deactivate button on the Hypertext Feature Bar. After editing, reactivate hypertext by clicking the Activate button on the Feature Bar.

Editing the Appearance of a Button

A hypertext button, by default, contains no text. It appears as a gray box with no text to designate what it will do. It might be necessary to edit the appearance of the button. This button is really a graphic box and can be edited as any other graphic box by double-clicking the box. At that time, the Text Box Editor opens and enables you to type and format the text to appear in the button. Be aware that some browser programs cannot display a button.

To edit the appearance of a button:

1. Be sure hypertext is deactivated by clicking Deactivate on the Feature Bar.
2. Double-click the graphic button image. You are taken into the Text Box Editor.
3. Type and format the desired text for the button
4. Click outside the graphic box to deselect it.

NOTE

If you are in Draft view instead of Page view, click Close on the Feature Bar to exit the Text Box Editor.

Linking Graphic Images

Most of the time you create a hypertext link by selecting a block of text such as "Click here for more information." Linking is not limited to text, however. In the earlier section, "Creating a Hypertext Link," I discussed how to use a button instead of text, but you can also create a link with a graphic image.

Usually, graphics just lay on the page—looking quite nice, but doing nothing. You can make your web page graphics interactive with hypertext links. With a graphic being interactive, your reader can click the image and jump to a different location.

To link a graphic image:

1. Insert the graphic image into the HTML document, as discussed earlier in the section, "Adding Graphics."

2. Click the graphic image once to select it. Do not double-click it, or you are taken into the drawing program to actually edit the graphic. When it is selected, you see eight small "handles" around it. These are also the sizing handles discussed in the section, "Adding Graphics."

3. With the graphic selected, choose <u>T</u>ools, Hypertext/<u>W</u>eb Links. The Hypertext Feature Bar appears.

4. Click the Crea<u>t</u>e button.

5. Specify the name of the <u>B</u>ookmark to jump to, or select a different HTML <u>D</u>ocument and (if desired) its Bo<u>o</u>kmark to jump to. Notice that because you have preselected a graphic image in the Appearance portion of this dialog box, the text option is not available.

6. Choose OK.

7. Deselect the graphic image by clicking anywhere else in your document.

8. If the Hypertext feature has been deactivated, click the <u>A</u>ctivate button on the Feature bar to reactivate hypertext.

Notice now as you move your mouse pointer over the picture of the graphic it turns into a small hand with a pointing finger. Click anywhere on your graphic, and it jumps to the bookmark or location you specified.

Finishing Your Document

The document is almost complete. There are a few tasks left to do, however. One is to spell check the document and check the grammar. Make sure the text is correct, and make sure the page is in a logical format with headings and subheadings.

Ask someone to review your page. Sometimes it helps to have a coworker or a consultant look at it for structural errors you might have overlooked. Make sure the page is really relaying the information you intended it to. It's better to have a friend point out an error than one of your readers. Readers can notice any mistake in the document and, unfortunately, they don't usually forget it.

Publishing to HTML

As you are working on the HTML document, you can view it with your Netscape browser. This gives you a different perspective of the document from the way WordPerfect is presenting it to you. You might notice some features that appear in WordPerfect but don't appear in the browser—for example, underlining. Note that the browser is the bottom line—how it appears in the browser is how the reader sees it.

The first step to seeing the document in the browser is to save it in an HTML format. This is the step that actually converts the document from WordPerfect format to HTML. At this point, WordPerfect converts all styles to HTML tags. You must save the document first as a WordPerfect document, then as an HTML document.

To publish to HTML:

1. Choose File, Save to save the WordPerfect document.
2. Choose File, Internet Publisher, Publish to HTML. The dialog box shown in figure 24.20 appears, prompting you for a file name. The default choice is to keep the same file name as given in WordPerfect, but assign it an extension of HTM.

Fig. 24.20
WordPerfect creates a separate folder to store the HTML graphics files.

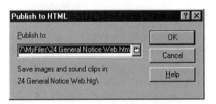

3. Choose OK to accept the default choice.

If you have graphics or hypertext link buttons in your HTML document, they are saved in a separate folder that WordPerfect creates for you. The default choice is to create a folder called *FILENAME*.HTG.

To illustrate this, say the name of your WordPerfect document is MYHOME.WPD and is stored in the C:\OFFICE\MYFILES folder. The HTML document is called MYHOME.HTM and is also stored in the C:\OFFICE\ MYFILES folder. Any graphics or buttons, however, are stored by

WordPerfect in the C:\OFFICE\MYFILES\MYHOME.HTG folder. WordPerfect establishes file names for the graphics such as 0.JPG or 1.JPG. This is controlled exclusively by WordPerfect's Internet Publisher.

CAUTION

Let WordPerfect do its job. Changing the file names or folders may cause the Internet Publisher to not function properly.

Viewing in Netscape

To view the document in your Netscape Web browser:

1. Click the View in Web Browser icon or choose File, Internet Publisher.

2. Choose Browse the Web.

If you click the icon from the toolbar instead of going through the menu, the Netscape browser appears with your document already loaded. You can view the document in the same way your readers will view it. When viewed in the Netscape browser, the document shows a path on the top line similar to

```
C:\WINDOWS\TEMP\WP}00001.TMP
```

This path generally points to your temporary file directory as specified in your computer's AUTOEXEC.BAT file. The file is named WP}*NNNNN*.TMP where *NNNNN* is a file number specified by WordPerfect. When your document is actually published and out on a server, the path points to the server's name and address. An example might be:

```
http://www.1stclass.com/index.html
```

After viewing your document in the browser, you should exit the browser program as you normally would before returning to WordPerfect to make any editing changes.

From Here...

This chapter showed you how to create a page for the intranet using WordPerfect. I introduced you to the features provided in WordPerfect Internet Publisher. However, there are many more things you can do with an intranet page, such as creating interactive forms for your readers to fill out and return to you via e-mail, or being able to download an employee manual from your page.

To accomplish these tasks, you need a clear understanding of the HTML language found in earlier chapters of this book:

- Chapter 2, "HTML Primer: Planning a Document," reviews the basic HTML tags.
- Chapter 3, "Formatting Documents," deals with more advanced HTML tags and linking.

You can also learn about these custom HTML tags from several other books available on the market today. Among these books are Que's *Using HTML* or *Special Edition Using HTML*. You will find a wealth of information in them regarding the additional codes you could use in creating your HTML document.

25

Microsoft FrontPage

By Rick Darnell

FrontPage is a new web management tool developed by Vermeer Technologies, a division of Microsoft. FrontPage eliminates virtually all programming tasks previously associated with constructing a web site, including gathering feedback and registration, and managing content. Knowledge of HTML, Perl, CGI and other languages is not needed for creating pages, so anyone from a programmer to an accountant can develop attractive, interactive pages.

The creation, implementation, and continuing management of web sites is simplified and, thanks to multi-author and administrator capability, spread over a larger group of people. Managing a large web site is also simplified with FrontPage Explorer, which provides a visual, intuitive interface that keeps track of links, pages, and other page components within a web site.

NOTE

Which Explorer is which? With the introduction of FrontPage, Microsoft now has three products with "Explorer" as part of their title. FrontPage Explorer is a web site management tool covered in this chapter, while Internet Explorer is a web browser, and Explorer is a file management tool. References to Explorer in this chapter are to FrontPage Explorer.

FrontPage Editor, another key part of the package, is a powerful creation tool for HTML pages. Changes are made to elements on the page using menus and toolbars, eliminating the need for a designer to remember HTML tags.

Interactivity is added to web pages with FrontPage Editor with Web Robots, also called Web Bots. There are 12 Web Bots included with FrontPage for managing complex, interactive tasks such as managing discussion groups, conducting full-text searches, and adding surveys and registration forms. A few clicks to select and configure a Web Bot replaces once-required custom scripts or complicated HTML commands.

In this chapter, you learn to

- ● Create a web site with a template or wizard
- ● Change author and user permissions
- ● Create and format a web page without knowing HTML
- ● Add links to text and graphics
- ● Include forms for ordering, feedback, and other information
- ● Implement Web Bots for interactive features

Creating and Managing a Web Site with FrontPage Explorer

Perhaps the strongest feature of FrontPage is the ability to quickly assemble the pages and links that compose a local web. FrontPage Explorer provides visual access and editing to the structure of your web.

Depending on your company's size and organization, there are several ways to organize a web site. To start, it's easier to have one site for the entire company. If a department has a specific need or function for the intranet, such as a knowledge base or project information, additional sites can be added. If all sites are located on the same server, they are referenced using the same http domain address, such as **http://www.amalgamated.com/**, followed by the name of the web site.

TIP

Web site organization should reflect the way your company works. If activities happen along department lines, then it makes more sense to users if the web site is organized that way. If your company is project or product-oriented, users expect that reflection in the site. Either way, be sure to include a "road map" accessible from the root directory to display your site's layout.

Start Explorer by clicking its icon.

NOTE

Explorer won't operate without a web server, such as the Personal Web Server included with FrontPage, running in the background. Start the Web Server by clicking its icon before beginning Explorer.

After Explorer is up and running, choose File, New to create a new web. There are several options for creating a new web (see fig. 25.1). When creating a new web, you have the choice of using a template or wizard to construct your web site.

Fig. 25.1
The New Web dialog box gives you access to templates and wizards for creating preconstructed webs.

Enter the name of the server (see fig. 25.2). If you are working through a stand-alone server on your computer using the Personal Web Server, this will probably be **localhost**. If you're operating through a network, enter the name of the server identified by your network administrator. You also need to type a name for the new web.

Fig. 25.2
When creating a new web, the only required information is a web name. This name becomes the name of the directory holding the web contents.

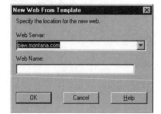

After identifying the server and naming the web, you are prompted for an administrator name and password before proceeding (see fig. 25.3). The person entered here will be the primary administrator for the new web.

Fig. 25.3
An administrator name and password is required for creating a new web on a server. Permission to create or delete webs is granted from the root web.

NOTE

The name of the web is also the name of the folder created in FrontPage's content folder. The name must conform to the naming requirements of your system in regard to length and allowable characters.

Using a Template

Templates are preconstructed webs with a predetermined set of pages already in place. The following templates are available for selection from the New Web dialog box:

- *Normal Web.* Creates a web consisting of a single blank page.
- *Customer Support Web.* Especially useful for companies with a high volume of technical support inquiries, such as software companies, this web helps improve customer service.
- *Empty Web.* For starting completely from scratch, a web without pages.
- *Personal Web.* This is a simple starting point for personal home pages.
- *Project Web.* Creates a web for a specific project, and includes member lists, status reports, schedules, archives, and discussions.

After selecting a template, FrontPage loads the predefined pages and displays the results. The pages are already linked, and only require customization by the user.

Using Web Wizards

Web Wizards prompt the user for information through an interview process, then create a web with specific page formats based on the answers provided. The dialog-driven process can dramatically shorten the time needed to get a web site up and running. These are the Web Wizards available from the New Web dialog box:

- *Corporate Presence Wizard.* Helps create a professional presence for your department or company. It can include products, services, department information, mission statements, and personnel.
- *Discussion Web Wizard.* A web for supporting discussion groups, complete with threads, tables of content, and full-text searching capabilities.

Viewing the Web

Explorer's initial view is a type of web control panel. It shows your web in two different formats (see fig. 25.4). On the left side of the screen is an

Outline view, showing each page that is included as part of the site, whether it contains links to any other pages or not. Clicking a page in the Outline view puts the selected page as the focus of the Link view.

Fig. 25.4
Clicking a page in Outline view makes it the starting point for the graphic display in Link view.

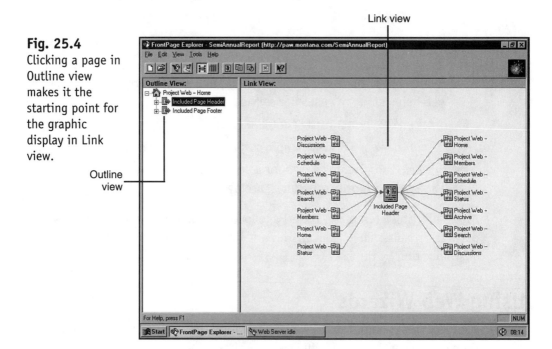

On the right side of the screen is a Link view of the web showing the home page and all pages linked to it. All pages on the left of the central page in Link view contain links to the source, while pages on the right are called from the source.

In Outline or Link view, any page with links not currently displayed are marked with a plus sign (+). Clicking this symbol expands the view with links contained in the page.

 For a directory-type listing of all files on a web, select the Summary view button on the toolbar (see fig. 25.5). This view replaces the Link view with a list of page titles and file information, including who last modified a file and when.

Fig. 25.5
The Summary view gives a detailed listing of all pages on the web without any link information.

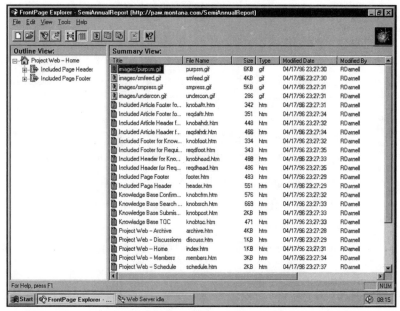

On the toolbar, there are three buttons for controlling which links on a page are displayed:

 🔵 *Images.* This shows all links to images used in your document, whether they're used for hotspots or general illustration.

 🔵 *Repeated Links.* If there is more than one link to the same location on a page, this view displays each separate occurrence of the link. When this isn't selected, only one link is displayed, even if multiple calls exist to the same location.

 🔵 *Inside Page.* Choosing this button displays any links to bookmarks or anchors within a page. For example, a "Frequently Asked Questions" page typically includes a table of contents with a multitude of links to topics contained within. Showing Inside Page links causes Explorer to display a link for each reference from the table of contents to the answer.

Including Other Webs

Once a web is created, new webs can be added to its structure. For example, if you wanted to add a discussion group to a current web, you would choose the Discussion Web Wizard in the New Web dialog box and select the Add to Current Web checkbox.

Adding a New Web

To add a web to the current web, follow these steps:

1. Choose File, New Web to open the New Web Dialog box.

2. Select the type of web you want to add, and click the Add to the Current Web checkbox.

3. Choose OK. The pages from the template or wizard are added to the web.

N O T E

If the inserted template or wizard includes a file that already exists in the current web, you are prompted to confirm the operation before the existing file is replaced.

If a file name in the new web duplicates a file that already exists in the web, you are prompted to choose whether you want to replace the existing file.

Copying an Existing Web

You can also copy the current web into an existing web or server by following these steps:

1. Open the source web.

2. Choose File, Copy Web.

3. From the dialog box (see fig. 25.6), select the server and web destination. If you are copying a web on the same server, the only input needed is the web destination.

Click the Add to Existing Web checkbox if it's being sent to a standing web. If there are permissions associated with the current web, they can also be preserved with the transfer.

Fig. 25.6
To copy the current web to another web or server, identify the server and the name of the destination. Security settings can be maintained through the transfer.

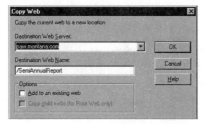

CAUTION

You should change the name of the home page in the source web from `"index.htm"`. Explorer does *not* prompt if there are any duplicate pages in the destination, and any duplicate files are automatically overwritten by the source. Since every web created by Explorer includes a file named `"index.htm"` for its home page, the home page in the destination could be eliminated.

Secure Updating and Editing

Each web has at least one administrator who is identified with a name and password when the web is first created. This administrator controls access to the web by setting permissions for end users, authors, and other administrators of the web. Web security is inherited from the server's root web. The default root web is located in the Content folder on the computer where the server is based. All administrators, authors, and end users defined for the root web are valid for any other web created under the root web, unless otherwise specified.

Permissions are checked for each access to the web site, including attempts to add or edit pages. By including permission information, only authorized users are allowed to alter web site content.

To add or change user permissions, follow these steps:

1. After opening the web, choose Tools, Permissions.

2. You'll see a tab in the Web Permissions dialog box for each type of permission (see fig. 25.7). Choose among the various options:

Fig. 25.7
Web permission settings can be defined for administrators, authors and end users by name and passwords, IP addresses, or a combination of both. In addition, each web can have its own unique set of permissions.

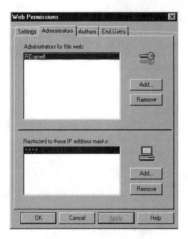

Use the *Administrators tab* to set up or remove administrators from a web. Administrators have permission to create and delete webs and pages, designate other administrators and authors, and restrict end users from accessing a web.

Authors are limited to creating and deleting pages. They can only change pages and content, and cannot completely remove a web from the server.

The *End Users tab* is used to limit access to the web. By default, a web is open to everyone. However, if it is necessary to control who has access to the web, use this tab to identify individuals with permission to browse. When a browser opens a protected web, the user is prompted for their name and password. If these are invalid entries, access is denied.

In addition to basic name and password information, all permissions can be screened by entering a mask IP address. By entering a range of numbers and/or wildcards in this tab, access is restricted to specific computers. This serves as a "double-safe" on password systems. Even if a name and password combination becomes known, the user must still use the right terminal in order to gain administrator access.

3. Choose OK to accept the security options.

Creating and Editing Pages with FrontPage Editor

Creating attractive and user-friendly web pages is easy with the FrontPage Editor object-based design. Creating HTML tags is not necessary, even for complicated pages with forms and other special items. As you add each item, it appears the same as when viewed with a browser, relieving the need to visualize HTML coding.

In addition to launching from the Start button, you can alternatively start Editor from Explorer by selecting its button or double-clicking a page.

Creating a Page

Creating a page with Editor is similar to creating a web with Explorer. A set of templates and Page Wizards are available to ease the task of creating and developing page formats and content.

To create a page, follow these steps:

1. Choose File, New.
2. Pick the type of page from the list of templates and Page Wizards (see fig. 25.8).
3. Choose OK. The new page is displayed and ready for editing.

Fig. 25.8
The New Page dialog box allows the user to start with a blank sheet or select a preformatted page.

Templates

Page templates include formatting and sample text already in place. Many also include generic links to other web pages. These links can be edited to real locations by the user. Templates that come with FrontPage Editor are:

- ● *Normal Page.* Creates a blank page.
- ● *Bibliography.* A listing of printed or electronic works.
- ● *Confirmation Form.* Used to acknowledge user input from forms.
- ● *Directory of Press Releases.* Creates a directory of press releases, sorted by date. These can be imported from compatible word processor files.
- ● *Employee Directory.* Alphabetized list of employees in your company or department, complete with a hot-linked table of contents.
- ● *Employment Opportunities.* Manages a list of job openings along with a registration form to get more information.
- ● *Feedback Form/Guest Book/Survey Form.* A place for users to submit comments on your web site or provide other information for your use.
- ● *Frequently Asked Questions (FAQ).* A question and answer document with bookmarks to answer common questions on a topic.
- ● *Glossary of Terms.* A page of definitions, divided into sections alphabetically.
- ● *Hot List/Table of Contents.* A list of links to favorite sites divided into sections, or a generated index to all pages on a web.

- *HyperDocument Page.* This page is designed to serve as one section of a hyperlinked manual or report. Fill-in links are available for the hyperdocument's home page and Table of Contents page.
- *Lecture Abstract.* This provides an outline of a lecture or presentation topic, and is especially useful when linked to the Seminar Schedule.
- *Office Directory.* A page listing the physical and electronic locations of company offices.
- *Press Release.* Creates a press release page which can be linked into the Directory of Press Releases page.
- *Product Description/Software Data Sheet.* A listing of features, benefits, and specifications for a specific product or software package.
- *Product or Event Registration.* Allows user to register for product support or attendance at an upcoming event.
- *Search Page.* A very powerful page which allows a user to search for keywords in all documents on a web.
- *Seminar Schedule.* Creates a listing of events and lectures for a seminar.
- *User Registration.* Creates information to let a new user into a web site. This will also help the user, by using the information on the registration form to fill in other forms on the web. This page is only effective from the root web.
- *What's New.* A list of new documents, features, files, links, and other items of interest on a web.

Page Wizards

Page Wizards gather information about the content and intent of your page, and then create the elements on the page based on your answers. Here are the page wizards that come with FrontPage Editor:

- *Form Page Wizard.* Creates a form by deciding what types of information you need to collect.
- *Personal Home Page Wizard.* This creates a single page designed to meet your personal and professional needs for a presence on the web.

Opening a Page

If a web is active in Explorer, you can open pages from it by choosing File, Open from Web. To edit pages not associated with the current web, select Open from File.

The page is displayed as it will appear in a browser. If you're interested in seeing how the page would look with HTML tags, select View, Source HTML.

Adding Titles

Basic page information is changed by selecting Edit, Page Settings (see fig. 25.9). The title of the page is what appears at the top of the browser when the page is loaded. If you have specific color requirements for your page, they are also defined here. Keep in mind, however, the different monitors and systems that your page may be viewed on. What looks pleasing on one monitor may become an unreadable dithered mess on another.

Fig. 25.9
The Page Proper-
ties sheet allows
the user to edit
items applying to
the entire docu-
ment, such as the
page title and link
colors.

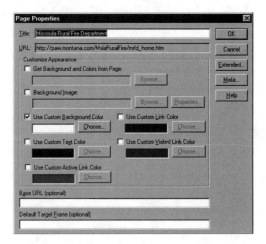

Adding Formatting

On a basic level, Editor is similar to any other word processor. It allows typing, cutting, and pasting of any text on the page. Formatting the text for appearances on a web browser is accomplished by highlighting text, and then choosing the appropriate style from a menu.

Any format allowed by HTML is accessible from Editor. To help define sections of the page, begin with headings. There are two ways to add formatting text: by changing the appearance of existing text or inserting a new item with the required attributes.

To change existing text:

1. Highlight the text you want to change.

2. Choose the new format from the style list on the top left of the menu bar. Changes to the selected text take effect immediately.

To insert a new line with new formatting:

1. Position the insertion point at the point where the new item should be.

2. Choose Insert, Heading. A list of menu choices appears from 1 to 6, largest to smallest (see fig. 25.10). Click to choose.

Fig. 25.10
Inserting formatted text is a simple matter of selecting the type and style of text from the Insert menu.

3. Type your heading or other text. Any text typed on this line will reflect the applied style. The process used for creating headings also applies for lists, definitions, and paragraph styles.

Horizontal lines are another feature used by many web pages, and are also simple to insert from Editor:

1. Position the insertion point where the line should be inserted.

2. Choose Insert, Horizontal Line. The new line appears with its default settings.

3. To change the appearance of a line, choose <u>E</u>dit, Pr<u>o</u>perties to display its attributes (see fig. 25.11).

Fig. 25.11
The attributes of a horizontal line are altered from this dialog box, which allows total control of the line's appearance.

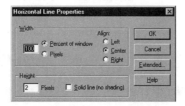

4. Select among the options to change the line. The line can be shortened, widened, justified with the left or right margin, or changed to a solid black line.

5. Choose OK to save the changes and view the results.

Creating Links and Bookmarks

One of the key items for any web page is a link or multiple links to other pages, web sites, and important items on the current page. There are two ways to create links to other pages.

Inserted Links

The first way to create a link is by manually inserting it into the current document:

1. Select the text which will become the link.

2. When the text is highlighted, the link button becomes active. Click this button to create the link, or choose <u>E</u>dit, <u>L</u>ink.

3. The Create Link dialog box includes four tabs, depending on the source of the link (see fig. 25.12). Choose among the options on these tabs:

Fig. 25.12
Links to any page
on your server or
World Wide Web
are defined by
choosing the tab
representing its
basic location.

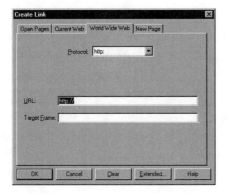

Open Pages. Pages already open under Editor.

Current Web. Pages from the current web in Explorer. A link to a book-mark on the current page can also be selected from this tab.

World Wide Web. Pages from the World Wide Web. A complete URL is needed, including the type of page (HTTP, ftp, MAILTO).

New Page. If you are referencing a page before creating it, there are two options. Editor opens a new page with the name and title you specify. Or, it adds an item to the To Do list. This allows you to post-pone the task or assign it to someone else.

4. After selecting the page, click OK. The highlighted choice is in a new color and underlined. The destination appears in the bottom status bar when the mouse is over the link.

5. To check the link, select Tools, Follow Link, and Editor loads the page for viewing or editing.

Drag-and-Drop Links

Links can also be included on a page by dragging icons from Explorer:

1. Reduce the size of the Editor screen and make sure you can see the screen for Explorer. You will need to see the page icons in Explorer, and the point where you want them inserted in Editor.

2. Click and hold on the desired page in Explorer and drag it onto the Edi-tor page. The pointer changes from a page to a link.

3. When the pointer is at the correct position, release the mouse button. The new link has the same title as the page title. You can edit the text of the link the same as any other formatted text, although editing from either end of the text or highlighting and replacing will remove the link.

Defining Bookmarks

Bookmarks are used to create links within a page. This is often used for "Frequently Asked Questions" documents, which have a hot list of questions at the top of the page that link to answers on the same page.

To create bookmarks (or anchors in HTML) from Editor:

1. Select the text for the bookmark.
2. Choose Edit, Bookmark to view a dialog box for naming the bookmark.
3. Type a name for the bookmark and choose OK. The bookmark is identified with a dashed underline.

Creating a link to a bookmark is similar to manually inserting a link to another page:

1. Highlight the text which will be linked to the bookmark.

2. Choose the Link button, or choose Edit, Link.
3. From the Open Pages tab, click the current page. Then, click the List button next to the Bookmarks field.
4. Pick the desired target from the list of defined bookmarks, and click OK.

Graphics

Including graphics is a simple matter of telling Editor where to find the graphic file. Hotspots can also be created from imported images. Hotspots are similar to image maps, which define multiple links within an image. By clicking different areas of the image, a different destination is selected. This is especially useful for items like menu and navigation bars.

Importing a Graphic

FrontPage can import graphics from many of the common formats, including GIF, JPEG, PCX, TIFF, PostScript, and WordPerfect. Images other than GIF and JPEG will be translated into GIF if 256 colors or less, and JPEG if more than 256.

To import a graphic, follow these steps:

1. Choose Insert, Image.
2. If you are using an image from another web, choose From URL and enter the address. If it's an image from your local drive, choose From File.
3. To complete the process from a file, select the file type from the list at the bottom of the dialog box (see fig. 25.13) and navigate to the folder that contains the image.

Fig. 25.13
Any image file accessible from your computer can be included as part of a web page.

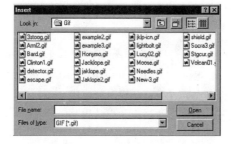

4. Select the file, and choose OK.
5. When the page is saved, you are prompted to save the image file in its new format in a subdirectory to your web. Choose OK to complete the process.

Turning a Graphic into a Hotspot

After importing an image, you can turn the entire picture or just portions of it into links to other pages or bookmarks.

To create a link with the entire picture, click the image and follow the directions for creating links.

To create a hotspot:

1. Click the image to select it. The hotspot buttons on the top right of the menu bar are activated. Hotspots can be square, round, or freehand.

2. Click and hold the left mouse button while drawing the lines around the desired portion of the image. When using the freehand tool, click the mouse button to anchor a line, move the mouse to the next point, and click again. Repeat the process to outline the shape.

3. Choose the Link button, and pick the destination for the spot (see "Creating Links and Bookmarks" earlier in this chapter for more information).

4. Choose OK.

5. Repeat Steps 2 through 4 for additional hotspots within the same image.

Forms

Simplified form creation and handling are probably FrontPage's strongest editing features. Like the other editing features, form elements are displayed as they'll appear on a browser. After adding form elements such as text boxes, radio buttons, and checkboxes, you'll make choices on how contents are handled when the Submit button is clicked.

Form Page Wizard

The simplest way to create a form is to open a new document and choose the Form Page Wizard. Through a series of questions and checkboxes, the wizard will ask which kinds of information need to be collected, and then construct the elements into a finished form. The final product can be used as a stand-alone page, copied and pasted into another page, or inserted at runtime using the Include Web Bot.

Manual Form Creation

Creating a form is like creating any other item on a page, and the full range of form features are at your disposal, including single- and multiple-line text boxes, buttons, and checkboxes. Each element is created by selecting Insert,

Form Field, and then selecting a specific item from the list. Basic item information is entered on a dialog box, and the resulting form element is inserted on the page.

When the first form item is created, it's surrounded by dotted lines (see fig. 25.14). This denotes the size of the individual form. More form elements and text can be included on the form, or a new form can be created by moving outside the dotted lines and inserting another form item.

Fig. 25.14
A new form is created by inserting a form element. The new form is defined by a dashed line around all form elements and text.

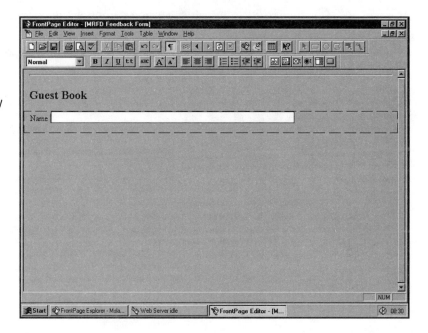

Each form item requires basic information to function:

- *Text box.* The name is how the item is referred to within the form (see fig. 25.15). No spaces are allowed. The value is any text that should appear in the box when the user first views the form. All text boxes require a width (in characters), while scrolling text boxes also require a height. One-line text boxes can accept input beyond their width, defined in maximum characters. Any information typed beyond the width of the box will scroll across until the maximum character limit is reached. Selecting the password option results in masking user input with asterisks (*).

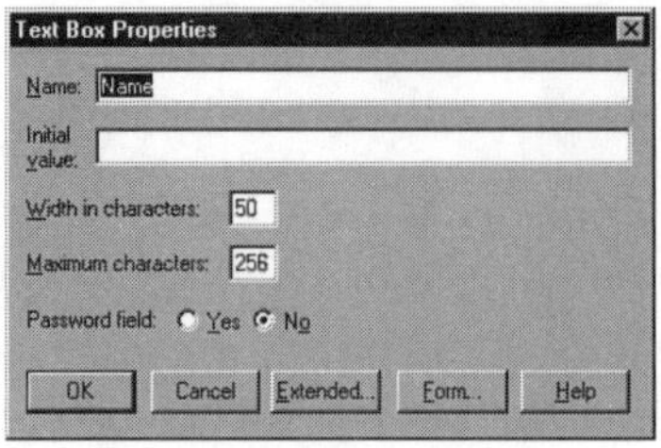

Fig. 25.15
The size and capacity of one-line and scrolling text boxes are controlled through their respective dialog boxes.

● *Checkbox/Radio buttons.* Enter a name for the checkbox, and indicate whether the box should be selected when the form is loaded (see fig. 25.16). For radio buttons, all related items are linked together by using the same name. Each individual button will have the same group name, and a different value. You can also indicate if a button is already selected when the form is viewed. The value is what will be recorded as the result when information from the form is submitted.

Fig. 25.16
Radio buttons and checkboxes require a value to return when they are marked.

● *Push Buttons.* The value of a push button (see fig. 25.17) is the title that will appear on the button, such as Order Now or Reset Form. The purpose of the button is selected by clicking the appropriate function.

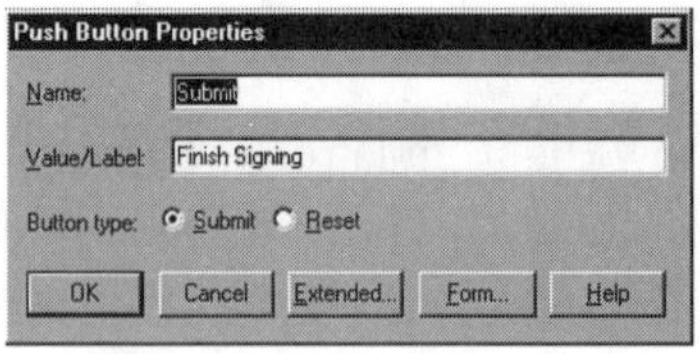

Fig. 25.17
Push buttons come in two varieties, submit or reset. The value is the name that appears on the button.

Web Bots

Web Bots are *helper applications*, also referred to as applets. There are 12 bots included with FrontPage to add functionality to your web pages that normally require extensive and complicated HTML commands or CGI programming. These Web Bots add interactive features such as navigation bars, discussion groups, full-text searches, and registration forms—all with just clicks of the mouse. Four of the most useful and powerful Web Bots are described in the following sections.

Include

This simple but effective bot inserts a working version of another web page as part of the current web page. This is useful when creating a navigation bar with links leading to other web pages. Instead of copying and pasting navigation bar text into each page, the navigation bar is created on its own HTML page. The Include Bot includes a copy at runtime on the destination pages. Any changes to the navigation bar page are automatically included anywhere it is called by the bot.

To insert an Include Bot on a page:

1. Choose Insert, Bot.
2. A dialog box requests the URL of the page to include (see fig. 25.18). If you don't know the exact URL, select Browse. From the browse screen (see fig. 25.19), you can choose another page from the current web to include.
3. Click OK to complete the entry.
4. The new page is inserted into the current page. You can't edit the imported version from the host page. It can only be altered by opening the original source. Moving the mouse over the area of the imported page changes the pointer into a little robot, to indicate how it was generated.

Fig. 25.18
Type the URL for
the page that the
Include Bot will
include in the
current page at
runtime, or
choose Browse to
complete the
entry if you don't
know the com-
plete URL.

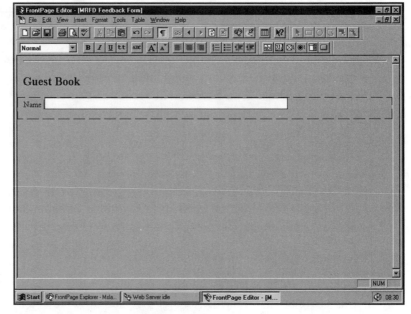

Fig. 25.19
All pages from the
current web are
available to
choose for the
Include Bot.

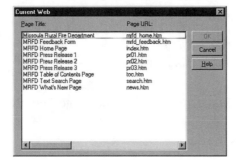

Save Results

The Save Results Bot takes input from a form and saves it to a user-defined
location, usually another HTML page. This makes it easy to collect items such
as comments, feedback, questions, and other end-user entered information.

To add a Save Results Bot to a page:

1. To add a bot to a form, click an existing form item.

2. Choose Edit, Properties to view the properties for the specific form item. Choose Form to view the form properties.

3. At the top of the Form Properties box (see fig. 25.20), there is a selection list of different ways of handling this form. By default, all forms look for a CGI script. Click the arrow next to the box, and choose Save Results Bot from the list.

Fig. 25.20
Depending on the type of form, there are three Web Bots to choose from to handle the results. Custom CGI scripts are also supported by FrontPage.

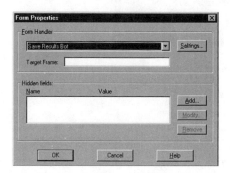

4. Form Web Bots need basic information to know how to function. Select Settings to view the setup options (see fig. 25.21). If the results will be used with other web pages or viewed with a browser, enter a file name and select HTML. If the information will be collected and entered into a database for other use, then additional formats are available, including comma or tab-delimited lists. Both formats can be used by selecting the Advanced tab, and including another file name and type to hold results.

Field names given to each form item can be included, along with additional information such as the time and date of submission, a user name or computer name, and the type of browser used. A confirmation page is used to inform the user that the page was submitted, and typically provides a link back to the form or to the next step in the process.

Fig. 25.21
In order to save
the results from a
form, the Web Bot
needs a file name
and file type. A
confirmation page
provides feedback
to the user after
the contents of a
form are success-
fully submitted.

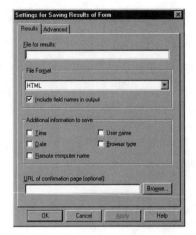

5. Click OK to return to the page.

Discussion

This Web Bot manages threads of a discussion group, creates an index, and generates a table of contents. Functionally, it creates a web version of a newsgroup.

A Discussion Bot is added to a page in a similar manner to other bots:

1. Create a form that contains two basic elements: a one-line text box for the subject, and a scrolling text box for the message or comments.

2. Click one of the form elements, and then choose Edit, Properties. From the Form Item Properties box, select Form.

3. The default form handler is CGI Script. Click the selection arrow next to this field, and choose Discussion Bot.

4. Click Settings to configure the Web Bot.

5. From the Discussion tab (see fig. 25.22), there are two key items to include: Title and Directory. The title entered here will appear at the top of all articles submitted for discussion. To store the contents of a discussion, FrontPage creates a subdirectory to hold submitted articles. The name must be eight characters or less, beginning with an under-score (_).

Fig. 25.22
The table of
contents for a
discussion group
can include
several items to
help identify who
provided the
comments and
when.

The table of contents layout is also defined from this tab. Subject is the default name for the one-line text box with the comment topic. Enter the name of the subject field entered in step 1, along with any other fields you want to include in the table of contents, separated by spaces. Time, Date, Remote Computer Name, and User Name can also be part of the listing.

The default order provides the most recent articles at the top of the list. Selecting Oldest to Youngest sorts the articles in the order they were posted.

A confirmation page acknowledges receipt of user. This is typically a short page with a link back to the home page or to the discussion table of contents.

6. Select the Article tab to format the page that contains each discussion entry. It can include a header and footer page, which is useful for providing navigation bars and feedback capabilities, in addition to the date, time, remote computer name, and user name of the person who made the entry.

7. After all operation and formatting choices are made, click OK until you return to the main document.

Search

By using a Search Web Bot in conjunction with a search form, the user creates a runtime list of links to pages containing key words. Adding a search form to your web allows users to easily find pages that contain topics that interest them. For example, if a web contains several projects with input from the same department, the user could locate the project pages that mention a specific department by entering the department's name in a search form.

To add search capabilities to your page:

1. Open the page in your web on which you want to create the search form. A common location is on the web's home page, or a page directly linked to the home page on a navigation bar.

2. Position the insertion point where the search form will be located, and choose Insert, Bot.

3. When the Insert Bot dialog box opens, select Search. The Search Bot Properties dialog box opens (see fig. 25.23).

Fig. 25.23
Parameters for collecting search key information and how to display search results are entered in the Search Bot Properties dialog box.

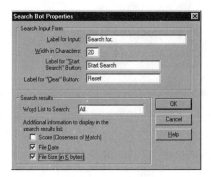

4. The Search Bot creates a one-line text box field to collect input. In the Label for Input field, enter a title for this field or accept the default, Search for.

   For the Width in Characters field, enter the width of the input field, or accept the default.

In the Label for Start Search button field, enter a title for the push button field that starts the search, or accept the default, Start Search.

In the Label for Clear Button field, enter a title for the push button that clears the form, or accept the default, Reset.

In the Word List to Search field, indicate where the Search Bot will look for the user's input. To search the entire web except discussion groups, specify All. To search a single discussion group, specify the directory for the discussion group preceded by an underscore (_).

5. When the Search Bot returns with its results, additional information can be included about the matches.

Score indicates the quality of the match.   Document Date indicates the date and time the document containing the match was modified. Document Size indicates the size of the document containing the match.

6. Choose OK to accept your selections.

To Do List

The FrontPage To Do List is integrated with the creation of webs and web pages (see fig. 25.24). In addition, items can be added manually to the list, or by the creation of links to non-existent pages. Once a task is added to the list, it can be named, described, prioritized, and assigned. Tasks can be started from the To Do list, and when completed or saved, are prompted for removal.

Fig. 25.24
FrontPage Editor can be launched from the To Do list by double-clicking a task.

One Site, Multiple Authors

A corporate web can include many different departments and individuals. Rather than trying to create pages and manage content for each group, each department can maintain its own section of the web without relying on a single point of contact.

When the web is created, each department is given its own home page or web, and links to these pages are created on the corporate home page. Each web site can have its own administrator and individual authors, reducing the demands on the primary web administrator. If all pages and webs are managed from the same server, links are verified when Explorer starts.

Personal Web Server

To test and view your web, FrontPage is equipped with a Personal Web Server. Depending on your hardware and software combination, it configures itself for 16- or 32-bit operation. This slows down the operation of Explorer and Editor when changes are made to the web site. However, it allows you to access and test your site using a browser such as Netscape or Mosaic the same way an end user would.

From Here...

Creating and managing an intranet site means preplanning and coordination with everyone who needs to contribute. FrontPage lets you worry about the "big picture" by taking the hassle out of the details.

While a sophisticated and powerful application, FrontPage provides a simple and easy-to-use interface for effectively managing large web sites involving complicated functions such as discussion groups. With the basic information provided in this chapter, even novice webmasters can develop a new web in a matter of hours, not days.

- Chapter 1, "Understanding Your Intranet Site," explains the basic mechanics of what an intranet is and how it functions.

- Chapter 3, "Formatting Documents," gives guidance on making your site and individual pages easy to use.

- Chapter 8, "Planning and Using Intranet Forms," offers advice on when to use forms, and how to make them effective tools.

26

InterNotes Web Publisher

By Jane "JC" Calabria

Good management is the key to a successful web site. The most visually stimulating, graphically intense, professionally designed pages on a web site are only effective on the first visit. For electronic commerce, you need to keep people coming back. On a company intranet, you need to keep your information current. This is accomplished through constant creation and updating of content, directories, templates, forms, and information. The InterNotes Web Publisher is the key to good management of your intranet.

In this chapter, you'll learn about Lotus InterNotes Web Publisher, a set of tools that permits the conversion of documents in Lotus Notes databases into HTML formatted files stored on an HTTP server. You will learn how this process works and what sort of effort is necessary to make it happen. If you already have Lotus Notes in your organization, this will be very useful information to you. If you're not yet familiar with Notes, we try to illustrate what Notes is and how Notes and InterNotes Web Publisher can streamline the management of your web site, as well as the powerful synergy that exists between Lotus Notes and web technology.

Your Company Wide Web

To understand how Notes and InterNotes Web Publisher can help you make your company intranet a truly powerful management tool, it might help to step back and look at the current and future benefits of your company intranet. We'll refer to your intranet as your Company Wide Web.

What's Right with Your Company Wide Web

The original and still primary benefit of web technology is the elegant and inexpensive way it provides for disseminating information far and wide. Management can use it to publish all sorts of important information to its employees. For example, suppose your company training department wants to publish its course offerings and class schedules to the rest of the company. They could distribute them on paper and post them on non-computerized bulletin boards. They could flood the network with e-mail. Or, they could publish them on the Company Wide Web, making them widely and conveniently available to anyone with a connection to the network and a web browser.

What's Wrong with Your Company Wide Web

The mere publishing of the course schedule solves only one of many problems for the training department. Employees still need to call the training department to enroll in class, find out more about class content, or request an approval form for their manager to sign. A really effective Company Wide Web would allow for interactivity—with online registration, automatic notification of enrollment acceptance, automatic mailing of approval forms, and up-to-the-minute details of class enrollment. A really useful web application would publish information stored in back-end databases on the web, and would receive information entered in the web browser back into the back-end databases for further processing.

While it's possible to marry web technology to other programs in this way, it's no trivial undertaking. It requires some pretty sophisticated programming in one or more database languages as well as one or more scripting languages such as CGI, SSI, or Perl. Or you may let Lotus Notes and InterNotes Web Publisher do all the work for you.

Furthermore, while cheap and widely available web browsers make retrieving information on the Internet/intranet wonderfully easy, publishing that information and managing a web site full of interconnected pages is a major undertaking. Someone has to create all those HTML documents. Someone has to maintain all the links between those documents. Doing these things by hand quickly becomes impossible as a web site grows beyond a couple dozen pages.

There are many tools available to help you code links to back-end databases, to automate the creation of HTML documents, and to manage a web site full of interlinked documents. Some tools are cheap and adequate. Others are expensive and elegant. Most require that you have some degree of expertise in HTML, CGI, and maybe other scripting languages. Lotus Notes does the whole job for you, and it does it elegantly, at low cost, and without CGI programming on your part.

What Is Lotus Notes?

Lotus Notes combines databases with e-mail and a rich programming environment. Notes users can *communicate* with each other via e-mail; they can *collaborate* with each other in projects by maintaining shared tracking databases; and they can *coordinate* their mutual efforts with Notes workflow applications. Workgroups may develop their own applications; they may customize applications that come with Notes; or they may buy applications or customization from a third-party developer. They can refine their applications as necessary using Notes' built-in development tools. Notes includes:

- *Tracking Databases*. The heart of Notes is its shared database technology. Groups of Notes users can keep track of on-going projects in Notes databases. For example, in our training department we can schedule classes, then track the progress of enrollments and department approvals. We know exactly who to notify if a class needs to be rescheduled. Because this is all stored in a shared Notes database, this information is available to our entire department.

- *Electronic Mail.* Notes users can communicate with each other by e-mail and with non-Notes users through mail gateways. However, NotesMail is different from other e-mail systems because it is an extension of the Notes database technology, not a shared file system as are other mail systems. That is, Notes mail documents are stored in Notes databases and the mailing of documents from one user to another is really the mailing of a document from one Notes database to another. So, we can mail our Notes list of attendees to contracted trainers who might not otherwise have access to our Notes applications. We can mail approval requests to the managers of prospective students. And our databases can mail notices to us automatically, triggered by the passage of time or occurrence of events.

● *Workflow Applications.* Because Notes databases can mail documents to each other, and because it includes a rich, integrated programming environment, Notes is an ideal platform for creating workflow applications. For example, a trainer might fill out an expense report. When the trainer saves and closes the expense report, Notes mails it automatically to an expense-tracking database, and mails a notice to the trainer's manager that the expense report requires review and approval.

The notice includes a link to the expense report in the tracking database. By double-clicking the link, the manager opens the expense report. When the manager approves and saves the expense report, Notes mails a notice to the accounting clerk responsible for paying the expenses, and so the cycle continues.

If either the manager or the accounting clerk neglects a pending task, Notes sends a reminder. If the person designated to complete a task is unavailable for any reason, a substitute might automatically be appointed. Because all of this is stored in a central-tracking database, anyone involved in the transaction can see its status simply by looking there.

● *Development Tools.* In addition to its tracking databases and mail capability, Notes provides a rich programming environment that offers you a selection of programming languages, from simple (the Notes @function language) to more powerful and complex: LotusScript↔, an ANSI BASIC compliant language similar to Visual BASIC™; the Lotus Notes API, a library of C functions; HiTest Tools™ for Visual BASIC™; numerous third-party programming tools; and, due to be available in the summer of 1996, an implementation of Java™.

● *Client/Server technology.* Notes implements as a client/server system. Notes servers store Notes databases, provide multiple levels of security, and make information in the databases available to people and other servers according to their access rights.

People use the Notes client to access the data on the servers. The Notes client can access Notes servers via network connections or remotely by modem. Notes Release 4 makes connections to servers almost foolproof for the user by allowing Notes administrators to predefine connection procedures from different locations.

For example, if a salesman is in the office, he connects to the LAN, tells Notes he is in the office, and Notes automatically uses the LAN to connect to the server. Then the salesman goes on the road, arrives in a hotel room, connects his modem to a telephone line, and tells Notes he is located in a hotel. Notes automatically calls the server using the modem and a standard hotel phone system dialing sequence.

- *InterNotes Web Navigator.* In addition to InterNotes Web Publisher, which allows publication of Notes databases to an HTTP server, Notes Release 4 includes InterNotes Web Navigator. This is a tool that permits Notes users to access the World Wide Web from within Notes.

  In effect, it turns the Notes client into a web browser. However, it is a web browser with a difference. It uses an InterNotes server as a gateway to the web, and the server can be configured to limit web access to approved sites and approved access times. The InterNotes server can also cache selected HTML documents as documents in Notes databases, so that especially valuable web content is available much quicker than if one always had to reach across the Internet for the information.

- *Connectivity.* Notes was designed from the ground up to work with whatever other software tools you may use. You can pull information into Notes documents from all of your desktop productivity applications as well as from databases located on PCs and mainframes. You can also export information to your back-end databases. Also, Notes runs on a variety of platforms including Windows, Windows 95, Windows NT, Macintosh, OS/2, NetWare, and UNIX. It can use all major networking protocols including TCP/IP, SPX/IPX, NetBEUI/NetBIOS, AppleTalk, and Banyan VINES.

Notes Documents and Fields

Lotus Notes databases bear only the most superficial resemblance to standard computer databases. They do have records and fields in them, as do standard databases, but the resemblance ends right about there. The records, known as *documents* or *notes*, look and feel more like word processor documents than database records. Notes fields do not have a fixed length and the length of any one field varies from document to document depending on the field's actual contents. Not all documents in a database even have to have the same array of fields. Document A might have fields one, two, and three, while document B has fields one, two, and four. And a document might acquire fields one and two when created, then have fields three and four added at a later date.

Notes Forms

When you create, edit, or read a Notes document, you do so using a template known as a *Form*. Forms define what fields may be added to a document when created or edited. They define what fields may be seen when reading the document. They also define how the document will be formatted.

You may use one form to create a document and another to read it. Or I may read a document with Form A while you read it with Form B. The result might be that I, the trainer, would see some fields and you, the student, would see others. Notes databases typically have multiple forms.

Notes Views and Full-Text Search

To find information in a Notes database, you could either browse Notes views or you could use Notes' full-text search engine to locate documents. A Notes view is a tabular listing of documents. The documents appear in rows, and information from the documents appears in columns. Most Notes databases include multiple views, allowing you to use the one most suited to your search. For example, in a training department database, you might view classes by date in one view and by subject in another view. A third view might show only a subset of documents. For example, one view might show only the classes scheduled for this week.

What's Right with Notes

Lotus Notes is a powerful tool for the rapid development and deployment of applications that enhance the ability of groups of people to communicate with each other, work together on projects, and coordinate their activities. It includes an integrated programming environment. There are numerous third-party products available, including end-user applications, application development tools, and server-enhancing add-ins. All of these features combine to make Notes the only truly comprehensive groupware product on the market.

What's Wrong with Notes

Until Notes Release 4 arrived in January 1996, Notes was a closed system. You had to have a Notes client, available only from Lotus, to gain full access to Notes databases, or you could gain limited, customized access to Notes databases with some of the Notes add-in tools, such as Notes ViP. Also, until Notes Release 4 arrived, these tools were much more expensive than the browsers necessary to implement a company intranet.

Of course, Notes Release 4 has eliminated much of the downside of implementing Notes. Not only has Release 4 dramatically increased the functionality and interconnectivity of Notes with the inclusion of such tools as InterNotes Web Publisher and InterNotes Web Navigator, but Lotus has also slashed its pricing to bring Notes servers and clients in line with Internet servers and browsers. For example, a single Notes server now costs about $700. InterNotes Web Publisher (which cost $7,500 when first released in January 1995) is at this writing a free download from Lotus's website (**http://www.lotus.com**), and will probably be included in the box with the server software by the time you read this. And a Notes Desktop™ client, which includes all Notes functionality except server administration and application design, runs around $100 per desktop, less if purchased in quantity.

What Is InterNotes Web Publisher?

The InterNotes Web Publisher is an add-in product to Lotus Notes. It publishes Notes databases as linked HTML pages to an HTTP server. It also publishes Notes forms, then accepts data entered into the forms in a web browser, converting it into documents in the underlying Notes database. It distributes web page authorship to anyone who can create a Notes document. And InterNotes Web Publisher promotes the maintenance of your HTML document-base because every time a Notes document changes, InterNotes Web Publisher republishes it, refreshing its links in the process.

InterNotes Web Publisher is available at no charge as a download from the Lotus website (**http://www.lotus.com**). That's a big improvement over its price tag when it was first released in January 1995. Version 2.x works with Notes Release 3 servers. Version 4.x works with Notes Release 4 servers.

InterNotes Web Publisher is the answer to what's wrong with your Company Wide Web and what's wrong with Lotus Notes. It marries them nicely. InterNotes Web Publisher features:

- *Document conversion.* InterNotes Web Publisher converts Notes documents and views into HTML pages, and data entered into HTML forms into Notes documents.

- *HTML publishing.* InterNotes Web Publisher publishes Notes databases as HTML pages on HTTP servers.

- *HTML maintenance.* InterNotes Web Publisher maintains the Notes-originated HTML pages and their links by updating them whenever the underlying Notes database is updated.

- *Search engine.* InterNotes Web Publisher extends Notes's full-text search capability to web users. They enter a query into a field in a search form. InterNotes Web Publisher conveys the query to Notes, which conducts the search. InterNotes Web Publisher then conveys the results of the search to the user as a list of links to the HTML pages that meet the search criteria.

- *Information retrieval.* InterNotes Web Publisher publishes Notes forms as HTML forms, fillable in web browsers. When a web user submits a form, InterNotes Web Publisher conveys it to the underlying Notes database as a standard Notes document. That document could then become a part of a standard Notes workflow application, or it could in turn be republished by InterNotes Web Publisher as an HTML document

- *Discussion site.* Because InterNotes Web Publisher permits the republishing of forms completed by web users as HTML documents, your web site can be used as a discussion database. You can effectively extend the utility of Notes's discussion databases to your web users.

InterNotes Web Publisher converts Notes documents and databases into directories of HTML documents. Then it maintains those HTML documents by automatically updating them whenever the underlying Notes documents change. It establishes the links among the Notes-published pages, based on their relationships in the Notes database as well as on links inserted in the documents by their authors. And it updates the links, again based on changes that occur in the Notes databases.

Finally, it permits the publishing of forms. A reader can complete the form in his web browser. InterNotes Web Publisher then takes the information from the form and converts it back into a Notes document. That Notes document could in turn be republished as a web page, or it could become part of a pre-defined Notes workflow, wherein the information entered into it is processed and integrated with other information stored in Notes and back-end data-bases.

InterNotes Web Publisher certainly seems like a seamless step in marrying Notes to the web. And it really is as easy as it looks! To understand how InterNotes Web Publisher can do what it does, it helps to compare Notes itself to the World Wide Web.

Notes and the World Wide Web

Notes and the World Wide Web complement each other nicely. Each has strengths where the other has weaknesses. Where Notes is proprietary and requires both the publisher and the reader to use Notes software, the World Wide Web is based on open, published standards. Anyone can develop a web server or browser program simply by writing it to comply with the standards. (And it seems like just about everyone has done so.) So it has been much easier and cheaper to participate in the web publishing phenomenon than in the Notes publishing phenomenon.

On the other hand, where the World Wide Web makes it easy to retrieve in-formation with cheap, widely available web browsers, the publishing side of the World Wide Web is not so easy. Publishing documents on the web and maintaining a web site properly can be a fearsome task. Each time a docu-ment is added to a web site, it must be linked to the other documents in that web site and perhaps in other web sites. Each time a document is removed from a web site, links to it in other documents must be updated so that they no longer point to the deceased document. As the number of pages stored on a server grow from a few to a few hundred to a few thousand, the mainte-nance task grows from painstaking to onerous to nearly impossible.

Notes, however, was designed from the ground up to ease the creation, main-tenance, linking, and retrieval of hundreds, thousands, even millions of docu-ments. So the marriage of Notes and the web is a natural match. And Lotus

InterNotes Web Publisher is the tool (along with the InterNotes Web Navigator) that weds Notes and the web.

Also, the World Wide Web is essentially a one-way communication tool. It's great at publishing information widely. But if the publisher wants to get information back from the reader, they must resort either to e-mail or to some serious programming efforts. And to relate that retrieved information to the publisher's back-end databases requires even more programming. Thus web publishing, once it gets past the one-way publishing stage, is not for amateurs. In Notes, publishing is inherently a two-way process. Anyone who can fill in a form can author a Notes document and publish it in a Notes database. Relating the information in that form to data in back-end databases is also inherent in the design of Notes.

As you can see, Notes is much more than a tool for distributed electronic publishing. Notes documents are stored not as separate files, as HTML documents are, but rather in Notes databases. Notes databases, furthermore, are designed not only to make Notes documents readily available to the reader, but also to facilitate the creation of those documents, and to facilitate various business processes via the manipulation of those documents. But the fact remains that Notes and the WWW both do a superb job of making information widely available electronically.

An Example Notes Application

Using the example of our Training department, we're going to walk you through a typical Notes application. Once we explain the application and how it works in Notes, we'll show you what happens when we publish that application through the InterNotes Web Publisher to our Company Wide Web.

Our Training department maintains its class schedule in a Notes database (see fig. 26.1). When someone telephones the department to inquire about a class, the Training department employee looks up the information in a Notes database.

If the caller then decides to enroll in the class, the Training department employee fills in a Notes form and stores it in the Notes database (see fig. 26.2).

Fig. 26.1
Lotus Notes
Release 4 displays
the Training
Department
database, with a
list of views on
the left and a
view of available
classes on the
right.

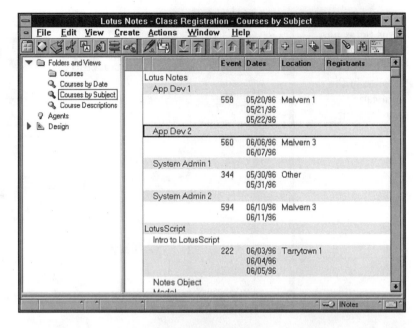

Fig. 26.2
Lotus Notes
displays the
database enroll-
ment form in edit
mode. Corner
brackets surround
fields where the
user enters data.
No brackets
surround fields
completed
automatically by
Notes.

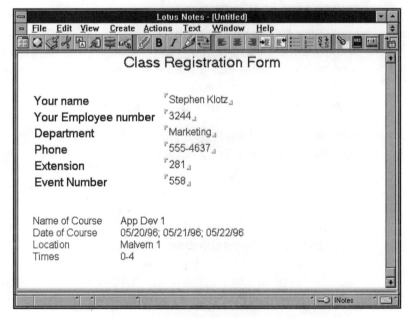

Upon completion of the enrollment form, the Training department employee
can see the enrollee listed in the Notes view (see fig. 26.3).

Fig. 26.3

Lotus Notes now displays the name of the new enrollee in the Application Development class.

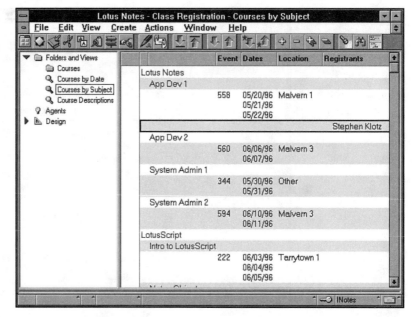

Notes provides *views* for seeing collections of documents. Notes views look like tables you see in a relational database. Each document constitutes one or several rows of the view. Each column conveys specific information about the document, probably culled from one or more of the fields. A given database usually has multiple views. In our example, we could view classes by course date, by event, or by course description.

Our example Training department application works well, is efficient, and takes little time to learn to navigate. But there's a catch. Any person in our organization who needs to see or retrieve information from our Notes database must, of course, have Lotus Notes installed. That's not as expensive as it sounds—we could purchase Notes Desktop for each of our users, enabling them to receive mail, and access our server. At a cost of about $70 to $100 per workstation (depending on quantity purchased), that sounds pretty affordable. But we have an established Company Wide Web. A more cost-effective approach to accessing our Training database would be through our Company Wide Web.

Fig. 26.5

The Company Wide Web home page is displayed here in Microsoft Internet Explorer, a web browser. This page originated as the "About [database name]" document in a Lotus Notes database.

Every database that you publish with the InterNotes Web Publisher has a home page. By default, the home page is a list of all the views in the database, with links to each view. The home page automatically supports navigation of published files through web browsers.

You'll want a home page for your entire site. On this site home page, you can add links to the database home page document of every database you publish. You can tell the InterNotes Web Publisher which of your home pages is the home page for the entire site.

From the site database home page, we navigate to the Training department home page (see fig. 26.6).

Because this page incorporates a search bar, it originated as a Notes form designed specifically to be published on the web. If we did not need the search bar, we could have simply used a standard Notes document, the "About Class Registration" document, of the "Class Registration" Notes database.

Now we can take a look at the course offerings by clicking the hypertext, "Course Offerings" (see fig. 26.7).

Fig. 26.6
The Training department home page is displayed here in Microsoft Internet Explorer, a web browser.

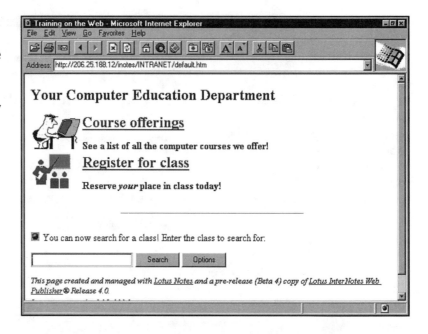

Fig. 26.7
The course listing is displayed in Microsoft Internet Explorer, a web browser. This page originated as a view in the Training department's "Class Registration" Notes database.

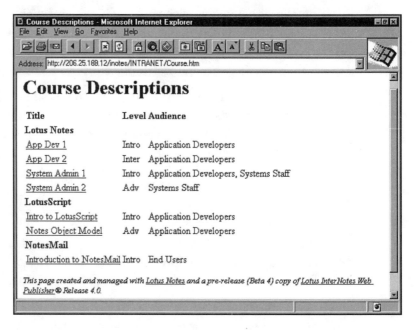

We are interested in App Dev 1. Clicking its URL takes us to a document that describes the course in detail (see fig. 26.8).

Fig. 26.8
A document
describing a
course is dis-
played in the
web browser.

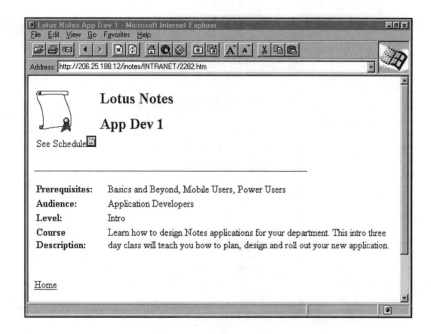

This page originated as a document in the Training department's "Class Reg-istration" Notes database. If we want to enroll, we can click the "See Sched-ule" URL to find out when the course is scheduled.

If we want to enroll in the course, we can click the "See Schedule" icon. A list of courses and their scheduled times appears as shown in figure 26.9.

If we click the URL for one of the scheduled dates, the Class Registration Form appears (see fig. 26.10).

This form originated as a form in the Training department's "Class Registra-tion" Notes database. When the enrollee submits the form, it will generate a document in the Notes database. If we desire, it could also be published back to the web.

As you can see, our Notes databases look very much like they did when we viewed them in Notes, and Notes doesn't care which web browser you are using.

Fig. 26.9
This list shows the dates, times, and locations of the offered courses.

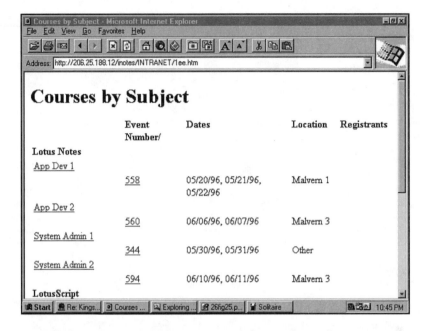

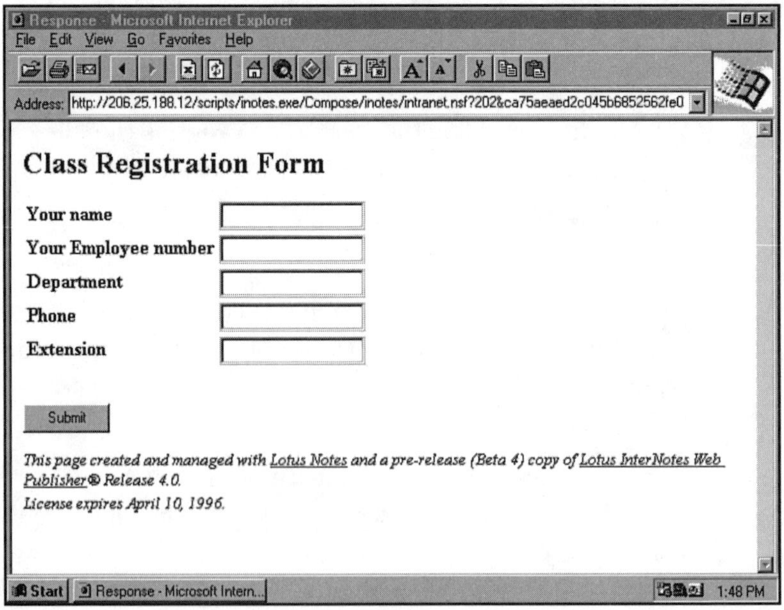

Fig. 26.10
The Class Registration Form is displayed here.

A Closer Look at What Happens When You Publish with InterNotes

In the preceding example, when the database was published, InterNotes did the following:

- Published the About Database document from our Training database (TRAINING.NSF) and made it the home page for the database
- Listed our database views as hypertext links on the home page
- Converted each Notes document into an HTML file
- Converted our Notes forms into HTML forms
- Converted our Notes DocLinks into hypertext links
- Converted our Notes tables into HTML tables
- Converted bitmaps in our Notes documents into online GIF files
- Preserved the full-text index so users could search the database and view the search results from our Company Wide Web
- Preserved attachments to Notes documents so users could download them from the Web with a browser

Configuring Your Site

To set up Lotus InterNotes Web Publisher, you must have both a Lotus Notes server and an HTTP server. You can run both servers on the same computer or on separate computers. But, the computers must be able to communicate with each other on a TCP/IP network. You lose the interactivity features (form inputs and full-text searches) if both servers are not on the same computer. Therefore, we recommend that you run your Notes server, InterNotes Web Publisher, and your HTTP server all on one computer, as illustrated in figure 26.11.

Fig. 26.11
This diagram illustrates two possible InterNotes Web Publisher site configurations, using either two computers or one.

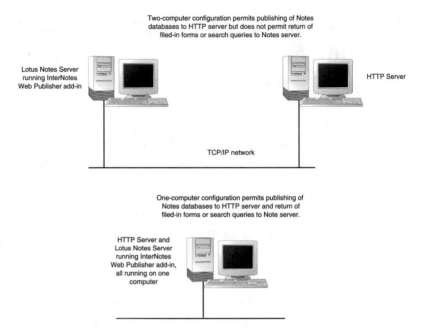

Two-computer configuration permits publishing of Notes databases to HTTP server but does not permit return of filed-in forms or search queries to Notes server.

Lotus Notes Server running InterNotes Web Publisher add-in

HTTP Server

TCP/IP network

One-computer configuration permits publishing of Notes databases to HTTP server and return of filed-in forms or search queries to Note server.

HTTP Server and Lotus Notes Server running InterNotes Web Publisher add-in, all running on one computer

In the two-computer configuration the HTTP server runs on one computer and the Notes server runs on the other. In the one-computer configuration, both servers run on one computer. The one-computer configuration is preferable because only it permits the HTTP server to return information to the Notes server.

NOTE

As of March 25, 1996, Lotus had announced the release of InterNotes Web Publisher 4.0, intended to run on Notes Release 4.x servers on the following platforms: OS/2, Windows NT and Windows 95, IBM AIX, and Sun Solaris. Lotus also announced the release of InterNotes Web Publisher 2.1, intended to run on Notes Release 3.x servers on the OS/2 and Windows NT platforms.

To benefit from the interactive features of InterNotes Web Publisher, that is, full-text search and the submission of forms back into Notes databases, the Notes server and web server must be running on the same computer. If your web server runs under any other operating system than those listed above, InterNotes Web Publisher can publish to it, but your web server cannot return information to your Notes server.

The Lotus Notes server is actually a group of programs that share the same memory space on the computer and work cooperatively with each other. The mix of programs that constitutes a given Notes server varies according to the tasks it must perform. Thus, one Notes server may act as a gateway to other mail systems and so would run mail gateway software that other Notes servers would have no need to run. The other Notes servers, when they have mail to deliver outside Notes' mail system, would simply deliver it to the gateway server.

A Lotus InterNotes server is itself a gateway server. It transfers information back and forth between its Notes domain and the web server with which it is paired. The InterNotes Web Publisher program runs on the Notes server as a Notes server add-in program. InterNotes Web Publisher consists of two programs, a configuration database, a log database, a help database, and a couple of sample databases. One of the programs, called WEBPUB.EXE, is the main server add-in program that actually accomplishes the conversion of Notes databases to HTML files. It resides on-disk in the Notes program directory and in memory with the other Notes server modules.

The other program, called INOTES.EXE, is the interactivity module. It's a CGI program that publishes Notes forms to the web server and converts information entered into the forms by web surfers into documents in Notes database. There are actually two copies of it. One copy resides on-disk in the Notes program directory and in memory with the other Notes server modules. This copy publishes Notes forms to the web server. The second copy resides on-disk in the web server's CGI script directory. The web server calls it into memory when necessary to convert HTML user input to a Notes document.

In addition to the add-in programs, there is a Notes database, the Web Publisher Configuration database, in which you store configuration data. One of the documents in this database is the WebMaster Options document. Here you set global variables that affect all of your published databases. For each published database there is also a Database Publishing Record document that defines the "local" variables of the publication of that database.

Understanding Directories

Notes doesn't do all of your web site management for you. You still get to use some of the skills you learned elsewhere in this book. For example, if you publish multiple Notes databases, you have to link them to each other manually. Also, if you want to integrate Notes-published pages into a preexisting web site, already occupied by non-Notes-generated pages, you have to take measures to insure that the Notes-generated pages don't overwrite the non-Notes pages, especially the site home page. And you need to link your non-Notes home page to your Notes home pages.

When you configure your web server, you typically specify a directory as the root directory of your web site. Depending on which brand of web server you are running, this may be called \HTTP or \WWWROOT. Your site home page resides here, and has a file name that your web server will look for whenever anyone requests your site home page. Typically, it's called DEFAULT.HTM or something equally clever and original. Your site home page will have links embedded in it that will lead eventually to every other publicly available page in your site, as well as to pages at other sites. And the pages on your site will typically reside in subdirectories of the site root directory. Thus, the structure of your site might look something like what's shown in figure 26.12.

Fig. 26.12
This diagram illustrates the data directory structure of an HTTP server in which all HTML pages are derived from Lotus Notes databases.

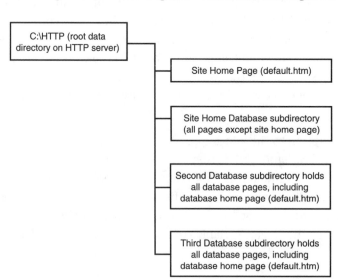

When you configure your InterNotes server, you have to go through the same exercise. That is, you have to specify an output directory for the HTML files that Notes will generate. And you have to specify a filename for your Notes home pages, that is, for each published Notes database's home page. You do these things in Notes, in the WebMaster Options document in the Web Publisher Configuration database (see fig. 26.13).

Fig. 26.13
This WebMaster options document tells InterNotes Web Publisher to publish to C:\INETSRV\ WWWROOT\INOTES, to name Notes home pages DEFAULT.HTM and all other pages with the extension HTM, and to look for INOTES.EXE in the /SCRIPTS virtual directory.

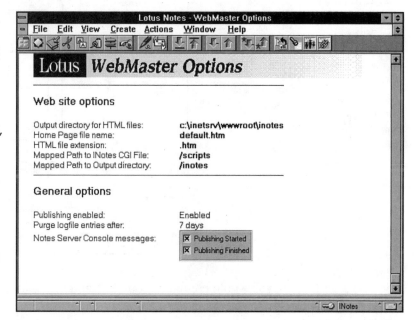

When you publish each Notes database, you have the opportunity to designate it as the "Home Page Database." That is, you may designate the home page of any one Notes-published database as either the site home page, from which all public documents on the site can be reached, or as the home page from which all other Notes home pages can be reached. If you only generate pages with InterNotes Web Publisher, your site directory structure will look something like figure 26.13 of the Notes web site.

Alternately, if you are adding Notes-generated pages to an established web site, your site directory structure might look like figure 26.14.

Fig. 26.14
This diagram
illustrates the
data directory
structure of an
HTTP server in
which only some
HTML pages are
derived from
Lotus Notes
databases. In this
diagram, Notes-
derived pages
occupy directories
branching off
from the "NOTES"
directory.

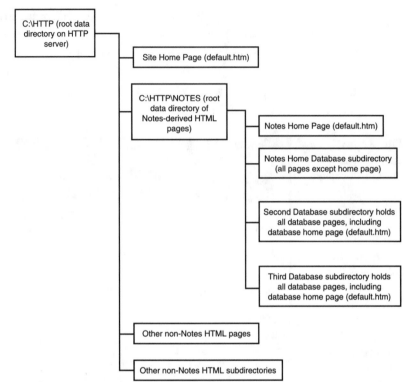

To set this up, you would configure your web and InterNotes servers to recognize a subdirectory of your site root directory as the output directory for
your Notes HTML pages. You would designate one Notes database (and *only*
one Notes database) as the Home Page Database. When InterNotes publishes
the database, InterNotes creates a subdirectory for each database beneath
the InterNotes output directory. Then, with one exception, it publishes all
pages for each database into that database's designated subdirectory. The
one exception is the home page for the Home Page Database; *it alone* would
reside in the main Notes output directory.

You would have to craft a pointer from your site home page to the home page
of the Notes Home Page Database. And you would have to create pointers
from the Notes Home Page database's home page to the home pages of all
your other Notes home pages.

You can insert links by hand in Notes documents or Notes forms in several
ways, all of them illustrated in figures 26.15 and 26.16.

Fig. 26.15
This figure shows a form in Notes in design mode. It includes four examples of the same URL: a DocLink, a text URL, a graphic URL, and a hotspot link URL.

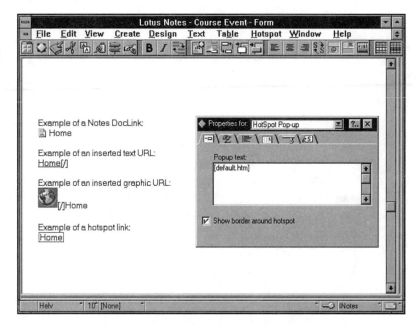

All the examples in figure 26.15 include the word "Home," which is descriptive, intended to tell the reader what document this URL will return. The notation "[/]" is the URL; it points to the home page of the current web server. The Properties Infobox shows the URL for the hotspot link.

Fig. 26.16
This figure shows how the examples in figure 26.15 appear in a web browser.

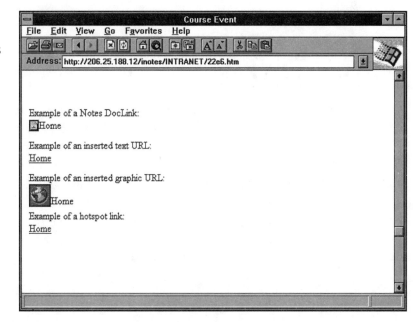

First, you could insert standard Notes DocLinks. In Notes Release 3, you can only link Notes *documents* to each other this way. Beginning in Release 4, you can link Notes documents to other Notes documents, Notes views, or other Notes databases. Notes 4 also allows you to insert hotspots, which act like doclinks.

Second, you could insert URL references into Notes documents. These could link to any page in your site, to a Notes view, or to another web site. You can do this either as a text link or a graphic link. To create a text link, you could underline a block of text, then insert the URL reference, enclosed in square brackets, immediately following the underlined text. To create a graphic link, you can embed a graphic image in your Notes document, followed by the URL reference enclosed in square brackets. Figure 26.15 shows how text links and graphic links appear in a Notes form in design mode. Figure 26.16 shows how they appear in a web browser.

Third, in Notes 4.x you could create a hotspot link in a Notes document or form. In a form in design mode, or in a rich text field of a document in edit mode, you enter a block of text and select it. Then, in the menu, choose Create, Hotspot, Text Popup. A box appears around the selected text and an Infobox appears, called Properties for HotSpot Pop-up. On the first tabbed page of the Infobox, in the Popup text field, enter the URL surrounded by square brackets (refer to fig. 26.15).

Searching Notes Databases from Within a Web Browser

Lotus Notes, being a repository of information, naturally comes with a lot of tools intended to make it easy to find the information you need. One of the most powerful is its full-text search engine. To enable it, you have to create a full-text index of the database to be searched. You create the index by selecting options in the Notes menu or, in Notes Release 4, by selecting an option when you create the database. After you have created the index, you can use Boolean search terms ("x and y," "x or y," and so on) to search for any text string that appears anywhere in any document in the indexed database.

InterNotes Web Publisher extends this powerful tool out to the web. You can insert a search bar into a Notes-generated home page or view page. A user who brings up the page in his or her browser can enter a search string into the text field in the search bar, then click the Search button (see fig. 26.17).

Fig. 26.17
This is the Training department home page, as seen in a web browser. Note the search input field.

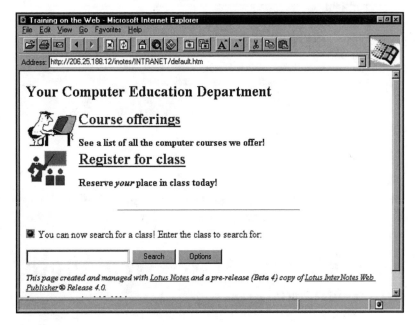

InterNotes Web Publisher conveys the search string to the Notes server, which performs the search. InterNotes Web Publisher takes the search results and displays them to the user as a linked list of HTML documents. Those having the most "hits" appear at the top of the list. Click the link for any document to display it in the usual fashion.

This search bar was embedded in our Notes form by adding a field to a form called $$ViewSearchBar, as shown in figure 26.18. The Notes Help Description of this field is the name of the Notes view we wish to search.

Fig. 26.18
This is a Notes document in design mode, displaying the search bar field ($$ViewSearchBar), which becomes the search input field illustrated in figure 26.17.

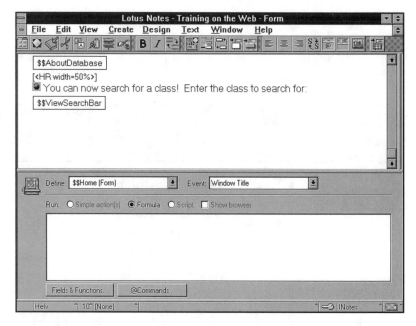

Building Interactive Web Applications with Notes Forms

As you can see, Notes users use Notes forms as templates to create new documents. InterNotes Web Publisher permits the webmaster to publish Notes forms as HTML forms, that people can fill out in their browsers. When a user clicks the Submit button on the form, InterNotes Web Publisher submits the form to the Notes server, which then stores the form in a Notes database as a standard Notes document. If you don't create a Submit button on the form, InterNotes Web Publisher automatically creates it for you.

What Notes does with that document next is solely up to the Notes database designer. The document might be republished as yet another HTML document, now available for anyone to view in their browser. Or it might be internally processed by Notes and become part of a workflow in the everyday business of the company. Either way, the webmaster has just extended Notes functionality to non-Notes users, either in the form of a web-based discussion database, or as a Notes workflow application.

You enable the submission of responses from web users to the Notes database by a simple, two-step process. First, you create the response form as you would create any form in Notes. Then you add a field named $$Response to the main form (the one to which the user responds). The $$Response field points to the response form, and appears as a URL link in the main document. When the user clicks the URL link, the response form appears.

You can also capture information from Web users by adding CGI environment variables to the response form. These fields, such as Server_Software, Remote_User, and so on, can be marked as "hide when Editing" so that users cannot enter information into them. But when the user submits the form, INOTES.EXE populates them with the appropriate information, which can then be used by Notes to process the response appropriately.

System Requirements

Since the InterNotes Web Publisher resides on the same server as Lotus Notes, the system requirements are the same as Lotus Notes, except that more memory is required. The Lotus Notes server can run on several platforms including Windows NT, OS/2, and several versions of UNIX. InterNotes Web Publisher, version 2.1, for Lotus Notes version 3.x, runs on the OS/2 and Windows NT platforms. InterNotes Web Publisher version 4.0, for Lotus Notes version 4.x, runs on Windows NT, Windows 95, OS/2, Sun Solaris, and IBM AIX operating systems. Versions of Lotus Notes server also run on Windows 3.x, HP-UX, SCO UNIX, and Novell NetWare platforms, but at the time of this writing there was no version of InterNotes Web Publisher available to run with those Notes servers.

Hardware

InterNotes Web Publisher runs on whatever hardware platform its underlying operating system runs on, which may include an Intel® 80486 or greater microprocessor (33MHz or higher) or a RISC-based processor. Lotus recommends a minimum of 48M of RAM (but preferably 64M) and a 1G (or greater) hard disk drive. Part of the reason the RAM requirement is so high is because you will be running Notes, InterNotes Web Publisher, and your HTTP server at the same time. For this book, we ran on an NEC PowerMate V100 with a 100MHz Pentium processor, 80M RAM, and a 1G hard disk drive.

Software

The InterNotes Web Publisher version 2.1 (for Lotus Notes 3.x) requires Windows NT Advanced Server version 3.1 or later, and Notes server for Windows NT version 3.2 or later. It requires OS/2 version 3.0 or later, and Notes Server for OS/2 version 3.31 or later.

Lotus has announced plans to incorporate the HTML, HTTP, and Java protocols into release 4.2 of Lotus Notes, due to be released the summer of 1996. This will effectively turn the Notes server into a Web server. In the meantime, you will need a Web server to make the translated HTML documents available to Web clients. InterNotes Web Publisher works with standard HTTP servers and browsers.

We have successfully run InterNotes Web Publisher version 4.0 with Lotus Notes 4.0 on Windows NT 3.51 (Service Pack 3). We ran it with both the Microsoft Internet Information Server release 1.0 and the beta 2 release of the Netscape FastTrack HTTP server.

We had difficulty getting the HTTP servers to run properly until we removed Novell's NetWare Directory Service client from the computer. We also had difficulty configuring the InterNotes Web Publisher to work properly with the Microsoft Internet Information Server, and had to seek help on the Lotus InterNotes web site to solve our problems. We were working with beta versions of InterNotes Web Publisher at the time and Lotus was still hammering out both the code and the documentation of InterNotes Web Publisher. Presumably Lotus will properly document the configuration procedure in the "final customer ship" version of the product.

Summary

We have demonstrated only a small part of the power of Lotus Notes and the InterNotes Web Publisher. Many of the skills that you've acquired throughout this book can be applied in the design of your Notes documents and databases, or you can elect to have Notes do the conversion for you! In our examples, we added very little HTML code to our documents. And we did so simply to demonstrate that we could—not that we had to.

InterNotes Web Publisher integrates Notes and the World Wide Web in a robust web application and hosting environment. Lotus Notes has set the standard for messaging and groupware. InterNotes Web Publisher just might have the same affect on the World Wide Web.

27

Overview of Internet Studio

By Tony Wasson

Internet Studio is a high-end electronic publishing tool from Microsoft. Using Internet Studio, there is no need to spend hours learning HTML tags and the tricks of UNIX. Internet Studio allows one person to gather stories, lay out graphics, add links, provide a table of contents, and use multiple means of navigation. Using Internet Studio, writers can concentrate on writing, and artists can concentrate on making art. Then the Internet Studio user can drag and drop these elements to form a complex HTML document and eventually an entire site.

The strength of Internet Studio lies in its use of Object Linking and Embedding, commonly called OLE (pronounced olay). All the primary Microsoft Office products (Word, Excel, PowerPoint, Access) can exchange information using OLE, and Internet Studio capitalizes on this. Microsoft Office is deployed at a majority of business desktops.

While getting a company intranet running may be difficult, the real chore lies in keeping all the information current and up-to-date. If you are responsible for maintaining a portion of the site (or even more fun, all of it) using Internet Studio could save large amounts of time.

Setting up a site in Internet Studio is relatively simple. The Project Editor helps you organize your intranet by using a file and folder setup. Internet Studio allows you to combine stories, graphics, and other forms of multimedia to create a visually pleasing page. This chapter is being written before Microsoft releases the product, so this is just an overview of some of the functions of Internet Studio.

In this chapter, you learn

● What you need to start using Internet Studio for your intranet

● How to link and lay out content

● How to update content using Internet Studio

● When to upgrade to Internet Studio

Setting Up a Site

Internet Studio provides a rich, easy-to-manage intranet. All the information already in PC-based applications can be dragged and dropped together. Making a page involves laying out frames and filling them with text, graphics, and other media forms. Internet Studio makes pages easy to create via a WYSIWYG screen.

Who doesn't have enough job responsibilities? Everyone has a long list of things they need to do. Care to add Learn HTML to that list? Most people don't, yet they want the benefit of easily distributing information. Using a browser and an intranet is an excellent way to distribute information.

Internet Explorer is the preferred browser for pages created with Internet Studio. Just as many sites on the Web are best viewed with Netscape, Internet Studio sites are best viewed with Internet Explorer. With Internet Explorer available for Macintosh, Windows 3.1, Windows 95, and Windows NT machines, Internet Studio can be used in a mixed machine network environment.

Here's what you'll need to run an intranet using Internet Studio:

● A computer that has Internet Studio software on it (at least a 486 with 16M of RAM)

● A server running a Web server program

● Copies of Internet Explorer on each workstation to view what's on the intranet

● A network that allows employees to use Internet Explorer to connect to the server

See Chapter 1, "Understanding Your Intranet Site," and Chapter 11, "Making Content Available on the Server," for more on the necessities for an intranet.

Organizing Content

Internet Studio uses a folder metaphor to lay out content. There are actually three levels with an Internet Studio project—sections, folders, and the actual page. Content like text, graphics, and sound are placed within folders for easy access when making a page.

Internet Studio content is imported into a web-usable format and a link is placed to the original file. A new page can be started at any time and any content within the current project can be used within the page. Pages can be fixed page size (like magazines) or of varying length (like WWW pages).

T I P

While you can import, remove, create, and delete pages as you desire, I've found it very useful to spend some time storyboarding the site and figuring out what existing content I can make use of and what I'll need to make from scratch. Within the company intranet, have an assigned person in each department update their own content (Word files, Excel sheets, graphs, and so on).

Working with Projects

Each Internet Studio file is called a *project*. Marketing could be its own project, a new product could be a project, it doesn't really matter—except that a huge project file will be harder to update and take longer to load and edit in Internet Studio. Within each project are sections that group together folders.

A project needs to contain links to all the content it will use. You can't use content linked in a different project; each project must have its own links.

N O T E

Putting an entire intranet in one project could result in a very large file, so breaking it down to the department level or below is a good idea.

Each project has a number of folders in it. The folders organize the content and make graphics easily available.

Assuming you've figured out how the intranet will be designed, you can move on. Creating pages in Internet Studio is very easy.

First, assemble the content pieces in folders. After getting the content into the folder, you can start making the pages. This is rather simple—draw frames, place text and graphics, and try the pages out by following links and checking the layout.

Text can be created in Word and transformed into HTML or made in another HTML editor. Graphics can be made in a variety or formats and converted to the web standard GIF or JPEG. Sounds can be dropped on pages with instructions only to play when a certain event happens (like clicking a button).

Internet Studio includes a Microsoft template with all the appropriate styles. Just as you use styles within Word documents to show different text attributes, Internet Studio uses the styles to make everything from hyperlinks, bold words, strong sections, and appropriate header sizes.

Maintaining a Site

Anyone who's ever made a web page knows that getting it online is only half the battle. Keeping it current is the real challenge. Internet Studio provides two ways of updating the content. One, by manually running Internet Studio and updating all the files via OLE. Two, by creating a Visual Basic script that automatically updates the pages via OLE.

Usually, when something big is changing, there's no time to crank out the HTML and create new artwork. With Internet Studio, you could just open Word, edit the page's text and then have it update the content.

Adding Content

Adding content is just like setting up the pages for the first time. If you just want to add content, you can make folders, link to graphics and text, and lay out the pages. If you want to create an entirely new project, that's no problem either.

Updating Content

Internet Studio lets you update content in two ways—manually or automatically. When you start a manual update, Internet Studio follows the OLE links and pulls in the changed files to refresh your web site. Manual updates may be done any time.

Taking the manual updates a step further, Visual Basic scripts can be written to fully automate updating existing content. New pages and information will still need to be added, but the current material will be updated as the original files on the network are updated.

Figure 27.1 shows how the OLE updates work.

Fig. 27.1
OLE can do the
repetitive updates
for a site.

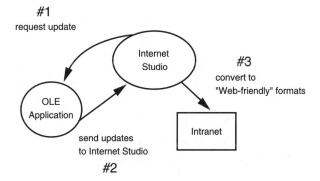

OLE certainly sounds tempting to use. However, Internet Studio isn't a fire-and-forget solution. If someone isn't in charge of making sure the information stays current and that new areas and topics are added, the intranet could fall into disuse. Internet Studio takes a lot of the grunt work out of creating and updating HTML pages.

Internet Studio is also very adaptable. It can be modified by a programmer who knows C/C++ through the use of OLE controls. Custom controls are ready-made, reusable elements of Windows applications that developers can use to build applications fast.

Most Windows programmers are familiar with OLE and the OLE controls. OLE is a way to integrate two or more programs in a seamless way. Intranet browsers see all the content roped together in one window.

Weighing the Cost of Internet Studio

An intranet shouldn't be installed because it's the latest buzz in technology. Company-wide intranets are about letting people get back to doing their job instead of wading through piles of reports, memos, and sales figures. If they need to know the latest on a certain project, they can hit the intranet.

Internet Studio takes that idea one step farther. Why bother spending lots of time converting digital files to HTML format? Let software worry about which tag will work best where or how to align that graphic. Internet Studio provides an easier way to publish and update information so you don't have to spend valuable time manually updating information.

Internet Studio requires nothing besides an installed base of OLE programs. It can easily place images, charts, and figures. Pages can be designed once and updated with new numbers, text, and pictures.

If you've created an HTML page, you know that it's easy to spend a long time getting the text looking decent, and the graphics aligned like you want. Usually, it means switching between an editor and a viewer. With Internet Studio, What You See Is What You Get (WYSIWYG). Draw a frame and fill it with text—you'll see text filling the frame. Drop in a company graphic across the top and a few links to other pages and you've got a ready to publish page.

Internet Studio was updated to publish to all web servers. No longer is an NT server required—UNIX is welcomed.

How can you figure out when to upgrade to Internet Studio? One sign is that you dread updating the site. Once a site gets beyond a certain size it becomes very difficult to manage manually. Internet Studio is also very useful to get content from other people. They can stay in their Windows-based world, create content in the programs they are comfortable with and you don't have to worry about the formats—Internet Studio does that for you.

From Here...

Internet Studio is a powerful tool for creating both web pages and intranet information. As Internet Studio nears its shipping date, more details will be available both in the trade papers (like *PC WEEK* and *INFOWORLD*) and on Microsoft's Web site (**http://www.microsoft.com**).

PART

VI

Appendixes

What's on the CD

Knowing how to write your own HTML and use other people's intranet pages is only half the battle. Writing your code efficiently, keeping your site operating smoothly, and having access to all the information on your intranet can require a host of programs and utilities. We've put together a collection of the best shareware and freeware available to help you.

The CD-ROM accompanying this book has everything you need to make an effective intranet site. From HTML editors to server software, graphics viewers to voice chat utilities, this CD has it all. In addition, we've included links to all of the World Wide Web locations listed in Appendix C, "For Further Reading," (so you don't have to type in the URLs by hand) and many HTML code examples from the text.

As noted above, there are two types of programs on the CD: shareware and freeware.

Shareware programs are not free. They are provided for you to try out before you buy them. You have a certain period of time to evaluate the program and decide if it meets your needs. If, after that trial period, you want to keep using the program, you are obligated to license the program from its author. Paying this registration fee often gives you additional benefits such as notification of updates, a printed manual, technical support, or in some cases a more powerful version of the program. Each shareware program is provided with documentation, either on the CD or in the program itself, explaining the registration procedure.

Freeware programs, on the other hand, are provided by the author free of charge. You have no obligation to pay the author anything for the use of the program (though many of them would appreciate a note telling them that you like the program and how you are using it).

Each program comes with documentation telling you which category it fits into. If you find a program especially useful and want to distribute it around your company, check with the author about site licenses (if shareware) or any restrictions that may apply. Most program's documentation includes the e-mail address, phone number, or mailing address of the author.

Using The CD

To make the CD easier to use (and to give you some ideas on how you can organize your own intranet site) we have created the installation program in the form of an HTML document. This works just the same as any document you might find on your intranet. If you're unfamiliar with using your intranet, you may want to review Appendix B, "Using an Intranet."

The CD-ROM incorporates Windows 95's autostart feature so all you have to do is load the CD into your computer's drive. Windows 95 automatically starts your existing browser (if you have one) and you then can navigate the drive and find the programs and resources that interest you. If you don't have a browser loaded yet, you will be given instructions for installing Microsoft Internet Explorer from the CD so you can be up-and-running quickly.

Many of the programs we've included can run directly from the CD. This is especially useful if you're running low on local hard drive space or just want to check out a program without installing it.

To make navigation easier, we've arranged the CD to correspond to this chapter. When you find a program in this appendix that you're interested in, just pop the CD into your computer and follow the links to the following section.

Must Haves

The CD contains more programs than you may want or need. This is an excellent collection, and all of these programs come highly recommended. You may want to start your intranet publishing work by using the basic programs recommended in the following list. If you want, you can explore others later to see whether they better meet your needs or working style.

Internet Explorer 2.0

Internet Assistant for Word

Internet Assistant for Excel

Internet Assistant for PowerPoint

Internet Assistant for Access

HotDog

HoTMetaL

Paint Shop Pro

LView Pro for Windows 95

Library of clip art and graphic images

Color Machine

PowerPoint Player and Publisher

Nick Bicanic's Server Push Animation Script

Microsoft Internet Information Server

CuteFTP

WinZip

HTML Editors and Utilities

The following editors can make writing your intranet documents much easier. Each can help automate inserting tags and updating. You might want

to try a few of them to find out which one best suits your needs before set-
tling on your favorite.

▶ **See** "Working with Text Files," **p. 84**

TIP

Each editor has its own strong points and you may find that you'll want
to use two or three, based on what type of pages you are making. Also,
you might use one to write one portion of your page and another to write
another portion.

All the HTML editors mentioned in Chapter 4 are included on the CD, with
the exception of Netscape Navigator 2.0 Gold, which you may download
directly from Netscape at **http://www.netscape.com**.

● ANT_HTML
● Color Machine
● Color Manipulation Device
● Colorwiz
● CU_HTML
● HotDog
● HoTMetaL
● HTML Assistant Pro
● HTML Author
● HTML Builder
● HTML Easy! Pro
● HTML Notepad
● HTML Writer
● HTMLed
● Internet Assistant for Access
● Internet Assistant for Excel

- Internet Assistant for PowerPoint
- Internet Assistant for Word
- Kenn Nesbitt's WebEdit
- <Live Markup> PRO
- PowerPoint Player and Publisher
- Viewer for Excel
- Viewer for PowerPoint
- Viewer for Word
- Webber
- WebForms
- WebMania
- WEB Wizard

> You can obtain the latest versions of the Internet Assistants from Microsoft at the following WWW page:
>
> **http://www.microsoft.com/IntDev/AUTOOLS.HTM**

Clip Art

The CD-ROM contains a complete collection of buttons, images, backgrounds, and other graphic elements for your intranet pages. These elements have been culled from the best clip art available on the World Wide Web. Our clip art and graphics collections are provided courtesy of Martin Gleeson of the University of Melbourne and Chris Stevens of the Medical College of Virginia. You can reach updates to these libraries at **http://www.unimelb. edu.au/images/archive.html** and **http://128.172.69.106:8080/gifs/ bullet.html,** respectively.

- Clip art collection
- Graphics collection

Graphics and Multimedia Viewers and Editors

This group of utilities will help you add, convert, and retouch graphics for your intranet pages. In addition, viewers are included to use as helper applications for many popular video formats.

- ACDSee
- Acrobat Reader
- GoldWave
- LView Pro
- Map THIS!
- MPEGPLAY
- Nick Bicanic's Server Push Animation Script
- Paint Shop Pro
- PolyView
- QuickTime
- Streamworks
- VMPEG Lite
- VuePrint
- WinECJ
- WinJPEG

▶ **See** "Using Inline Graphics," **p. 127**
▶ **See** "Using Server Push Animation," **p. 145**

You can obtain the latest versions of the Office viewers from Microsoft at the following WWW page:

http://www.microsoft.com/Internet/PRODUCTS.HTM

FTP Utilities

File Transfer Protocol (ftp) is the standard used to transmit files through an intranet. Ftp through an intranet page is automatic, but there may be times when you need one of the following utilities to gain access to certain files:

- CuteFTP
- FTP Serv-U
- POPT Secure FTP
- Win FTP
- Windows FTP Daemon
- WS_FTP

Servers and Server Utilities

The following programs and utilities are for the system administrator charged with setting up and maintaining an intranet:

- HotJava Browser
- Microsoft Internet Explorer 2.0
- Microsoft Internet Information Server
- NCompass ActiveX Netscape Plug-in

> To get the latest version of the Internet Information Server, point your browser at:
> **http://www.microsoft.com/infoserv/iisinfo.htm**

IRC and Voice Chat Utilities

IRC (Internet Relay Chat) permits two or more people on the network to write back and forth in real time. The voice chat utilities allow users to actually talk to one another over the network provided their hardware is adequate (and the network administrator doesn't mind the increased traffic).

- ● Trumpet IRC
- ● Visual IRC
- ● WinTalk
- ● WS-IRC

General Utilities and Other Software

As the title implies, these utilities are for general maintenance, file compression/decompression, control, setup, and so on:

- ● AnzioLite
- ● Drag & Zip
- ● Internet Control Center
- ● NetTerm
- ● Surfer Central
- ● Trumpet Telnet
- ● UUCode
- ● WinCode
- ● WinZip
- ● WinZip Self Extractor

Database Utilities

As described in Chapter 9, "Creating Interactive Databases," you can use database applications to make a variety of intranet services, from threaded discussion groups to product databases. The following "turn-key" programs can help make intranet database publishing much easier. Note, however, they are for the advanced database user, though the applications you create can be used by any intranet user.

- ● Cold Fusion
- ● R:Web

B

Using an Intranet

By Paul Bodensiek

Programs like Microsoft Internet Explorer and Netscape Navigator let you "browse" your company's intranet to find and use almost any information contained in the network.

The initial installation and setup of your browser should be done by your company's Information Technology (IT) department to make sure the appropriate internet protocols and system numbers are properly configured. However, using and customizing your browser to make your work easier isn't difficult, and these are things that you can do on your own.

The instructions included in this appendix are based on Microsoft Internet Explorer and Netscape Navigator. If you are using another browser application, these instructions are still appropriate, but some dialog boxes' appearance and menu locations may be different.

In this chapter, you learn to

- Recognize and use links to other intranet pages
- Add bookmarks to often visited pages
- Download files referenced by intranet pages
- Configure helper applications
- Search for specific content on an intranet
- Change the appearance of your browser
- Change your browser's home page

Using a Browser

Once your company's intranet is operational, you can begin browsing to find out what information is available to you and how you can use this new communications tool to help you do your job better. If you have read the remainder of this book and created your own intranet pages, this section should be just a refresher for you.

Typically, when you start your browser, the first page you see is your corporate intranet home page (see fig. B.1). This page generally provides a list of other locations that give more information about a specific department. This list gives you direct access to the information through *links* that tell the browser to display a different file.

Fig. B.1
Your company's home page may look different, but generally you'll see a list linking you to each department's intranet site.

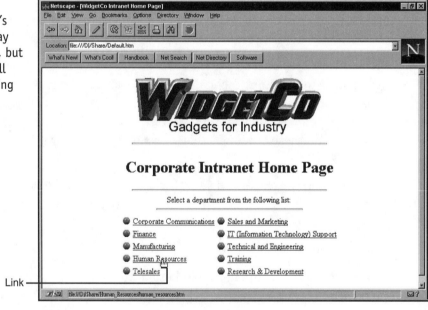

Link

Note that the appearance of an intranet page can vary, depending on the browser program being used. Figure B.2 shows the same intranet page shown in figure B.1 viewed by a different software program.

Fig. B.2
Even though a page may look different depending on the browser used, it will still act in the same way.

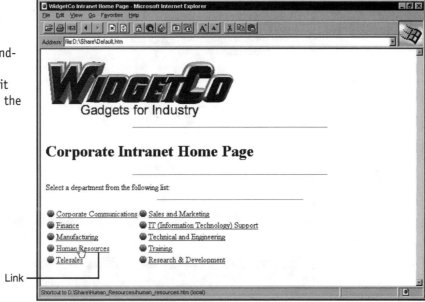

Link

Using Links

Links provide quick access to related information on an intranet. A page on employee benefits, for example, may contain links to pages concerning profit sharing, sick days, vacation pay, and medical packages (see fig. B.3).

To tell your browser to display the linked page, simply click the link. Your browser sends a message to the server software and requests it to transmit the appropriate file, which your browser then displays on your screen (see fig. B.4).

Fig. B.3
An intranet page contains links to related information contained in other pages.

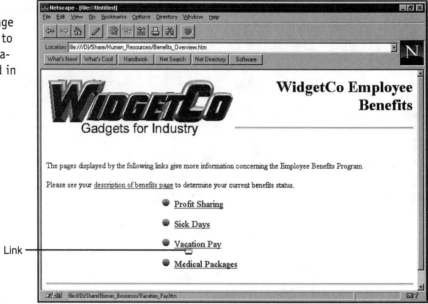

Link —

Fig. B.4
Clicking a link displays a new page. The Vacation Pay link shown in figure B.3 brings you to this page.

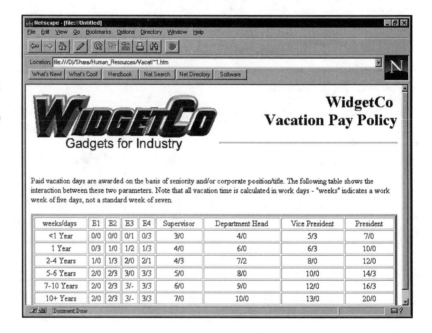

Moving Forward and Backward

If you have used a link and accessed a new page, you may return to the previous page using the back button on most browser's button bar (see fig. B.5). This button is usually a left-hand arrow. If you have gone back, you can return "forward" to the page you left using the forward button, usually a right-hand arrow.

Fig. B.5
The Forward and Back buttons let you navigate between pages you have already visited.

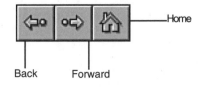

If pages are arranged in a linear fashion (in other words, you should travel from one to the next, without any branching) the author usually includes a set of VCR style buttons that let you go forward and backward as well as jump to the first page or last page in the sequence (see fig. B.6).

Fig. B.6
Use VCR style buttons to navigate pages that are arranged in a linear fashion.

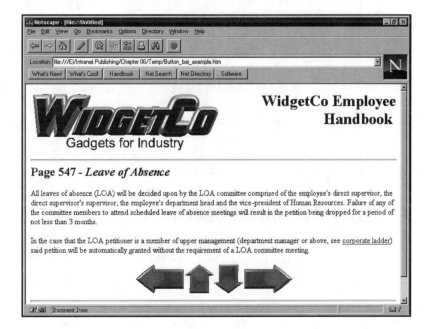

Storing Locations

You may find yourself visiting some pages over and over. Rather than following the same links from your corporate home page through six or seven levels of pages to find the one you want, most browsers let you create menu shortcuts to these pages. Netscape Navigator calls these shortcuts *bookmarks* and Microsoft Internet Explorer calls them *favorites*. Other programs have their own names, but they are generally easy to figure out from context.

Adding Stored Locations

To add a stored location in Netscape Navigator:

1. Load the page whose location you want to store (use links, enter the address directly, and so on).

2. Choose Bookmark, Add Bookmark (or press Ctrl+D).

   The title of the viewed page serves as the title of the saved location and is automatically placed at the bottom of the bookmark list.

To add a stored location in Microsoft Internet Explorer:

1. Go to the page whose location you want to store.

2. Choose Favorites, Add to Favorites. The Add To Favorites dialog box opens.

3. Click the Add button to add this location to your list.

   The title of the viewed page serves as the title of the saved location and is automatically placed at the bottom of the favorite list.

Other browsers have similar procedures.

Accessing Stored Locations

To jump to a stored location using Netscape Navigator, choose Bookmark and then choose the location from the list (see fig. B.7).

Fig. B.7
Stored locations,
called Bookmarks
in Netscape
Navigator, are
reached through
the Bookmarks
menu.

To jump to a stored location using Microsoft Internet Explorer, choose
Favorites and then choose the location from the list (see fig. B.8).

Fig. B.8
Stored locations,
called Favorites in
Microsoft Internet
Explorer, are
reached through
the Favorites
menu.

Deleting Stored Locations

If you find your stored locations menu getting too long or some pages have
moved or been removed from the system, you may want to do some house-
cleaning and delete unused locations.

To delete a stored location in Netscape Navigator:

1. Choose Bookmarks, Go To Bookmarks (or press Ctrl+B). The Bookmarks editor window opens (see fig. B.9).
2. Select the stored location you want to delete.
3. Choose Edit, Delete (or press the Delete key). The location is removed
   from the list.
4. To close the Bookmarks Explorer window and return to Netscape Navigator, choose File, Close (or press Ctrl+W).

Fig. B.9
The Bookmarks editor window provides direct access to your bookmarks, letting you change them at will.

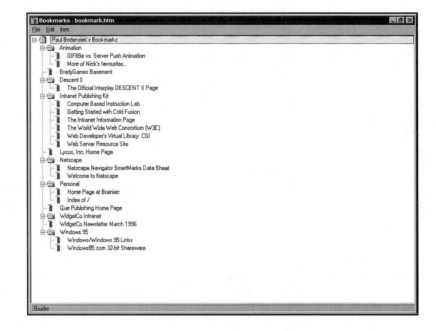

To delete a stored location in Microsoft Internet Explorer:

1. Choose F<u>a</u>vorites, <u>O</u>pen Favorites. The Favorites Explorer window opens (see fig. B.10).

Fig. B.10
The Favorites Explorer window provides direct access to your saved locations, letting you change them at will.

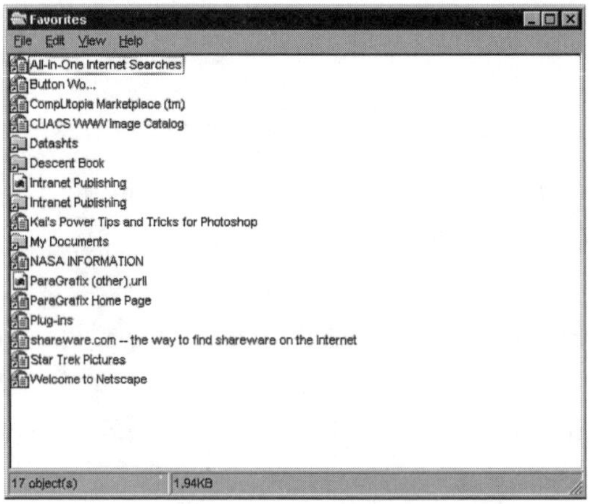

2. Select the stored location you want to delete.

3. Choose File, Delete (or simply press Del). The Confirm File Delete dialog box opens.

4. Click the Yes button to delete the stored location.

5. To close the Favorites Explorer window and return to Microsoft Internet Explorer, choose File, Close (or press Alt+F4).

Accessing and Using Intranet Files

Many files that may be accessed over your intranet can't be displayed on a browser. Remember that a browser may only display graphics files in GIF and JPEG formats and text files that are either pure text or have been formatted using HTML tags. (Other types of files such as Java scripts interact with your browser like a new program.)

There are many other types of files that do not fall into these categories (for example, spreadsheets, computer-aided design drawings, and so on). See Chapter 4, "Creating Content with Your Desktop Applications," for other examples.

When a browser encounters any file it doesn't know how to display or work with, it gives you the option to either save the file to your hard drive or configure a program to use this type of file with. You can tell your browser how you want to deal with specific files when it encounters them.

Downloading Files

You may want to download (copy) the file to your local hard drive for later viewing or editing. All browsers include options for doing this and the actions you take will be similar to those outlined below even if you are not using MS Internet Explorer or Netscape Navigator.

To download a file using your browser:

1. Click the link to the file. When using Netscape Navigator, the Unknown File Type dialog box opens (see fig. B.11). When using Microsoft Internet Explorer, the Confirm File Open dialog box opens (see fig. B.12).

Fig. B.11
The Unknown File
Type dialog box
gives you the
option of saving a
downloaded file
to your hard
drive.

Fig. B.12
The Confirm File
Open dialog box
lets you decide
what you want to
do with a down-
loaded file.

2. To save the file to your hard drive, click either the Save File or Save <u>A</u>s
button (depending on the program). The standard Windows 95 Save As
dialog box opens.

TIP

To help keep track of your file downloads, create a folder named Download using the Create New Folder button located in the Save dialog box.

3. Navigate your hard drive to select a folder to store the file in and click
the Save button to save the file.

NOTE

Often, the file you've downloaded is a program or program installation
file. In this case, you may want to save the file to a new folder titled
Installation or some similar name. This should help you keep track of
exactly what files go with this new application.

Once you have installed the program to its final location, you can delete
the files in the Installation folder so that it's ready for the next application you download.

Configuring Helper Applications

TIP

If the file is compressed, such as a ZIP file, you may still want to save it to your hard drive and run a decompression program, such as PKUnzip, on it later rather than configuring a program to work with the zipped file. This lets you keep the original file on your drive if anything goes wrong.

Instead of just saving a downloaded file to disk, you can have your browser automatically launch a program to view or edit the file. These programs are called *helper applications*.

With its close ties to Windows 95 and the Registry, Microsoft Internet Assistant is already configured to launch any program you have installed on your system. After you've clicked a link to a file and the Confirm File Open dialog box opens (see fig. B.12), click the Open button to launch the appropriate helper application.

Netscape Navigator, however, is not automatically configured by the Registry and you have to tell it which program is associated with what file type. To configure a helper application:

1. Click the link to the file. The Unknown File Type dialog box opens (refer to fig. B.11).

2. Click the Pick App button to open the Configure External Viewer dialog box (see fig. B.13).

Fig. B.13
The Configure External Viewer dialog box lets you tell Netscape Navigator which program you want to automatically run certain types of files.

3. Either enter the path and file name of the helper application, or click the Browse button and search for the application. When you have found it, click the file to select it then click OK. You return to the Configure External Viewer dialog box.

4. Click the OK button to close the Configure External Viewer dialog box and return to Netscape Navigator. The helper application will automatically load and display the file that was downloaded.

Depending on your network rights, if you have edited the file you downloaded, you may either save it to its original location in the network or to your personal hard drive for later viewing and editing.

Searching for Content

Depending on the size of your corporate intranet, it may be very difficult to find exactly the information you are looking for. Knowing this, your IT department may have created a database that keeps track of the majority of pages on your intranet and a series of descriptive words and phrases about these pages (called *keywords*). These databases are called *search engines* and are what makes all the content on the World Wide Web accessible to millions of people.

If such a search engine is available on your system, your IT department may have configured your viewer so that clicking the Search or Net Search button links you directly with that page. If your browser cannot be updated in this way, add the location of the search engine to your list of saved locations as outlined earlier in this chapter.

The search engine displays a standard intranet form that asks you to input one or more keywords concerning the topic you are interested in (see fig. B.14). (Chapter 9, "Creating Interactive Databases," includes information on creating databases that can be used as intranet search engines.) After you have entered your keyword(s), click the submit button to have the computer perform you search. Note that the submit button may be named "Search Now" as shown in the figure, or another self-explanatory name. Once the search has finished, its results are displayed on a new page as shown in figure B.15.

Fig. B.14
This is the
InfoSeek search
engine for the
World Wide Web.
Your search
engine may look
slightly different.

Enter keywords here ——————

Fig. B.15
Once you have
entered your
keyword(s), the
search engine
displays a series
of links to pages
that match your
criteria.

Links to
related pages

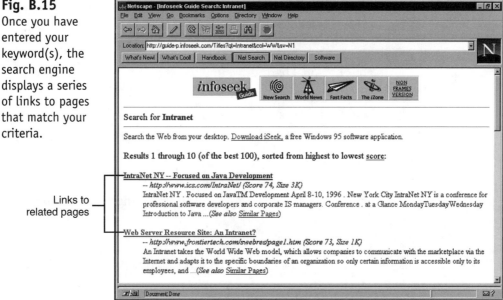

Changing Your Home Page

If you are creating a web page or site on your personal computer, you may want to make it the first page your browser displays when it's started—your home page. This can make the page easier to edit by always bringing up your latest changes automatically.

TIP

If you don't want to set the page you are editing as your default page, consider adding it to your stored locations list.

Alternatively, you may want to set your department page as your home page instead of the overall corporate page.

To set the default home page in Netscape Navigator:

1. Start Netscape Navigator.

2. Navigate through the intranet to find the page you want to use as your home page, or, to choose a file on your local drive, follow these steps:

   Choose File, Open File in Browser (or press Ctrl+O). The Open dialog box appears.

   Navigate your personal hard drive until you find the page you want to use.

   Click Open to load that page.

3. Click once in the Location text box in the button bar to highlight the file and path.

4. Copy this text to the Clipboard by pressing Ctrl+C.

5. Choose Options, General Preferences. The Preferences dialog box opens.

6. Select the Appearance tab.

7. Click the Home Page Location radio button so that it is activated (the circle is filled).

8. Highlight all the text in the text box below the <u>H</u>ome Page Location radio button.

9. Paste your new home page location by pressing Ctrl+V. Your new home page location appears in the text box (see fig. B.16).

Fig. B.16
Enter a new home page location to set the page your browser automatically loads when you start the program.

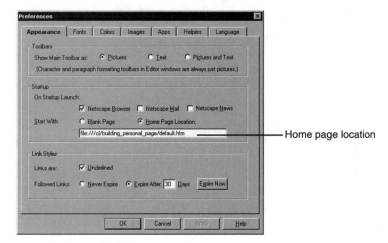

Home page location

10. Click the OK button to return to Netscape Navigator.

To set the default home page in Microsoft Internet Explorer:

1. Start Microsoft Internet Explorer.

2. Navigate through the intranet to find the page you want to use as your home page, or, to choose a file on your local drive, follow these steps:

Choose <u>F</u>ile, Open <u>F</u>ile in Browser (or press Ctrl+O). The Open Internet Address dialog box appears.

Click the Open <u>F</u>ile button. The Open File dialog box opens.

Navigate your personal hard drive until you find the page you want to use.

Click the <u>O</u>pen button to load that page.

3. Choose <u>V</u>iew, Options. The Options dialog box opens.

4. Select the Start and Search Pages tab (see fig. B.17).

Fig. B.17
Enter a new home page location to set the page your browser automatically loads when you start the program.

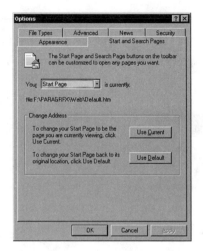

5. Click the Use Current button to set your home page to the current page.

6. Click the OK button to return to Microsoft Internet Explorer.

Altering the Appearance of Your Browser

In the same way that you can change many visual attributes of your Windows desktop, you have a broad range of control over the appearance of your browser.

In Microsoft Internet Explorer, choose View, Options to open the Options dialog box. Under the Appearance tab you can set various controls to change the default background color, font type and color, and even how the browser displays links. The Use Larger Font and Use Smaller Font buttons on the button bar increase and decrease the default font size for the browser (see fig. B.18).

Use larger font   Use smaller font

Fig. B.18
Change the
default colors,
type size, and
font to make your
browser easier to
read.

Define display fonts

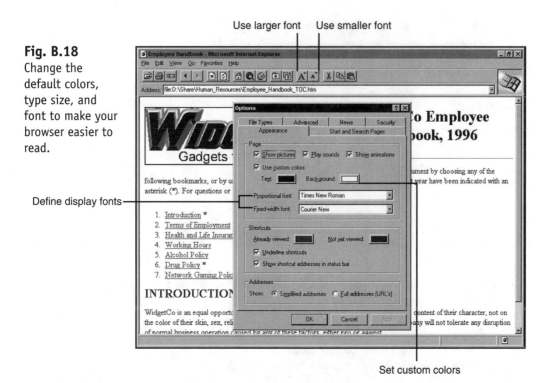

Set custom colors

In Netscape Navigator, you can set the default font and text size in the
Choose Base Font dialog box, accessed from the Fonts tab in the Preferences
dialog box (see fig. B.19). You can set default colors under the Colors tab in
the Preferences dialog box (see fig. B.20).

TIP

Some of your coworkers may set specific colors for their pages' backgrounds and text. Don't select Always Use My Colors, Overriding Document
as this may make some pages look really bad, depending on the graphics
and backgrounds used.

Fig. B.19
You can change the font and type size to make text easier to read on your browser.

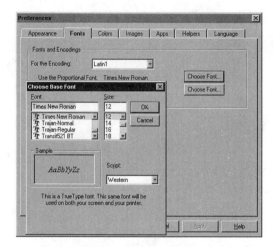

Fig. B.20
Although you can change the default colors that your browser uses, some pages will override these choices.

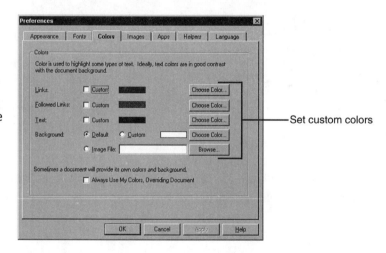

Set custom colors

For Further Reading

By Paul Bodensiek

Although we have made every effort to make *Intranet Publishing* as complete a reference as possible, the shear magnitude of information available on intranets, and their parents, the Internet and World Wide Web, makes a single comprehensive volume impractical.

The following books and World Wide Web sites provide additional material that you may find helpful. You'll also find the Web site addresses shown in this appendix on the CD. Because of the constantly changing nature of intranets and the Internet, we have arranged the books in chronological order, showing the newest (or forthcoming) books first and limiting the age to one year before *Intranet Publishing* is published.

HTML and Page Design

HyperText Markup Language seems to change daily and the tools used to write the code change almost as fast. The following books and World Wide Web sites will help you expand your knowledge and get new ideas for creative HTML coding.

Books

    Special Edition Using Microsoft FrontPage, Neil Randall and Dennis Jones, Que, July 1996

- *Special Edition Using Intranet HTML*, Mark Brown and John Jung, Que, July 1996

- *HTML By Example*, Todd Stauffer, Que, June 1996

- *Teach Yourself Netscape Web Publishing with HTML 3.0 in 14 Days, Premier Second Edition*, Laura Lemay, sams.net, June 1996

- *10 Minute Guide to Intranets*, Galen Grimes, Que, May 1996

- *Enhancing Netscape Web Pages*, Andy Shafran, Que, May 1996

- *HTML Visual Quick Reference, Second Edition*, Dean Scharf, Que, May 1996

- *Special Edition Using HTML, Second Edition*, Tom Savola, Que, April, 1996

- *The Complete Idiot's Guide to Creating an HTML Web Page*, Paul McFedries, Que, February 1996

- *Designing Web Graphics*, Lynda Weinman, New Riders Publishing, January 1996

- *HTML 3.0 Manual of Style*, Larry Aronson, Ziff-Davis Press, January 1996

- *Teach Yourself Web Publishing with HTML 3.0 in 14 Days, Premier Edition*, Laura Lemay, sams.net, January 1996

- *Using HTML*, Neil Randall, Que, January 1996

- *Web Site Construction Kit*, Christopher L. T. Brown and Scott Zimmerman, sams.net, January 1996

- *Creating Your Own Netscape Web Pages*, Andy Shafran, Que, November 1995

- *Web Publishing with WordPerfect for Windows*, Gordon McComb, Que, November 1995

- *Instant HTML Web Pages*, AUSE, Ziff-Davis Press, October 1995

- *Mbone: Interactive Multimedia on the Internet*, Vinay Kumar, New Riders Publishing, October 1995

- *Create Your Home Page*, Tonya and Adam Engst, Hayden, September 1995

- *World Wide Web Design Guide*, Steven Wilson, Hayden, September 1995

- *10 Minute Guide to HTML*, Tim Evans, Que, July 1995
- *Teach Yourself Web Publishing with Microsoft Word in a Week*, Herb Tyson, sams.net, July 1995
- *10 Minute Guide to Internet Assistant for Word*, J. Michael Roach, Que, June 1995

On the World Wide Web

- Macmillan SuperLibrary, Macmillan Computer Publishing, **http://www.mcp.com**
- *Creating Web Sites*, Netscape, **http://home.netscape.com/assist/net_sites/index.html**
- *The Intranet Journal*[SM]*—Bringing the Web home...*, **BES/Internet Services, http://www.brill.com/intranet/**
- *CWIS and WWW Information*, University of Melbourne, **http://www.unimelb.edu.au/cwis-info.html**
- *Guides to Writing HTML Documents*, National Center for Supercomputing Applications (NCSA), University of Illinois, **http://www.ncsa.uiuc.edu/SDG/Presentations/Conf/Create/style.html**
- *F.A.Q. Publishing: Page Creation: Graphics*, Clever Computers, Inc., **http://clever.net/self/faq/graphics.html**

System Security and Setup

Implementing, securing, and maintaining an intranet system doesn't have to be a full-time job. The following books and World Wide Web sites provide all the information you'll need to keep your system running at peak efficiency and security with the least effort.

Books

- *Inside Internet Information Server*, New Riders Publishing, May 1996
- *Introducing Intranets*, Gordon Benett, Que, May 1996

🌑 *Internet Security Professional Reference*, Chris Hare, et al., New Riders Publishing, March 1996

🌑 *Building a Windows NT Internet Server*, Eric Harper, Matt Arnett and R. Paul Singh, New Riders Publishing, October 1995

🌑 *Actually Useful Internet Security Techniques*, Larry Hughes, New Riders Publishing, September 1995

🌑 *Implementing Internet Security*, New Riders Development Group, New Riders Publishing, June 1995

🌑 *Web Page Construction Kit*, Sams Software, Sams, June 1995

🌑 *Web Publishing with Word for Windows*, Ron Person, Que, June 1995

On the World Wide Web

🌑 *Creating Private Intranets: Challenges and Prospects for IS*, David Strom, Inc., **http://www.strom.com/pubwork/intranetp.html**

🌑 *NIST Computer Security Resource Clearinghouse—Prototype*, National Institute of Standards and Technology, **http://www.first.org/**

🌑 *On Security*, Netscape, **http://www.netscape.com/newsref/ref/ internet-security.html**

🌑 *RSA Data Security, Inc.'s Home Page*, RSA Data Security, Inc., **http:// www.rsa.com/**

🌑 *The Server-Application Function and Netscape Server API*, Netscape, **http://www.netscape.com/newsref/std/server_api.html**

Browsers

Browsers change even more frequently than HTML code. There are also a lot more browsers out there than we could possibly introduce in this book. The following books and World Wide Web sites provide complete instructions for using the most popular browsers and downloading new versions when they are available.

Books

- *Netscape Navigator 6-in-1,* Jennifer Fulton and Nat Gertler, Que, June 1996
- *Netscape Unleashed*, Neil Randall, Selby Bateman, and David Wade, sams.net, February 1996
- *Special Edition Using the Internet with Windows 95*, Mary Ann Pike, et al., Que, February 1996
- *Guide to Netscape Navigator 2.0*, James Barnett, Ziff-Davis Press, January 1996
- *Special Edition Using Netscape 2*, Mark R. Brown, Que, January 1996
- *The Complete Idiot's Guide to Netscape Navigator for Windows 95*, Joe Kraynak, Que, January 1996
- *Using Netscape 2 for Windows 95*, Peter Kent, Que, January 1996
- *10 Minute Guide to Microsoft Internet Explorer*, J. Michael Roch, Que, November 1995
- *Using Microsoft Internet Explorer*, Peter Kent, Que, November 1995

On the World Wide Web

- *The Online Handbook*, Netscape, **http://home.netscape.com/eng/ mozilla/Gold/handbook/index.html**
- *Netscape—Frequently Asked Questions*, Netscape, **http:// home.netscape.com/eng/mozilla/2.01/faq.html**
- *Frequently Asked Questions About Microsoft Internet Explorer 2.0*, Microsoft, **http://www.microsoft.com/ie/feedback/ie20faq.htm**
- *Help!*, Art & Science W3 Development, Ltd., **http://www.chiba.com/ help.html**

CGI and Other Intranet Programming

Custom intranet programming can help bring your sites alive with capabilities far beyond those available from straight HTML. The examples given in this book just scratch the surface of CGI scripting and other programming methods. The following books and World Wide Web sites are a complete library of the most current information and examples.

Books

- ⬤ *Java By Example*, Clayton Walnum-®Ç&E, June 1996
- ⬤ *CGI Manual of Style*, Ziff-Davis Press, May 1996
- ⬤ *Special Edition Using CGI*, Michael Erwin and Jeffry Dwight, Que, April 1996
- ⬤ *Special Edition Using Java*, Alex Newman, Que, April 1996.
- ⬤ *Java Unleashed,* Charles Perkins, sams.net, April 1996
- ⬤ *Teach Yourself Java in 21 Days*, Laura Lemay and Charles Perkins, sams.net, January 1996
- ⬤ *Java!*, Tim Ritchey, New Riders Publishing, September 1995
- ⬤ *HTML & CGI Unleashed*, John December and Mark Ginsburg, sams.net, October 1995
- ⬤ *Presenting Java*, John December, sams.net, September 1995
- ⬤ *Building Internet Applications with Visual Basic*, Michael Marchuk, Que, June 1995

On the World Wide Web

- ⬤ *Introduction to CGI Programming*, University of Utah, **http://ute.usi.utah.edu/bin/cgi-programming/counter.pl/cgi-programming/index.html**
- ⬤ *WPD—Grok This—Programming, Little Blue Productions* (Web Professionals Digest), **http://www.littleblue.com/webpro/docs/programming.html**
- ⬤ *Writing Java Programs*, Sun Microsystems, Inc., **http://java.sun.com/doc/programmer.html**
- ⬤ *Gamelan: EarthWeb's Java Directory*, EarthWeb, LLC., **http://www.gamelan.com/**

Index

B

<B> tag, 33-34

background colors, assigning via Internet Publisher, 388-389

backward/forward buttons (browsers), 489

<BASEFONT> tag, 57-58

<%BEGINDETAIL%> tag, 204

benchmarks (research and development sample site), 355

benefits information (human resource sample site), 291-293

Berners-Lee, Tim, 10

Bibliography template (FrontPage Editor), 417

Bicanic, Nick, 146

billing/accounting procedures (legal and finance sample site), 326

bitmaps, 98, 129

blink text, 382

<BLOCKQUOTE> tag, 70

blueprints (research and development sample site), 355

body section (HTML pages), 30

body text, writing via Internet Publisher, 380-381

boilerplate materials (sales and marketing sample site), 286

bold tag, 33-34

bonus plans (human resources sample site), 295

bookmarks, 490-493
FrontPage Editor, 423
internal links, 117-118
Internet Publisher, 395-397

borders
removing from graphics, 141
tables, 156

bots, *see* Web Bots

 tag, 32

briefs (legal and finance sample site), 323

brochures (corporate communications sample site), 274-275

browsers, 11, 486-487
client/server architecture, 192-193
configuring helper applications, 495-496
customizing, 500-501
default home pages, 498-500
downloading files, 493-494
forward/backward buttons, 489
headings, 381-382
Internet Explorer, 41-42, 470
InterNotes Web Navigator, 441
intranet overview, 11-13
links, 487
Netscape, viewing WordPerfect documents in, 403
path statements
relative compared to absolute, 120-121
UNIX notation, 119-120
search engines, 496

stored locations
accessing, 490-491
adding, 490
deleting, 491-493

budgets (legal and finance sample site), 329

bug fixes
customer service and IT support sample site, 367
research and development sample site, 355

built-in variables (HTML templates), 206

bulleted lists, creating via Internet Publisher, 386-387

bulletin boards
documentation sample site, 348-349
education and training sample site, 310
manufacturing sample site, 334-335
research and development sample site, 361
sales and marketing sample site, 288

bullets (unordered lists), 64-66

buttons
editing in Internet Publisher, 400
inline graphics as links, 141-142

C

calendars (corporate communications sample site), 275-276

<CAPTION> tag, 154

catalogs (education and training sample site), 306-307

Check out Que® Books on the World Wide Web
http://www.mcp.com/que

As the biggest software release in computer history, Windows 95 continues to redefine the computer industry. Click here for the latest info on our Windows 95 books

Make computing quick and easy with these products designed exclusively for new and casual users

Examine the latest releases in word processing, spreadsheets, operating systems, and suites

The Internet, The World Wide Web, CompuServe®, America Online®, Prodigy®—it's a world of ever-changing information. Don't get left behind!

Find out about new additions to our site, new bestsellers and hot topics

In-depth information on high-end topics: find the best reference books for databases, programming, networking, and client/server technologies

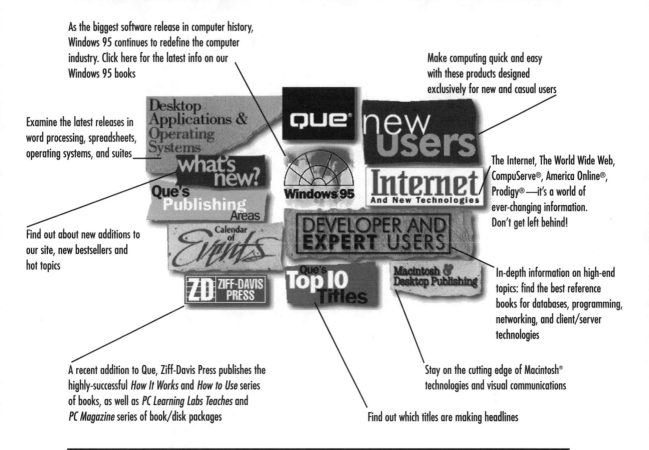

A recent addition to Que, Ziff-Davis Press publishes the highly-successful *How It Works* and *How to Use* series of books, as well as *PC Learning Labs Teaches* and *PC Magazine* series of book/disk packages

Stay on the cutting edge of Macintosh® technologies and visual communications

Find out which titles are making headlines

With 6 separate publishing groups, Que develops products for many specific market segments and areas of computer technology. Explore our Web Site and you'll find information on best-selling titles, newly published titles, upcoming products, authors, and much more.

- Stay informed on the latest industry trends and products available
- Visit our online bookstore for the latest information and editions
- Download software from Que's library of the best shareware and freeware

GET CONNECTED
to the ultimate source of computer information!

The MCP Forum on CompuServe

Go online with the world's leading computer book publisher! Macmillan Computer Publishing offers everything you need for computer success!

Find the books that are right for you!
A complete online catalog, plus sample chapters and tables of contents give you an in-depth look at all our books. The best way to shop or browse!

➤ Get fast answers and technical support for MCP books and software

➤ Join discussion groups on major computer subjects

➤ Interact with our expert authors via e-mail and conferences

➤ Download software from our immense library:
  ▷ Source code from books
  ▷ Demos of hot software
  ▷ The best shareware and freeware
  ▷ Graphics files

Join now and get a free CompuServe Starter Kit!

To receive your free CompuServe Introductory Membership, call **1-800-848-8199** and ask for representative #597.

The Starter Kit includes:
➤ Personal ID number and password
➤ $15 credit on the system
➤ Subscription to *CompuServe Magazine*

Once on the CompuServe System, type:

GO MACMILLAN

for the most computer information anywhere!

MACMILLAN
COMPUTER
PUBLISHING

CompuServe

QUE® has the right choice for every computer user

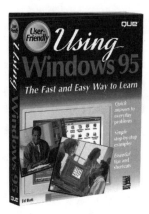

From the new computer user to the advanced programmer, we've got the right computer book for you. Our user-friendly *Using* series offers just the information you need to perform specific tasks quickly and move onto other things. And, for computer users ready to advance to new levels, QUE *Special Edition Using* books, the perfect all-in-one resource—and recognized authority on detailed reference information.

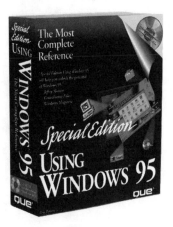

The *Using* series for casual users

Who should use this book?

Everyday users who:

- Work with computers in the office or at home
- Are familiar with computers but not in love with technology
- Just want to "get the job done"
- Don't want to read a lot of material

The user-friendly reference

- The fastest access to the one best way to get things done
- Bite-sized information for quick and easy reference
- Nontechnical approach in plain English
- Real-world analogies to explain new concepts
- Troubleshooting tips to help solve problems
- Visual elements and screen pictures that reinforce topics
- Expert authors who are experienced in training and instruction

Special Edition Using for accomplished users

Who should use this book?

Proficient computer users who:

- Have a more technical understanding of computers
- Are interested in technological trends
- Want in-depth reference information
- Prefer more detailed explanations and examples

The most complete reference

- Thorough explanations of various ways to perform tasks
- In-depth coverage of all topics
- Technical information cross-referenced for easy access
- Professional tips, tricks, and shortcuts for experienced users
- Advanced troubleshooting information with alternative approaches
- Visual elements and screen pictures that reinforce topics
- Technically qualified authors who are experts in their fields
- "Techniques form the Pros" sections with advice from well-known computer professionals

Complete and Return this Card
for a *FREE* Computer Book Catalog

Thank you for purchasing this book! You have purchased a superior computer book written expressly for your needs. To continue to provide the kind of up-to-date, pertinent coverage you've come to expect from us, we need to hear from you. Please take a minute to complete and return this self-addressed, postage-paid form. In return, we'll send you a free catalog of all our computer books on topics ranging from word processing to programming and the internet.

Mr. ☐   Mrs. ☐   Ms. ☐   Dr. ☐

Name (first) [ ] (M.I.) [ ] (last) [ ]

Address [ ]

[ ]

City [ ] State [ ] Zip [ ] [ ]

Phone [ ] Fax [ ]

Company Name [ ]

E-mail address [ ]

Please check at least (3) influencing factors for purchasing this book.

Front or back cover information on book .... ☐
Special approach to the content .... ☐
Completeness of content .... ☐
Author's reputation .... ☐
Publisher's reputation .... ☐
Book cover design or layout .... ☐
Index or table of contents of book .... ☐
Price of book .... ☐
Special effects, graphics, illustrations .... ☐
Other (Please specify): _____ ☐

How did you first learn about this book?

Saw in Macmillan Computer Publishing catalog .... ☐
Recommended by store personnel .... ☐
Saw the book on bookshelf at store .... ☐
Recommended by a friend .... ☐
Received advertisement in the mail .... ☐
Saw an advertisement in: _____ ☐
Read book review in: _____ ☐
Other (Please specify): _____ ☐

How many computer books have you purchased in the last six months?

This book only .... ☐   3 to 5 books .... ☐
books .... ☐   More than 5 .... ☐

4. Where did you purchase this book?

Bookstore .... ☐
Computer Store .... ☐
Consumer Electronics Store .... ☐
Department Store .... ☐
Office Club .... ☐
Warehouse Club .... ☐
Mail Order .... ☐
Direct from Publisher .... ☐
Internet site .... ☐
Other (Please specify): _____ ☐

5. How long have you been using a computer?

☐ Less than 6 months   ☐ 6 months to a year
☐ 1 to 3 years   ☐ More than 3 years

6. What is your level of experience with personal computers and with the subject of this book?

	With PCs	With subject of book
New	☐	☐
Casual	☐	☐
Accomplished	☐	☐
Expert	☐	☐

Source Code ISBN: 0-7897-0803-5

7. Which of the following best describes your job title?

Administrative Assistant .... ☐
Coordinator .... ☐
Manager/Supervisor .... ☐
Director .... ☐
Vice President .... ☐
President/CEO/COO .... ☐
Lawyer/Doctor/Medical Professional .... ☐
Teacher/Educator/Trainer .... ☐
Engineer/Technician .... ☐
Consultant .... ☐
Not employed/Student/Retired .... ☐
Other (Please specify): _____ ☐

8. Which of the following best describes the area of the company your job title falls under?

Accounting .... ☐
Engineering .... ☐
Manufacturing .... ☐
Operations .... ☐
Marketing .... ☐
Sales .... ☐
Other (Please specify): _____ ☐

9. What is your age?

Under 20 .... ☐
21-29 .... ☐
30-39 .... ☐
40-49 .... ☐
50-59 .... ☐
60-over .... ☐

10. Are you:

Male .... ☐
Female .... ☐

11. Which computer publications do you read regularly? (Please list)

_____
_____
_____
_____
_____
_____
_____
_____
_____

Comments: _____
_____
_____

Fold here and scotch-tape to mail

MISCELLANEOUS

If you acquired this product in the United States, this EULA is governed by laws of the State of Washington.

If this product was acquired outside of the United States, then local laws may apply.

Should you have any questions concerning this EULA, or if you desire to contact Microsoft for any reason, please contact the Microsoft subsidiary serving your country, or write Microsoft Sales Information Center/One Microsoft Way/Redmond, WA 98052-6399.

This program was reproduced by Macmillan Computer Publishing under a special arrangement with Microsoft Corporation. For this reason, Macmillan Computer Publishing is responsible for the product warranty and for support. If your CD-ROM is defective, please return it to Macmillan Computer Publishing, which will arrange for its replacement. PLEASE DO NOT RETURN IT TO MICROSOFT CORPORATION. Any product support will be provided, if at all, by Macmillan Computer Publishing. PLEASE DO NOT CONTACT MICROSOFT CORPORATION FOR PRODUCT SUPPORT. End users of this Microsoft program shall not be considered "registered owners" of a Microsoft product and therefore shall not be eligible for upgrades, promotions, or other benefits available to "registered owners" of Microsoft products.

IMPORTANT—READ CAREFULLY: This Microsoft End-User License Agreement ("EULA") is a legal agreement between you (either an individual or a single entity) and Microsoft Corporation for the Microsoft software accompanying this EULA, which includes computer software and may include associated media, printed materials, and "online" or electronic documentation ("SOFTWARE PRODUCT" or "SOFTWARE"). By exercising your rights to make and use copies of the SOFTWARE PRODUCT, you agree to be bound by the terms of this EULA. If you do not agree to the terms of this EULA, you may not use the SOFTWARE PRODUCT.

SOFTWARE PRODUCT LICENSE

The SOFTWARE PRODUCT is protected by copyright laws and international copyright treaties, as well as other intellectual property laws and treaties. The SOFTWARE PRODUCT is licensed, not sold.

1. GRANT OF LICENSE. This EULA grants you the following rights:

- **Installation and Use.** You may install and use an unlimited number of copies of the SOFTWARE PRODUCT.

- **Reproduction and Distribution.** You may reproduce and distribute an unlimited number of copies of the SOFTWARE PRODUCT, provided that each copy shall be a true and complete copy, including all copyright and trademark notices, and shall be accompanied by a copy of this EULA. Copies of the SOFTWARE PRODUCT may be distributed as a standalone product or included with your own product.

2. DESCRIPTION OF OTHER RIGHTS AND LIMITATIONS

- **Limitations on Reverse Engineering, Decompilation, and Disassembly.** You may not reverse engineer, decompile, or disassemble the SOFTWARE PRODUCT, except and only to the extent that such activity is expressly permitted by applicable law notwithstanding this limitation.

- **Separation of Components.** The SOFTWARE PRODUCT is licensed as a single product. Its component parts may not be separated for use on more than one computer.

- **Software Transfer.** You may permanently transfer all of your rights under this EULA, provided the recipient agrees to the terms of this EULA.

- **Termination.** Without prejudice in any other rights, Microsoft may terminate this EULA if you fail to comply with the terms and conditions of this EULA. In such event, you must destroy all copies of the SOFTWARE PRODUCT and all of its component parts.

3. COPYRIGHT. All title and copyrights in and to the SOFTWARE PRODUCT (including but not limited to any images, photographs, animations, video, audio, music, text, and "applets" incorporated into the SOFTWARE PRODUCT), the accompanying printed materials, and any copies of the SOFTWARE PRODUCT are owned by Microsoft or its suppliers. The SOFTWARE PRODUCT is protected by copyright laws and international treaty provisions. Therefore, you must treat the SOFTWARE PRODUCT like any other copyrighted material.

4. U.S. GOVERNMENT RESTRICTED RIGHTS. The SOFTWARE PRODUCT and documentation are provided with RESTRICTED RIGHTS. Use, duplication, or disclosure by the Government is subject to restrictions as set forth in subparagraph (c)(1)(ii) of the Rights in Technical Data and Computer Software clause at DFARS 252.227-7013 or subparagraphs (c)(1) and (2) of the Commercial Computer Software Restricted Rights at 48 CFR 52.227-19, as applicable

LIMITED WARRANTY

NO WARRANTIES. Microsoft expressly disclaims any warranty for the SOFTWARE PRODUCT. The SOFTWARE PRODUCT and any related documentation is provided "as is" without warranty of any kind, either express or implied, including without limitation, the implied warranties or merchantability, fitness for a particular purpose, or noninfringement. The entire risk arising out of use or performance of the SOFTWARE PRODUCT remains with you.

NO LIABILITY FOR CONSEQUENTIAL DAMAGES. In no event shall Microsoft or its suppliers be liable for any damages whatsoever (including, without limitation, damages for loss of business profits, business interruption, loss of business information, or any other pecuniary loss) arising out of the use of or inability to use this Microsoft product, even if Microsoft has been advised of the possibility of such damages. Because some states/jurisdictions do not allow the exclusion or limitation of liability for consequential or incidental damages, the above limitation may not apply to you.

Continues on previous page

About the Intranet Publishing CD-ROM

The CD-ROM that accompanies this book contains all the tools you need to publish on your intranet site. The Intranet Publishing CD-ROM includes the following tools (and more), as well as files that contain the examples shown in the text, and direct links to valuable resources on the Internet:

- **Microsoft's Internet Explorer**—one of the most popular browsers available.

- **Microsoft's Word Internet Assistant**, **Excel Internet Assistant**, and **PowerPoint Internet Assistant**—for quickly converting your word processing documents, spreadsheets, and presentations into HTML format.

- Other popular HTML editors—including **Hot Dog** and **SoftQuad's HoTMetaL**. Hot Dog is a text-based editor for creating the most basic type of HTML pages. HoTMetaL is an extended text-based editor that uses icons to represent HTML tags.

- **LView Pro for Windows 95**—a shareware program that converts image files from one format to another.

- A collection of graphic accents, icons, and buttons to help you put together interesting pages with a minimum of effort.

- The **Color Machine** utility—generates hexadecimal numbers for any color you want to use. Saves lots of HTML coding time.

- **CuteFTP**—makes transferring files to the server easier.

- **WinZip**—creates compression files and maintains your folder structure.

Continues on previous page